This book studies the dollar–sterling exchange rate from 1791 to 1931. The gold standard is examined from the perspective of the precise location of the exchange rate. Professor Officer begins with a historical perspective of the monetary standards of the United States and Britain, following which he develops new data on exchange rates, mint parity, and gold points.

The data are used to investigate three important features of Anglo-American monetary history. First, the integration (degree of perfection) of the American foreign-exchange market is examined; enhanced integration over time is observed. Second, market efficiency (the behavior of private parities in response to the profit opportunities offered by a gold standard) is studied; it is proved that gold-point arbitrage is markedly more efficient than either interest arbitrage or forward speculation. Third, regime efficiency (the viability of an existing gold standard) is explored from the standpoints of both private agents and policy-makers; the 1925–31 gold standard, though less durable than the prewar standard, is nevertheless shown to be surprisingly stable.

The book presents and examines new data on the exchange rate and related variables, and will serve as a dollar–sterling handbook for those interested in this important aspect of international monetary history. In its presentation of theories and results centred on the precise location of the exchange rate, the book breaks new ground in our understanding of the gold standard.

Between the dollar–sterling gold points

Studies in Monetary and Financial History

Editors: Michael Bordo and Forrest Capie

Between the dollar–sterling gold points

Exchange rates, parity, and market behavior

LAWRENCE H. OFFICER
University of Illinois at Chicago

Published by the Press Syndicate of the University of Cambridge
The Pitt Building, Trumpington Street, Cambridge CB2 1RP
40 West 20th Street, New York, NY 10011-4211, USA
10 Stamford Road, Oakleigh, Melbourne 3166, Australia

© Cambridge University Press 1996

First published 1996

Printed in Great Britain at the University Press, Cambridge

A catalogue record for this book is available from the British Library

Library of Congress cataloguing in publication data
Officer, Lawrence H.
    Between the dollar–sterling gold points: exchange rates, parity,
and market behavior / Lawrence H. Officer.
        p.   cm. – (Studies in monetary and financial history)
    Includes bibliographical references and index.
    ISBN 0 521 45462 X (hc)
    1. Gold standard–History.   2. Foreign exchange rates–United
States–History.   3. Foreign exchange rates–Great Britain–History.
4. Money–United States–History.   5. Money–Great Britain–History.
I. Title.   II. Series.
HG297.035   1996
332.4'56'0941–dc20   95-34575 CIP

ISBN 0 521 45462 X hardback

This book is dedicated to my sons

ARI JOSEPH OFFICER
JONATHAN DAVID OFFICER

"The child is father to the man."

Contents

Figures

Tables

Preface

This book is a labor of love. I can think of nothing more intellectually stimulating than studying the broad sweep of the dollar–sterling exchange rate from 1791 to 1931. The existence of gold, or other metallic, standards during most of this period provides the background to the foreign-exchange market. Even when such a system was inoperative and a paper standard reigned, in almost all such episodes the exchange rate can be measured in such a way that the gold standard can be deemed to exist. Therefore the dollar–sterling exchange rate is studied from the universal standpoint of a gold standard.

The outcome is this volume, a dollar–sterling handbook for the economic historian. The book is a contribution to Anglo-American monetary history over the 140-year period 1791–1931. It is based on two fundamental premises of the behavior of the exchange rate under a gold standard. First, the dollar/pound exchange rate cannot be considered apart from exchange-rate parity and gold or specie points. Second, the precise location of the exchange rate is of importance; much information is lost – indeed, some important questions cannot even be answered – if the exchange rate is measured by the dollar/sterling mint parity (as is customary) rather than by the "actual value" of the exchange rate, difficult though it may be to obtain this "actual value."

These premises lead to a reconsideration of data on all three variables: exchange rate, parity, and gold points. Newly generated such data are then put to use examining the integration of the foreign-exchange market, the behavior of private participants in the market, and the role of policy authorities in influencing the stability of the gold standard.

The book is a culmination of over a decade of study of the history of the dollar–sterling foreign-exchange market. I thank Academic Press, Cambridge University Press, and the University of Chicago Press for permission to use material from my articles and essays previously published by these presses. However, this volume emanates from new research and exhibits new results. My former writings on the dollar–sterling exchange rate reflect earlier methodology and findings – both of which were in a state of flux – and deal with only segments of the 1791–1931 period. Presenting a consistent methodology and new results, the book conducts more an original than a revisited investigation of the entire 140-year span.

I am grateful to Michael Bordo and Forrest Capie, editors of the series *Studies in Monetary and Financial History*, who encouraged me to proceed with the study. Patrick McCartan, of Cambridge University Press, provided sound advice during the two-year process of generating the manuscript. The assistance of Pamela Pinnow enabled the completion of the project much quicker than otherwise. My wife, Sandra Diane Officer, was both understanding and helpful.

Finally, I thank some people whom I have never met and who may not, or could not, have known of the preparation of this book: Arthur H. Cole, Lance E. Davis, Jonathan R. T. Hughes, and Edwin J. Perkins. These historians were the true pathbreakers in the history of the dollar–sterling foreign-exchange market. It was their great work that inspired me to study the dollar–sterling market in the first place. This book builds on their pioneering research rather than replaces it.

Lawrence H. Officer

Symbols*

APP applicable, current preferred exchange-rate series, percentage deviation from mint parity (6, 3.10)

*BA*14 percentage premium of specie over currency, Baltimore [1814–17] (6, 3.8)

BHD Bank of England holdings of dollars, end of month, millions of dollars (15, 4)

*BW*1 band width relative to band mid-point, percentage of gold-point spread (14, 2)

*BW*2 band width relative to spread mid-point, percentage of gold-point spread (14, 2)

C broker's commission in foreign-exchange market, dollars per pound (6, 3.6)

CIA covered interest arbitrage (12, 3)

CX cost of gold-export arbitrage or gold-effected outward transfer of funds, percent (8, 4)

*CX** *CX* redefined as deviation from spread mid-point, percent (10, 1)

CM cost of gold-import arbitrage or gold-effected inward transfer of funds, percent (8, 4)

*CM** *CM* redefined as deviation from spread mid-point, percent (10, 1)

D dollar price paid for bill of exchange (6, 3.4)

E exchange rate corrected for paper-currency depreciation, dollars per pound (8, 4.1, n. 6)

E_L^{cia} exchange-rate gain of covered interest arbitrage in favor of pound, *ad valorem* per *N*-month period (12, 6.1)

E_L^{uia} expected exchange-rate gain of uncovered interest arbitrage in favor of pound, *ad valorem* per *N*-month period (12, 5.2)

E_U^{cia} exchange-rate gain of covered interest arbitrage in favor of dollar, *ad valorem* per *N*-month period (12, 6.2)

---

* Chapter(s) and section(s) where the symbol is defined are in parentheses.

E_U^{fs} expected exchange-rate gain of forward speculation in favor of dollar, *ad valorem* per N-month period (12, 7.2)

E_U^{uia} expected exchange-rate gain of uncovered interest arbitrage in favor of dollar, *ad valorem* per N-month period (12, 5.3)

EI external integration, average of CX and CM, percent (10, 1)

$EMINT$ joint exchange-market intervention of Bank of England and Federal Reserve banks, millions of dollars (15, 3)

$ENG19$ percentage premium of pound over gold [1919–25] (6, 3.8)

$ENG97$ percentage premium of pound over Spanish dollar [1797–1821] (6, 3.8)

$ENG97A$ average of quarterly values of ENG97 [1797–1821] (6, 3.8)

ERC exchange-rate cost of gold-point arbitrage or gold-effected transfer of funds, percent (9, 2.3.3)

EXP American exports of specie, New York to London [indicator of direction] (9, 2.1.1)

EXT extended, former or later component of long-run exchange-rate series, percentage deviation from mint parity (6, 3.10)

$FRHP$ Federal Reserve holdings of pounds, end of month, millions of dollars (15, 4)

FS forward speculation (12, 3)

g number of days of grace in making payment of time bill of exchange (6, 2)

GM gold-import point, dollars per pound (8, 4)

GPA gold-point arbitrage (8, 1)

GTF gold-effected transfer of funds (8, 1)

GX gold-export point, dollars per pound (8, 4)

i interest-rate, percent per year (6, 3.5; 9, 2.2.2, 2.4.1)

I *ad valorem* interest rate for duration of time bill over that of demand bill (6, 3.5)

I_L interest return of interest arbitrage in favor of pound, for $t_{US} = t_{UK}$, *ad valorem* per N-month period (12, 5.4)

I_{BR} Bank Rate, percent per year (15, 2)

I_{DR} Federal Reserve Bank of New York discount rate, percent per year (15, 2)

I_{La} interest return of interest arbitrage in favor of pound, for $t_{US} < t_{UK}$, *ad valorem* per N-month period (12, 5.2)

I_{Lb} interest return of interest arbitrage in favor of pound, for $t_{US} > t_{UK}$, *ad valorem* per N-month period (12, 5.2)

I_U interest return of interest arbitrage in favor of dollar, *ad valorem* per N-month period (12, 5.3)

I_{UK} London interest rate, *ad valorem* per N-month period (12, 5.2)

I_{US}	New York interest rate, *ad valorem* per N-month period (12, 5.2)
IC	interest cost of gold-point arbitrage or gold-effected transfer of funds, percent (9, 2.4.1)
II	internal integration, percent of parity (10, 1)
IMP	American imports of specie, London to New York [indicator of direction] (9, 2.1.1)
k	Broker's commission, *ad valorem* (6, 3.6)
K	parity of raw exchange-rate series (6, 3.4)
L	time loss for bullion deposit at New York Assay Office, number of days (9, 2.2.2)
m	proportion of specie-shipment value subject to interest (9, 2.4.1)
M	mint parity, dollars per pound (6, 3.7)
MC	marginal cost (9, 2.2.2)
MER	market exchange rate, dollars per pound (9, 2.3.3)
n	note
N	horizon of interest arbitrageurs and forward speculators, number of months (12, 5.1)
$NY37$	percentage premium of specie over currency, New York [1837–8] (6, 3.8)
$NY57$	percentage premium of specie over currency, New York [1857] (6, 3.8)
$NY62$	percentage premium of gold over greenbacks, New York [1862–78] (6, 3.8)
p	dividend-payout ratio, ratio of dividends to gross profit (12, 5.1)
P	pound face-value of bill of exchange (6, 3.4)
$PH15$	percentage premium of specie over currency, Philadelphia [1815–17] (6, 3.8)
$PH37$	percentage premium of specie over currency, Philadelphia [1837–42] (6, 3.8)
PR	forward premium on pound, dollars per pound (9, 2.3.3; 13, 4.2.2)
Q	percent of estimated value of bullion received upon deposit at New York Assay Office (9, 2.2.2)
r	risk-premium parameter, pure number (12, 5.2)
R	exchange rate corrected for paper-currency depreciation, percentage deviation from mint parity (6, 3.8)
R^*	R re-expressed as deviation from spread mid-point, percentage points of parity (10, 1)
R_L^{fs}	risk premium of forward speculation in favor of pound, *ad valorem* per N-month period (12, 7.1)
R_L^{uia}	risk premium of uncovered interest arbitrage in favor of pound, *ad valorem* per N-month period (12, 5.2)

R_U^{fs} risk premium of forward speculation in favor of dollar, *ad valorem* per N-month period (12, 7.2)

R_U^{uia} risk premium of uncovered interest arbitrage in favor of dollar, *ad valorem* per N-month period (12, 5.3)

RF foward exchange rate, dollars per pound (12, 6.1; 13, 4.2.2)

RF_L^{fs} lower efficiency point of RF under forward speculation (12, 7.1)

RF_U^{fs} upper efficiency point of RF under forward speculation (12, 7.2)

$RF8$ eight-day forward selling rate, dollars per pound (9, 2.3.3)

RM mid-point of gold-point spread, dollars per pound (10, 1)

RS exchange rate, mid-point of buying and selling rates, dollars per pound (12, 4.1)

RS^e expected spot rate, dollars per pound (12, 5.2)

RS_{La}^{cia} lower efficiency point of RS under covered interest arbitrage, for $t_{US} < t_{UK}$ (12, 6.1)

RS_{Lb}^{cia} lower efficiency point of RS under covered interest arbitrage, for $t_{US} > t_{UK}$ (12, 6.1)

RS_{Lx}^{cia} RS_{La}^{cia} or RS_{Lb}^{cia} (12, 6.1)

RS_{La}^{j} lower efficiency point of RS under joint operation of forward speculation with covered interest arbitrage (indirect uncovered interest arbitrage), for $t_{US} < t_{UK}$ (12, 7.3)

RS_{Lb}^{j} lower efficiency point of RS under joint operation of forward speculation with covered interest arbitrage (indirect uncovered interest arbitrage), for $t_{US} > t_{UK}$ (12, 7.3)

RS_{Lx}^{j} RS_{La}^{j} or RS_{LB}^{j} (12, 7.3)

RS_L^{uia} lower efficiency point of RS under uncovered interest arbitrage, for $t_{US} = t_{UK} = r = I_L = 0$ (12, 5.4)

RS_{La}^{uia} lower efficiency point of RS under uncovered interest arbitrage, for $t_{US} < t_{UK}$ (12, 5.2)

RS_{Lb}^{uia} lower efficiency point of RS under uncovered interest arbitrage, for $t_{US} > t_{UK}$ (12, 5.2)

RS_{Lx}^{uia} RS_{La}^{uia} or RS_{Lb}^{uia} (12, 5.2)

RS_U^{cia} upper efficiency point of RS under covered interest arbitrage (12, 6.2)

RS_U^{j} upper efficiency point of RS under joint operation of forward speculation with covered interest arbitrage (indirect uncovered interest arbitrage) (12, 7.3)

RS_U^{uia} upper efficiency point of RS under uncovered interest arbitrage (12, 5.3)

RSM deviation of spread mid-point from parity, percentage of half gold-point spread (10, 1)

S exchange rate, percentage deviation from mint parity (6, 3.7)

SM	mid-point of gold-point spread, percentage deviation from mint parity (10, 1)
t	maturity length of time bill of exchange, number of days (6, 2, 3.5)
T	interest duration under gold-point arbitrage or gold-effected transfer of funds, number of days (9, 2.4.1)
t_{UK}	UK effective income-tax rate, *ad valorem* (12, 5.1)
t_{UK}^{n}	UK income-tax rate, *ad valorem* (12, 5.1)
t_{US}	US corporate tax rate (12, 4.1)
TC	transactions cost of interest arbitrage or forward speculation, *ad valorem* (12, 5.2)
TOT	total time needed for gold-import arbitrage using demand bill as foreign-exchange instrument (9, 2.4.2)
UIA	uncovered interest arbitrage (12, 3)
V	exchange rate, mid-point of buying and selling rates, dollars per pound (6, 3.6)
VOY	duration of round-trip Atlantic voyage, number of days (9, 2.4.2)
W	exchange rate, buying rate of brokers or dealers, dollars per pound (6, 3.6)
X	raw exchange-rate series, percentage deviation from parity (6, 3.4)
Y	exchange rate, time bill for exchange, dollars per pound (6, 3.5)
Z	exchange rate, selling rate of brokers or dealers, dollars per pound (6, 3.5–6)
π_{L}^{fs}	expected economic profit of forward speculation in favor of pound, *ad valorem* per N-month period (12, 7.1)
π_{La}^{cia}	economic profit of covered interest arbitrage in favor of pound, for $t_{US} < t_{UK}$, *ad valorem* per N-month period (12, 6.1)
π_{Lb}^{cia}	economic profit of covered interest arbitrage in favor of pound, for $t_{US} > t_{UK}$, *ad valorem* per N-month period (12, 6.1)
π_{Lx}^{cia}	π_{La}^{cia} or π_{Lb}^{cia}
π_{La}^{uia}	expected economic profit of uncovered interest arbitrage in favor of pound, for $t_{US} < t_{UK}$, *ad valorem* per N-month period (12, 5.2)
π_{Lb}^{uia}	expected economic profit of uncovered interest arbitrage in favor of pound, for $t_{US} > t_{UK}$, *ad valorem* per N-month period (12, 5.2)
π_{Lx}^{uia}	π_{La}^{uia} or π_{Lb}^{uia} (12, 5.2)
π_{U}^{cia}	economic profit of covered interest arbitrage in favor of dollar, *ad valorem* per N-month period (12, 6.2)
π_{U}^{fs}	expected economic profit of forward speculation in favor of dollar, *ad valorem* per N-month period (12, 7.2)
π_{U}^{uia}	expected economic profit of uncovered interest arbitrage in favor of dollar, *ad valorem* per N-month period (12, 5.3)

1 Introduction

The main theme of this volume is that, under a gold (or any metallic) standard, the *precise* location of the exchange rate is of importance – and this is so whether the exchange rate is within the gold-point spread (the range of the exchange rate delimited by the gold points) or outside the spread. This viewpoint is contrary to the traditional approach, which is dichotomous in nature, checking only whether the exchange rate is inside or outside the spread. The traditional approach typically analyzes the gold standard as a fixed exchange-rate regime. While the existence of a gold-point spread is recognized (if only implicitly), the location of the exchange rate is deemed irrelevant as long as the rate remains within the spread.[1]

The common procedure, then, is simply to represent the exchange rate by the mint parity, a practice justified by long-term automatic adjustment processes that eliminate balance-of-payments disequilibria that can exist only at (or beyond) a gold point. For example, the interwar dollar–sterling gold standard is almost universally viewed as involving a pound substantially overvalued at the mint parity but with corrective processes stymied by altered circumstances and policies compared to the prewar period, eventually leading to the demise of the gold standard. So the existing studies of the stability of the interwar gold standard are long run in nature, making no reference to the gold-point spread or the movement of the exchange rate within it.[2]

In this book a different focus is adopted. The functioning of a gold standard in general – with the dollar–sterling historical experience as the case study – is analyzed from the standpoint of models in which the specific location of the exchange rate plays the central role, with the variation and movement of the exchange rate also of interest.

A second theme of the present study is that specific gold-standard episodes are best examined only in their long-run context. To that end, part I provides histories of the monetary standards of the United States and Britain from the beginnings, with continuous detail from the mid-sixteenth century for Britain and from the mid-1780s for the United States. Treatises

1

of old – for example, Bolles (1894), Del Mar (1899), Watson (1899), Laughlin (1900), Hepburn (1924), Nussbaum (1957), and Feavearyear (1963) – concentrated on these histories for their own sake. In contrast, the purpose of the monetary history here is to provide background, context, and particular information for the remaining parts of the volume.

Data development is crucial to this study. Without appropriate data substantive issues cannot properly be explored. The third theme of the volume is itself threefold. First, data cannot be generated and assembled appropriately outside the institutional context. Second, existing data and their studies must be explored and their advantages/limitations understood before new work can be justified. Third, generation of data continuously for a long time period – taken here to be 1791–1931 with 1950–66 adopted as a comparison period – is the preferred approach over period-specific undertakings. With these orientations adopted, time series of exchange-rate parity (a norm value of the exchange rate), the exchange rate itself, and gold points are developed in parts II and III.

The remainder of the book is concerned with substantive issues, in both theory and practice. In empirical investigation, the 1791–1931 period is divided into subperiods – decadal to 1910 (1791–1800 through 1901–10), then 1911–14, 1919–25, and 1925–31, with the addition of 1950–66.[3]

Integration – the extent of perfection – of the American foreign-exchange market in its dollar–sterling manifestation is studied from two aspects: external and internal. External integration, which ignores the exchange rate and observes only gold points or the gold-point spread, is considered in part IV. Internal integration has three dimensions: geographic, temporal, and placement integration – integration across space, across time, and with respect to the mid-point of the gold-point spread, respectively. First, geographic integration, the focus of which is the decentralised nature of the early foreign-exchange market, is examined in part II. Second, temporal integration, which involves exchange-rate variation and movement, is treated in parts II and IV. Finally, placement integration, concerned with the location of the exchange rate rather than the variation in the rate, is considered in part IV.

Geographic integration is of interest only for the early part of the 1791–1931 period. External, temporal, and placement integration are investigated for the entirety of 1791–1931, 1950–66, except that data limitations sometimes force omission of the 1801–20 and 1919–25 subperiods.

Market efficiency, the topic of part V, involves the behavior of private parties in response to the profit opportunities afforded by the gold standard. Interest concentrates on those operations either (1) specific to a gold standard (gold-point arbitrage), (2) the pattern of which is essentially influenced by that standard (uncovered interest arbitrage, forward speculation), or (3) the working of which is intertwined with activities already included (covered interest arbitrage). Because of the strict information and data requirements that the testing of market efficiency involves, only the specially selected periods 1890–1906, 1925–31, and 1950–66 are examined for gold-point arbitrage and only 1925–31 for the other operations.

Regime efficiency pertains to the probability of maintenance of the gold standard with the existing mint parity, and is the viewpoint of part VI. The roles of both private parties and domestic authorities are explored in this context, and the entire 1791–1931, 1950–66 period is considered (absent 1801–20 and 1919–25).

To assist the reader, part VII provides summaries and conclusions of the entire study, organized in the following categories: institutions, theory, measurement, data, and empirical results. For each point, reference is made to the appropriate chapter section(s).

Part I
Monetary standards

2 The various monetary standards

1 Types of monetary standards, and exchange-rate consequences

Any given period in Anglo-American economic history can be characterized by the quintuplet (1) domestic monetary standard in Britain, (2)
domestic monetary standard in the United States, (3) international monetary standard in Britain, (4) international monetary standard in the United
States, and (5) exchange-rate system involving the two countries' currencies.

The *domestic monetary standards* that have entered American or British
economic history are basically distinguished as metallic versus paper standards, where a metallic standard is founded on metallic money and a paper
standard on paper currency. Metallic standards are either monometallic,
subdivided into gold or silver standards, or bimetallic, meaning that both a
gold and a silver standard are involved. A domestic metallic standard is
called a specie standard, because it is based on coined money, an archaic
word for which is "specie."[1]

The corresponding *international monetary standards* for a given country
are also divided into metallic or paper standards. A metallic standard, in
addition to the gold, silver, or bimetallic breakdown, can be divided into a
specie standard, as above, or a bullion standard, meaning a foundation on
bars rather than coin.

The domestic and international monetary standards as just defined are
country-specific dependent. The *exchange-rate system* between two countries is a joint characteristic of the international monetary standards of the
countries involved and is also a function of the exchange-market intervention policies of the countries' authorities. If the countries are each on an
international metallic standard, then there results a fixed exchange rate,
meaning a rate with an upper and lower bound.

If one of the countries is on a metallic and the other on a paper standard,
then the exchange rate is fixed, managed floating, or freely floating, according as the paper-standard authority pegs its currency against the other

country's currency, engages in exchange-market intervention short of pegging, or absents itself from the foreign-exchange market. If both countries are on a paper standard, then just one of the countries can bring about a fixed rate or managed float by appropriate intervention. Only if both countries restrain from exchange-market intervention will a free float result.

2   Domestic conditions for a metallic standard

Consider now the general conditions for a gold standard, whether of the specie or bullion variety. *Domestic conditions* are: (1) A well-defined and fixed gold content of the domestic monetary unit (although occasional discrete changes in the gold content are acceptable). For example, the dollar or pound would be defined as a specified number of ounces of pure gold. (2) The readiness and ability of the monetary authority to transact in gold in some form or forms (domestic coin, foreign coin, or bars) for domestic currency (coin or paper money) based on (though not necessarily equivalent to) that gold content, in unlimited amounts and in both directions. (3) The absence of restrictions on the use of gold by private parties, in particular, on the melting of gold (except that privately created gold money may be prohibited) and on the purchase or sale of gold (whether privately or on an organized market).

Within these three conditions, a gold-coin (specie) standard has the following special characteristics. (1a) Gold coin circulates as money, with unlimited legal-tender power (meaning compulsorily acceptable means of payment of any amount in any transaction or obligation). (2a) Privately held government or central bank (paper) currency is convertible into gold coin at the government (Treasury or mint) or central bank. (2b) Privately owned bullion (gold in mass or foreign coin considered as mass, or gold in the form of bars) is convertible into gold coin or currency at the government (mint) or central bank. (2c) Banknotes and deposit liabilities of private (commercial) banks are convertible into gold coin, government or central bank currency, or private banknotes the gold convertibility of which is government-guaranteed, at the issuing institution and at the fixed gold content of the currency. (3a) Gold coin may be melted into bullion and utilized or transacted as the private owner wishes.

The following private versus government/central bank transactions, though not requirements of a gold-coin standard, might also occur, as the option of the government or central bank: (2d) exchange of privately held domestic gold coin or government/central bank currency for gold bars, (2e) exchange of privately held foreign gold coin *not considered bullion* for government/central bank currency, (2f) exchange of privately held government/central bank currency for foreign gold coin *not considered bullion*.

If "gold" is replaced by "silver" in the above characteristics, a silver specie standard results. If the conditions pertain (separately) to both gold and silver, then there is a bimetallic standard. Under bimetallism, condition (1) involves a well-defined and fixed content of the domestic monetary unit both in gold and in silver. This establishes a fixed gold/silver price ratio. Condition (2) establishes potential transactions in both directions either in gold or silver (the form of specie – gold or silver – corresponding to the bullion in transaction (2b) and at the discretion of the government, central bank, or commercial bank in transactions (2a) and (2c)). This maintains the gold/silver price ratio.

Under a gold-bullion standard, condition (2) takes a restricted form. Gold coin does not circulate as money and is not transactable between the government or central bank and private parties. Government or central bank currency is transactable for gold bars in both directions, but the government may establish a minimum amount of privately held currency that must be offered for convertibility into bars.[2] Silver and bimetallic bullion standards are definable under similar lines. For ease of expression, where bullion versus specie standard is not the issue, the word "specie" will be used to denote gold or silver in any form.

3   International conditions for a metallic standard

Thus far only the "domestic conditions" for a gold (or silver or bimetallic) standard have been outlined, and these conditions define the specified domestic standard. An international gold (or silver or bimetallic) standard requires, in addition to the domestic conditions, that certain "international conditions" be fulfilled: (4) freedom of foreign-exchange transactions (that is, the absence of exchange control), (5) absence of exchange-market intervention (no exchange-rate management involving the authority transacting between the domestic and foreign currencies), and (6) freedom of international gold flows (no restrictions on the export or import of gold, or silver, or both).

Strictly speaking, a domestic gold (or silver or bimetallic) standard does not require conditions (4) to (6). Indeed, stipulation (6) is essentially irrelevant if no other country is on a metallic standard. However, the rationale for a bullion standard purely domestic in nature is hard to envisage. More generally, the international (which incorporates the domestic) rather than just the domestic metallic standards are the focus of this volume.

A paper standard involves an alteration of condition (2) so that one of the directions of the transaction is eliminated. Privately held government and central bank paper currency are not convertible into coin or bars; nor are private banknotes or deposit liabilities transferable into coin. Therefore a paper standard was called an "inconvertible paper currency." Other conditions of a gold (or silver or bimetallic) standard may be fulfilled; but it is nevertheless a paper, and not a specie or bullion, standard. If condition (5), no exchange-market intervention, holds for both countries involved – true for Britain and the United States in the 1791–1931 span – then there is a freely floating exchange rate between their currencies, irrespective as to whether the other country remains on a metallic standard.[3]

4   Legal versus effective monetary standard

Finally, the effective monetary standard (domestic or international) of a country must be distinguished from the legal standard. What actually operates could differ from what is mandated by statute. Three possible reasons for the difference are: (1) a divergence between the law and market forces, which could lead, for example, to legal bimetallism becoming effective monometallism; (2) the statute suspended or made inoperative by new legislation or administrative order; and (3) the government, central bank, or commercial banks simply not honoring legal commitments to convert paper currency or deposits into specie. Instances of each of the three events occur in Anglo-American history.

3 American monetary standard

1 Unit of account

Until the mid-1790s the monetary system of colonial times continued to exist in its basic form in the United States. The most important feature of that system was the dichotomy between the medium of exchange and the unit of account. The "Spanish dollar" – a silver coin produced in Mexico and Peru as well as Spain, and therefore sometimes called the "Mexican dollar" – was the dominant coin in transactions. Known in Spanish as the peso or piastre, it was termed the "dollar" or "piece of eight" in England and the colonies. The word "dollar" is a corruption of "thaler," an abbreviation of "Joachimsthaler," a silver coin produced in 1517 in a Bohemian county of the same name.[1] The smallest subdivision of the peso was the "real," one-eighth of a dollar. The term "piece of eight" flowed naturally for the entire peso.[2]

In contrast, the unit of account was based on the English system of pounds (£), shillings (s.), and pence (d.), where £1 = 20s. and 1s. = 12d. The phrase "based on" rather than "equivalent to" is used advisedly, because "a shilling from the British mint was not a shilling in any colony" (Carothers, 1930, p. 34). Instead of a national, homogeneous, standard of value, the individual states, as the colonies before them, had their own units of account. For example, a British shilling (1s.) was equal to 1s. 6d. in Massachusetts but 2s. in New York (Carothers, 1930, pp. 34, 47; Stewart, 1924, p. 19).

These properties of the colonial monetary system continued to exist after General Cornwallis surrendered at Yorktown in 1781, ending the American Revolutionary War, and even after the Articles of Confederation were superseded by the US Constitution in 1789. However, reform of the standard of value was on its way. In 1782 Robert Morris, Superintendent of Finance under the Confederation (equivalent to Secretary of the Treasury under the Constitution), submitted a report – in response to a directive from Congress but apparently already completed and by his assistant,

Gouverneur Morris (no relation) – that recommended a decimal system of currency, with "units" (mills), "cents" (100 units), and "marks" (1000 units). Morris understood the concept of a unit of account; for he notes that "there is no necessity that this money unit be exactly represented in coin."[3] Morris was the first author in history to suggest a monetary framework (unit of account and medium of exchange) based on a decimal system.

The monetary reform of Congressman Thomas Jefferson, probably writing in 1783, also involved a decimal system, with the dollar as the basic unit, a "tenth [of a dollar]" or "bit," forerunner of the dime, and the smallest coin a copper "hundredth [of a dollar]," what would be called the cent.[4] The Jefferson plan was embodied in a report dated May 13, 1785, of the Congressional Committee on Finance ("Report of a Grand Committee on the Money Unit"), which also allowed for a copper piece of 1/200th of a dollar. The first legislation on the subject occurred on July 6, 1785, when Congress resolved that the money unit of the United States should be the dollar with a decimal system of coinage ("the several pieces shall increase in a decimal ratio") and smallest coin a copper 1/200th of a dollar. It was followed by the Act of August 8, 1786, which specified "that the money of account . . . proceed in a decimal ratio," with mills (1000 to the money unit), dimes (ten to the unit), cents (100 to the unit), and dollars (the money unit).[5]

On April 15, 1790, the House of Representatives directed that Alexander Hamilton, Secretary of the Treasury, prepare a report on the establishment of a mint. Hamilton reported to the House on January 28, 1791, with a recommendation for a decimal system of account implicit in his coinage: the dollar, "tenth part" of the dollar, and "hundredth part" of the dollar (and also a "two-hundredth" part of the dollar).[6] Still, the standard of value remained as it had been in colonial America.

Finally, on April 2, 1792, Congress passed the Mint Act, which declared that "the money of account of the United States shall be expressed in dollars or units, dismes or tenths, cents or hundredths, and milles or thousandths." The decimal system was adopted! Further, for implementation: "all accounts in the public offices and all proceedings in the courts of the United States shall be kept and had in conformity to this regulation."[7] As commented by Stewart (1924, p. 18):

At one fell swoop with a few chosen words the English system of accounting with pounds, shillings, and pence that had been used by the people under the Colonial government of Great Britain and continued after the Declaration of Independence, as a matter of necessity down to the passage of this momentous Act of Congress, was obliterated as far as public records were concerned.

It took until about 1800 for the private sector to follow the government and courts in moving to the uniform national decimal accounting system from their states' specific pound–shilling–pence units of account.[8]

2   Metallic content of the dollar and coinage denominations

It also took a long time for the United States to reform the media of exchange that it inherited from colonial times. The new nation continued to rely on foreign coin, with the Spanish dollar and its fractional parts dominant. This dollar was rated by the individual states at differing values in terms of the local unit of account (although some valuations were common to several states – Stewart, 1924, p. 19). A silver standard was in effect, then, and its basis was the Spanish dollar. It is true that the dollars in circulation tended to vary greatly in weight and fineness (ratio of pure metal to total weight). This was because of the practice of sending the full-bodied coins abroad to settle balance-of-payments deficits, the lack of quality control at the Spanish mints in Mexico and Peru, and the private clipping and sweating of coins (in order to remove particles of silver prior to recirculation). Yet a dollar coin, irrespective of its condition, was acceptable "by tale" everywhere in the United States (as it had been in the colonies), that is, at its full assigned nominal value in local currency. While some gold coins did circulate, they were rated in dollars according to actual pure metal content.[9] This practice also dated from colonial times.[10]

The reform offered by Robert Morris involved a silver standard with the money unit only 0.25 grain of silver and equal to 1/1440th of the Spanish dollar.[11] The largest-denomination coin, the mark, would equal 1000/1440th of the dollar. The number 1440 was selected so that the shilling of each state (excluding South Carolina, an outlier due to paper-money inflation) could be converted into the smallest whole number of units based on the state's valuation of the Spanish dollar. Thus Morris would effect a reconciliation of the Spanish dollar, the new national unit, and the individual states' existing units of account. "The Morris plan was not only ingenious, but the most cumbersome scheme for coinage ever devised by Man" (Taxay, 1966, p. 16).

In contrast, Jefferson advocated as the monetary unit the dollar, equal in value to the Spanish dollar and composed of 365 grains of pure silver (purported to be the fine-metal content of the newest Spanish dollar). He would coin also a silver half-dollar and lesser denominations, along with a $10 gold piece. Thus there would be a bimetallic standard, and the gold/silver price ratio (ratio of silver to gold per dollar coinage) would be set at 15. The British fineness (ratio of pure metal to total weight) of 11/12th would be adopted. The Finance Committee report of 1785 modified Jefferson's plan, principally by having a 362 rather than 365-grain silver dollar and a $5 rather than $10 gold coin. It was followed by three reports on coinage and a mint, produced by the Board of Treasury, that took over the responsibilities of the Superintendent of Finance after Morris resigned. The Act of August 8, 1786 was heavily influenced by these reports.[12]

On October 16, 1786, Congress passed its first bill to establish a mint, in accordance with the Act of August 8, 1786, which authorized the coinage of a silver dollar and half-dollar, and a $10 gold piece, called the eagle, and a half-eagle, plus smaller denominations. Table 3.1 assembles all legislation and practice on the gold and silver value of the dollar from the first Mint Act to 1934. The final column of table 3.2 presents the most important element in table 3.1, the fine-metal content of the dollar, to the present day.

The specified amount of fine (pure) metal in a coin is the product of the standard fineness and standard weight. The standard fineness is the stipulated proportion of the weight consisting of pure metal, the remainder being alloy and considered worthless. The standard weight is the specified gross weight (pure metal plus alloy). Gold or silver of standard fineness is called "standard gold" or "standard silver." It is the relative amount of fine metal in gold and silver coins for a given valuation (say, a dollar) that defines the gold/silver price ratio (called the mint ratio), which was 15.25 under the 1786 legislation. However, except for a few copper pieces produced by a private contractor, the legislation was not put into effect and the mint was not established.

Yet the impetus for change was strong. In his report of January 1791, Hamilton investigated the specie market value of the Spanish dollar in the United States. Merchants valued the dollar at 24.75 grains of fine gold, while examination of the existing dollar coins in circulation revealed a gross weight of 416 grains on average and a fine weight of 368 and 374 grains for the two most recent dollars minted. These figures yield market gold/silver price ratios of 14.87 and 15.11, leading Hamilton to suggest a mint ratio of 15, resulting in a dollar of 24.75 grains of pure gold and 371.25 grains of pure silver. With fineness of 11/12th, standard weights would be 27 grains for the gold dollar and 405 for the silver.[13] Hamilton also recommended the minting of a $10 gold piece but not a half-dollar silver coin. The reverse coinage was inconceivable. Given the high valuation of gold relative to silver, a $10 silver coin would have been much too large and a half-dollar gold coin too small.

On March 3, 1791, Congress ordered that a mint be established, and on April 2, 1792 it passed the second Mint Act in US history but the first under the Constitution. Relying heavily on Hamilton's recommendations, Congress nevertheless deviated from them in authorizing the coinage also of gold half-eagles and quarter-eagles and of silver half-dollars and quarter-dollars. Also, incredibly, it legislated a cumbersome fineness of the silver dollar, at 1485/1664th (see table 3.1).[14]

Table 3.1 Gold and silver value of American dollar, 1786–1934

Authority	Date	Type of specification	Gold dollar				Silver dollar				Gold/silver price ratio[a]
			Fineness	Weight (grains)			Fineness	Weight (grains)			
				Standard	Fine			Standard	Fine		
Act of Congress	August 8, 1786	Legal	11/12	26.8656[b]	24.6268[b]		11/12	409.7891	375.64		15.25
Act of Congress	April 2, 1792	Legal	11/12	27[b]	24.75[b]		1485/1664	416	371.25		15.00
US Mint	Oct. 15, 1794[c]	Mint practice	11/12	27[b]	24.75[b]		9/10	416	374.4		15.13
Act of Congress	June 28, 1834[d]	Legal	116/129	25.8[b]	23.2[b]		1485/1664	416	371.25		16.00
Act of Congress	Jan. 18, 1837	Legal	9/10	25.8[b]	23.22[b]		9/10	412.5	371.25		15.99
Act of Congress	Feb. 12, 1873	Legal	9/10	25.8	23.22		—	—	—		
Act of Congress	Feb. 28, 1878	Legal					9/10	412.5	371.25		15.99
Act of Congress	March 14, 1900	Legal	9/10	25.8	23.22						
Presidential Proclamation	Jan. 31, 1934	Legal	9/10	15 5/21	13 5/7						

Notes:
[a] Ratio of fine-silver to fine-gold content of dollar.
[b] Weight of gold dollar is 1/10 of eagle ($10 gold piece).
[c] Terminated October 28, 1795.
[d] Effective July 31, 1834.

Sources: Huntington and Mawhinney (1910, pp. 475, 496–7, 502, 534–5, 579, 610), International Monetary Conference (1879, p. 450), Krooss (1969, p. 2805), Select Committee on Coins (1832, p. 17).

Table 3.2 *Effective American monetary standards, 1791–present*

Time period	National standard	Exceptional standard	Fine metal in dollar[a] (grains)
Jan. 1, 1791–March 2, 1794	silver	—	371[b]
March 3, 1794–Oct. 14, 1794	"	—	371.25
Oct. 15, 1794–Oct. 28, 1795	"	—	374.4
Oct. 29, 1795–Aug. 29, 1814	"	—	371.25
Aug. 30, 1814–Feb. 19, 1817	paper	silver (New England)[c]	"
Feb. 20, 1817–July 30, 1834	silver	—	"
July 31, 1834–Jan. 17, 1837	gold	—	23.2
Jan. 18, 1837—May 9, 1837	"	—	23.22
May 10, 1837–May 9, 1838	paper	—	"
May 10, 1838–Oct. 9, 1839	gold	paper (Philadelphia)[d]	"
Oct. 10, 1839–March 17, 1842	paper	gold (New England and New York)[e]	"
March 18, 1842–Oct. 13, 1857	gold	—	"
Oct 14, 1857[f]–Dec. 13, 1857	paper	gold (Alabama, Kentucky, and New Orleans)	"
Dec. 18, 1857[g]–Dec. 29, 1861	gold	paper (Philadelphia, Baltimore, and South)[h]	"
Dec. 30, 1861–Sept. 24, 1873	paper	gold (West Coast)[i]	"
Sept. 25, 1873–Oct. 22, 1873	currency[j]	gold (West Coast)	"
Oct. 23, 1873–Dec. 31, 1878	paper	"	"
Jan. 1, 1879–Aug. 2, 1893	gold	—	"
Aug. 3, 1893–Sept. 2, 1893	gold[k]	—	"
Sept. 3, 1893–Oct. 30, 1907	gold	—	"
Oct. 31, 1907–Dec. 30, 1907	gold[k]	—	"
Dec. 31, 1907–April 5, 1917	gold	paper (New York)[l]	"
April 6, 1917–March 17, 1922	paper	—	"
March 18, 1922–March 5, 1933	gold	—	"
March 6, 1933–Jan. 30, 1934	paper	—	"
Jan 31, 1934–Aug. 14, 1971	"	gold (official foreigners)[m]	13 5/7
Aug. 15, 1971–Dec. 17, 1971	"	—	"
Dec. 18, 1971–Feb. 12, 1973	"	gold (official foreigners)[m]	12 12/19
Feb. 13, 1973–present	"	—	11.3684

Notes:

^a Metallic dollar, even during periods of paper standard.

^b Average weight of two Spanish-dollar issues in circulation, as computed by Alexander Hamilton.

^c Also, silver standard continued in Ohio and Kentucky until January 1, 1815, and in Nashville, Tennessee, until Augut 1815.

^d Until August 13, 1838. Also, banks in the South and West.

^e Also, in Pennsylvania January 15–February 3, 1841, and elsewhere around that time.

^f Date pertains to New York. September 24–6 in Baltimore and Philadelphia. A large part of the banks in Pennsylvania, Virginia, Maryland, and Rhode Island also suspended before New York.

^g Date pertains to New York. Baltimore and Philadelphia returned to gold February 3–5, Virginia May 1, 1858.

^h Virginia, Baltimore, and Philadelphia banks suspended November 20–2, 1860, followed by St. Louis, South Carolina, and Georgia banks November 28–30. Philadelphia and Baltimore banks resumed February–March 1861.

ⁱ Also, Ohio, Indiana, and Kentucky banks did not suspend until January 1861, March 1861, and March 1862, respectively.

^j Notes only, excluding certified checks.

^k Obtainable at par from currency only, not certified checks.

^l August–October 1914.

^m US Treasury bought gold from anyone but sold it only to foreign monetary authorities and licensed industrial users.

Sources: Bolles (1894, vol. II, pp. 264–5, 322, 328), Brown (1940, p. 37), Calmoris and Schweikart (1991, pp. 822–3), Chandler (1958, pp. 103–4), de Vries (1985, vol. I, pp. 66, 69), Dunbar (1904, pp. 280–4, 288, 309–10), Friedman and Schwartz (1963, pp. 7, 27, 471), Hammond (1957, pp. 227, 246–8, 481), Knox (1900, pp. 76, 504–5, 512, 514), McGrane (1965, p. 201), Mitchell (1903, pp. 40–1, 141, 144–7), Nussbaum (1957, pp. 174–80), Secretary of the Treasury (1830, p. 47; 1838, p. 5; 1920, pp. 181–2; 1922, p. 72), Smith and Cole (1935, pp. 26–9), Sprague (1910, pp. 57, 67, 187, 280–2; 1915, p. 528), Sumner (1874, pp. 68, 74, 140, 144–6, 151–2), Temin (1969, p. 113), Yeager (1976, pp. 65, 580–1). Also, table 3.1 and see text.

The first coinage of the mint consisted of experimental half-dimes, probably produced in July 1792.[15] While coinage of minor copper coins began the following year, gold and silver could not be processed until the assayer and chief coiner posted a $10,000 bond, under the Mint Act, and the appointees were unable to do so. Thomas Jefferson as Secretary of State wrote to President Washington about the problem, and on March 3, 1794 Congress reduced the amount of the bond required.[16]

With the posting of bonds, the mint could effectively function. The first deposit of bullion (which was silver), however, did not take place until July 1794, and its coinage was completed on October 15.[17] This began an amazing episode in American monetary history. For over a year – overlapping the tenure of two directors of the mint – silver was coined at a convenient fineness of 9/10th rather than the slightly lower fineness of 1485/1664th specified by law (see table 3.1). The practice was quite deliberate, though with the expectation that the law would be changed to correspond to mint practice. Instead, in the short run, the mint practice changed to correspond with the existing law; for, when the third mint director took office on October 28, 1795, he ordered that the legislated fineness be followed.[18] However, 42 years later, the law would be amended to conform to the 1794–5 mint practice.

On June 28, 1834 Congress passed legislation (effective July 31) that drastically changed the mint ratio, from 15 to slightly over 16. The silver dollar was left unchanged, but the standard and fine weights of the gold dollar were reduced non-proportionately, resulting in an unwieldy fineness of the gold dollar (116/129th) to accompany that of the silver dollar (1485/1664th). These deficiencies were removed with the legislation of January 18, 1837, when the fineness of both gold and silver coins was changed to 9/10th, the former by increasing the fine metal in a dollar's worth of coin, the latter by reducing the standard weight of a silver dollar. The mint ratio now moved slightly below 16.[19]

The *mint price* of gold or silver is the value of domestic money that the mint will coin per physical unit of bullion deposited with it. The standard weight of the gold dollar established in the legislation of 1837 was to remain until 1934 (see table 3.1). From the standard weight, one can obtain the mint price of standard gold: the price per "standard ounce" (meaning ounce of standard fineness) at which bullion is converted into coin by the mint. From 1837 to 1934, the mint price of standard gold was $18.604651 + per ounce, obtained as the ratio 480/25.8, where the numerator is the number of grains per ounce, the denominator the standard weight of the dollar in grains, and "+" represents additional decimal places. Taking 10/9th of that price, where 10/9th is the reciprocal of the standard fineness, the mint-price equivalent per ounce of fine gold was $20.671834 +.

The Act of March 3, 1849 authorized coinage of gold dollars and double-eagles ($20 coins). The former was not popular, in part because of its small size, in part because of the introduction of subsidiary silver coinage in 1853 (see section 3), with less than $20 million produced in total until the coin was discontinued by the Act of September 26, 1890. The Act of February 21, 1853 allowed for coinage of a $3 gold piece, an unusual denomination, that also was discontinued by the 1890 legislation, with less than $2 million having been struck. In contrast, the double-eagle was enormously success-ful, and the preferred coin of those engaged in international gold operations (see section 2.2.1(2) of chapter 9); almost $3.5 billion of this coin was pro-duced in total. The Act of February 12, 1873 summarized the coinage authorizations and standards for gold. Both this act and that of March 14, 1900 are distinguished by defining the dollar directly in terms of gold, whereas all earlier legislation had established the weight of the gold dollar implicitly via the eagle.[20]

Even World War I did not disturb the established weight of the gold dollar. However, the Act of May 12, 1933 authorized the President to reduce the gold content of the dollar to a minimum of 50 percent of its existing weight. Subsequently, the Gold Reserve Act of January 30, 1934 amended that provision by authorizing the President by proclamation to fix the weight of the dollar at any level between 50 and 60 percent of its current weight. On January 31, 1934 President Roosevelt reduced the weight of the dollar to 59.06 percent of its existing level. With the 9/10th fineness retained, the fine weight of the dollar became $13.7142+$ ($13 5/7$) grains of gold and the "mint-price equivalent" $480/(13.7142+) = \$35$ per fine ounce.[21]

Turning to table 3.2, the Smithsonian Agreement of December 18, 1971 increased the price of pure gold to $38 an ounce, implying a fine gold weight of the dollar equal to $480/38 = 12.6315+$ ($12 12/19$) grains. The final official action on the dollar/gold price occurred on February 13, 1973, when the dollar was devalued to $42.22 ... per ounce, equivalent to $480/42.22 ... = 11.3684+$ grains of pure gold in a dollar (where "..." indicates an infinitely recurring pair of numbers, in this case "22").

3   Legal-tender status of coin

The Mint Act of 1792 established full legal tender for all gold and silver coins issued by the mint, those of less than full weight at values proportional to their weight. With the other prerequisites of a specie standard satisfied (see section 2 of chapter 2), bimetallism was legally installed. The Act of 1837 declared legal tender at full nominal value, with no reduced value for lightweight coin – a status received also by the new denominations of gold coins in the Acts of 1849 and 1853.

In the meantime the legal-tender status of foreign coin, particularly the Spanish dollar, required attention. After all, foreign coin had been the only coin of consequence in the colonies and the United States until the US mint began full functioning. Also, Hamilton had recommended gold and silver values of the US dollar derived from market values of the Spanish dollar, and the 1792 Mint Act had declared the value of the US silver dollar to be equal to that of the then current Spanish dollar.

Hamilton suggested a maximum three-year period for circulation of foreign coin. One month after the Mint Act of 1792 was passed, a committee was appointed to consider the role of foreign coin, leading to the Act of February 9, 1793, which provided for the full legal tender of (1) gold coins of certain countries at stipulated valuations in proportion to their weights (2) the Spanish silver dollar, if minimum weight of 415 grains, at 100 cents (that is, equal to the US dollar), and in proportion for parts of the dollar, and (3) the French silver crown, similarly treated. Three years after the mint began coinage, the date to be proclaimed by the President, all foreign coins except the Spanish dollar and its subdivisions would cease to be legal tender. The proclamation was made by President John Adams on July 22, 1797; but the termination date of October 15, 1797 did not stand, and various Acts between 1798 and 1834 continued the legal-tender status of foreign coin.[22]

The legislation addressing the legal-tender position of foreign coin was confusing and unhelpful to US monetary development. Foreign gold coins, no matter how worn, possessed full legal tender; but the dominant foreign coin, the Spanish silver dollar, was required to be at least 415 grains (with parts in proportion) to have this power. "The impossibility of weighing coins in retail trade meant that the entire mass of Spanish coins would be accepted as legal coins" (Carothers, 1930, p. 67). The provisions for legal tender of parts of the Spanish, later Mexican, silver dollar were inconsistent and unclear. Irrespective of legislation, the public apparently considered all foreign coin to be full legal tender. In fact, until July 31, 1834, with the coming into effect of the 1834 mint legislation, the Spanish dollar was the dominant coin in the United States (see section 8 below, section 3 of chapter 5, and section 2.2.1 of chapter 9), and only in 1853, when US silver coins below a dollar became subsidiary in nature (see below), did the parts of the Spanish dollar lose substantial circulatory power. Finally, the Act of February 21, 1857 terminated the legal-tender status of all foreign coin.[23]

As mentioned, the legal position of silver coins changed in 1853, when an Act of February 21 provided for fiduciary coinage of silver pieces below a dollar, reducing their weight (but not fineness) by 6.91 percent and limiting their legal-tender power to $5.[24] It appears obvious that the purpose of the Act was to render a proper subsidiary coinage, and indeed that was its effect. Nevertheless, some observers see the legislation as paving the way to formal gold monometallism, even though the silver dollar coin is not even mentioned in the Act.

Watson (1899, p. 107) writes: "When this bill was being discussed in Congress it was claimed that it would result in establishing the gold standard, and it clearly appears from the debates as published in the *Congressional Globe* that such was the evident purpose of the bill, and that there was no desire to conceal it." Laughlin (1900, p. 92) declares: "This, then, was the act which really excluded silver dollars from our currency." Myers (1970, p. 34) comments: "The debates in Congress show quite clearly that the intention of the Act of 1853 was abandonment of the bimetallic standard."

Rather, Carothers (1930, pp. 120, 136) is on the mark in stating: "it was not the intention of Congress to demonetize silver, and the law did not effect this result . . . the subsidiary coinage law of 1853 did not establish the gold standard and was not intended to establish it." But he does concede that "it paved the way to the gold standard." Martin (1973, p. 841) notes: "Although the Act of February 21, 1853 did not repeal completely the de jure bases of bimetallism, it did terminate de facto bimetallism in the United States."

Twenty years later, the Act of February 12, 1873 ended coinage of the silver dollar. A "trade dollar," of 420 grains, was to be coined freely (that is, from any depositor of silver bullion), but it was included with subsidiary coins and given the $5 legal-tender restriction. While the standard silver dollar was no longer to be issued, the full legal-tender power of existing silver dollars remained undisturbed. Legislation of June 22, 1874 revised the statutes so that [all] silver coins of the United States should have limited tender of $5 in any payment.[25] It was this 1874 action that accomplished the true demonetization of silver.

Nevertheless, it was the 1873 exclusion of silver dollars from coinage that is viewed as the formal end of bimetallism in the United States.[26] The Act of February 12, 1873 became known as the "Crime of 1873," and silver coinage became a domestic political issue.[27] Friedman (1990b, pp. 1165–6) shows that there was no crime in the legal sense, but the standard silver dollar was omitted from the coinage list intentionally, deliberately to demonetize silver. The most incisive comment on the matter is made by Watson (1899, p. 119): "no one seemed to have discovered that the Act of 1873 omitted the silver dollar until some years later when the price of silver bullion began to fall. Then the agitation began in the silver States about the omission of the dollar from the act, and it was charged that a crime had been committed."

It is ironic that the move from formal bimetallism to a legal gold standard, whether in 1873 or 1874, occurred during the greenback, *paper* standard, with a dual legal and effective gold standard not reached until 1879 (see sections 4 and 9). Meanwhile, silver legislation proceeded. The Act of July 22, 1876 ended both the legal-tender power and the free coinage of the trade dollar. In fact, the Secretary of the Treasury terminated coinage of the trade dollar in 1878, except for trivial amounts over the next five years. Less than $36 million had been coined in total.

Free coinage of silver was never restored. The Bland–Allison Act of February 28, 1878 directed the Secretary of the Treasury to purchase $2–4 million of silver bullion monthly, to be coined into standard silver dollars of unlimited legal tender. In fact, the Treasury purchased silver in minimum amounts, and "the coins were very badly received" (Carothers, 1930, pp. 282–3). The Sherman Purchase Act of July 14, 1890 changed the monthly amount of silver bought to 4.5 million ounces, with payment to be made by the issuance of Treasury notes (see section 4). The Act of November 1, 1893 repealed these provisions, but coinage of silver dollars continued to 1904.[28]

The legal gold standard was established in the Act of February 12, 1873 which stipulated that the gold dollar of standard weight "shall be the unit of value." Consistent with the 1792 Act, US gold coins were to be legal tender in all payments at nominal value when not below standard weight and limit of tolerance, otherwise at valuation in proportion to their actual weight. The Gold Standard Act of March 14, 1900 declared the gold dollar of 25.8 grains 9/10ths fine to be "the standard unit of value." It was not until January 30, 1934, with the passage of the Gold Reserve Act, that the gold standard was legally terminated. All gold coin was to be withdrawn from circulation and no further gold coining was to occur.

4   Convertibility of government/central bank paper into coin

The first US government paper currency convertible into coin on demand was the Treasury demand notes authorized by the Acts of July 17, 1861 and February 12, 1862. By the Act of March 17, 1862 these notes were made receivable for all payments due to the United States and for all claims and demand against the United States except for interest on bonds and notes, which were to be paid in coin. Also, they were made legal tender for all payments (except for interest payable by the United States, as aforementioned).

Four Acts (February 25 and July 11, 1862; January 17 and March 3, 1863) authorized the Treasury to issue United States notes, the famous "greenbacks". These legislations are called the "legal-tender acts," because, for the first time, they gave legal-tender power to paper currency (US notes and Treasury demand notes). The legal tender of US notes excluded both payment of import tariffs and interest on the public debt. The notes were not redeemable in coin until January 1, 1879, as provided by the Resumption Act of January 14, 1875.[29] The Gold Standard Act of March

14, 1900 repeated this obligation of the Treasury, and stipulated gold coin of the weight and fineness fixed in the Act, which was the standard weight and fineness.

The Act of March 3, 1863 provided a third government paper currency: gold certificates, issued in response to gold coin and bullion deposited with the Treasury and payable in such gold on demand. The amount issued could be up to 20 percent higher than the value of gold deposited. By the Act of July 12, 1882, (1) only gold coin was so depositable and payable, (2) the certificates were made receivable for customs, taxes and all public dues, and (3) the certificates were to be pure warehouse receipts, with no excess of issuance over deposits.[30] The Act of March 2, 1911 extended the allowable deposits to foreign gold coin and gold bars produced by US mints or the New York assay office. The certificates were a convenience to those dealing in gold. It was not until the Act of December 24, 1919 that they were made legal tender.[31]

The fourth government paper currency was the Treasury notes of 1890. The Act of July 14, 1890 established that these notes were to be a full legal tender (except where otherwise expressly stipulated by contract) and receivable for customs, taxes, and all public dues. The notes were made redeemable on demand, in gold or silver coin at the discretion of the Treasury. The Act of March 14, 1900 specified gold coin, of standard weight and fineness (as for US notes).

Federal Reserve notes, authorized by the Federal Reserve Act of December 23, 1913, were a central bank currency to be redeemed in gold at the Treasury on demand. The notes were made receivable by all Federal Reserve banks, member banks of the Federal Reserve System, and national banks, and also for all taxes, customs, and other public dues. However, they were not given legal-tender status until June 5, 1933.[32]

5   Nature of coinage

Coinage of private bullion has three characteristics: openness (delineation of the depositors for whom coinage would be provided), cost (with charges possible for mint expenses and for seigniorage, the monopoly profit of the mint), and speed (the duration between receipt of bullion and delivery of coin to the depositor).

Regarding openness, the Mint Act of 1792 specified free coinage (open to bullion from any person or persons) and for both gold and silver, while that of 1873 declared free coinage only for gold (with a $100 minimum) and silver trade dollars. The Federal Reserve Act of 1913 permitted Federal Reserve banks to deal in gold coin or bullion and to exchange Federal Reserve notes for gold, gold coin, or gold certificates. This provision meant, in particular, that the owner of gold bars or foreign gold coin could always convert it into American gold coin at the mint or, if a Federal Reserve bank was prepared to transact, could exchange the bullion for gold-convertible Federal Reserve notes. The Federal Reserve Bank of New York did exercise its right to purchase gold bars, and from all comers, at least from 1925 onward. Even throughout World War I the Treasury continued its open policy of buying gold according to statute.

Turning to the mint charge, Robert Morris suggested that it be almost 3.5 percent, while the Acts of August 8 and October 16, 1786 set it at almost 2 percent for silver and slightly above that for gold.[33] The Mint Act of 1792 involved no mint charges except if the depositor and mint were to agree to an immediate exchange of coins for standard bullion, in which case there would be a charge of 0.5 percent. This provision was pursuant to a recommendation in the Hamilton report. The Act of June 28, 1834 repeated the 0.5-percent charge, but changed "immediate" exchange to payment within five or forty days, in contradictory sentences within the same section of the Act.[34]

Neither the 1792 nor 1834 Acts assessed the depositor for the cost of mint procedures to bring deposited bullion to standard: melting (required for various other procedures), assaying (determination of the fine-gold and/or fine-silver content of bullion), alloying (addition of alloy to reduce the fineness of overly fine bullion to standard), parting or separating (separation of gold from silver in bullion containing both in significant quantity), toughening (removal of metals unacceptable for coining that are intermixed with bullion), and refining (the specific processes by which parting and/or toughening take place).[35]

The Mint Act of 1837 marked an abrupt shift in the nature of mint charges. The 0.5-percent charge was dropped, and the only charges permitted were for separating, toughening, refining, and for the metal used for alloy, the rates to be fixed from time to time so as not to exceed the actual expense of the mint. However, the Act of February 21, 1853 added seigniorage of 0.5 percent, with no reciprocation of quick coinage. The Mint Act of 1873 reduced seigniorage to 0.2 percent (for converting standard gold bullion into coin), and the Resumption Act of 1875 eliminated seigniorage. From that time on, coinage was gratuitous (meaning no seigniorage charge for standard bullion), but the Act of 1873 specified charges for melting, refining, toughening, and copper alloy, to be fixed from time to time, at actual average cost.

The speed of coinage was dismal until the second half of the nineteenth century. In 1803 the annual report of the mint stated that the certificates for deposits of bullion were sold to the banks at 0.25–0.5 percent discount for delay of coinage (Bolles, 1894, vol. II, p. 165, n. 4), and a 0.5-percent discount for about this time is noted by Stewart (1924, p. 50). In 1831 the delay in coinage was said to be two months, equivalent to an interest loss of 1 percent (Sumner, 1874, pp. 104–5). As late as 1850, a lag of 52 days between deposit and coinage was experienced, equal to nearly a 1-percent loss of interest (Committee on Commerce, 1850, p. 4). An additional delay and cost emanated from the location of the mint in Philadelphia, whereas the international commercial center of the country had become New York City and there was no branch mint there. In 1850 the transport cost for shipment of bullion from New York to Philadelphia was reported at 0.25 percent.

It is not surprising, then, that the mint was little used by private parties. For enhanced business, two reforms were needed. First, funds had to be appropriated by Congress for the mint for the purchase of bullion in advance of deposits. Without such a "bullion fund," the provisions of the 1792 and 1834 Acts for speedy exchange of coin for bullion were inoperative: "the depositor of bullion had to wait weeks and even months for his coins" (Carothers, 1930, p. 73). As early as 1797 the Committee of Congress on the mint recommended a bullion fund (Stewart, 1924, p. 50), and in 1836 the Secretary of the Treasury requested that Congress authorize him to establish such a fund, even temporarily, in the amount of $100,000 (Secretary of the Treasury, 1836, p. 1). The Mint Act of 1837 directed the Secretary to keep in the mint a bullion fund of up to $1 million (when the state of the Treasury so permitted) for the purpose of paying depositors as soon as practicable after the value of bullion had been ascertained. The Act of May 23, 1850 permitted the President to transfer funds to the mint for the same purpose (Huntington and Mawhinney, 1910, p. 509). A bullion fund was in fact established (Bolles, 1894, vol. II, p. 514).

The second required reform was the institution of a mint branch or equivalent office in New York. The Act of March 3, 1853 provided for the establishment of an "assay office" in that city (Huntington and Mawhinney, 1910, pp. 514–16). To private parties in New York, dealing with the assay office was the same as dealing with the mint, except that the element of distance and associated expense was eliminated.[36] The New York Assay Office opened for business in October 1854, and from that date dealing with the mint (via the Assay Office) was a practicable opportunity for private parties centered in New York.

The Federal Reserve Act gave the Federal Reserve banks the right to deal in gold coin and bullion and, in particular, to exchange Federal Reserve notes for gold bars. At least in the 1925–31 period, the Federal Reserve Bank of New York purchased bars from private parties at the mint price (see section 2.2.2 of chapter 9). So owners of gold bars could receive for them either coin at the New York Assay Office or Federal Reserve notes (exchangeable into coin) at the Federal Reserve Bank of New York.

6   Provision of bars

The Act of May 26, 1882 authorized the mints and the Assay Office in New York to provide gold bars in exchange for US gold coin, with a $5000 minimum. The Act of March 3, 1891 specified that this exchange could occur only with the approval of the Secretary of the Treasury, and allowed the Secretary to impose a charge equal to the cost of manufacturing the bars. Finally, the Act of March 3, 1901 allowed a charge of any amount.[37]

On June 1, 1882, the 1882 Act went into effect (*New York Times*, July 2, 1882, p. 9). The bars provided by the Treasury were much prized, because they were "Assay bars," that is, bars with the fineness (also weight and value) stamp of the New York Assay Office. From March 1928, if not earlier, the bars were obtainable also from the Federal Reserve Bank of New York (see section 2.2.1 of chapter 9).

7   Convertibility of banknotes and bank deposits

Though the monetary system of the American colonies extended into the United States, indeed as far forward as the 1790s (see sections 1 and 2), there was one respect in which the US system differed. Commercial banks did not exist in the colonies. During the Confederation period (1781–8), three banks were established in the United States. By the end of 1790 four banks were open for business, and by the end of 1791, six. Then the growth of banking accelerated. In 1800 29 banks were operating; in 1816, 246.[38]

Historically, banks were of four types: federal, private, state, and national. Some early banks (Bank of North America, First and Second Bank of the United States) were federal in the senses that enabling legislation was by Act of Congress and the banks performed some functions of a central bank. Private banks were unchartered and unincorporated. State banks were chartered by individual states, and national banks by Congressional Acts of February 25, 1863 and June 3, 1864.[39] In 1913 the Federal Reserve Act created a true central banking system, the Federal Reserve banks.

Because the notes issued and deposits created by banks were debts of the institution, the banks had the legal obligation of extinguishing these debts in legal tender, at par (meaning at face value, without discount) and, by contractual obligation (for notes and demand deposits), on demand. Until 1862, the only legal tender was gold and silver coin; so banks had to redeem their notes and deposits in that medium. Then there arose the concept of "lawful money," meaning money usable as legal bank reserves against note and deposit liabilities. In addition to legal-tender coin, lawful-money status was extended to US notes (Act of February 25, 1862), Treasury demand notes (Act of March 17, 1862), gold and silver certificates (Act of July 12, 1882), and Treasury notes of 1890 (Act of July 14, 1890).[40]

By the enabling legislations, the legal reserves of national banks could consist only of lawful money, and Federal Reserve notes were redeemable at the Federal Reserve banks in lawful money. While national banknotes were redeemable in lawful money at the issuing bank, the Act of June 20, 1874 provided also for their redemption, in US notes, at the Treasury, based on a 5-percent redemption fund (in lawful money) maintained there by the issuing banks (Huntington and Mawhinney, 1910, pp. 418–21). For state banks, acceptable legal-reserves media were determined by state legislation. In most states, not only lawful money but also national banknotes were permissible reserves (Friedman and Schwartz, 1963, pp. 21, 781–2). In sum, all banks stood ready to cash their deposits and banknotes at par in coin or in paper currency redeemable in coin.

In addition to Federal Reserve notes, the Federal Reserve Act authorized circulating notes of individual Federal Reserve banks (known as Federal Reserve banknotes). They were similar to national banknotes, but never replaced them and were not a popular currency. Although made legal tender (with Federal Reserve notes) on June 5, 1933, their issuance was terminated by the Act of June 12, 1945.[41]

8   Legal versus effective metallic standards

With no restrictions on the melting or use of gold and silver, all the domestic conditions for a metallic standard in general and for a specie standard in particular were legally fulfilled in the United States from 1786 onward. The one exception was a functioning mint to convert bullion into coin, which did not begin until March 1794. The lack of a mint also meant that the monetary legislation of 1786 was inoperative.

Formally, the United States was on a bimetallic standard from 1786 to 1873. However, although the Congressional legislations of 1786, 1792, 1834, and 1837 all involved a bimetallic standard, it happened that even under these laws the United States was in fact either on a gold or a silver standard but never both. The reason is that a mint gold/silver price ratio different from the market (world) ratio provides incentive for (1) the undervalued metal, whether bullion or coin, to be sold on the world market, and (2) the overvalued metal to be coined and utilized as domestic money. Indeed, if the undervalued metal is exchanged for the overvalued one, a process of arbitrage occurs that in principle can change the market ratio so that it comes sufficiently close to the mint ratio to eliminate the incentive for the transactions. In practice, there is generally insufficient supply of the undervalued metal available domestically to alter the world ratio significantly.[42]

The "world" market gold/silver price ratio for 1791–1834 is shown in column 2 of table 5.2 (in chapter 5), which may be compared to the American ratio listed in the last column of table 3.1.[43] It was only from March 1794 that the United States possessed a functioning mint to support its legislation. So the Mint Act of 1786 was irrelevant and that of 1792 applicable only from March 1794. Until that last date, a silver standard based on the Spanish dollar reigned in the United States by default (see section 2). From March 1794 until July 30, 1834, the American legal mint ratio, at 15 – and even the slightly higher unauthorized ratio in 1794–5 – was continuously below the world ratio. This meant that gold was undervalued and silver overvalued in the United States relative to world markets, and an effective silver standard resulted, notwithstanding legal bimetallism supported by a functioning mint. Interestingly, the result was unintentional. Hamilton had recommended a mint ratio that he thought was close to market rates both in the United States and abroad, and in this he was at least temporarily successful.[44]

The situation was reversed in 1834 when Congress deliberately established a mint ratio (at 16.00) above the world ratio (15.73), so that gold would be overvalued and silver undervalued. From 1834 to 1873 the world gold/silver price ratio was consistently below 16. Beginning July 31, 1834, then, it was economically unsound for a private party to provide silver for coinage and economically sound for the party to withdraw from circulation any silver previously coined, melt it down for its metal content, sell it for gold on the open market, and present the gold to the US Mint for coinage. The only metallic standard that could effectively exist and persist in the United States was the gold standard.[45] The fact that the world gold/silver price ratio rose above 16 in 1874 is irrelevant, because in 1873–4 silver was legally reduced to a subsidiary coinage (see section 3) and in any event the United States was then on the paper greenback standard.[46] Five years later the United States was on not only a legal but also an effective monometallic gold standard. In summary, disregarding episodic paper standards (and eventually a lasting one), the United States was on a silver standard until July 30, 1834 and on a gold standard thereafter.

9   Paper standards

Table 3.2 shows the time periods of effective monetary standards of the United States from 1791 to the present. A metallic standard, gold or silver, was subject to interruption by a paper standard. In each case the movement off specie was initiated by commercial banks "suspending specie payments" in the face of an experienced or feared increased demand for specie on the part of the public, a demand that could not be satisfied given the fractional-reserve system under which banks operated. One scenario was for the banks to run out of reserves or virtually so, to close their doors, and to declare bankruptcy. The alternative, and preferred, scenario was for the banks to refuse to pay specie for their outstanding notes and deposits at the par (dollar-for-dollar) value but nevertheless to remain open and sometimes even to expand their note and deposit liabilities. As Temin (1969, p. 115) observes: "Suspension as practiced in the nineteenth century was not bankruptcy; one might say it was an alternative to bankruptcy." For a bank to refuse to convert its note and deposit liabilities into legal tender (or, later, lawful-reserve money for national banks and legislated acceptable money for state banks) was not only in general violation of a contract but also specifically illegal in many states. However, "the laws on this matter were seldom enforced" (Temin, 1969, p. 114).

With "suspension of specie payments," markets developed in which the notes of suspending banks traded at a discount in terms of specie. The existence of such markets meant that Gresham's Law was inoperative. Specie and its equivalent (notes and deposits of non-suspending institutions) circulated together with notes and deposits of the suspending institutions, but a fixed exchange rate ("parity") between the two types of money was not imposed.[47]

From 1861, with the issuance and circulation of government currency, followed by national banknotes and, after the Federal Reserve Act, central-bank currency, inconvertibility involved not only commercial-bank but also government behavior. For the government to cease to honor its redemption commitments could make the banks declare suspension. It was also true that the government standing fast could induce the commercial banks to avoid suspension. However, the existence of currency issues directly or indirectly government-guaranteed could foster banking panics by providing alternatives beyond specie for local banknotes and deposits.[48]

Suspension of specie payments did not generally occur in all regions of the country: it was not a national phenomenon. In the affected states, a floating exchange rate between (1) the paper dollar (note or deposit) and (2) specie and foreign exchange resulted. In the states where banks continued to honor the specie-convertibility commitment, the specie standard was disturbed neither within regions nor internationally but only against regions where suspension occurred. The floating exchange rate led to a currency depreciation only in those areas where banks suspended payments.

As table 3.2 shows, widespread bank suspensions occurred in 1814–17, 1837–42 (accurately characterized as a series of suspensions), 1857, and 1861–78, with localized suspensions in 1860–1.[49] The experience of December 30, 1861–December 31, 1878 is noteworthy for several reasons.

First, it was the first occasion in which not only the banks but also the government suspended; for on December 30, 1861 the Treasury refused to honor the right of holders of its demand notes to redeem the notes in gold. Second, this episode involved government issuance of legal-tender paper currency, US notes or "greenbacks," whence the name "greenback period." As the Treasury demand notes were received by the Treasury for customs duties (a property that US notes lacked), they were replaced by greenbacks in accordance with the greenback legislation. Third, a free market for gold not only developed in terms of the irredeemable dollar (Treasury demand notes and banknotes, and later greenbacks) but also was institutionalized, with a formal gold market in New York City and banks offering both gold deposits (that is, deposits payable in gold) and ordinary (greenback) deposits.[50]

In the postbellum period to World War I, the experienced bank suspensions beyond the greenback period involved the withholding of the obligation to convert deposits into both currency and specie rather than specie alone. In this respect the 1873 experience has been called a "suspension within a suspension" (Martin, 1898, p. 40), as specie payments had been suspended since the end of 1861 and now banks refused to cash their deposits into currency as well. Suspension of currency (and specie) payments also occurred in 1893 and 1907. In these three episodes a premium on currency in terms of certified checks developed. The currency-premium experiences involved an appreciation of currency against deposits (certified checks), but not a depreciation of currency against gold and foreign exchange (except as already was occurring during the greenback period).[51]

In April 1917, when the United States entered as a belligerent in World War I, another paper-standard period ensued. The Treasury and the Federal Reserve banks, though always claiming that they obeyed the statutes guaranteeing redemption in gold coin of all US paper money and Federal Reserve notes on demand, in fact imposed effective, though informal, restrictions on redemption from April 6, 1917 to March 17, 1922.[52] Commercial banks cooperated with the Federal Reserve by converting their notes and deposits only into currency and not gold, a perfectly legal restriction (Cross, 1923, p. 377).

The final, and still current, US paper standard began on March 6, 1933, when President Roosevelt suspended gold redemption and prohibited banks from paying out gold. Subsequently, an Executive Order of March 10 prohibited gold payments by banks and non-banks unless licensed by the Secretary of the Treasury. The Congressional Joint Resolution of June 5, 1933 declared "gold clauses" – provisions for payment in gold or in US money measured in gold – to be invalid in the sense that such obligations were dischargeable in any legal tender, and it conveyed legal-tender status on all coins and currencies of the United States (including Federal Reserve notes).

From September 8, 1933 the official gold price was fixed daily at the world market price less shipping and insurance cost, but only for the purpose of the Treasury purchasing gold from domestic mining companies. This set the stage for the Gold Reserve Act of January 30, 1934 and the Presidential Proclamation the next day that established a fixed dollar price for gold at $35 per fine ounce. However, the existing paper standard was not disturbed in any real sense. Indeed, the Gold Reserve Act forbade redemption of any US currency in gold.

Rather, from January 31, 1934 the United States was only on a "limited gold-bullion standard" (Yeager, 1976, p. 65, n. 12). The Treasury purchased gold bars from all comers at $35 − 0.25 percent ($34.9125) and sold them to foreign monetary authorities and licensed industrial users, *but to no one else*, at $35 + 0.25 percent ($35.0875) per fine ounce. "Rather than being the basis of the monetary system . . . [gold became] a commodity whose price is officially supported" (Friedman and Schwartz, 1963, p. 472).[53] Treasury sales of gold were suspended by President Nixon from August 15 to December 17, 1971, and were terminated on February 13, 1973. The official gold price became irrelevant.

All paper standards except the last, that beginning in 1933, were generally considered by contemporaries as temporary aberrations from the previously applicable metallic standard. In fact, in every case (except 1933) the paper standard eventually came to an end, whereupon the existing metallic value of the dollar regained its effectiveness. The paper standards differed in their effect on the foreign-exchange market. Some periods involved noticeable disturbances to the market: 1814–17, 1837–42, 1861–78. Bank suspensions in other periods, especially later in the century, did not significantly affect the local foreign-exchange market, for any of a variety of reasons: the limited number of banks involved, the brief time span of suspension, and especially the development of a more-integrated foreign-exchange market.[54] The 1857, 1873, 1893, and 1907 suspensions were of this nature. In the 1873, 1893, and 1907 periods, only the "deposit dollar" – not the "currency dollar," on which the exchange rate is based – noticeably depreciated against gold and foreign exchange. To the extent that the 1917–22 and 1933–present paper standards involved fixed or managed exchange rates, exchange-rate variation was restricted.

Besides currency inconvertibility, divergences from the conditions for an international gold standard occurred during and around the paper standard occasioned by World War I, as shown in table 3.3, and also with adoption of the 1933 paper standard. From August to October 1914, there was an informal embargo on the export of gold on the part of New York banks

Table 3.3 *Deviations from international gold standard, 1914–25*

Deviation	Time period	
	Britain	United States
Currency inconvertibility	Aug. 1914–April 27, 1925[a]	April 6, 1917–March 17, 1922
Payments moratorium	Aug. 2, 1914–Nov. 3, 1914	—
Restriction of gold exports	April 1, 1919–Sept. 11, 1919[b]	Aug. 2, 1914–Oct. 1, 1914
		Sept. 10, 1917–June 8, 1919
Prohibition of gold imports[c]	Dec. 5, 1916–March 31, 1919	—
Commandeering of gold imports	Aug. 1914–Sept. 11, 1919	—
Prohibition of gold melting	Dec. 5, 1916–March 31, 1919[d]	—
Prohibition of buying or selling gold at a premium	May 18, 1918–Dec. 30, 1925	—
Exchange control	Dec. 24, 1914–Jan. 14, 1924	Jan. 26, 1918–June 24, 1919
	Nov. 1924–Nov. 3, 1925	
Exchange-rate management	Aug. 1915—Jan. 12, 1916	—
Exchange-rate pegging	Jan 13, 1916–March 19, 1919	—

Notes:

[a] Currency convertibility restored on April 28, 1925, only for export of gold, not for domestic circulation.

[b] Prohibition of export of gold produced outside British Empire continued to April 27, 1925.

[c] Gold sold to Bank of England excluded.

[d] Prohibition for non− Empire gold continued to April 27, 1925.

Sources: Atkin (1970, pp. 325–31), Beckhart (1924, pp. 267–8, 272–3), Brown (1929, pp. 6, 7, 20, 31, 37–41, 47–8, 227–9; 1932, pp. 201, 204–6, 241–3, 248; 1940, pp. 31, 35, 37, 60, 180, 184, 378), Bullock, Williams, and Tucker (1919, p. 242), Cross (1923, pp. 377–81), Fraser (1933, pp. 33, 40–1, 45–6), Jaeger (1922, p. 24), Keynes (1930, vol. I, p. 19), Kirkaldy (1921, pp. 6–9, 33–4, 421), Morgan (1952, pp. 12–13, 23, 64, 197–8, 261–5), Sayers (1976, pp. 55–6, 80–2), Spalding (1922, pp. 176–7), Taus (1943, p. 155).

(Brown, 1932, pp. 201–6). On September 7, 1917, by Presidential Proclamation, an embargo effective September 10 was imposed on exports of coin, bullion, and currency. Supported by the Treasury, Federal Reserve Board, and Postmaster General, the embargo lasted until June 9, 1919, when the Federal Reserve Board announced that licenses for the export of gold and currency would be freely granted (with rare geographical exceptions).[55] In 1933, on March 6 President Roosevelt suspended gold exports and on April 20 prohibited them (except by license).[56]

Complete exchange control was imposed under the paper standard of World War I: from January 1918 to June 1919, all foreign-exchange transactions required approval from the Federal Reserve Board (Taus, 1943, pp. 154–5). Prohibition of bank dealings in foreign exchange was temporarily imposed under the 1933 paper standard.

Impounding of gold was a third common feature of the two paper standards. Through a combination of moral suasion and creative legislation over 1916–18, gold and gold certificates were given up by commercial banks and concentrated in the Federal Reserve banks.[57] President Roosevelt's Proclamation of April 5, 1933 required all bank and non-bank owners of gold coin, gold bullion, or gold certificates to deliver all their present and future holdings, with minor exemptions, to a Federal Reserve bank, either directly or through commercial banks (member banks of the Federal Reserve system), to be paid for at par.[58] A subsequent proclamation, of August 28, 1933, forbade any one other than a Federal Reserve Bank from acquiring or holding gold in the United States or exporting gold, except under license. On December 28, 1933, the Secretary of the Treasury ordered that all gold be delivered to it at the official price of $20.671835 per fine ounce, resulting in almost a 70-percent profit with the $35 price instituted January 31, 1934. Throughout the 1934–71 "limited gold-bullion standard," the holding of gold was forbidden to US residents, with minor exceptions.

In sum, the final two paper standards of the United States differed from all previous such episodes in that "suspension of specie payments," historically the only deviation from a metallic standard, was supported by a variety of other divergences from the international gold standard.

4   British monetary standard

1   Unit of account

The pound, shilling, and pence schemata as the unit of account began prior to the Norman Conquest, in the Anglo-Saxon period, when the only coin in existence was the silver penny.[1] With rare and temporary exception, the penny was the only coin in circulation until the late thirteenth century. The term "penny" is believed to emanate from a coin issued by King Penda of Mercia in the seventh country. In the ninth century the penny was in all the Saxon kingdoms and 240 pennies always constituted a pound. Even though the weight of the penny varied across kingdoms and over time, "the intention was that the pound weight of silver and the pound of money should be the same and that the pound of silver should be minted into 240 pennies" (Feavearyear, 1963, pp. 7–8). The abbreviation for penny, d., is from the Latin *denarius* (a Roman coin and unit of account), which until the fourteenth century meant both a pennyweight and the face value of the penny coin.

According to Feavearyear, the Saxons may have applied the term "scilling," later "shilling" and meaning "a piece cut off," to pieces of broken silver added to the scale to compensate for underweight coin. Over time, the shilling became equal to a definite number of pennies, eventually 12, the preference of William the Conqueror. Following Roman nomenclature, the Normans determined the unit of account as the *libra* (the ancient Roman pound, weight measure, abbreviated as £), equal to 20 *solidi* (a Roman coin, abbreviated as s.), with the *solidus* equal to 12 *denarii*. In English: pound, shilling, and pence.[2]

2   Mint price and coins struck

In sharp contrast to the American experience, in which a national mint was not functioning until 1794, the minting of coined money had been undertaken by British monetary authorities more or less continuously since

34

Roman times.[3] The penny declined in size steadily over time from 24 grains in the eighth century to a third that weight in 1601. Notwithstanding its role in the unit of account, the shilling as a coin was not issued until 1504; a variety of other silver coins before and after were also produced (Feavearyear, 1963, p. 439). With rare exception, (1) all silver coins were made of "sterling silver," that is, they were of 37/40th (or 0.925) fineness, and (2) the value/weight ratio of the other coins was proportional to that of the penny. Coining of silver was prohibited by the Act of June 21, 1798, but restored by the Act of June 22, 1816 (known as Lord Liverpool's Coinage Act).[4]

Gold coins were first issued in 1257, and more than a dozen different coins subject to varying weight and denomination were produced until the two final and most important: the guinea and sovereign, which entered circulation in 1663 and 1817, respectively (Feavearyear, 1963, pp. 437–8).[5] The guinea had initial value and the sovereign continuous value of 20 shillings (as did the old sovereign from 1489 to 1526, the first coin with such valuation), thus representing the pound. Other denominations of these two basic coins were also produced. The fineness of gold coins varied with the specific coin until the guinea, when an 11/12th (or 0.9166 . . .) fineness was established and retained for the sovereign.

In 1560 silver was coined at 60d. per standard ounce (stated as: sterling silver coined at 60d. per ounce). Two gold coins, with different valuations, were in existence: the angel and crown, coined at 723.7d. and 720d., respectively, per fine ounce. The mint (gold/silver price) ratio was the gold valuation [723.7d. or 720d.] divided by the silver valuation converted to a fine basis $[(60d.)\cdot(40/37)]$: 11.16 for the angel and 11.10 for the crown. On September 29, 1601, both metals were increased in value at the mint (all coins reduced in weight), silver in particular to 62d. per standard ounce and gold proportionately less, so the mint ratios fell to 10.95 and 10.90. Further increases in the value of gold, holding silver constant, then increased the mint ratio to 14.25 and 14.21 for the angel and crown, respectively, by 1662 (Horsefield, 1960, p. 75).

Considered another way, the mint indenture of 1601 involved one pound Troy, or 5760 grains, of standard silver coined into 62 shillings, whence the silver weight of the pound sterling was $(20/62)\cdot(5760)\cdot(37/40) =$ 1718.7096+ (1718 22/31) fine (pure) grains. On December 24, 1663, King Charles II ordered the guinea to be coined.[6] By the Order, one pound Troy, or 5760 grains, of standard gold was made into 44.5 guineas, implying a guinea weight of 129.4382+ (129 39/89) grains, and the value of the guinea was set at 20 shillings. At this valuation, the gold weight of the pound sterling was $(129.4382+)\cdot(11/12) = 118.6516+$ (118 58/89) fine grains. The silver-weight to gold-weight ratio is the mint ratio, which was 14.49.

Only government offices had to respect the official rating of the guinea (or of any gold coin); private transactions took place at market rates. On March 7, 1696, in an effort to reduce the market price, an Act was passed forbidding any person from transacting in guineas at a rate higher than 26 shillings per guinea, effective March 25, 1696. The gold weight of the £ became $(129.4382+)\cdot(11/12)\cdot(20/26) = 91.2705+$ (91 313/1157) fine grains, and the mint ratio increased to 18.83. A subsequent Act lowered the price ceiling to 22 shillings from April 10, 1696.[7] This resulted in a £ gold weight of $(129.4382+)\cdot(11/12)\cdot(20/22) = 107.8651+$ (107 77/89) fine grains and a mint ratio of 15.93.

On February 15, 1699, the Treasury ordered that, in the receipt of taxes, guineas be accepted at no more than 21s. 6d., the day before Parliament agreed to a report to that effect.[8] The £ gold weight became $(129.4382+)\cdot(11/12)\cdot(20/21.5) = 110.3736+$ (110 1430/3827) fine grains, and the mint ratio fell to 15.57. In response to a Parliamentary resolution of December 21, 1717, a Royal Proclamation was issued the next day lowering the maximum price of the guinea in transactions to 21 shillings.[9] This valuation established the gold content of the £ at $(129.4382+)\cdot(11/12)\cdot(20/21) = 113.0016+$ (113 1/623) fine grains and the resultant mint ratio at 15.21.

The Coinage Act of 1816 stated that the weight and fineness of gold coin should be that prescribed by the existing mint indenture (meaning that for the guinea). On July 1, 1817 a Royal Proclamation revealed the ordering of coinage of the sovereign, weighing 123.274 grains of standard gold, to have the valuation of 20 shillings.[10] The accurate weight of the sovereign consistent with the guinea is rather $(129.4382+)\cdot(20/21) = 123.274478+$ (123 171/623), which the Coinage Act of April 4, 1870 expressed truncated to five decimal places, as 123.27447.[11] That Act decreed that 934.5 sovereigns should be coined from 20 pounds, or $(20)\cdot(5760)$ grains, of standard gold. The gold weight of the pound is then $(1/934.5)\cdot(20)\cdot(5760)\cdot(11/12) = 113.0016+$ (113 1/623) grains of pure gold, the same as that established in 1717. In fact, the Act of 1870 specifically continues the mint indenture of the Coinage Act of 1816, which was that for the guinea.

The Coinage Act of 1816 did reduce the weight of silver coins, with one pound Troy coined into 66 rather than 62 shillings, but silver became a subsidiary coinage and the mint ratio ceased to have economic meaning. The gold content of the pound, like that of the dollar, remained unchanged through World War I and even after 1925, the last year in which gold was coined. With 123.2744+ (123 171/623) grains of standard gold constituting £1 and 480 grains to the ounce, the mint price of standard gold from December 22, 1717 onward was $480/(123.2744+) = £3.89375$, or £3 17s. 10.5d. per ounce.

3 Legal-tender status of coin

Until the late eigthteenth century, the legal-tender quality of coin is found not in specifically oriented statutes but in Royal Proclamations, mint indentures, and incidental passages in legislation.[12] Phrases such as "current coins," "lawful coin," and "current money" established or accepted the legal-tender status of gold and silver coin produced by the Royal Mint. It follows that with the coinage of gold as well as silver, legal bimetallism resulted. However, because of the practice of expressing the legal denomination of gold coins in terms of shilling and pence, in a sense there was an underlying silver standard.

Formal bimetallism was disturbed by the Act of May 10, 1774, which temporarily limited the legal tender of silver coin to £25; above that amount it could be tendered only by weight and at a maximum valuation of 62 pence an ounce. The act was renewed but allowed to lapse on May 1, 1783, then renewed on June 21, 1798, and made perpetual on July 12, 1799.[13] The Coinage Act of 1816 restored the legal tender of silver coin but only up to £2 and eliminated its tender by weight. Gold coin was made the only standard of value and its legal tender was explicitly stated as unlimited. Britain was now legally on the gold standard. The Coinage Act of 1870 repeated the legal-tender provisions of the 1816 legislation. Ironically, the statute that placed Britain on the gold standard occurred during a paper-standard regime, the Bank Restriction Period (see section 9 below), just as the formal American move to a gold standard happened during the greenback paper-standard period.

4 Convertibility of government/central bank paper into coin

Immediately after its founding in 1694, the Bank of England issued banknotes. Of course, like any debtor, the Bank was required to discharge this liability in legal tender, namely, gold or silver coin. It was only with the Resumption Act (Peel's Act) of July 2, 1819 that specific statutory content was given to the obligation of the Bank to redeem its notes in gold coin on demand. The Bank of England Act of August 29, 1833 made Bank of England notes for sums above £5 legal tender (beginning August 1, 1834), as long as the Bank continued to pay its notes in coin on demand. Finally, the Currency and Bank Notes Act of July 2, 1928 made the Bank's notes legal tender in any amount.

Government paper money was not authorized until the Currency and Bank Notes Act of August 6, 1914, which permitted the issuance of currency notes with full legal-tender status and cashable into gold coin on demand at the Bank of England. The 1928 Act declared that currency notes are deemed to be Bank of England notes, thus amalgamating the two paper currencies.[14]

5   Nature of coinage

Traditionally, coinage at British mints was open to all, although from the late twelfth to the fourteenth century silver could be coined only at king's exchanges, which levied an additional fee. "An Act for encouragement of coinage," effective December 20, 1666, kept continuously in force by subsequent legislation (except for a temporary lapse in 1680–5) and made perpetual in 1768, explicitly stated freedom of coinage for everyone: "whatsoever person or persons, native or foreigner, alien or stranger."[15] The Act of June 21, 1798, made perpetual by the Act of July 12, 1799, terminated the coinage of silver. Free coinage of silver was technically restored in the Coinage Act of 1816 – but only subsequent to a Royal Proclamation to that effect, which was never issued – and formally eliminated in the Coinage Act of 1870.

Free coinage of gold was undisturbed by the 1870 Act; but the minimum amount of bullion required was always much higher than in the United States, where, prior to the Mint Act of 1873, there was no minimum, and by that Act bullion of value less than $100 could be refused. The British minimum is stated as £10,000 for 1817–20 (Craig, 1953, p. 289) and £20,000 in the mid-nineteenth and the twentieth centuries (Seyd, 1868, p. 158; Spalding, 1928a, p. 86).

In England, as in every other country, there was a charge for coinage, consisting of mint expenses plus seigniorage for the king. The charge was variable over time and, with the important exception of part of the sixteenth century, generally low in percentage terms.[16] The Act of 1666 abolished mint charges, specifically those for melting and coining, for both gold and silver. England thus became the first country to have free and gratuitous coinage. Further, whether the fineness of bullion was above or below standard, no charge was to be made and payment was to be altered proportionately. The assayer and porter received "small fees" (Craig, 1953, p. 239). Also, the mint charged for melting into bars, if the bullion was not already in ingot form. The Act of 1870 repeated the absence of mint charges for gold bullion, but provided that the mint could refuse bullion that required refining to achieve standard fineness.

The Act of 1816 established that silver would be coined at 66 shillings per pound Troy but depositors would be paid the old rate of 62 shillings. Thus there would be a seigniorage of 6.06 percent for silver coinage. However, this provision was a dead letter, because the necessary proclamation to permit private depositing of silver at the mint was never issued.

Waiting time at the mint could be eliminated between the late twelfth and sixteenth centuries by paying an extra charge at the king's exchanges. In the fourteenth century the delay between deposit and coinage was stated as only a week (Craig, 1953, p. xvii), but "long delays" are cited elsewhere for the period prior to the Act of 1666 (Feavearyear, 1963, p. 3). In the eighteenth century three months was the norm. In 1817 the delay was only five to six weeks, and reduced further until 1820 by immediate payment for three-quarters of the bullion in bills discountable at fourteen days. In 1829–31 an even more favorable policy was followed, with depositors receiving three-fourths payment immediately and the remainder after assaying. A two-week delay was stated in 1868, and two to three weeks became the ultimate norm (Seyd, 1868, p. 158; Whitaker, 1919, p. 503; Cross, 1923, p. 376).

The Bank of England Act and Charter, each of 1694, gave the Bank the right to buy or sell bullion.[17] Early on, the Bank offered to buy gold from all comers at a fixed price. From 1717 to 1829 this price was £3 17s. 6d. per ounce of standard gold, and from 1829 onward it was £3 17s. 9d. The latter price was institutionalized in the Bank Charter Act of July 19, 1844, which required the Bank to purchase gold bullion from anyone with its notes at that rate. The Bank was entitled to require the bullion to be assayed and melted into bars at the expense of the seller. The statutory price was a minimum; the Bank could, and sometimes did, offer a higher price.[18]

Therefore gold-bullion owners wishing to dispose of their asset had a choice: the mint or the Bank. The Bank's statutory price was 0.1605 percent lower than the mint price (£3 17s. 9d. versus £3 17s. 10.5d.); but waiting time (and therefore forgone interest) at the Bank was much less than that at the mint, because only weighing and assay (and possible melting into bars), but not coinage, was required. By the mid-eighteenth century, it became clear that the net return to bullion was greater at the Bank, and no private party went to the mint.[19] In 1817–20 and 1829–31 favorable arrangements resulted in use of the mint by some large bankers and bullion brokers. Between these periods private coinage at the mint was minimal, and after 1831 only two such transactions are known. Each transaction was small in amount and, as expected, involved an interest loss beyond the 0.1605-percent price advantage.

6   Bank provision of bars and foreign-exchange dealings

At some point, probably in the mid-nineteenth century, the Bank began selling gold bars, permitted but not required by its Charter and the Bank of England Acts. The Bank frequently varied its selling price, rather than keeping it steady at the mint price. Winston Churchill's famous Budget Speech of April 28, 1925, announced the introduction of a bill, the Gold

Standard Act of 1925, which was passed on May 13 and obliged the Bank of England to sell gold bars to any person at the fixed price of £3 17s. 10.5d. per ounce of standard fineness, the mint price. Payment could be made in any legal tender. A minimum transaction size was specified, 400 ounces of fine gold, which was slightly over £1699 in value.[20]

Unlike the US Treasury, the Bank of England dealt directly in American eagles and other foreign coin, pricing them by weight, an alternative to treating them as bullion. The Bank began this practice in 1852 or possibly earlier (Sayers, 1986, pp. 48–9). For many years the Bank set its buying and selling prices of eagles (and other foreign coin) at levels to leave transactors indifferent between eagles and other forms of gold (bars or sovereigns). Beginning in 1890 it made prices more favorable for private parties and also more variable. With the British mint price at 77s. 10.5d. per ounce 11/12ths fine, the equivalent mint price for American gold coin, only 9/10ths fine, was 76s. 5.50909 . . . d. (5 28/55d.) per ounce. Almost always the Bank's purchase price was below and always its selling price was above the mint-price equivalent.

7   Convertibility of banknotes and bank deposits

Unlike the American experience, banking was in existence in England from the mid-seventeenth century, beginning, and most developed, in London.[21] The most important bank, of course, was the Bank of England, founded in 1694, and which performed the functions of both a commercial and central bank. It had a legal monopoly of joint-stock banking (meaning organization with more than six partners) throughout England (but not Scotland, which had a separate banking system) and an effective monopoly of note issue in and around London.

The earliest banks were the private banks in London, said to be 24 in 1725, 52 in 1785, and nearly 70 in 1800. There were also country banks (located outside London), their number estimated at 12 in 1750, 119 in 1784, and 230 in 1797. Legislation of 1826 permitted joint-stock banking outside 65 miles of London and the Act of 1833 allowed joint-stock banking in London absent note issuance. Bank of England notes served as well as coin as bank reserves, even though the notes did not receive legal-tender status until 1833.

8   Legal versus effective metallic standards

Britain was legally on a silver standard until gold was coined in the mid-thirteenth century, on a bimetallic standard until 1816 (or perhaps 1774, when the legal tender of silver was first limited; or 1798, when free coinage of silver was terminated), and then on a gold standard. Just as for the United States, legal bimetallism translated into effective monometallism. Until the end of the seventeenth century, the British mint ratio was generally below European gold/silver price ratios; so a silver standard was in effect. The annual Soetbeer data exist only from 1687; from that year to 1696 the UK mint ratio (14.49) established in 1663 was uniformly below the Hamburg market ratio.

For a few years at the turn of the eighteenth century, England actually had effective bimetallism: "for a while there were in circulation plenty of full-weight coins of both kinds" (Feavearyear, 1963, p. 152). However, foreign gold/silver price ratios had been falling and, after having been increased greatly in 1696, the British mint ratio was not subsequently reduced enough to compensate. At 15.57 the British ratio from 1699 to 1717 was higher than the Hamburg market ratio in all years. It was also higher than the ratio in most European countries – 16 in Spain and Portugal, but 15 in France and below 15 in seven other countries – and much higher than the ratio in the Far East, 9–10 in China and Japan and 12 in India.[22]

With gold so overvalued and silver undervalued in England, bimetallism could be only transitory. Arbitrageurs did not take long to adjust to the new situation, exporting silver and importing gold, and Britain shifted to a *de facto* gold standard. In 1702 silver coinage dwindled to almost nothing, and silver coinage was insignificant in amount in almost every year thereafter until 1816.[23]

Why Britain formally adopted the gold standard in 1816 is controversial. Four explanations have been offered. The conventional view is that Liverpool's Act merely ratified the prevailing effective gold standard that had been in existence since the beginning of the seventeenth century. As Li (1963, p. 174) comments: "It is certain that England did not establish the gold standard by any conscious or deliberate act. Nor was it foreseen by anyone that the gold standard would be established. It was established in practice first and then recognized officially later."

In contrast, Redish (1990) declares that the abandonment of legal bimetallism occurred because of new mint technology and policy, which permitted a gold standard with subsidiary silver coinage. New technology produced coins not readily counterfeitable, and new policy guaranteed the convertibility of all coins at face value. Friedman (1990a), however, argues that the achievement of a silver token coinage was not a sufficient reason for the adoption of a gold rather than a silver standard or even for the maintenance of bimetallism when Britain left the then paper standard in 1821. It might have been mere chance that a monometallic gold rather than silver standard replaced the inconvertible pound. David Ricardo, who had great influence, happened to favor a gold standard in 1819. If he had argued rather for silver, that might have been the standard adopted. Britain, with its dominant economic and financial power in the world, might even have made bimetallism work.

Finally, Feavearyear (1963, p. 214) asks what would have transpired under the 1816 Act had there been issuance of the proclamation to permit free coinage of silver at the fixed rate of 62 shillings per pound Troy (with actual coining at 66 shillings). Because of the low market price of silver, massive amounts of silver would have been presented to the mint and a silver standard, albeit with a seigniorage of 6.06 percent, would have resulted. According to Li (1963, p. 166), the provision for free coinage was based on the assumption that the eighteenth-century experience of a silver market price between 62 and 66 shillings per pound Troy would continue. Instead, the market price fell below 62 shillings. The mint practice of buying all its silver in the open market in lieu of free coinage not only yielded higher profits but also preserved the gold standard.

9   Paper standards

In contrast to the American experience, prior to World War I, Britain had only one episode of a paper standard. On February 27, 1797, acting on government orders issued the previous day (a Sunday), the Bank of England suspended specie payments, that is, it refused to pay out gold for its notes. The note-issuing commercial banks of England and Scotland followed, and the entire country was on a paper standard. The Bank Restriction Act of May 3, 1797 confirmed the suspension, and successive continuing Acts kept it in force until May 1, 1821, when payment resumed, ending the Bank Restriction Period.[24]

With the onset of World War I, the requirement of the Bank of England to redeem in gold coin both its own notes and Treasury currency notes was effectively abrogated by moral suasion, legalistic action, and regulation; and a paper standard resulted.[25] Contrary to the American experience and, ironically, convertibility of paper currency was legally terminated when the country "returned to the gold standard." The Gold Standard Act of 1925 ended both the Bank of England's obligation to pay its notes in coin and the right of holders of currency notes to redemption in coin.[26] The Gold Standard Act also put a legal end to free coinage, permitting use of the mint only by the Bank of England. This provision simply codified a practice that had existed for many years.

Brown (1929, pp. 229–30) writes with justice: "Thus free interchangeability between Bank of England notes and gold and between gold bullion and gold coin was for the first time legally suspended. And this by the very act

Table 4.1 *Effective British monetary standards, 1791–present*

	Standard	
Time period	Domestic	International
Jan. 1, 1791–Feb. 26, 1797	gold	gold
Feb. 27, 1797–April 30, 1821	paper	paper
May 1, 1821–August 1914	gold	gold
August 1914–April 27, 1925	paper	paper
April 28, 1925–Sept. 19, 1931	"	gold
Sept. 20, 1931–present	"	paper

Sources: Brown (1940, pp. 34–5), Cannan (1925, pp. xi, xxxiv), Yeager (1976, pp. 321–2, 342).

that restored England to a gold standard." Therefore the *international* dollar–sterling gold standard that began in 1925 was complemented by a *domestic* gold standard (involving circulation of gold coin) in the United States but not in Britain. The Bank's legal obligation to transact in gold pertained exclusively to bars – a form of gold suitable for international movement but hardly for domestic circulation. Table 4.1 summarizes the British monetary standards from 1791 to the present.

The obligation of the Bank of England to purchase bars with its notes at 77s. 9d. per standard ounce was not repealed until the Currency and Bank Notes Act of February 28, 1939 (Public General Acts, 1940, pp. 27–8). Its obligation to sell gold bars at the mint price was suspended by government instruction announced on September 20, 1931 (a Sunday) and terminated by the Gold Standard (Amendment) Act the following day.[27] The gold-bullion standard instituted by Churchill's famous Budget Speech was over. The UK gold standard, running from April 28, 1925 to September 19, 1931, delineated the dollar–sterling international gold standard of the time, because the UK, inner, period was enveloped by the American, which ran from March 18, 1922 to March 5, 1933 (see table 3.2)

Divergences from an international gold standard occasioned by World War I were even more extensive for Britain than for the United States, as shown in table 3.3. Further, unlike the United States, Britain had a long history of such deviations. Import of bullion was first prohibited by the Act of 1774, but only domestic silver coin and of less than standard fineness was affected. The purpose was to restrict supply, thus maintaining the value of silver coins in spite of light weight and the refusal of the government to recoin them. In fact, the silver coinage was so clipped, sweated, and naturally worn that it became no longer profitable to melt it down and sell it at the market price for silver bullion. An, albeit unsatisfactory, subsidiary silver coinage was in existence even before the currency reform instituted by the Coinage Act of 1816.

From early in World War I to April 1919, gold imports were restricted extra-legally by the simple expedient of the Bank of England purchasing all imported gold. This was accomplished principally by arrangement with South Africa to sell all gold to the Bank at the price of 77s. 9d. per standard ounce. From December 5, 1916 to March 31, 1919 imports were prohibited by Royal Proclamation except for gold sold to the Bank. Beginning September 12, 1919, gold could again be freely imported and sold in London at the market-determined price.

Restriction of export of gold and silver goes back to the turn of the thirteenth century; but the restraints were often evaded. "Act after Act and proclamation after proclamation attempted to prevent the export of coin and, later, of precious metal in any form. . . . For a long period death was the penalty for those found exporting good English money . . ." (Feavearyear, 1963, pp. 3–4). The king could override any export prohibition by license. Such a license was required to export gold or silver of any kind until the Act of August 1, 1663, which permitted the free export of gold and silver bullion and the re-export of foreign coin.

An Act of 1696 required export of bullion to be stamped and an oath taken that it was not produced from domestic coin. Of course, lying permitted melted British coin to be exported under the Act. Peel's Act of 1819 repealed all restrictions on the melting and exporting of British gold coin and all but one for silver. The remaining restriction, concerning taking an oath that bullion to be exported was not produced from clippings of silver coin, was removed by an Act of 1821.

During World War I, gold exports were restricted solely by extralegal means (apart from Trading with the Enemy legislation), not only by the Bank of England commandeering all gold imports but also by effective moral suasion of bankers and bullion brokers. The London bullion market suspended operations (Brown, 1929, p.6; 1940, pp. 36, 1014; Cross, 1923, pp. 377–8; Jaeger, 1922, p. 21). On April 1, 1919, just when imports were liberalized, an Order in Council under the Customs (Exportation Prohibition) Act of 1914 was issued forbidding the export of gold coin and bullion except by license. Beginning September 12, 1919, the Treasury agreed to provide licenses for the reexport of gold, and the London gold market reopened.

The Gold and Silver (Export Control, etc.) Act of December 23, 1920 prohibited the export of gold with the important exception of gold produced within the British Empire and imported under any arrangement approved by the Treasury. The Act was to continue in force until December 31, 1925. Churchill's Budget Speech of April 28, 1925 superseded the Act by giving the Bank of England a general license to export gold, which was in effect an obligation to provide bars to private exporters.

At the beginning of August 1914, by proclamations, international (and domestic) payments were postponed – the so-called "Moratorium." This embargo on payments, which lasted until November 4, constituted an extreme type of exchange control and, because of the importance of London in financing international trade and payments, made the international gold standard non-operational.[28] Conventional exchange control was in existence in England from the twelfth to the seventeenth century, varying in intensity and only partially effective (Einzig, 1970, pp. 104–8, 157–60).

With World War I, exchange control took several forms. First, beginning July 1915, there was a mobilization of foreign securities, at first by taxation and moral suasion, ultimately by order. Second, in 1916 and 1917 regulations were promulgated that prohibited the export of capital in any form; they were removed in August 1919. Third, beginning December 24, 1914, overseas investment taking the form of new issues of capital was tightly controlled by the Treasury. From November 1919 the control of new issues was done through moral suasion on the part of the Bank of England. Removed, reinstituted, and removed again in 1924–5, the control was reintroduced in 1929, relaxed and then reimposed in 1930.

As a result of strong moral suasion, the Bank of England achieved even greater impounding of domestic gold holdings in World War I than did the US Treasury. Both commercial banks and the public exchanged their coin for Bank of England notes.[29]

As mentioned above, until 1819 British coin could not legally be melted into bullion for the purpose of export. During World War I, on December 5, 1916, a regulation under the Defense of the Realm Act prohibited the melting of gold coin or its use other than as currency. This restriction continued under the Gold and Silver (Export Control, etc.) Act of 1920, which provided for exceptions upon license from the Treasury. On May 18, 1918 a regulation prohibited buying or selling gold coin at a premium in Britain, which restriction may in effect have been incorporated in the 1920 Act under the phrase "use otherwise than as currency." The purpose of both regulations, absent from the American experience, was to remove any incentive to redeem Bank and currency notes.

Britain also engaged in intervention in the dollar–sterling exchange market in World War I. From August 1915 to January 12, 1916 intervention took the form of exchange-rate management. This practice was followed by exchange-rate pegging, at first between $4.765 and $4.77, after

May 1916 between $4.764375 ($4.76 7/16) and $4.765625 ($4.76 9/16) per pound. Intervention continued after the war, ending in March 1919. So, during 1914–25, when an international gold standard did not exist, the dollar–sterling exchange rate did not float freely until almost half the period was over.

Part II

Exchange rate

5   Parity

1   Concept of parity

Parity between two currencies is a hypothetical exchange rate involving equivalence in value. So parity is also called exchange-rate parity. Parity is not the actual exchange rate (except by accident), nor it is even a central tendency of exchange-rate values. Rather, it is an exchange-rate norm.

Four uses of parity can be distinguished. First, parity is a frame of reference from which to assess the level of the exchange rate. Second, parity appropriately defined is an exchange rate about which and by means of which "specie points" (bounds to the exchange rate outside of which arbitrage opportunities exist) are constructed. Third, expressing the exchange rate as the percentage deviation from parity (or, equivalently, as an index number with parity as the base) makes it easier to follow the movement of the exchange rate over time and enhances interpretation. Fourth, parity provides an invariant exchange-rate standard and therefore is of practical use in contracts and in courts of law (Nussbaum, 1950, p. 333).

There are two types of parity, metallic and legal, each with subcategories. The metallic (also called "mint") parity is the relative pure-specie content of the two countries' currencies or, equivalently, the ratio of the countries' mint prices expressed in common fineness. The mint price, it may be recalled, is the value of domestic money that the country's authority would coin per ounce of gold deposited with it. It is *the only price consistent with mint parity* at which the country's authority could buy or sell gold for domestic currency.

If both countries are on the same metallic standard, then mint parity, either gold or silver, is readily defined. If the countries are on a bimetallic standard, then both a gold and silver parity can be computed, but both are meaningful only if there is effective bimetallism in each country. Simplicity vanishes if the countries are on different monometallic standards, one gold and the other silver, or if the effective standard under bimetallism differs in

49

the two countries. Metallic parity must then be defined to incorporate the divergent standards.

2   Report of John Quincy Adams

In 1817 the United States Senate requested that John Quincy Adams, Secretary of State 1817–25 (and President 1825–9), prepare a report on weights and measures. Submitted in 1821, the report includes a remarkable discussion of the various concepts of exchange-rate parity between the American dollar and the British pound. Despite a few conceptual errors, Adams' report is so sophisticated and comprehensive that it provides the most convenient framework for discussion of dollar-sterling parity.[1] Table 5.1 presents all of Adams' parity computations (with corrections of his errors) in a logical schemata. The applicable time period of some measures terminates beyond 1821, which could not, of course, be foreseen by Adams.

Adams distinguished three concepts of mint parity: (I) gold par, based on the legal gold value of each country's currency; (II) silver par, based on their legal silver values; and (III) medium par, the average of the two. Many observers – both contemporary and later – considered the gold par to be the appropriate measure for the 1792–1834 period.[2] In fact, this parity was often called "real par." However, until July 31, 1834, all three measures were deficient, because they ignored that Britain and the United States were effectively on two different metallic standards, gold and silver. If the medium par involves a recognition of and an attempt to adjust for the divergent standards, the measure provides a crude correction at best.[3]

Adams noted (IV) two values of dollar-sterling parity based on legal declarations of exchange value of currencies. One emanates from a Royal Proclamation. On June 18, 1704, Queen Anne declared that "Sevill Pieces of Eight, Old Plate" and "Mexico Pieces of Eight" had a "just Proportion" to British coin of 4s. 6d., based upon assays at the mint.[4] A Spanish dollar worth 54d. implies a $240/54 = \$4.4444$ . . . ($4.44 4/9) valuation of the pound. This rate became known as the "nominal par," both in contemporary usage and in later reference.[5] Originally founded on a true mint parity between English and Spanish silver coin, the $4.4444 . . . rate was used as the parity against which exchange-rate quotations were measured long after the Spanish dollar underwent successive reductions in metallic content, long after it gave rise to the American dollar, and long after England switched from a silver to a gold standard. In addition to the contemporary term "nominal par," then, the descriptions "technical par" and "customary par" have been suggested.[6]

The second legal declaration of parity noted by Adams was the Congressional determination in the Act of July 31, 1789 (repeated in the

Acts of August 4, 1790 and March 2, 1799) that, for the appraisal of British merchandise in computing tariffs, the pound sterling should be rated at $4.44, likely a truncated form of nominal par.[7]

Another set of legal parities delineated by Adams was (V) the exchange value of the pound implied by Congressional ratings of British coin. The Acts of 1789 and 1790 stated that tariff payments could be made in English gold and silver coin at specified rates, that for gold corresponding to a parity close to the gold par, that for silver equivalent to a $4.44 parity. On February 9, 1793, Congress passed the first of a series of legal-tender acts for foreign currency (see section 3 of chapter 3). British gold coin, but not silver, was granted legal-tender status. The implied exchange rate was the gold par. This rating recurred in five Acts over 1799 to 1823.[8]

3   Mint parity, 1791–1934 and 1950–66

To study the dollar–sterling exchange rate as an international specie standard, metallic parity is the relevant concept, and in this section and the next I generate a quarterly series of true mint parity over the time period 1791–1934, shown in table 5.2. Beginning July 31, 1834, when the United States joined Britain on an effective gold standard, gold par was clearly the appropriate measure of parity, computable as the ratio of the American to the British mint price, each expressed per fine ounce of gold.

For Britain, the mint price since 1717 is given by £3.89375·(12/11) = £4.247727 per fine ounce, where £3.89375 is equivalent to £3 17s. 10.5d. From 1834 to 1837, while the US 1834 coinage law was in effect, the US fine-gold mint price is calculated as 480/23.2 = $20.689655 per fine ounce, where 480 is the number of grains per ounce and 23.2 the number of grains of pure gold in the dollar. Beginning January 18, 1837, under the 1837 Coinage Act, the mint price is 480/23.22 = $20.671835 per fine ounce. True parity is $4.8707588+ for July 31, 1834 to January 17, 1837 and $4.8665635+ thereafter. The latter parity correctly rounds up to $4.8666, whereas both official and private statements almost invariably cite $4.8665 as the number.[9]

With Britain and the United States legally on a bimetallic monetary standard until 1816 and 1873, respectively, and thence on a gold standard, a gold mint parity is in a formal sense calculable also prior to July 1, 1834 (and a silver parity prior to 1816), as performed by Adams. Indeed, some writers remain comfortable with the gold parity for this earlier period (see note 2). However, Cole (1929a, pp. 406–7, n. 1; 1929b, p. 204, n. 2) and Davis and Hughes (1960, p. 54) claim that no true parity exists. The reasons given are three. First, the differing metallic standards of Britain and the United States require a silver–gold comparison, which would depend on the gold/silver price ratio. However, in fact an excellent price series is provided by the

Table 5.1 *Parity measures presented by John Quiney Adams*

Basis of parity		Parity (dollars per £)	Applicable time period	Method of construction
Act of Congress	Act of Parliament			
I Mint parity: gold par				
Aug. 8, 1786	Dec. 22, 1717[a]	4.58856[b]	Aug. 8, 1786–Apr. 1, 1791	113.0016/24.6268[c]
April 2, 1792	,,	4.565721[d]	Apr. 2, 1792–July 30, 1834	113.0016/24.75[c]
II Mint parity: silver par				
Aug. 8, 1786	Sept. 29, 1601	4.575417[e]	Aug. 8, 1786–Apr. 1, 1791	1718.710/375.64[f]
April 2, 1792	,,	4.629521[g]	Apr. 2, 1792–June 21, 1816	1718.710/371.25[f]
	June 22, 1816	4.348943	June 22, 1816–Feb. 11, 1873	1614.545/371.25[h]
III Mint parity: medium par				
,,	,,	4.457331	June 22, 1816–July 30, 1834	$(4.565721 + 4.348943)/2$
IV Ratings of pound sterling				
—	June 18, 1704[a]	4.44 4/9	June 18, 1704–Mar. 2, 1873	240/54[i]
July 31, 1789[j]		4.44	July 31, 1789–Mar. 3, 1833	
V Ratings of British coin				
July 31, 1789[k]	—	4.57143	July 31, 1789–June 30, 1793	0.89 × 5.1364[l]
July 31, 1789[k]	—	4.44[m]	,,	1.11 × 4[n]
Feb. 9, 1793[o]	—	4.56572	July 1, 1793–July 30, 1834	0.88 8/9 × 5.1364[p]

Notes:

^a Royal Proclamation.

^b Not presented by Adams but implicit in his argument.

^c Numerator is obtained by Adams from 5280/(11,214/240), where (as described by Adams) 5280 is the number of grains of gold in one pound Troy weight [5760 grains] of standard gold [and 5280/5760 = 11/12, the fineness of gold], 11,214 is the number of pence equal in valuation to the gold coined, and 240 is the number of pence per pound sterling. However, Adams wrongly computes the numerator as 113.0014.

^d Computed by Adams as 4.565720.

^e Computed by Adams as 4.575445.

^f Following Adams (1816–73 period), numerator obtained from 5328/(744/240). See note *h*.

^g Computed by Adams as 4.62955.

^h Numerator is obtained by Adams from 5328/(792/240), where (as described by Adams) 5328 is the number of grains of silver in one pound Troy weight [5760 grains] of standard silver [and 5328/5760 = 37/40, the fineness of silver], 792 is the number of pence equal in valuation to the silver coined, and 240 is the number of pence per pound sterling.

ⁱ Royal Proclamation established "just Proportion" of Spanish dollar to British coin as 4 shillings and 6 pence. With the Spanish dollar thus rated at 54 pence and the pound sterling equalling 240 pence, the reciprocal of 54/240 is the dollar value of the pound.

^j Restated in Acts of August 4, 1790 and March 2, 1799.

^k Restated in Act of August 4, 1790.

^l English gold coin rated at 89 cents per pennyweight, with the pound sterling containing 5760/((11,214/240)/24 = 5.1364 pennyweights of standard gold (see note *c*). Adams does not describe the computation, but this is the spirit of his calculations of gold and silver par.

^m Misconstrued by Adams as $4.575445.

ⁿ English silver crown rated at $1.11, with the pound sterling equal to 4 crowns.

^o Restated in Acts of March 2, 1799, April 10, 1806, April 29, 1816, March 3, 1819, and March 3, 1823.

^p British gold coins rated at 100 cents for every 27 grains, equivalent to 24/27 = 88 8/9 cents per pennyweight, with the pound sterling containing 5.1364 pennyweights of standard gold.

Source: See text and table 3.1.

Table 5.2 *Computation of parity, 1791–1934*

(1) Year	(2) World gold/silver price ratio	Fine-metal value of dollar (number of grains)		(5) Parity (dollars per pound)
		Silver (3)	Gold (4)	
1791	15.05	371.00	24.65	4.5840
1792	15.17	"	24.46	4.6206
1793	15.00	"	24.73	4.5688
1794				
Jan. 1–March 2	15.37	"	24.14	4.6815
March 3–Oct. 14	"	371.25	24.15	4.6783
Oct. 15–Dec. 31	"	374.40	24.36	4.6390
1795				
Jan. 1–Oct. 28	15.55	"	24.08	4.6933
Oct. 29–Dec. 31	"	371.25	23.87	4.7331
1796	15.65	"	23.72	4.7636
1797	15.41	"	24.09	4.6905
1798	15.59	"	23.81	4.7453
1799	15.74	"	23.59	4.7910
1800	15.68	"	23.68	4.7727
1801	15.46	"	24.01	4.7057
1802	15.26	"	24.33	4.6449
1803	15.41	"	24.09	4.6905
1804	"	"	"	"
1805	15.79	"	23.51	4.8062
1806	15.52	"	23.92	4.7240
1807	15.43	"	24.06	4.6966
1808	16.08	"	23.09	4.8945
1809	15.96	"	23.26	4.8579
1810	15.77	"	23.54	4.8001
1811	15.53	"	23.91	4.7270
1812	16.11	"	23.04	4.9036
1813	16.25	"	22.85	4.9462
1814	15.04	"	24.68	4.5779
1815	15.26	"	24.33	4.6449
1816	15.28	"	24.30	4.6509
1817	15.11	"	24.57	4.5992
1818	15.35	"	24.19	4.6723
1819	15.33	"	24.22	4.6662
1820	15.62	"	23.77	4.7544
1821	15.95	"	23.28	4.8549
1822	15.80	"	23.50	4.8092

Table 5.2 (*cont.*)

| (1) Year | (2) World gold/silver price ratio | Fine-metal value of dollar (number of grains) | | (5) Parity (dollars per pound) |
		Silver (3)	Gold (4)	
1823	15.84	371.25	23.44	4.8214
1824	15.82	"	23.47	4.8153
1825	15.70	"	23.65	4.7788
1826	15.76	"	23.56	4.7971
1827	15.74	"	23.59	4.7910
1828	15.78	"	23.53	4.8031
1829	"	"	"	"
1830	15.82	"	23.47	4.8153
1831	15.72	"	23.62	4.7849
1832	15.73	"	23.60	4.7879
1833	15.93	"	23.31	4.8488
1834				
Jan. 1–July 30	15.73	"	23.60	4.7879
1834 (July 31)– 1837 (Jan. 17)			23.20	4.8708
1837 (Jan. 18)– 1934 (Jan. 30)			23.22	4.8666ᵃ

Note:
ᵃ To greater accuracy, 4.8665635+.
Sources: Column (1) – see text and table 2.2. *Column (2):* Soetbeer (1879, pp. 130–1). *Column (3):* table 2.2. Values for transitional quarters, computed as weighted averages of adjacent quarters, are: 1794(1), 371.08; 1794(4), 373.92; 1795(4), 372.21. *Column (4), 1791 to 1834 (January 1–July 30):* ratio of column (3) to column (2). Values for transitional quarters are: 1794(1), 24.14; 1794(4), 23.33; 1795(4), 23.94. *Column (4), 1834 (July 31)–1934 (January 30):* table 2.2. Values for transitional quarters, computed as weighted averages of adjacent quarters, are: 1834(3), 23.33; 1837(1), 23.22. *Column (5), 1791–1834 (January 30):* (480/column (4))/((12/11)·3.89375), where 480 is the number of grains per ounce, 12/11 is the reciprocal of the fineness of British gold coin, and £3.89375 is the British mint price per standard ounce. Values for transitional quarters are: 1794(1), 4.6805; 1794(4), 4.6449; 1795(4), 4.7208; 1834(3), 4.8434; 1837(1), 4.8674.

Soetbeer data. The statement that "there was no 'true' par during the period before 1834" – made by Cole and quoted approvingly by Davis and Hughes – is correct only providing the word "true" is replaced by "constant."

Second, it is argued that the coinage of silver dollars was suspended in the United States in 1805; it was not resumed until after the 1834 legislation that brought the United States to the gold standard.[10] This objection is invalid, because the silver standard remained to produce the large number of half-dollars coined in place of the dollar.[11] Similarly, although the United States was on a gold standard from July 31, 1834, the gold dollar itself was not minted until 1849.[12] Even in gold-standard England, no coin was the equivalent of a pound sterling until 1817, when the gold sovereign was issued.[13]

Third, the existence of a paper standard in England in 1797–1821 (and, the authors might have added, in the United States in 1814–17) removed the metallic basis that the very definition of mint parity requires. Still, the parity based on coined money retains its applicability as a frame of reference, as the paper standards were generally considered by contemporaries as temporary aberrations from the metallic standard. In both cases (as in all paper standards in the two countries until the 1930s), specie payments were indeed resumed at the original mint price, corresponding to the original par value. Under a paper standard, however, mint parity ceases to be applicable as an exchange value about which specie points can be expected to envelope market exchange rates. To restore this function of parity, the observations of the exchange rate (based on the paper standard)must be adjusted for depreciation of the paper currency in terms of specie.[14]

Abstracting from periods of paper standards, Britain was on an effective gold standard from the early eighteenth century and the United States on an effective silver standard until July 31, 1834. True mint parity is nevertheless calculable for 1791–1834, as seen in table 5.2. This parity involves the effective metallic standard for each country and employs the ratio of the market price of gold to silver to make the divergent monetary standards comparable.

The technique has two steps. First, the silver content of the dollar [number of grains of silver per dollar, column (3)] is divided by the world market price of gold in terms of silver [column (2)] to yield the equivalent gold amount of the dollar [number of grains of gold per dollar, column (4)]. Second, the result is divided into 480 (the number of grains per ounce) to obtain the American mint-price equivalent for gold (number of dollars per fine ounce of gold), which itself is divided by the British mint price (£4.247727, the number of pounds sterling per fine ounce of gold) to yield parity [number of dollars per pound, column (5)].

Taking the silver content of the dollar for appropriate subperiods, proper attention is paid not only to the varying gold/silver market price but also to

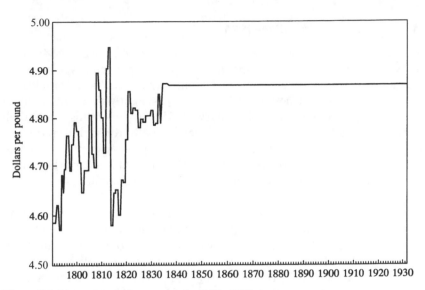

Figure 5.1 True mint parity, quarterly, 1791–1931

the unique episodes of the non-functioning American mint in 1791–4 (when the Spanish dollar served as the monetary standard) and the overly fine silver dollar of 1794–5. Because the best available gold/silver price measure (the Soetbeer data) is an annual series, the resulting parity is not a constant but varies annually (and also intra-annually when there is a change in the silver content of the dollar – values for transitional quarters are in the *Sources* to the table). The originality of table 5.2 lies not in the technique itself but, first, in applying it to the full 1791–1834 period rather than merely to isolated years, and, second, in using a source for the gold/silver market rate superior to the London data to which previous authors have resorted.[15]

True mint parity by quarters for 1791–1934 is plotted in figure 5.1. Very apparent is the contrast between the variability until 1834, when the countries were on different metallic standards, and the constancy for the following century (apart from the slight discrete change in 1837), when the countries were each on the gold standard. For the 1950–66 period (selected for comparison purposes), the much lower parity of $2.80 per pound, the par value of the pound at the International Monetary Fund, is applicable. Though not a mint parity, it was the effective parity (that governing exchange-rate movements) and, by the Articles of Agreement of the Fund, related the pound to the US dollar of weight and fineness in effect on July 1, 1944, which was that declared by proclamation on January 31, 1934 (equivalent to $35 per fine ounce).

4   Legal parity, 1834–1921

The final Act rating the gold coin of Britain is that of June 28, 1834, which provided legal-tender status at the rate of 94.8 cents per pennyweight, corresponding to a parity of $4.86934 per pound sterling (see note *l* of table 5.1 for the computational method).[16] This value was slightly above the new gold (and true) parity. The Act of February 21, 1857 repealed this Act and all others that made foreign coin legal tender. Actually, the various ratings of British coin had little practical effect. By far the predominant foreign coin in circulation was the Spanish, and later the Mexican, dollar, which, if of proper weight, was valued equivalent to the American dollar (see section 3 of chapter 3).

Of greater importance was the parity for converting sterling-denominated imports into dollars for the purpose of computing *ad valorem* tariffs. By the Act of July 14, 1832, this rate was increased from $4.44 to $4.80 per pound sterling effective March 3, 1833. The new rate is tantalizingly close to the computed mint parity of $4.7879 for 1832. It is strange that the 1832 law has been ignored in the literature. The Act of July 17, 1842, that changed the rate to $4.84, somewhat below mint parity of $4.86656, is usually cited as the successor to the 1789 legislation.[17] The 1842 Act changed the reach of the rate from tariffs alone to all payments by or to the Treasury involving computation of the value of the pound sterling. Finally, on March 3, 1873 Congress decreed that in all payments by or to the Treasury the pound sterling should be evaluated at $4.8665 (essentially the true mint parity).

Also not recognized in the literature is the Act of August 27, 1894, which states that the value of foreign coin expressed in dollars shall be that of the pure metal of such coin of standard value, and that this value shall be proclaimed quarterly by the Secretary of the Treasury and used to estimate the dollar value of imports. Essentially, this clause solidified the rate of $4.8665 per pound.

The Act of May 27, 1921 repealed these provisions of the Acts of 1873 and 1894. By the Secretary of the Treasury failing to proclaim a value of a foreign currency, conversion of that currency into dollars is to be made at the noon buying rate in the New York foreign-exchange market on the day of foreign export. Because of the depreciation of the pound after World War I, the 1921 Act made legal parity cease to be an operative concept.[18]

5   Expression of exchange rate

The mode of expression of exchange-rate quotations in relation to parity warrants discussion. First, by convention until World War I, the exchange rate was invariably *defined* as the dollar price of the pound instead of the reverse.[19] However, the exchange rate was not *expressed* that way. Rather, since the inception of a national dollar, exchange-rate quotations took the form of either a percentage premium/discount or an index number, with respect to nominal parity ($4.4444 . . . per pound) as the base – a practice fostered by the Act of July 31, 1789. For example, an exchange rate of $4.8888 . . . ($4.88 8/9) per pound was quoted as 110 or 10, meaning 110 with respect to nominal parity ($4.4444 . . . = 100) or a 10 percent premium over nominal parity. Note, however, that in this example the premium over true parity is only 0.46 percent.

Gold ("real") par, too, was cited as the divergence from nominal parity. Until the 1834 coinage legislation, real par, at $4.5657, was 2.73 percent above nominal par.[20] After the 1837 Coinage Act, gold par (and true mint parity) was 9.50 percent over nominal par, and was commonly expressed as 109 1/2 or 9 1/2-percent premium (rather than the true 100 or 0).[21] Between the 1834 and 1837 legislations, gold parity was 9.59 percent over nominal par.

Nominal parity provided an unrealistically low measured exchange value of the dollar (and of mint parity). "The result of using the legal rather than the true par made exchange on London seem always to be at a high premium, even though it might actually be at a discount" (Myers, 1931, p. 72). Nominal parity continued to be used to express the exchange rate, despite the legislations of 1832 and 1842 and despite several efforts in the private sector in the 1830s to have the pound quoted simply in dollars and cents.[22]

Finally, in a determined effort to change the absurd method of exchange-rate quotation, the Act of March 3, 1873 explicitly stated that the new rate "shall be the par of exchange" and that all contracts made after January 1, 1874, based on an assumed par of $4.4444 . . . "shall be null and void." The legislation had the desired effect; thereafter the value of the pound was stated simply in dollars and cents.

6 Exchange-rate data

1 Dispersion of American foreign-exchange market

Unlike England, where the foreign-exchange market always centered in London, in the United States the market developed in a dispersed fashion among the major port cities. These were Baltimore, Boston, New York, and Philadelphia – the four largest cities in the country – with New Orleans of lesser importance.[1] It is a good hypothesis that the foreign-exchange market had greatest volume and influence in the port city that was most developed economically, especially in the foreign-trade sector. Then the earliest foreign-exchange market probably was Boston, the most populous and economically developed town in early colonial America.[2]

Some time after 1725 Boston was overtaken by Philadelphia in economic activity, and in the 1780s Philadelphia clearly became the leading financial center of the United States. Almost certainly it already was the dominant market for foreign exchange. Baltimore's foreign-trade sector began to grow rapidly in that decade, and it could be that around the turn of the century that city was at least temporarily preeminent in foreign exchange, before Philadelphia again asserted itself.

It took a long time for New York to overtake Philadelphia as the dominant city – probably by about 1800 in foreign trade, 1825 in domestic economic activity, and 1835 in finance. As early as 1821, New York was described in the internal correspondence of a foreign-exchange dealer (the House of Brown) as "the greatest [foreign-exchange] market," and by the 1850s "conditions in the New York market usually had an overbearing influence on the firm's sterling rates" (Perkins, 1975, pp. 27, 184). However, it was only after the Civil War, and especially with the US return to the gold standard in 1879, that the city was said to have "a very active market" in foreign exchange (Einzig, 1970, p. 179). In the twentieth century New York could be described as "the dominating market for foreign exchange," "the only important market," and "since 1914 [the location of] most foreign exchange business" (Johnson, 1911, p. 511; Miller, 1925, p. 61; Einzig, 1970, p. 242).

60

2   Exchange-market instruments

Important as Anglo-American bilateral trade and payments were to the American colonies and to the subsequent United States, the reach of the dollar–sterling exchange market extended beyond to encompass almost the entirety of American economic transactions. Referring to the 1800–80 period (but just as well it could be colonial times to World War I), Perkins (1975, p. 6) writes: "In the United States, the British pound was so critical to the foreign trade sector that the term foreign exchange became almost a synonym for money obligations payable in sterling. American importers settled virtually all their international debts in sterling bills. . . . exporters drew the vast majority of their bills in sterling."

Then the predominant instrument in the American foreign-exchange market to World War I was a particular *order to pay a specified amount of money in cash*, the sterling bill of exchange. Drawn on a British party, denominated in pounds and payable in that currency, it was traded in the port cities via at first brokers and then exchange dealers, while in colonial times the ultimate buyer and seller of the bill, that is, American importers and exporters, transacted directly with each other.[3] The dollar–sterling exchange rate was given by the bill's dollar market-price/pound face-value ratio. The bill was then shipped to England for payment.

Typically, a bill was drawn up "t days sight," and was simply called a "t-day bill." This meant that sterling payment was required to be made by the English drawee $t + g$ days after "sight" or "presentation," that is, after the bill was presented to him, where g was the number of days of grace in making payment allowed by British law. One distinction was legal, between "time" bills ($t > 0$) and "demand" or "sight" bills ($t = 0$). Another distinction, based on usage rather than law and not stabilized until the late nineteenth century, was between "long" bills ($t \geq 60$) and "short" bills (originally $t < 60$, later $t \leq 8$).[4] The law on number of days of grace was $g = 3$ for $t > 3$, $g = 0$ for $t \leq 3$. Therefore, upon presentation, a demand bill was redeemed at its pound face-value immediately by the drawee, while a time bill was "accepted" (the drawee literally writing "accepted" on the bill with date and signature). The time bill was thereby turned into an "acceptance," which could be sold ("discounted") in the London discount market, and at $t + g$ days (for example, for a 60-day bill, 63 days) after acceptance delivered to the drawee for payment.[5]

Fundamental to the dollar–sterling exchange market was the practice of drawing sterling bills in the American port cities on London and the absence of drawing dollar bills in England on American port cities.[6] This led to flourishing American markets for sterling bills of exchange but no corresponding London market for dollar bills. Development of the

American foreign-exchange market was enhanced relative to the London market.

With the laying of the Atlantic cable in 1866, the "cable" ("cable transfer" or "telegraphic transfer") provided an alternative to the bill of exchange for an order to pay sterling. A cable involved dollar payment in New York (as did the bill of exchange), with sterling in a London bank transferred upon receipt of the cabled order, generally on the same business day (Whitaker, 1919, p. 89; Cross, 1923, p. 349).

Each exchange-market instrument had its own price, or exchange rate (dollar-price per pound). The relationship among these rates is derivable as follows. The purchasers of all types of sterling made dollar payment immediately, but received their pounds the same day only in the case of cable. With demand bills, a delay for oceanic shipment and presentation was necessary. With t-day time bills, an additional wait of $t + g$ days was involved. Therefore the buyer suffered no interest loss with the cable, an interest loss calculated from the time of purchase in the United States (dollar outlay) to the estimated time of presentation of the bill in England (receipt of pounds) with the demand bill, and an additional $t + g$ days' loss of interest with the time bill. The cable exchange rate (dollar-price of the pound) was highest, followed by the demand bill, and then time bills with the rate varying inversely with t.

The price of bills of exchange varied directly with the quality of the bill. The greater the subjective probability of payment by the drawee, which meant in effect the more esteemed the British party upon which the bill was drawn, the higher the exchange rate. "First class" or "A 1" bills, drawn on esteemed British firms specializing in acceptances, were the most prized and the subject of exchange-rate quotations, with "good but not well-known Bills" purchasable "for a fraction less" (*Bankers' Magazine*, March 1848, p. 532; February 1852, p. 599).[7] Bankers' bills, meaning bills of exchange drawn on British banks, eventually became the epitome of the bill of exchange. Once accepted, they were termed "bankers' acceptances" and enjoyed a thriving discount market in London to World War I. The quality of cables did not vary and was as high as bankers' bills, because of the speed of cable and its development into bank-to-bank transfer of funds.

Which exchange-market instrument was dominant? Until the Civil War the long bill prevailed, usually in the form of the 60-day bill, although on occasion bills of 30 or 90 days were employed.[8] Regular quotations by exchange dealers and in the financial press began only in 1865–6 for 3-day bills and sight bills.[9] Davis and Hughes (1960, p. 59) argue that the use of short bills was retarded by a delayed response to the increased speed and enhanced reliability of ocean transport that had occurred in the preceding decades. Perkins (1975, pp. 184, 189, 291, ns. 24, 34; 1978, pp. 406–7) provides a more convincing explanation, which involves discriminatory pricing by exchange dealers. Because of the high cost of portfolio adjustment, exchange dealers charged purchasers (but not sellers) of short bills a substantial penalty rate. By the late 1860s the discriminatory penalty had been dropped for 3-day bills; but it continued against demand bills until 1879, when its removal let the demand bill become the standard short bill and the dominant exchange-market instrument.

Although cable was available from 1866, its use was discouraged by discriminatory rates on the part of exchange dealers. Indeed, cable rates were not quoted in the financial press until 1879 and even after that date exchange dealers continued their practice of charging discriminatorily high rates for the purchase of cable relative to bills of exchange.[10] Perhaps for that reason, perhaps by tradition, the cable was dominated by bills of exchange until World War I.[11] After the war, however, cable became "by far" the dominant exchange-market instrument, at least in the interbank market, although bills continued to be important in bank-to-customer transactions (Einzig, 1970, p. 238). Under the gold-exchange standard after World War II (incorporating 1950–66, the period selected in this study for comparison purpose), the cable rate was not only the basic exchange rate in the New York market but also was the rate under which the Bank of England intervened in the foreign-exchange market.[12]

It is not entirely clear why a market for dollar drafts failed to develop in the United States prior to World War I. The literature provides several answers.[13] First, there was the long and powerful tradition, going back to colonial times and cemented by bank–customer and bank–bank relations, of financing trade with bills drawn on London. Second, British importers and exporters were themselves unwilling to transact in dollars (or other foreign currency) until after World War I. Third, until the Federal Reserve Act of 1913, American banks were not allowed to engage in the acceptance business and there was no discount market for foreign acceptances, meaning that dollar bills would have had to be held to maturity.

All the while, the balance-of-payments strength of the United States was growing, and along with it resentment of foreign-exchange dependence on London, which financed US trade even with third parties.[14] Net monetary gold flows – the *balance* of payments – were negative from 1889 to 1895 but positive for all years but one from 1896 to 1913. The balance on goods and services (net foreign investment) was negative in 12 of the 15 years from 1881 to 1895, but positive continuously thereafter (Bureau of the Census, 1975, pp. 867–8). In the 1890s attempts were made on the part of New York to rid itself of dependence on sterling bills, but failed because of domestic political considerations.

3   Exchange-rate series

In this section I generate a long-run time series of the dollar–sterling exchange rate. Criteria for an ideal exchange-rate series are laid down in sequence, and the series is developed to satisfy these standards step-by-step.

3.1   Time span

The series should cover all periods of an Anglo-American international specie standard plus floating-exchange-rate episodes with a free gold market that intervened between such periods. Also, the period 1950–66 should be incorporated, for comparison purposes.

The earliest possible observation would be when a dollar/sterling (as distinct from individual-state shilling/English shilling) exchange rate was first continuously provided. In the early years, the "dollar" against sterling might be the Spanish dollar; but no matter, because it was the medium of exchange prior to institution of the American dollar and was set equal in value to that dollar by the Act of 1793. The series cannot extend beyond September 19, 1931, after which Britain left the gold standard never to return. There is one discernible gap, August 1914 to September 11, 1919, during which time the London gold market was non-operational.

3.2   Frequency

A quarterly series is desired for the entire time span, and also a monthly series for 1890–1906, 1925–31, and 1950–66. Quarterly presntation of data allows for intra-annual movement while averaging out atypical observations. Monthly series are needed for detailed examination of three comparable exchange-rate regimes: the classical gold standard (January 1890–December 1906), the interwar gold standard (May 1925–August 1931), and the postwar gold-exchange standard (January 1950–December 1966).[15]

3.3   Exchange-market instrument

The series should pertain to the dominant generic exchange-market instrument. That is the bill of exchange prior to World War I and the cable after the war (see section 2).

3.4   Rapporteur, city, and representativeness

Exchange-rate data should emanate from actual transactions. Secondly, the data should pertain to the dominant foreign-exchange center of the country.

Ideally (prior to World War I), bills should be of high quality and should be uniform in quality. Traditional nineteenth-century dollar–sterling exchange-rate series are quoted rates, based on published or advertised prices of bills of exchange for sale. The reliability of such series is questionable compared to recorded prices of actual transactions. While it is also logical that, for any given time subperiod, the series should have as its locus the city dominant in the foreign-exchange market, the standard of true transaction prices is primary. Underlying the exchange-rate series, high and uniform quality is a desirable quality for bills and a natural characteristic of cables.

The entire period for the exchange-rate series may be divided into sub-periods each with a specific data source or alternative sources. For *1919–31 and 1950–66*, monthly averages of daily rates for cable transfers payable in pounds are taken from Board of Governors of the Federal Reserve System (1943, 1976). These are New York market buying rates or dealer selling rates (prices paid by the purchaser of the cable in the interbank market), based on actual transactions, and are expressed in dollars per pound.

For *1896–1914*, the *Commercial and Financial Chronicle* recorded daily the range of the actual rate at which bankers' sight bills on London was quoted in New York. "Actual rates" are "those for actual business" and therefore possess the transactions characteristic desired in the data. The recorded rates are the prices (in dollars per pound) at which demand bills were sold in large-scale transactions by the New York international banks, principally amongst themselves. So again the rates are prices paid by the purchaser. Proximate sources of the data are Andrew (1910, pp. 195–208) for 1896–1909 and the *Financial Review*, the annual compendium volume of the *Chronicle*, for 1910–14. Before processing the figures, obvious misprints or misrecordings were corrected. Replacing daily ranges by their mid-points, quarterly averages of daily rates were computed for 1896–1914 and monthly averages for 1896–1906.

Perkins (1978, pp. 413–15) provides quarterly averages of daily rates in the *Financial Review* for 1870–1900, and his series is taken for the *1870–95* period. The Perkins series differs from those for 1896–1914 in three ways. First, the Perkins data pertain to demand bills from 1879, but to 3-day bills for 1870–8.[16] Second, they are "posted" rather than "actual" rates throughout.[17] Third, they are expressed as the percentage deviation from (percentage premium over) a $4.8665 "par."

Monthly averages of the Andrew data are taken for 1890–5, as well as for 1896–1906. The early period involves posted rather than actual rates (Andrew, 1910, pp. 189–94).

"Actual" rates were wholesale prices, applicable to large-scale transactions; "posted rates" were "formal prices announced by the leading international bankers as maxima, and employed only for casual business and for small dealings in exchange" (Cole, 1929b, p. 214). Fortunately, as the *Financial Review* regularly stated, posted rates were only "fractionally higher as a rule than those for actual business." Nevertheless, to fulfil strictly the criterion of an exchange-rate series based on actual transactions, I convert the posted rates so they are fully equivalent to actual rates (see section 3.6).

The firm of Nathan Trotter, a nineteenth-century Philadelphia metals importer, kept records of 2789 sterling bills of exchange, of various but specified maturity, that it purchased over 1803–95.[18] Davis and Hughes (1960) use these records to develop several quarterly exchange-rate series, of which the one relevant here runs from 1835 to 1895, retains the original maturity dates, and is expressed as the percent premium over a $4.8665 "par" (wrong though this parity is until January 18, 1837).[19] The underlying data are compelling, and so are used for the *1835–69* component of the exchange-rate series, for two reasons. First, the data are clearly records of actual transactions, showing the prices paid by the purchaser of the bills. Second, there is evidence that the quality of Trotter's bills was high during this period. Thirteen acceptors, all well-known, constituted about 45 percent of the total value of the bills from 1834 to 1865, and only ten for the entirety of the bills thereafter (Davis and Hughes, 1960, p. 68).

An alternative data source for this time period is Martin (1898, pp. 28, 51ff.), who provides a monthly exchange-rate series at New York for 60-day bankers' bills for 1835–97.[20] The series is expressed as the percent premium over nominal par through 1873, in dollars per pound thereafter. The advantages of the Martin over the Trotter series are that its city of quotation is the foreign-exchange center and the bills are of highest quality. Its disadvantages are also twofold. From 1835 to 1861, the series pertains to only one day in the month.[21] More important, Martin's data are quotations rather than actual rates – the definitive deficiency leading to selection of the Trotter series.

For the *pre-1835* period, no one source can provide all the observations, and data in all the major port cities of the time are assembled. Davis and Hughes (1960, pp. 76–7) present a Trotter series for 1803–34 (expressed in contemporary fashion as the percent premium over nominal par); but it has twenty missing observations, as Trotter did not purchase bills in these quarters. Also, the bills were of relatively low quality.[22]

Another series based on actual transactions pertains to Baltimore rather than Philadelphia. In November 1829 John White, Cashier of the Second Bank of the United States, provided the Secretary of the Treasury with a monthly 60-day bill exchange-rate series, running from January 1791 to October 1829, remarkable for its time in several respects.[23] First, the data are described as "compiled chiefly from the average monthly sales effected by two mercantile houses of high standing" and "compiled chiefly from actual sales effected by two highly respectable mercantile houses" (Secretary of the Treasury, 1830, pp. 67, 78). The series therefore emanates from actual transactions, a feature that Davis and Hughes (1960, pp. 53–4) claimed for their series alone.

Second, the source of White's data is directly foreign-exchange dealers (rather than newspapers or magazines), and White takes pains to say this four times: twice as quoted above, in the table as "Authorities – Two Respectable Mercantile Houses," and in a derivative table for 1814–17 as "a Baltimore broker" (Secretary of the Treasury, 1830, p. 92).[24] Exchange dealer as seller is suggestive of high-quality bills. Third, especially noteworthy, the exchange rate is expressed not only as the percent premium over nominal parity but also as the number of dollars per pound.[25] Fourth, the series is continuous, with no missing observations even in the unsettled conditions of paper standards.

Exchange-rate series for the remaining port cities are quotations rather than actual-transactions data. All the series are monthly, expressed as the percent premium over nominal par, and pertain to 60-day bills. Where there is a range for the month, the mid-point is taken. For Boston, Smith and Cole (1935, pp. 187–9) compile a series derived from one-day-a-month quotations in specified newspapers and magazines and running from September 1795 to December 1824. The series can be supplemented with that in Martin (1898, pp. 10–28), available from June 1798 to December 1834, but used only from January 1824 (allowing a year's overlap with the later, and therefore presumed superior, Smith–Cole series).[26]

For New York, *Bankers' Magazine* (March 1848, p. 532; February 1852, p. 599) tabulates a series beginning in January 1822 and running to 1850, though of interest only to December 1835 (allowing for a year's overlap with the 1835–69 Trotter data). Quotations are "the rate charged for A1 bills."

For Philadelphia, the latest-published series, available from May 1825 to April 1838 (but of interest only to December 1835), is that of Levi Woodbury (Secretary of the Treasury, 1838, pp. 64–83). Woodbury was Secretary of the Treasury from 1834 to 1841. For three missing months in 1834, the Woodbury series is estimated by averaging figures for the two adjacent months. The Woodbury series is supplemented with that of Samuel Moore (Secretary of the Treasury, 1830, pp. 52–7). Moore was Director of the mint from 1824 to 1835. The Moore series runs from May 1815 to September 1829 (of interest to June 1826, allowing for four quarters' overlap with the Woodbury series), with two missing observations estimated as above. The Moore series is also available annually for 1802–4 and 1811–14.

For Baltimore, the only pre-1838 series other than White is offered by Woodbury and is annual, available for 1800–10 (Secretary of the Treasury, 1838, p. 137).

It is reasonable to assume that the Martin and all pre-1835 series are dealer selling rates (market buying rates) – as are the other series, for which this property is expressly stated.

Two initial manipulations of the series are performed. The Martin 1835–70 series and all the pre-1835 series other than Trotter are monthly; so they are averaged to obtain quarterly frequency (but the monthly Andrew 1890–1906 and Board of Governors of the Federal Reserve System 1925–31, 1950–66 series are also retained). Then the data not already in dollars per pound but rather expressed as the percentage deviation from "parity" (all series except Andrew, *Financial Review* unprocessed by Perkins, and Board of Governors of the Federal Reserve System) are reexpressed in that form by means of the formula $Y = (1 + 0.01 \cdot X) \cdot K$, where X is the quarterly or annual series under consideration, Y is the corresponding series in dollars per pound, and the value of K is 4.8665 for the Trotter 1835–70 and Perkins 1870–1900 series, 4.4444 . . . for the other series. Letting P denote the pound face-value of a bill of exchange and D the dollar price paid for the bill, $Y = D/P$.

3.5   Uniform bill maturity

A consistent pre-World War I exchange-rate series requires that all observations pertain to bills of a given maturity t. Logically, $t = 0$, the series should refer consistently to sight bills, for two reasons. First, the demand bill became the ultimate dominant instrument prior to the ascendancy of cable. Second, if the objective is to obtain a bill-of-exchange rate measure as close as possible to the postwar hegemonic cable rate, then the interest component of the bill is to be minimized, wherefore $t = 0$.[27] So all the time-bill exchange-rate series developed in section 3.4 are to be converted to a demand-bill basis. This is achievable by formula.

Let Y denote the exchange rate of a time bill, Z the exchange rate of the corresponding demand bill (both rates in dollars per pound), and I the *ad valorem* (one-hundredth the percentage) interest rate for the duration of the time bill over that of the demand bill. The interest element (I) depends on the percentage interest rate per year (i) and the maturity length of the time bill in days (t): $I = (i/100) \cdot (t/365)$. Then $D = Y \cdot P = Z \cdot (1 - I) \cdot P$. It follows that $Z = Y/(1 - I)$.[28] Because the dollar-purchaser of a time bill obtains his pound-funds later than the purchaser of an equivalent sight bill, the interest component of the time bill reduces the exchange rate: $Y < Z$.

To factor out the interest component of a t-day time bill, an annual interest rate (i) is needed. Davis and Hughes (1960, pp. 53, 56) use American rather than British short-term interest rates for this purpose, because the purchaser of the bill (Trotter in their case) was in effect providing credit to the seller and had the investment alternative of the American money market. Perkins (1978), however, argues that this argument is incorrect and that, rather, British short-term interest rates should underlie construction of i. His argument is fourfold. First, the motive of American importers in purchasing bills was to settle a near-term foreign debt, not to invest surplus funds. The American money market, therefore, did not provide an alternative opportunity, and American interest rates were irrelevant (Perkins, 1978, p. 405).

Second, "authors of some textbooks and practical business guides" state that the interest rate in the domicile or drawee city (London), where bills are payable – rather than in the drawer city (New York) – determines the interest component in time versus sight bills. This rule is presented as "an accepted fact, based on experience" (Perkins, 1978, p. 394).[29]

Third, Perkins (1978, pp. 394–6) notes that exchange dealers played both sides of the bill market and to them the absolute level of interest rates in the home (drawer) and foreign (drawee) countries was irrelevant. Competition among exchange dealers drove the implicit interest rate in bills of exchange down to that in the lower-interest-rate market, which empirically in the pre-World War I era was almost always London (coinciding with the drawee location) rather than New York or another American port city.[30]

Fourth, Perkins (1978, pp. 397–402) provides empirical evidence for years ranging from 1852 to 1899 that the implicit interest components derived from bills with varying maturities were clearly correlated with the British rather than the American short-term interest rate.[31]

The evidence for the British rather than American rate in adjusting for the interest component in time-bill data is overwhelming. So, for the required values of i, a quarterly British short-term interest-rate series running from 1791 to 1878 must be developed. In principle, one could select either the Bank of England rediscount rate ("Bank Rate") or the money-market rate of discount for this purpose. Perkins uses Bank Rate to reconvert the Trotter 1835–95 series of Davis and Hughes to a demand-bill basis.

Whereas the Bank Rate was set by the Bank of England, the money-market rate was a true competitive price, determined by the public's supply of bills to be discounted and the demand of bill brokers for the same. In fact, the Bank Rate "was usually maintained at a figure slightly above prevailing rates in the London discount market" (Perkins, 1978, p. 396). The money-market rate of discount is the better measure, and the series i constructed by selecting this market rate over the Bank Rate, data permitting, is exhibited in table 6.1.

Table 6.1 *British interest rate to convert time to demand bills (percent per year)*

Year(s)	First quarter	Second quarter	Third quarter	Fourth quarter
1791–1821	5.00	5.00	5.00	5.00
1822	5.00	4.88	4.00	4.00
1823	4.00	4.00	4.00	4.00
1824	3.50	3.50	3.50	3.50
1825	3.50	3.67	4.00	4.33
1826	5.00	4.83	4.17	4.00
1827	3.67	3.33	3.00	3.00
1828	3.00	3.00	3.00	3.17
1829	3.67	3.67	3.17	3.00
1830	2.92	2.58	2.50	3.25
1831	3.25	3.83	3.67	4.00
1832	3.58	3.25	3.00	2.75
1833	2.50	2.42	2.67	3.33
1834	3.08	3.17	3.50	3.75
1835	3.50	3.83	3.75	3.75
1836	3.67	3.50	4.50	5.33
1837	5.50	4.83	4.00	3.42
1838	3.17	2.67	2.92	3.25
1839	3.75	4.25	6.00	6.50
1840	5.17	4.58	4.58	5.58
1841	5.17	4.67	4.58	5.17
1842	4.33	3.50	2.92	2.58
1843	2.25	2.08	2.08	2.25
1844	2.08	1.92	1.92	2.58
1845	2.58	2.75	2.83	3.67
1846	4.50	4.00	3.50	3.17
1847	4.08	5.83	5.83	7.67
1848	3.75	3.33	3.00	2.75
1849	2.42	2.33	2.25	2.25
1850	2.25	2.08	2.17	2.50
1851	3.08	3.08	3.17	2.92
1852	2.25	1.88	1.75	1.75
1853	2.83	3.08	3.58	5.17
1854	4.75	5.25	5.08	4.67
1855	4.92	3.58	3.42	7.00
1856	6.83	6.00	4.42	6.83
1857	6.00	6.42	5.67	8.67
1858	3.75	3.00	3.00	2.83
1859	2.23	3.02	2.53	2.23
1860	3.42	4.26	3.84	4.48

Table 6.1 (*cont.*)

Year(s)	First quarter	Second quarter	Third quarter	Fourth quarter
1861	7.69	3.86	5.09	3.36
1862	2.26	2.42	1.93	2.39
1863	3.93	3.62	3.85	5.61
1864	6.51	6.80	7.24	7.45
1865	5.61	4.30	4.12	7.25
1866	6.79	7.71	7.32	3.82
1867	3.35	2.96	2.23	2.10
1868	2.35	2.35	2.35	2.80
1869	3.16	4.37	2.99	2.96
1870	3.17	3.17	4.14	2.64
1871	2.65	2.55	2.19	4.17
1872	2.98	3.97	3.53	5.84
1873	3.74	5.01	3.72	6.33
1874	3.54	3.29	2.91	4.51
1875	3.64	3.40	2.35	3.17
1876	3.63	1.94	1.74	1.74
1877	1.81	2.39	2.21	4.07
1878	2.36	2.71	4.15	5.14

Data and Sources: 1791–1823: Bank Rate, Clapham (1945, vol. I, p. 299; vol. II, p. 429). Rate for 1822 (second quarter) computed as quarterly average of daily rates. *1824–58:* quarterly average of monthly rates. *1824–57 (May)* – Overend-Gurney rate of discount for three-month bills, House of Commons (1857, p. 464). *1857 (June)–1858* – market rate of interest, Bigelow (1862, p. 205). *1859–78:* market rate of discount, three-month bank bills. Computed as QBR·(AMR/ABR), where QBR is the quarterly Bank Rate, AMR the annual market rate, and ABR the annual Bank Rate. QBR: quarterly average of daily rates. 1859–70 from Perkins (1978, p. 417), 1871–8 computed from data in Clapham (1945, vol. II, pp. 430–1).AMR: Williams (1912, p. 382). ABR: average QBR for year.

For the period 1824–58 a true market rate is used for i: the rate of discount for first-class bills charged by Overend and Gurney, an important London bill-broker.[32] For 1791–1823 no market series is available and resort must be made to the Bank Rate. The Bank of England discounted bills at 5 percent (until June 1822, when the Bank Rate was reduced to 4 percent); usury laws set a maximum interest rate of 5 percent; and private bill-brokers could find no loopholes to evade the law. Thus there is strong evidence that the Bank Rate represented the market bill-discount rate as a rule for the period 1791–1823.[33]

For 1859–78 the annual market rate of Williams (1912, p. 382) is converted to quarterly form by multiplication by the quarterly Bank Rate and division by the annual Bank Rate.

To compute I, one needs not only the annual interest rate (i), but also the maturity (t) for the specific time-bill exchange-rate series under consideration. All such series in section 3.4 have $t = 60$, with two exceptions: Perkins 1870–8, for which $t = 3$; and Trotter, for which t is variable. Davis and Hughes (1960, pp. 75–6) provide an annual table of the average term to maturity of the Trotter bills of exchange. Using this table together with the actual Trotter bills-of-exchange accounts, I constructed a quarterly series of the average maturity (t) of the bills of exchange for 1803–34, exhibited in table 6.2.[34] For 1835–70, the annual average, shown in table 6.3, is taken on a quarterly basis.

Having obtained the ingredients of I for every bill-of-exchange series, Y, the formula for Z is applied to convert these series to the sight exchange rate. Then Z may represent any series of section 3.4, after this stage of processing. So a given exchange-rate series, Z, pertains to a cable transfer or a demand bill (whether original or converted from time bills) and is expressed in dollars per pound.

3.6   Incorporation of broker's commission

All observed data on the exchange rate, and therefore all the exchange-rate series Z, represent the price at which pounds can be purchased, the selling rate of brokers or dealers. One can envisage a corresponding set of exchange-rate series W, calibrated as the price at which pounds can be sold, the buying rate of brokers or dealers. The difference between the two is the broker's commission, C, expressed (as is Z and W) in dollars per pound. So $Z - W = C$. Logically, the "true" exchange rate, V, if it is to be one number, is the mid-point of the buying and selling rates: $V = (W + Z)/2 = W + 0.5 \cdot C = Z - 0.5 \cdot C$. These equations enable computation of V from the observed exchange rate (Z) and broker's commission (C) ("the first formula for V"). Broker's commission, as part of the purchase price, is paid by the buyer of foreign exchange. If this commission is a percentage rate, $100 \cdot k$, then C and V may be obtained from the equations $C = k \cdot Z$ and $V = (1 - 0.5 \cdot k) \cdot Z$ ("the second formula for V").

Table 6.4 lists all available information on broker's commission in the American foreign-exchange market for 1791–1931 and 1950–66. Making some reasonable assumptions, a time series of broker's commission can be obtained for the entire period. The mid-point of the rate in the early 1820s, 1.25 percent, is projected back to 1791. Letting the "mid-1820s" begin January 1, 1824, the rate falls to 0.5 percent on that date, remaining to the end of 1873. So, for (1791–1823, 1824–73), $k = (0.0125, 0.005)$.

Table 6.2 *Average maturity of bills of exchange, Trotter series, 1803–34* *(days)*

Year	First quarter	Second quarter	Third quarter	Fourth quarter
1803	30	—	30	—
1804	60	52.5	60	50
1805	60	60	60	54
1806	60	55.7	60	52.5
1807	60	55.7	60	55
1808	60	30	—	50
1809	—	52.5	60	54
1810	60	50	60	40
1811	—	30	60	30
1812	30	—	—	60
1813	—	50	—	30
1814	—	—	—	—
1815	—	—	60	60
1816	—	38.6	60	50
1817	75	60	60	60
1818	54	50.2	60	60
1819	60	60	—	60
1820	30	60	—	60
1821	60	60	60	60
1822	60	60	60	—
1823	58.3	54	60	45
1824	60	60	60	60
1825	45	66.7	46	47.6
1826	54	50	45.7	44.1
1827	52.5	39.4	23.3	41.3
1828	47	30	37.5	42
1829	41.1	30	50	37
1830	36.3	45	42	60
1831	48	43.3	50	60
1832	55.7	57.3	56.3	56.3
1833	50	65	42.2	60
1834	50	60	—	60

Source: See text.

Table 6.3 *Average maturity of bills of exchange, Trotter Series, 1835–70*

Years	Maturity (days)					
1835–40	60.0	58.0	54.6	59.4	55.8	54.8
1841–45		57.9	59.3	59.3	65.9	56.8
1846–50		62.6	55.4	47.8	56.4	57.4
1851–5		57.4	57.3	56.3	56.6	60.0
1856–60		60.0	58.6	60.0	58.8	60.0
1861–5		55.7	48.8	54.0	42.0	43.7
1866–70		51.6	11.1	11.7	11.8	12.4

Source: Davis and Hughes (1960, pp. 75–6).

Beginning 1874, broker's commission became expressed in dollars per pound. $C =$ \$0.025 for 1874–8 and is taken as \$0.0125 (the mid-point of the observed range in 1879) for 1879–89, \$0.0025 (applicable some time before 1910) for 1890–9, and \$0.0005 (observed 1910–14) for 1900–14. The three latter intervals are obtained by dividing the period 1880–1909 into ten-year segments and allocating them to the observations enveloping 1879–1914.

After World War I a C of \$0.00125 from 1919 to March 1923 and \$0.000625 from April 1923 to 1931 reasonably occurred, with the switch deemed to happen two months after York proofread his textbook (see note g of table 6.4). For 1950–66, $C =$ \$0.0001.

Using the second formula for V, the "time series" of k (only two values) is used to convert all exchange-rate series in the 1791–1873 interval from Z to V format. Using the first formula for V, the time series of C is applied to transform all exchange-rate series in 1874–1966 from Z to V form.

The "posted rates" of the Perkins (1870–1900) quarterly series and of the 1890–5 segment of the Andrew (1890–1906) monthly series are now converted to actual rates. The average ratio of the *Financial Review* actual rate to the Perkins posted rate over the 20 quarters of 1896–1900, where the series overlap, is 0.9981, confirming that posted rates are "fractionally higher." The V series for Perkins (quarterly, 1870–1900) and Andrew (monthly, 1890–1906 – but only 1890–5 segment) are reconstructed by multiplication by 0.9981, resulting in "revised Perkins" and "revised Andrew" series.

3.7   Expression of exchange rate

The concept of true mint parity was developed in section 3 of chapter 5, and a quarterly series of that parity (dollars per pound) exhibited in table 5.2. The exchange-rate series V, in dollars per pound, are reexpressed as S, the

Table 6.4 *Broker's commission in foreign-exchange market, 1820s to 1969*

| Period | Commission rate | | Source |
	Dollars per pound	Percent	
Early 1820s		1–1.5[a]	Perkins (1975, p. 27)
Mid-1820s to Dec. 31, 1873		0.5[b]	Perkins (1975, pp. 188, 219, 270, n. 37)
Jan. 1, 1874 to beginning of 1879	0.025[c]		Perkins (1975, p. 219), Huntington and Mawhinney (1910, p. 209)
1879[d]	0.01–0.015[e]		Perkins (1975, p. 220)
Before 1910[f]	0.0025		Escher (1910, p. 61)
1910/1911/pre-World War I	0.0005		Escher (1910, p. 61)/ Johnson (1911, p. 523)/ York (1923, p. 433), Cross (1923, p. 100), Borts (1960, p. 224)
1918–23	0.000625–0.00125/ 0.00125		Cross (1923, p. 100)/York (1923, p. 433)
1923[g]/1925	0.000625		York (1923, pp. iv, 433, n. 1)/Miller (1925, pp. 61–2)
1969	0.0001		Federal Reserve Bank of New York (1969, p. 104)

Notes:
[a] Profit margin of House of Brown on foreign-exchange transactions.
[b] Buying rate of House of Brown set 0.5 percent below current selling rate.
[c] Brown's current selling rate minus buying rate, under new quotation system (dollars around parity rather than percentage deviations around 109.5).
[d] During First half of year, by April.
[e] Current selling rate minus buying rate of New York and Philadelphia foreign-exchange dealers.
[f] "Before the [foreign-exchange brokerage] business become overcrowded as it is now [1910]."
[g] "Since this was written [February 1, 1923]."

percentage deviation from true mint parity. Letting M denote this parity, $S = 100 \cdot (V - M)/M$.[35] S is the percent sterling premium (discount if negative) with respect to true parity, the percentage premium of the pound over the dollar.

3.8   Correction for paper-currency depreciation

Under a paper standard, mint parity is no longer an exchange value about which specie points can be expected to contain the current exchange rate. To restore this role of parity, the exchange rate must be converted from a paper-currency to a specie basis. This is done by correcting for depreciation of the currency in terms of specie, specifically, in terms of the effective metallic standard of the other country. In the case of Britain, there were two periods of a paper standard during the time period of interest. In 1797–1821 the exchange value of the paper pound (meaning Bank of England notes) is to be corrected for its movement against silver in general, leaving as the net (desired) series the pound's value against the American silver dollar. In 1919–25, the correction is against gold in general, with the resultant series the exchange value of the pound against the American gold dollar.

In the United States, until the 1890s, "suspension of specie payments" was usually a local rather than national occurrence, with a resulting floating exchange rate and currency (banknote) depreciation only in those areas where banks suspended payments.[36] Therefore adjustment for currency depreciation is made only for those exchange-rate series where suspension occurred in the city of quotation. This procedure not only restores the role of parity for exchange-rate variation with respect to specie points but also permits the reworked exchange-rate series potentially to be representative nationally. Of course, in cases where bank suspensions did not measurably affect the local foreign-exchange market – so that the link between currency inconvertibility and a floating exchange rate was broken – or where data on currency depreciation are lacking, there is no correction for depreciation of the paper currency. In all episodes where correction takes place, the paper dollar is adjusted for its valuation against gold, the effective metallic standard in Britain throughout 1791–1931. When both countries are on a paper standard – the situation in 1814–17, with incidentally a differing potentially effective metallic standard – then a double correction is to be made.

Table 6.5 presents quarterly time series of the percentage premium of the British pound over the Spanish dollar (representing silver in general, for which the direct data – on bars – are seriously incomplete) in 1797–1821 and over gold in 1919–25, these series denoted as ENG97 and ENG19, respectively. A negative premium (the usual case) denotes a discount of the pound.

Table 6.5 *Premium of British pound over Spanish dollar and gold, 1797–1821 and 1919–25 (percent)*[a]

Year	First quarter	Second quarter	Third quarter	Fourth quarter
1797	− 3.50	− 6.33	− 0.75	− 0.34
1798	− 1.10	− 1.04	− 1.17	− 1.17
1799	− 2.36	− 5.20	− 6.61	− 10.99
1800	− 10.46	− 11.59	−11.60	− 12.89
1801	− 13.60	− 15.72	− 15.29	− 14.84
1802	− 14.17	− 11.16	− 6.81	− 7.29
1803	− 8.51	− 9.37	− 6.29	− 9.21
1804	− 11.38	− 8.77	− 4.55	− 4.00
1805	− 7.10	− 4.35	− 6.34	− 10.41
1806	− 10.29	− 10.07	− 8.57	− 9.31
1807	− 9.92	− 8.97	− 8.77	− 8.61
1808	− 6.25	− 5.87	− 6.30	− 8.65
1809	− 8.59	− 8.30	− 10.45	− 9.96
1810	− 10.30	− 11.99	− 13.43	− 13.54
1811	− 15.20	− 16.59	− 17.20	− 19.00
1812	− 18.81	− 20.11	− 21.77	− 23.78
1813	− 24.24	− 25.92	− 28.51	− 29.02
1814	− 28.73	− 26.15	− 10.98	− 11.60
1815	− 14.06	− 24.50	− 11.05	− 6.37
1816	− 5.70	− 0.64	1.30	1.73
1817	− 0.20	− 3.81	− 3.94	− 5.87
1818	− 8.20	− 9.75	− 9.08	− 8.51
1819	− 11.16	− 5.54	− 1.44	− 1.30
1820	− 0.79	1.05	1.37	1.23
1821	1.29	0.74		
1919				− 17.13
1920	− 26.16	− 19.59	− 24.53	− 28.15
1921	− 20.66	− 19.69	− 24.20	− 17.50
1922	− 11.33	− 8.90	− 8.32	− 7.16
1923	− 3.98	− 4.53	− 5.93	− 8.85
1924	− 11.77	− 10.57	− 8.69	− 6.10
1925	− 2.27	− 0.56		

Note:
[a] A negative sign denotes a discount.
Source: Computed as 100·(PAR/PRICE − 1), where PAR and PRICE are expressed in pence per ounce of silver or gold. Sterling premium over parity is given by 100·[(1/PRICE − 1/PAR)/(1/PAR)] = 100· (PAR/PRICE − 1), where 1/PRICE and 1/PAR are in number of ounces of silver or gold per pence. For 1797–1821, par is 59.3, parity for the Spanish dollar in terms of the British pound [from Hawtrey (1950, p. 283)]. For 1919–25, par is 1019.4545..., computed as (12/11)·934.5, where 934.5 is the mint price per standard ounce of gold. For 1797–1821, PRICE is the average of weekly (sometimes biweekly) observations of the price of the Spanish dollar, from House of Commons (1819, pp. 336–54) and House of Commons (1832, pp. 98–100). For 1919–25, PRICE is the price of gold per fine ouce in the London market, quarterly average of daily rates in Shrigley (1935, pp. 93–104). PRICE is taken as PAR for (i) January 1–February 26, 1797 (with the price for February 27 obtained as the average of the February 24 and March 3 values), (ii) May 1–June 30, 1821, and (iii) May 1–June 30, 1925.

Table 6.6 *Premium of specie over currency, by city, 1817–57 (percent)*

Year–quarter	Baltimore	New York	Philadelphia
1814 (3)	6.67		
(4)	13.00		
1815 (1)	10.00		
(2)	13.33		4.90
(3)	19.67		14.07
(4)	18.17		17.65
1816 (1)	15.33		15.61
(2)	21.00		17.42
(3)	12.33		12.15
(4)	8.67		8.50
1817 (1)	1.83		2.92
1837 (2)		5.00	5.15
(3)		8.50	9.75
(4)		5.20	5.67
1838 (1)		3.03	4.44
(2)		0.53	2.76
(3)			0.33
1839 (4)			10.51
1840 (1)			6.50
(2)			4.67
(3)			3.13
(4)			2.75
1841 (1)			2.63
(2)			2.63
(3)			2.63
(4)			2.63
1842 (1)			2.23
1857 (4)		0.47	

Notes and Sources: Baltimore: 1814–17: Secretary of the Treasury (1830, p. 92). Quarterly average of monthly observations. *New York:* 1837–8, 1857: Computed as PG – 100, where PG is the quarterly average of the monthly currency value of gold, in cents. Data from Warren and Pearson (1932, p. 76; 1935, p. 154). Value of 100 imposed for June 1838. *Philadelphia:* 1815–17: Computed as $100 \cdot D/(100 - D)$, where D is the quarterly average of the monthly discount of currency in Philadelphia with respect to specie; data from Secretary of the Treasury (1830, pp. 52–3). Let D = discount of banknotes with respect to specie (percent, taken as positive, the observed series) and x = price of banknotes in terms of specie (number of specie dollars per banknote dollar). Then $D = 100 \cdot (1 - x)$. Let P = premium of specie over banknotes (percent, the desired series). With $1/x$ = price of specie in terms of banknotes (number of banknote dollars per specie dollar), $P = 100 \cdot (1/x - 1)$ $= 100 \cdot D/(100 - D)$. 1837–42: Average of monthly observations of premium of American gold. Data for May 1837 – April 1838 from Secretary of the Treasury (1838, pp. 80–3), May 1838 – December 1840 from Secretary of the Treasury (1841, pp. 18–27), January–December 1841 from Elliot (1845, p. 1172). Average of four observations for each of January–April and of two observations for June 1838. Value of zero imposed for April 1837. For May 1837, October 1839, weighted average of zero (days 1–10, 1–9) and recorded value (days 11–31, 10–31). For January 1841 – February 1842, mid-point of range for year 1841. For March 1842, weighted average of this range (days 1–17) and zero (days 18–31).

Table 6.7 *Premium of gold over greenbacks, New York, 1862–78 (percent)*

Year	First quarter	Second quarter	Third quarter	Fourth quarter
1862	2.60	3.80	16.20	30.60
1863	53.40	48.30	30.20	48.90
1864	59.00	86.60	144.90	122.70
1865	98.50	41.40	43.20	46.20
1866	36.30	35.90	48.60	42.90
1867	35.70	36.70	41.20	39.30
1868	39.80	39.50	43.90	35.60
1869	33.80	36.70	35.70	26.00
1870	17.80	13.60	16.50	11.60
1871	11.10	11.50	13.10	12.20
1872	9.80	12.90	14.10	12.80
1873	14.10	17.30	14.60	9.20
1874	11.90	12.40	9.80	10.90
1875	14.20	15.90	14.70	15.00
1876	13.50	12.70	11.00	8.90
1877	5.30	6.20	4.60	2.80
1878	1.70	0.70	0.50	0.30

Source: Constructed as PG – 100, where PG is the price of gold in greenbacks, in cents. Data from Mitchell (1908, pp. 5–13).

An annual series, ENG97A, is constructed as the average of the appropriate quarterly values of ENG97.

In table 6.6 quarterly time series of the percentage premium of specie over currency are shown for individual American port cities: Baltimore for 1814–17 (denoted as BA14), New York for 1837–8 and 1857 (NY37 and NY57, respectively), and Philadelphia for 1815–17 and 1837–42 (PH15 and PH37, respectively). Finally, table 6.7 exhibits a quarterly time series of the percentage premium of gold over greenbacks in New York for 1862–78, denoted as NY62.

In constructing these corrective series, both British and American, a zero value is imposed on either side of the paper-standard period. The British series (ENG97, ENG19) are expressed as the percent currency premium over specie (typically negative, because a discount), whereas the American series (BA14, NY37, NY57, PH15, PH37, NY62) are the percent specie premium over currency (typically positive). These respective formulations enable correction for paper-currency depreciation to be effected by subtraction from the exchange-rate series *S*, which have the form percentage deviation from parity in terms of the dollar price of the pound.

Exchange-rate series before Davis and Hughes (1960) did not generally correct for the depreciation of paper currency in terms of specie. The Martin series for New York is an exception, with "gold rates" rather than "quotations in currency" provided from 1865 to 1878. Davis and Hughes (1960, p. 55) convert the Trotter bills purchased in greenbacks during 1862–78 back to gold dollars, and Perkins (1978) corrects his *Financial Review* series for the paper-currency depreciation of the greenback period.[37] However, they do not apply such adjustment to the other paper-standard periods of the nineteenth century.[38]

The final exchange-rate series, denoted as R, are corrected for paper-currency depreciation and generated as follows: $R = S -$ ENG19 for Board of Governors of the Federal Reserve System (New York); $R = S$ for revised Perkins, revised Andrew, *Financial Review*, and *Bankers' Magazine* (all New York), Woodbury (Philadelphia), and Martin (Boston); $R = S -$ NY37 $-$ NY57 $-$ NY62, $R = S$, for Martin (New York) 1835–64, 1865–70; $R = S -$ ENG97 $-$ PH15 $-$ PH37 $-$ NY57 for Trotter (Philadelphia), with an annual series for 1803–4, 1811–13 obtained by averaging the available quarterly observations; $R = S -$ ENG97 $-$ BA14 for White (Baltimore), with an annual series for 1800–1810 obtained by averaging the four quarterly observations; $R = S -$ ENG97 $-$ PH15, $R = S -$ ENG97A for Moore (Philadelphia), quarterly, annual; $R = S -$ ENG97 for Smith and Cole (Boston), and $R = S -$ ENG97A for Woodbury (Baltimore). From 1857 onward, the paper-currency depreciation recorded in New York is applied nationally.

The exchange-rate series R are corrected for paper standards that noticeably affected the foreign-exchange market. Therefore the series can be interpreted as percentage deviations from the true metallic parity under the actually or potentially effective specie standard in each country. The quarterly R series for 1791–1834 and the annual R series for 1791–1813 are listed in tables 6.8 and 6.9, respectively. Table 6.10 presents the quarterly Trotter and Martin R series for 1835–69, and table 6.11 the selected New York R quarterly series for 1870–1966: revised Perkins (1870–95), Andrew and *Financial Review* (1896–1914), Board of Governors of the Federal Reserve System (1919–31, 1950–66). The New York monthly R series (1890–1906, 1925–31, 1950–66) are not tabulated, but are graphed in figures 16.1–16.3 in chapter 16.

For investigating the concerns of this volume, such as specie-point stability and exchange-market integration, the R series is preferred. However, for other purposes, such as data conversion and examination of floating exchange rates, adjustment for paper-currency depreciation is inappropriate. As users of the exchange-rate series will have a variety of objectives, the exchange-rate series in S form are obtainable, by applying tables 6.5–6.7 to decorrect the R series listed in tables 6.8–6.11.

3.9 Representativeness

The component subperiods of the long-run exchange-rate R series should be representative nationally. This property can be assumed for the New York series from 1870 onward, but needs to be checked for Trotter (1835–69), a Philadelphia series, versus New York, the foreign-exchange center. Comparing the Trotter and Martin R series for the 140 quarters of 1835–69 (table 6.10), there are only eight quarters with a divergence above two percent of parity, of which only one is above 5 percent.

Where there are deviations between two exchange-rate series, each corrected for the interest component in time bills of exchange and for paper standards, the explanation may reside in any of four factors.[39]

(a) *Underlying frequency of an observation.* Prior to 1862, the Martin monthly data are for one day, on or about the first of the month, whereas the Trotter data are always for all bills purchased over the quarter. Half of the mentioned divergences occur earlier than 1862, and the superior frequency property of Trotter could explain much of them.

(b) *Nature of the data.* Trotter (actual transactions) is clearly to be preferred to Martin (advertised or quoted rates), and this element helps to explain all divergences in Trotter's favor.

(c) *Place of quotation.* With New York the foreign-exchange center, this factor acts to resolve differences in favor of Martin.

(d) *Market participant providing the data.* The Trotter data are from the records of a purchaser of bills; the Martin series is probably quotations of dealers or advertised prices of sellers of exchange. This element is probably less important than (b).

All in all, the Trotter series tracks Martin remarkably well, with the divergences generally small and in any case substantially resolvable in Trotter's favor. The four largest divergences – ranging from 4.04 to 7.75 percent – happen during the greenback period, and are not so large, considering that currency-depreciation correction of 30–144 percent is applied to both series.

The pre-1835 component of the long-term exchange-rate series remains to be selected. The two principal candidates are the Trotter and White R series, and their quarter-by-quarter difference is shown in the second column of table 6.12. In the years 1803–10 there are sharp divergences between the two series, reaching as high as 34 percent of parity. Afterwards, only in four isolated quarters does the difference exceed 4 percent of parity (in 1815, 1816, 1823, and 1825). By 1827 the series become separated uniformly by less than 1 percent of parity.

Table 6.8 *Exchange-rate series, demand-bill basis, quarterly, 1791–1834 (percent sterling premium over parity)*[a]

Year-quarter	Derived from actual transactions		Based on published quotations		
	Philadelphia Trotter	Baltimore White	Boston Smith-Cole[b] Martin[c]	New York *Bankers' Magazine*	Philadelphia Moore[d] Woodbury[e]
1791 (1)		− 1.19			
(2)		− 0.71			
(3)		0.10			
(4)		− 0.71			
1792 (1)		− 2.94			
(2)		− 4.22			
(3)		− 2.62			
(4)		− 3.58			
1793 (1)		− 4.60			
(2)		− 2.49			
(3)		0.76			
(4)		1.09			
1794 (1)		0.10			
(2)		0.15			
(3)		2.85			
(4)		3.59			
1795 (1)		− 2.23			
(2)		− 2.86			
(3)		− 3.49			
(4)		− 6.26	− 6.34		
1796 (1)		− 14.58	− 11.07		
(2)		− 9.90	− 9.98		
(3)		− 8.50	− 6.86		
(4)		− 7.10	− 7.88		
1797 (1)		− 1.52	− 3.34		
(2)		0.68	4.00		
(3)		− 5.22	− 4.27		
(4)		− 4.68	− 6.90		
1798 (1)		− 5.01	− 6.73		
(2)		− 5.08	− 5.39		
(3)		− 6.83	− 6.83		
(4)		− 8.70	− 8.70		
1799 (1)		− 5.89	− 9.30		
(2)		− 11.11	− 7.86		
(3)		− 9.69	− 9.54		
(4)		− 3.14	− 2.29		

Table 6.8 (*cont.*)

Year-quarter	Derived from actual transactions		Based on published quotations		
	Philadelphia Trotter	Baltimore White	Boston Smith-Cole[b] Martin[c]	New York *Bankers' Magazine*	Philadelphia Moore[d] Woodbury[e]
1800 (1)		3.81	2.02		
(2)		7.43	7.12		
(3)		7.44	5.96		
(4)		9.04	7.56		
1801 (1)		6.38	4.81		
(2)		7.87	8.19		
(3)		8.07	6.80		
(4)		9.52	7.23		
1802 (1)		9.13	7.53		
(2)		7.08	5.48		
(3)		4.97	2.25		
(4)		4.48	3.28		
1803 (1)	2.53	3.81	4.52		
(2)		5.61	6.56		
(3)	− 25.64	4.43	2.77		
(4)		6.73	6.97		
1804 (1)	− 21.21	8.90	8.66		
(2)	− 22.47	6.44	5.02		
(3)	− 29.94	1.59	− 0.23		
(4)	− 30.58	− 0.07	0.41		
1805 (1)	− 31.28	− 1.13	− 0.67		
(2)	− 36.79	− 5.58	− 5.11		
(3)	− 18.36	− 4.83	− 6.07		
(4)	− 28.21	1.56	1.09		
1806 (1)	− 30.79	3.34	2.55		
(2)	− 27.18	3.75	5.00		
(3)	− 28.58	2.88	1.78		
(4)	− 28.23	3.62	2.28		
1807 (1)	− 29.39	3.83	4.23		
(2)	− 29.77	2.25	1.46		
(3)	− 30.55	3.63	− 0.17		
(4)	− 28.01	3.47	2.13		
1808 (1)	− 26.34	− 2.73	0.53		
(2)	− 26.17	0.54	1.98		
(3)		1.87	2.33		
(4)	− 19.80	5.44	4.91		
1809 (1)		6.42	6.03		

Table 6.8 (*cont.*)

Year-quarter	Derived from actual transactions		Based on published quotations		
	Philadelphia Trotter	Baltimore White	Boston Smith-Cole[b] Martin[c]	New York *Bankers' Magazine*	Philadelphia Moore[d] Woodbury[e]
1809 (2)	− 29.64	0.31	1.08		
(3)	− 25.38	3.48	3.61		
(4)	− 25.73	3.35	1.59		
1810 (1)	− 10.93	0.33	0.10		
(2)	7.13	1.09	1.86		
(3)	10.38	3.77	1.41		
(4)	− 3.20	2.33	− 0.30		
1811 (1)		0.02	− 0.06		
(2)	− 3.67	− 1.42	− 0.24		
(3)	− 7.44	− 4.26	− 7.01		
(4)	− 4.07	− 3.40	− 3.40		
1812 (1)	− 4.31	− 6.38	− 5.97		
(2)		− 7.51	− 7.51		
(3)		− 5.55	− 8.05		
(4)	− 1.75	− 1.11	0.06		
1813 (1)		− 1.30	− 1.41		
(2)	4.15	1.58	1.54		
(3)		3.87	5.45		
(4)	7.47	6.78	6.78		
1814 (1)		17.29	18.75		
(2)		19.90	14.14		
(3)		− 6.16	− 3.87		
(4)		− 2.78	− 5.19		
1815 (1)		1.89	− 2.74		
(2)		13.48	13.98		
(3)	1.47	− 0.23	0.01		2.17
(4)	− 5.24	2.02	− 0.87		− 1.30
1816 (1)		2.12	1.81		− 1.35
(2)	− 5.54	− 4.77	− 3.97		− 3.75
(3)	− 3.55	− 0.60	− 4.07		− 1.38
(4)	− 6.66	− 1.52	− 2.27		− 4.70
1817 (1)	− 3.52	0.07	− 2.69		− 3.92
(2)	2.60	3.42	2.82		2.94
(3)	3.12	3.07	2.66		2.50
(4)	5.39	5.65	4.60		4.68
1818 (1)	5.04	6.10	4.99		4.91
(2)	5.66	5.90	4.91		5.26

Table 6.8 (*cont.*)

Year-quarter	Derived from actual transactions		Based on published quotations		
	Philadelphia Trotter	Baltimore White	Boston Smith-Cole[b] Martin[c]	New York *Bankers' Magazine*	Philadelphia Moore[d] Woodbury[e]
1818 (3)	4.56	5.07	4.43		5.55
(4)	1.44	3.70	3.06		3.86
1819 (1)	6.60	6.32	5.60		5.36
(2)	0.98	2.61	1.41		2.45
(3)		− 1.97	− 1.61		− 2.29
(4)	− 0.63	− 0.67	− 1.43		− 0.67
1820 (1)	− 5.47	− 4.73	− 4.69		− 4.57
(2)	− 7.39	− 7.35	− 7.66		− 7.51
(3)		− 5.48	− 7.08		− 6.26
(4)	− 5.48	− 4.88	− 5.11		− 5.03
1821 (1)	− 4.30	− 5.55	− 5.36		− 5.24
(2)	− 0.79	− 1.02	− 1.71		− 0.64
(3)	− 0.02	0.18	− 0.20		0.48
(4)	1.13	1.55	1.59		1.25
1822 (1)	4.23	4.68	3.95	4.99	4.53
(2)	2.66	2.96	2.50	2.96	2.19
(3)	1.38	2.19	2.11	2.03	2.49
(4)		4.19	3.77	4.27	4.04
1823 (1)	− 3.66	2.24	1.85	2.85	1.93
(2)	− 4.08	− 2.53	− 2.80	− 3.76	− 2.99
(3)	− 1.54	− 0.99	− 1.57	− 1.76	− 1.15
(4)	− 0.63	− 0.53	− 0.92	− 0.84	− 0.84
1824 (1)	0.19	0.50	0.42	− 0.12	− 0.12
(2)	0.93	1.12	1.08	1.19	1.19
(3)	0.98	1.12	1.08	0.89	1.12
(4)	0.42	1.58	2.08	1.50	1.97
1825 (1)	− 2.17	2.36	2.32	2.28	2.67
(2)	− 1.48	0.05	1.06	0.36	− 0.41
(3)	1.45	− 0.51	− 0.98	− 0.82	− 0.90
(4)	1.67	2.35	2.58	2.51	2.19
1826 (1)	− 0.01	0.99	1.19	0.99	0.84
(2)	1.84	1.89	0.88	1.51	1.51
(3)	2.87	3.33	2.51	2.78	3.09
(4)	3.05	4.07	3.26	4.23	4.23
1827 (1)	2.71	3.21	2.98	2.98	3.83
(2)	2.45	2.84	2.73	2.84	2.77
(3)	2.25	2.78	2.67	2.63	2.74

Table 6.8 (*cont.*)

Year-quarter	Derived from actual transactions		Based on published quotations		
	Philadelphia Trotter	Baltimore White	Boston Smith-Cole[b] Martin[c]	New York *Bankers' Magazine*	Philadelphia Moore[d] Woodbury[e]
1827 (4)	3.25	3.25	3.52	3.40	3.40
1828 (1)	2.58	2.68	3.10	2.91	2.79
(2)	2.74	2.83	2.56	2.83	2.95
(3)	2.30	2.52	2.56	2.14	2.33
(4)	1.76	2.40	2.40	2.71	2.71
1829 (1)	0.70	1.09	1.02	0.55	1.25
(2)	0.88	1.09	1.36	1.25	1.52
(3)	1.17	1.47	0.46	1.39	1.24
(4)	1.25		1.32	1.83	1.75
1830 (1)	− 0.13		0.55	0.63	0.63
(2)	− 1.30		− 0.31	− 0.74	− 0.39
(3)	− 1.61		− 1.72	− 1.83	− 1.48
(4)	− 1.42		− 1.24	− 1.40	− 1.36
1831 (1)	− 0.79		− 0.65	− 0.85	− 0.88
(2)	1.49		1.04	0.81	0.96
(3)	2.63		2.65	2.65	2.33
(4)	2.96		3.09	3.02	2.74
1832 (1)	2.61		2.72	2.25	2.37
(2)	2.27		2.78	2.35	2.66
(3)	0.45		0.68	0.68	0.87
(4)	0.50		0.87	0.63	0.94
1833 (1)	− 1.34		− 0.60	− 0.83	− 0.60
(2)	− 0.66		− 0.42	− 0.53	− 0.42
(3)	− 1.25		− 0.26	− 0.41	− 0.34
(4)	− 3.90		− 2.22	− 1.76	− 1.83
1834 (1)	− 15.52		− 5.90	− 6.76	− 6.10
(2)	− 13.90		− 4.53	− 4.88	− 4.22
(3)			− 3.31	− 3.54	− 3.46
(4)	− 10.47		− 1.99	− 2.20	− 1.55

Notes:
[a] A negative sign denotes a sterling discount.
[b] 1795 (4) to 1824 (4).
[c] 1825 (1) to 1834 (4).
[d] 1815 (3) to 1825 (2).
[e] 1825 (3) to 1834 (4).
Source: See text.

Table 6.9 *Exchange-rate series, demand-bill basis, annual, 1800–13*
(percent sterling premium over parity)[a]

	Baltimore			Philadelphia		
Year	White[b]	Woodbury[c]	White minus Woodbury	Trotter[b]	Moore[c]	Trotter minus Moore
1800	6.93	6.38	0.54			
1801	7.96	8.59	− 0.63			
1802	6.41	6.97	− 0.56			
1803	5.15	4.99	0.16	− 11.55[d]	5.23	− 16.78
1804	4.21	3.82	0.40	− 26.05	− 4.49	− 21.56
1805	− 2.49	− 2.57	0.08			
1806	3.40	2.92	0.47			
1807	3.29	2.98	0.32			
1808	1.28	1.43	− 0.15			
1809	3.48	4.70	− 1.22			
1810	1.88	1.88	0			
1811				− 5.06[e]	5.59	− 10.65
1812				− 3.03[d]	− 5.29	2.26
1813				5.81[d]	2.58	3.23

Notes:
[a] A negative sign denotes a sterling discount.
[b] Derived from actual transactions.
[c] Based on published quotations.
[d] Average of two quarters.
[e] Average of three quarters.
Source: See text.

What of the large divergence between the series in the early years of their overlap? Can it be decided which series is unrepresentative? One possible test is based on the fact that both series are corrected for paper standards, wherefore the premiums and discounts that they exhibit are to be interpreted as deviations from mint parity under functioning specie standards in England and the United States. Unusual large absolute deviations from parity under these circumstances might arouse suspicion. For the common quarters of observation (see table 6.8), there are 25 instances of Trotter, and none of White, deviating from parity by more than 10 percent – and the Trotter figure reaches over 36 percent.

These statistics strongly favor White over Trotter, but the criterion is flawed. In the early nineteenth century the American foreign-exchange

Table 6.10 *Exchange-rate series, demand-bill basis, quarterly, 1835–69*
(percent sterling premium over parity)[a]

	First quarter		Second quarter		Third quarter		Fourth quarter	
Year	Trotter	Martin	Trotter	Martin	Trotter	Martin	Trotter	Martin
1835	− 2.19	− 1.79	0.50	− 0.13	0.12	0.16	− 0.15	0.47
1836	− 0.31	0.07	− 1.78	− 1.79	− 1.32	− 1.39	− 0.97	− 0.17
1837	− 0.42	− 0.07	− 0.09	− 2.27	− 0.65	1.20	− 0.36	− 0.12
1838	− 4.52	− 3.38	− 1.66	− 3.07	− 0.03	− 0.89	0.30	0.58
1839	0.05	0.02	− 0.25	0.22	1.18	0.53	− 1.79	0.73
1840	− 2.15	− 0.58	− 1.05	− 1.06	− 1.51	− 1.75	− 1.33	− 0.12
1841	− 2.09	− 0.58	− 0.18	− 1.20	0.10	− 0.22	1.76	0.80
1842	− 0.56	− 0.49	− 1.99	− 1.70	− 2.51	− 1.99	− 2.88	− 2.13
1843	− 3.60	− 3.40	− 1.34	− 2.02	− 0.53	− 0.27	− 1.00	− 0.62
1844	− 0.66	− 0.65	− 0.47	− 0.91	0.24	0.01	0.31	0.66
1845	0.28	0.58	0.41	0.38	0.40	0.47	− 0.70	0.01
1846	− 0.16	− 0.39	− 0.48	0.67	− 1.26	− 0.25	− 2.26	− 1.68
1847	− 2.87	− 2.83	− 2.25	− 2.30	− 2.11	− 1.84	1.22	1.32
1848	0.86	1.09	0.79	1.09	0.06	0.35	− 1.55	− 0.38
1849	− 1.44	− 0.67	− 2.18	− 1.06	− 0.30	0.06	− 0.40	0.45
1850	− 0.92	− 0.62	0.23	0.11	0.14	1.04	0.85	0.95
1851	0.77	0.82	1.13	1.16	0.86	1.10	1.04	1.13
1852	0.62	0.75	0.65	0.27	1.02	0.85	0.59	0.59
1853	0.35	0.43	0.49	0.29	0.12	0.41	0.78	0.61
1854	− 0.07	0.16	0.53	0.24	0.79	0.56	0.07	0.64
1855	− 0.06	− 0.20	0.98	0.79	0.72	0.57	− 0.03	0.20
1856	0.59	0.21	1.13	0.99	0.89	0.82	0.87	0.71
1857	0.05	− 0.12	0.83	0.49	0.36	0.51	0.10	− 3.13
1858	− 1.88	0.17	0.21	0.12	0.56	0.35	0.36	0.39
1859	0.28	0.21	0.85	0.69	0.91	0.80	0.65	0.59
1860	− 0.27	− 0.07	0.31	0.34	0.78	0.80	− 2.24	− 1.50
1861	− 2.94	− 3.06	− 3.13	− 2.41	− 0.83	− 1.78	− 0.75	− 1.19
1862	0.64	0.95	1.77	1.04	0.68	1.21	0.56	1.24
1863	2.96	3.59	− 2.10	1.94	− 0.14	3.08	0	1.96
1864	0.43	2.00	1.47	1.91	1.64	− 6.11	3.08	− 1.06
1865	0.74	− 0.12	1.41	0.10	0.04	0.10	0.72	0.36
1866	− 0.09	− 0.33	1.21	0.21	0.05	− 0.80	0.37	− 0.22
1867	− 0.03	− 0.32	0.58	0.47	0.56	0.40	0.92	0
1868	0.48	0.41	0.80	0.71	0.54	0.25	0.58	0.14
1869	− 0.22	− 0.04	0.32	0.17	0.62	− 0.11	− 0.04	− 0.40

Note:
[a] A negative sign denotes a sterling discount.
Source: See text.

Table 6.11 *Exchange-rate series, New York, quarterly, 1870–1966 (percent sterling premium over parity)[a]*

Year	First quarter	Second quarter	Third quarter	Fourth quarter
1870	− 0.58	0.01	0.53	− 0.14
1871	0.36	0.73	− 0.02	− 0.18
1872	− 0.12	− 0.25	− 0.61	− 1.09
1873	0.05	0.48	− 0.07	0.29
1874	− 0.18	0.36	0.15	0.18
1875	− 0.22	0.38	− 0.04	− 0.46
1876	0.21	0.28	− 0.01	− 0.84
1877	− 0.58	0.25	− 0.33	− 0.93
1878	− 0.57	− 0.07	− 0.28	− 0.36
1879	0.15	0.21	− 0.58	− 0.84
1880	− 0.31	0.13	− 0.66	− 0.96
1881	− 0.79	− 0.90	− 0.64	− 0.71
1882	0.22	0.39	. 0.19	− 0.52
1883	− 0.53	− 0.09	− 0.22	− 0.59
1884	0.14	0.03	− 0.57	− 0.64
1885	− 0.24	0.03	− 0.33	− 0.32
1886	0.34	0.31	− 0.38	− 0.68
1887	− 0.04	− 0.10	− 0.63	− 0.43
1888	− 0.12	0.21	0.08	0.15
1889	0.24	0.31	0.05	− 0.41
1890	− 0.18	− 0.01	0	− 0.31
1891	0.12	0.31	− 0.27	− 0.61
1892	0.01	0.26	0.24	0.03
1893	0.20	0.23	− 0.29	− 0.36
1894	0.15	0.39	0.11	0.20
1895	0.42	0.41	0.58	0.38
1896	0.32	0.38	− 0.07	− 0.25
1897	0.06	0.12	− 0.12	− 0.32
1898	− 0.45	− 0.36	− 0.35	− 0.39
1899	− 0.27	0.12	− 0.06	− 0.02
1900	0.04	0.16	0.12	− 0.43
1901	0.18	0.29	0.01	0.03
1902	0.15	0.20	0.08	0.01
1903	0.08	0.19	− 0.09	− 0.46
1904	− 0.12	0.11	0.13	− 0.04
1905	0.10	0.01	− 0.09	− 0.13
1906	− 0.08	− 0.33	− 0.49	− 0.40
1907	− 0.44	− 0.06	− 0.03	− 0.18
1908	− 0.08	0.07	− 0.03	− 0.04
1909	0.18	0.22	0.02	0.10

Table 6.11 (*cont.*)

Year	First quarter	Second quarter	Third quarter	Fourth quarter
1910	0.01	0.09	− 0.15	− 0.17
1911	− 0.12	− 0.09	− 0.11	− 0.03
1912	0.10	0.08	0.03	− 0.28
1913	0.13	− 0.01	− 0.08	− 0.27
1914	− 0.12	0.24		
1919				− 0.04
1920	0.01	− 0.09	− 0.16	− 0.60
1921	− 0.38	− 0.29	− 0.40	− 0.33
1922	0.11	0.06	− 0.31	− 0.19
1923	0.14	− 0.30	− 0.33	− 0.29
1924	− 0.17	− 0.17	− 0.01	0.56
1925	0.41	− 0.06	− 0.26	− 0.43
1926	− 0.13	− 0.07	− 0.17	− 0.34
1927	− 0.30	− 0.21	− 0.15	0.18
1928	0.20	0.30	− 0.23	− 0.34
1929	− 0.31	− 0.33	− 0.36	0.19
1930	− 0.05	− 0.13	− 0.02	− 0.20
1931	− 0.20	− 0.08		
1950	0.02	0.02	0.02	0.01
1951	0.01	0.02	− 0.03	− 0.06
1952	− 0.49	− 0.08	− 0.49	− 0.01
1953	0.56	0.53	0.39	0.32
1954	0.46	0.65	0.37	− 0.25
1955	− 0.48	− 0.21	− 0.51	− 0.05
1956	0.21	0.21	− 0.48	− 0.57
1957	− 0.16	− 0.36	− 0.53	0.10
1958	0.53	0.52	0.15	0.19
1959	0.34	0.52	0.29	0.09
1960	0.10	0.21	0.37	0.38
1961	0.04	− 0.22	0.03	0.47
1962	0.49	0.41	0.13	0.08
1963	0.10	0	− 0.02	− 0.10
1964	− 0.08	− 0.09	− 0.48	− 0.49
1965	− 0.25	− 0.17	− 0.26	0.10
1966	0.02	− 0.29	− 0.40	− 0.33

Note:
[a] A negative sign denotes a sterling discount.
Source: 1870–95: demand bills, revised Perkins data, posted rates converted to actual rates. *1896–1914:* demand bills, Andrew and *Financial Review* data, actual rates. *1919–31, 1950–66:* cable transfers, Board of Governors of the Federal Reserve System data, actual rates. See text for details.

market was not as integrated as it later became (see chapters 7, 10, and 11). It is indeed possible that the Trotter extreme figures, and not the moderate White data, are correct.[40]

Considering the criteria used to assess the later-Trotter versus Martin, (a)–(c) are neutral. The underlying frequency of an observation is unknown for White, dependent on the number of bills purchased for Trotter; both series are based on actual transactions; and while Philadelphia was the leading foreign-exchange center prior to the ascendancy of New York, Baltimore may very well have displaced Philadelphia temporarily for some years around the turn of the nineteenth century (see section 1). The criterion left is (d). Trotter emanates from the records of a purchaser of bills, whereas White comes from reports of dealers in exchange. This dichotomy may give rise to either a "Trotter peculiarity" or a "dealer peculiarity," rendering the particular series non-representative. To determine which specific characteristic is applicable, tests need to be performed to examine the extent of representativeness of each series, both nationally and within its own city of quotation.

An exchange-rate R series for the pre-1835 period is available for two other port cities: Boston (Smith and Cole for 1795–1824, Martin for 1825–34) and New York (*Bankers' Magazine*, for 1822–34). The differences Trotter *minus* Boston, Trotter *minus* New York, White *minus* Boston, and White *minus* New York are shown in table 6.12. There are unusually large divergences of Trotter against Boston in the 1803–10 period, exceeding 25 percent of parity in 21 quarters, and substantial divergences in 1834, the latter repeated against New York. There are also noticeable deviations (above four percent of parity) of Trotter against Boston in four isolated quarters in 1815, 1816, 1823, and 1825, repeated against New York when data exist (1823 and 1825).

In contrast, there are only two quarters of noticeable divergence between White and Boston (in 1814 and 1815, when data for Trotter are lacking). Furthermore, White tracks New York excellently, with only one deviation exceeding 1 percent of parity.

Therefore the Trotter series, and not White, is suspect for the years 1803–10. Trotter is also questionable for 1834 and for scattered quarters in other years. Does this non-representativeness reflect a "Philadelphia peculiarity" or a "Trotter peculiarity"; that is, is criterion (c) or (d) involved? The answer comes from comparing Trotter with two other Philadelphia R series, a quarterly series (Moore for 1815–25, Woodbury for 1825–34) and an annual series (Moore, comparable with Trotter 1803–4 and 1811–13). For completeness, the White series is compared with a Baltimore R series, Woodbury (annual 1800–10). Quarterly comparisons are in table 6.12, annual in table 6.9.

Table 6.12 *Comparisons of exchange-rate series, quarterly, 1795–1834 (percent sterling premium over parity)*

Year-quarter	Trotter minus White	Trotter minus Boston	Trotter minus New York	Trotter minus Phila.	White minus Boston	White minus New York	White minus Phila.
1795 (4)					0.08		
1796 (1)					− 3.51		
(2)					0.08		
(3)					− 1.64		
(4)					0.78		
1797 (1)					1.82		
(2)					− 3.32		
(3)					− 0.95		
(4)					2.22		
1798 (1)					1.72		
(2)					0.31		
(3)					0		
(4)					0		
1799 (1)					3.41		
(2)					− 3.25		
(3)					− 0.15		
(4)					− 0.85		
1800 (1)					1.79		
(2)					0.31		
(3)					1.48		
(4)					1.48		
1801 (1)					1.58		
(2)					− 0.32		
(3)					1.26		
(4)					2.29		
1802 (1)					1.60		
(2)					1.60		
(3)					2.72		
(4)					1.20		
1803 (1)	− 1.28	− 1.99			− 0.71		
(2)					− 0.95		
(3)	− 30.07	− 28.41			1.66		
(4)					− 0.24		
1804 (1)	− 30.11	− 29.87			0.24		
(2)	− 28.91	− 27.49			1.42		
(3)	− 31.53	− 29.71			1.82		
(4)	− 30.51	− 30.99			− 0.47		
1805 (1)	− 30.15	− 30.62			− 0.46		
(2)	− 31.21	− 31.68			− 0.46		

Table 6.12 (*cont.*)

Year-quarter	Trotter minus White	Trotter minus Boston	Trotter minus New York	Trotter minus Phila.	White minus Boston	White minus New York	White minus Phila.
1805 (3)	− 13.53	− 12.29			1.24		
(4)	− 29.77	− 29.31			0.46		
1806 (1)	− 34.13	− 33.35			0.79		
(2)	− 30.92	− 32.18			− 1.26		
(3)	− 31.46	− 30.36			1.10		
(4)	− 31.85	− 30.52			1.34		
1807 (1)	− 33.23	− 33.62			− 0.40		
(2)	− 32.01	− 31.22			0.79		
(3)	− 34.17	− 30.38			3.79		
(4)	− 31.48	− 30.13			1.34		
1808 (1)	− 23.61	− 26.87			− 3.26		
(2)	− 26.71	− 28.15			− 1.44		
(3)					− 0.46		
(4)	− 25.25	− 24.71			0.53		
1809 (1)					0.38		
(2)	− 29.95	− 30.72			− 0.76		
(3)	− 29.22	− 28.99			0.23		
(4)	− 29.07	− 27.31			1.76		
1810 (1)	− 11.26	− 11.03			0.23		
(2)	6.05	5.27			− 0.77		
(3)	6.61	8.97			2.36		
(4)	− 5.52	− 2.89			2.63		
1811 (1)					0.08		
(2)	− 2.25	− 3.43			− 1.18		
(3)	− 3.17	− 0.42			2.75		
(4)	− 0.66	− 0.66			0		
1812 (1)	2.07	1.66			− 0.42		
(2)					0		
(3)					2.50		
(4)	− 0.64	− 1.81			− 1.17		
1813 (1)					0.11		
(2)	2.57	2.61			0.04		
(3)					− 1.58		
(4)	0.69	0.69			0		
1814 (1)					− 1.46		
(2)					5.76		
(3)					− 2.29		
(4)					2.41		
1815 (1)					4.63		
(2)					− 0.50		
(3)	1.70	1.46		− 0.70	− 0.24		− 2.40

Table 6.12 (*cont.*)

Year-quarter	Trotter minus White	Trotter minus Boston	Trotter minus New York	Trotter minus Phila.	White minus Boston	White minus New York	White minus Phila.
1815 (4)	− 7.26	− 4.37		− 3.94	2.89		3.32
1816 (1)					0.31		3.47
(2)	− 0.76	− 1.57		− 1.79	− 0.80		− 1.03
(3)	− 2.95	0.53		− 2.17	3.47		0.77
(4)	− 5.14	− 4.39		− 1.95	0.75		3.19
1817 (1)	− 3.59	− 0.82		0.40	2.77		3.99
(2)	− 0.82	− 0.21		− 0.33	0.61		0.48
(3)	0.05	0.46		0.62	0.40		0.57
(4)	− 0.25	0.80		0.71	1.05		0.97
1818 (1)	− 1.06	0.05		0.13	1.11		1.19
(2)	− 0.24	0.75		0.40	0.99		0.64
(3)	− 0.51	0.12		− 0.99	0.64		− 0.48
(4)	− 2.26	− 1.63		− 2.42	0.64		− 0.16
1819 (1)	0.28	0.99		1.23	0.72		0.95
(2)	− 1.63	− 0.44		− 1.47	1.19		0.16
(3)					− 0.36		0.32
(4)	0.04	0.79		0.04	0.76		0
1820 (1)	− 0.74	− 0.78		− 0.90	− 0.04		− 0.16
(2)	− 0.04	0.27		0.12	0.31		0.16
(3)					1.60		0.78
(4)	− 0.61	− 0.37		− 0.45	0.23		0.16
1821 (1)	1.25	1.06		0.94	− 0.19		− 0.31
(2)	0.23	0.92		− 0.15	0.69		− 0.38
(3)	− 0.19	0.19		− 0.50	0.38		− 0.31
(4)	− 0.42	− 0.46		− 0.12	− 0.04		0.31
1822 (1)	− 0.45	0.28	− 0.76	− 0.30	0.73	− 0.31	0.15
(2)	− 0.30	0.17	− 0.30	0.47	0.46	0	0.77
(3)	− 0.81	− 0.73	− 0.66	− 1.12	0.08	0.15	− 0.31
(4)					0.42	− 0.08	0.15
1823 (1)	− 5.89	− 5.51	− 6.51	− 5.58	0.38	− 0.61	0.31
(2)	− 1.55	− 1.28	− 0.32	− 1.09	0.27	1.23	0.46
(3)	− 0.54	0.03	0.23	− 0.39	0.58	0.77	0.15
(4)	− 0.10	0.29	0.21	0.21	0.38	0.31	0.31
1824 (1)	− 0.31	− 0.23	0.31	0.31	0.08	0.62	0.62
(2)	− 0.18	− 0.15	− 0.26	− 0.26	0.04	− 0.08	− 0.08
(3)	− 0.14	− 0.10	0.09	− 0.14	0.04	0.23	0
(4)	− 1.16	− 1.66	− 1.08	− 1.54	− 0.50	0.08	− 0.39
1825 (1)	− 4.53	− 4.49	− 4.45	− 4.84	0.04	0.08	− 0.31
(2)	− 1.54	− 2.55	− 1.85	− 1.07	− 1.01	− 0.31	0.47
(3)	1.96	2.43	2.27	2.35	0.47	0.31	0.39
(4)	− 0.68	− 0.92	− 0.84	− 0.53	− 0.23	− 0.16	0.16

Table 6.12 (*cont.*)

Year-quarter	Trotter minus White	Trotter minus Boston	Trotter minus New York	Trotter minus Phila.	White minus Boston	White minus New York	White minus Phila.
1826 (1)	− 1.00	− 1.20	− 1.00	− 0.85	− 0.19	0	0.16
(2)	− 0.05	0.96	0.34	0.34	1.01	0.39	0.39
(3)	− 0.46	0.36	0.09	− 0.22	0.81	0.54	0.23
(4)	− 1.02	− 0.20	− 1.17	− 1.17	0.81	− 0.16	− 0.16
1827 (1)	− 0.50	− 0.27	− 0.27	− 1.12	0.23	0.23	− 0.62
(2)	− 0.39	− 0.27	− 0.39	− 0.31	0.12	0	0.08
(3)	− 0.53	− 0.41	− 0.38	− 0.49	0.12	0.16	0.04
(4)	0	− 0.27	− 0.15	− 0.15	− 0.27	− 0.16	− 0.16
1828 (1)	− 0.10	− 0.52	− 0.33	− 0.21	− 0.43	− 0.23	− 0.12
(2)	− 0.09	0.18	− 0.09	− 0.20	0.27	0	− 0.12
(3)	− 0.22	− 0.26	0.16	− 0.03	− 0.04	0.39	0.19
(4)	− 0.64	− 0.64	− 0.94	− 0.94	0	− 0.31	− 0.31
1829 (1)	− 0.39	− 0.32	0.15	− 0.55	0.08	0.54	− 0.15
(2)	− 0.21	− 0.48	− 0.36	− 0.64	− 0.27	− 0.15	− 0.43
(3)	− 0.30	0.70	− 0.23	− 0.07	1.01	0.08	0.23
(4)		− 0.08	− 0.58	− 0.50			
1830 (1)		− 0.68	− 0.76	− 0.76			
(2)		− 0.99	− 0.56	− 0.91			
(3)		0.11	0.22	− 0.13			
(4)		− 0.18	− 0.03	− 0.07			
1831 (1)		− 0.14	0.06	0.10			
(2)		0.45	0.68	0.53			
(3)		− 0.02	− 0.02	0.29			
(4)		− 0.14	0.06	0.21			
1832 (1)		− 0.11	0.35	0.24			
(2)		− 0.50	− 0.08	− 0.39			
(3)		− 0.23	− 0.23	− 0.42			
(4)		− 0.36	− 0.13	− 0.44			
1833 (1)		− 0.74	− 0.51	− 0.74			
(2)		− 0.24	− 0.13	− 0.24			
(3)		− 0.99	− 0.84	− 0.91			
(4)		− 1.68	− 2.14	− 2.07			
1834 (1)		− 9.62	− 8.77	− 9.43			
(2)		− 9.37	− 9.02	− 9.68			
(3)							
(4)		− 8.47	− 8.26	− 8.91			

Source: Table 6.8.

There are large discrepancies between Trotter and the annual Philadelphia series in 1803–4 and 1811. In 1834 there are noticeable differences between Trotter and the quarterly Philadelphia series. Furthermore, noticeable deviations of Trotter from quarterly Philadelphia occur in two of the four previously identified quarters in 1815–25. These results are consistent with the previous comparisons. The conclusion is unmistakable. The Trotter series is unrepresentative even for Philadelphia, let alone the other port cities, in 1803–4, 1811, possibly 1805–10, and for 1834 and some isolated quarters over 1815–25. In contrast, White tracks the Baltimore series very well. Further, the correspondence of White with quarterly Philadelphia is superior to that of Trotter.

In short, the Trotter series is deficient in representing exchange rates of the port cities, *including Philadelphia*, for much of the pre-1835 period. Trotter fails, and White passes, tests of representativeness not because of a "Philadelphia peculiarity" but rather because of a "Trotter peculiarity." The difference between Trotter and the other series in the periods of substantial deviation is always negative, meaning that the Trotter firm was somehow able to purchase bills of exchange at prices below – often far below – the market rate for these periods. The most logical explanation of this phenomenon is that Trotter purchased bills of inferior quality. Qualitative evidence may support this explanation for the earlier years, but not for 1834 (see note 22). Furthermore, it appears poor business practice consistently to risk non-payment of foreign debt in this manner.

An alternative explanation is that the foreign-exchange market was far from integrated in the pre-1835 period; but then why would market imperfections reveal themselves so markedly and exclusively in the Trotter data? One is left with the uneasy conclusion that an unidentified peculiarity of the exchange transactions of the firm, or of its records, is the explanation.

In any event, the White series is selected over Trotter for the pre-1835 period. Unfortunately, White ends in 1829 (third quarter). Fortunately, Trotter does appear to represent Boston, New York, and Philadelphia well from 1829 (fourth quarter) to 1833 (third quarter). As the only actual-transactions series available, it is chosen for that period.

What remains is 1833 (fourth quarter) to 1834 (fourth quarter), for which Trotter is unrepresentative (see table 6.12) and White unavailable. For the period 1822 (first quarter) to 1829 (third quarter), the mean absolute-value deviation of the Boston, New York, and quarterly Philadelphia series, respectively, from White is 0.37, 0.28, and 0.27 percent of parity. It is reasonable to select the quarterly Philadelphia (Woodbury) series for these five remaining quarters, as best corresponding to the most-reliable series

Table 6.13 *Exchange rate: component series*

Period	Series	City	Exchange-market-instrument	Type of price	Table listing series
1791 (1)–1829 (3)	White	Baltimore	demand bill	actual	6.8
1829 (4)–1833 (3)	Trotter	Philadelphia	"	"	"
1833 (4)–1834 (4)	Woodbury	"	"	quoted	"
1835 (1)–1869 (4)	Trotter	"	"	actual	6.10
1870 (1)–1895 (4)	revised Perkins	New York	"	"	6.11
1896 (1)–1914 (2)	Andrew, *Financial Rev.*	"	"	"	"
1919 (4)–1931 (2)	Board of Governors	"	cable transfer	"	"
1950 (1)–1966 (4)	"	"	"	"	"

(White). The selection has the additional advantage of a continuous Philadelphia presence from the end of Baltimore (1829, fourth quarter) to the beginning of New York (1870).

So the long-run exchange-rate series runs from 1791 to 1931 (second quarter) and also from 1950 to 1966. Properties of the component series are summarized in table 6.13. The series is in *R* form, meaning that it measures the percentage deviation of the exchange rate from the true parity – the percent sterling premium over parity – under the applicable specie standard of each country.

3.10   Homogeneity over time

Finally, overlaps between conjoining component series should be examined to ascertain overall homogeneity of the complete series. Table 6.14 shows one-year overlaps for the four instances when there was a switch in component series. The mean absolute-value difference between the (APP) applicable, current, preferred series and (EXT) extended, former or later series is 0.39 percent of parity in 1828–9 and falls precipitously to 0.04 percent in 1896. The component series are close to each other, but "how close is close?" An excellent basis for comparison is the buying versus selling price differential for bills of exchange, broker's commission, which was 0.5 percent between 1829 and 1870 (see section 3.6). The average overlaps are uniformly below 0.5 percent of parity, and only two of the sixteen quarters of overlap exceed this figure. One can conclude with confidence that the overall series passes the test of homogeneity over time.

Table 6.14 *Components of exchange-rate series, one-year overlaps (percent sterling premium over parity)*

Year-quarter	Applicable Series[a] (APP)	Extended Series[b] (EXT)	Absolute value of difference |APP–EXT|	
1828 (4)	2.40	1.76	0.64	
1829 (1)	1.09	0.70	0.39	
(2)	1.09	0.88	0.21	
(3)	1.47	1.17	0.30	
Mean				0.39
1835 (1)	− 2.19	− 1.71	0.47	
(2)	0.50	− 0.24	0.74	
(3)	0.12	0.20	0.08	
(4)	− 0.15	0.01	0.16	
Mean				0.36
1870 (1)	− 0.58	− 0.44	0.13	
(2)	0.01	− 0.02	0.03	
(3)	0.53	0.82	0.29	
(4)	− 0.14	0.01	0.15	
Mean				0.15
1896 (1)	0.32	0.33	0.01	
(2)	0.38	0.37	0.01	
(3)	− 0.07	0.05	0.12	
(4)	− 0.25	− 0.27	0.02	
Mean				0.04

Notes:
[a] 1828–9: White (Baltimore).
1835: Trotter (Philadelphia).
1870: Revised Perkins (New York).
1896: Andrew and *Financial Review* (New York).
[b] 1828–9: Trotter (Philadelphia).
1835: Woodbury (Philadelphia).
1870: Trotter (Philadelphia).
1896: Revised Perkins (New York).

Source: Tables 6.8, 6.10, 6.11. Also, see text.

7 Exchange-market integration

1   Geographic dispersion

Exchange-market integration has at least two dimensions: geographic and temporal. The geographic approach to integration is based on the decentralized nature of the early American foreign-exchange market. The exchange rate is compared by space and over time, with enhanced integration reflected in reduced dispersion of the rate in the various cities of quotation. Investigations of this nature, obvious though they may be, do not exist in the literature. The approach can be applied to the exchange-rate series developed in chapter 6 to derive an important conclusion.

The most fruitful comparison is between the Baltimore (White) and Boston series, for which a continuous overlap runs from 1795 to 1829. The mean of the absolute difference between the two series (from table 6.12), by period, is as follows: 1795–1800, 1.39 percent of parity; 1801–10, 1.21; 1811–20, 1.22; 1821–9, 0.36. The value for the 1820s is less than 30 percent of that in earlier decades. The implication is that there was a strong movement to exchange-market integration in the 1820s.

Further, in that decade the absolute level of integration was high, and uniformly so across all port cities. The mean absolute difference between both the White versus New York and the White versus Philadelphia exchange-rate series is 0.28 percent of parity. So, in the 1820s, the average difference between Baltimore, for which the data are for actual transactions, and the three other important port cities (Boston, New York, Philadelphia) in turn is well below 0.50 percent of parity, the buying–selling differential in the foreign-exchange market from the mid-1820s. Geographic integration was both strong and uniform even at that early date.

That conclusion is supported by qualitative information. Smith and Cole (1935, p. 26), in discussing the 1814–17 period, note "the ease with which foreign bills were sent from one American city to another." Internal correspondence of the exchange-dealing merchant-banking firm House of Brown in 1821 reports that, although New York was the "greatest market" for bills of exchange, "when exchange is stationary we have generally found Phila. and this place [Baltimore] full as good as New York" (quoted in Perkins, 1975, p. 27). While other comments about the pattern of exchange rates are made in the firm's records, "overshadowing all else in importance is the Browns' statement that exchange rates in the three key ports, Baltimore, Philadelphia, and New York, were normally about the same. . . . Indeed, the Browns' correspondence, taken in its entirety, demonstrates clearly that a regional market for sterling exchange was rapidly emerging in the Atlantic ports in the period from 1815 to 1825" (Perkins, 1975, pp. 28, 29).

The fact that "domestic exchange," that is, banknotes issued by banks in another city, were themselves subject to variation from par (face value) was an element preventing complete merging of exchange rates in the port cities, and makes the integration reached by the 1820s even more impressive.[1]

2   Seasonal variation

A purely temporal measure of exchange-market integration is based on exchange-rate seasonality. Integration is deemed to increase with a decrease in seasonal variation. Cole (1929b) assembles monthly exchange-rate data (60-day bills) from Martin for 1825–60 and the *Financial Review* and Andrew (1910) (3-day and sight bills) for 1865–1913. He plots month-to-month link relatives annually for May/April and August/July from 1825 and 1860, February/January and August/July for 1865 to 1913. Gold rates are taken for the greenback period.

Until 1850 exchange-rate movements were wide and erratic, and a seasonal index is not deemed derivable. The month-to-month link relatives stabilize in 1850–60 and do not reach steadiness again until the early 1880s. A period of changing seasonality follows until 1896. In 1897–1913 there is substantial stability again. So Cole plots seasonal indices (over the twelve months of the year) for 1850–60, 1880–6, and 1897–1913. There is a substantially equal spread of monthly high and low rates in the first two periods and a sharp reduction in the spread in the last period.

Myers (1931, p. 75) does not show her data, but notes a wide variation of the exchange rate in the antebellum period compared to afterwards. She plots the average exchange rate by month for three postbellum periods: 1879–88, 1889–1900, and 1901–13. Her data are identical to those of Cole. The range between high and low rate decreases over the three periods.

In sum, seasonality analysis suggests weak exchange-market integration prior to 1850, strong integration in the 1850s, not reached again until the early 1880s, conflicting evidence on whether integration increased or decreased from then to the late 1880s, followed by enhanced integration to 1900, reaching its highest level in 1901–13.

3   Intra-annual movement

A third approach to exchange-market integration centers on intra-annual movement of the exchange rate without reference to seasonal pattern. Smith and Cole (1935, pp. 24, 127) note the large month-to-month variability of the exchange rate in 1795–1820 and "a marked steadying of exchange rates" in 1848, persisting to about the Civil War. Cole (1929a, p. 406; 1929b, pp. 205, 213) describes contemporary commentary of erratic movement of the exchange rate in 1840, steadiness in 1845 compared to 1844, and increased stability in 1850. He observes that in the 1830s exchange rates moved over a wide range, about 4.5 percent during a year, falling to 0.76 percent in the early 1880s, steadily decreasing over 1897–1913, and ultimately reaching 0.30 percent just prior to World War I.

Myers (1931, pp. 341–2) plots the high and low sight exchange rate annually for 1879–1913. The difference during the last five years is "only a fraction" of that during the first five years.

This approach, in summary, indicates exchange-market integration that is low until 1845, much improved by the early 1880s, and gradually becoming stronger to World War I.

4   Decadal variation

Davis and Hughes (1960, pp. 58, 62–3) compute the range of their Trotter exchange-rate series by decade from the 1830s to the 1890s. From 18 percent of parity in the 1830s the range falls precipitously (excluding the 1860s) to 1 percent in the 1880s and 1890s. Davis and Hughes compute a second measure of variation, what they call the variance.[2] The finding is the same: a steady decrease in exchange-rate variability, interrupted only by the upheaval of the Civil War. From "fairly stable" in the 1850s, the exchange rate is "permanently stabilized" by the mid-1870s, so that the stability of exchange rates associated with the international gold standard emerged.

Exchange-market integration, then, is measured inversely by the variability of the exchange rate. The long-run exchange-rate series developed in chapter 6 is admirably suited for this analysis, because not only is it expressed as the percentage deviation from true mint parity but also it is corrected for paper standards (whence it has the interpretation of the percentage deviation from mint parity throughout). Neither property holds for the Davis–Hughes series.[3] Also, the long-run series runs from 1791 to 1931, continuing in 1950–66, whereas Davis-Hughes covers only 1835–95.

Figure 7.1 plots the exchange rate for the 1791–1931 time span. The Davis-Hughes result of reduced variability appears true for their time period and with their exception of the Civil War years. Prior to 1820

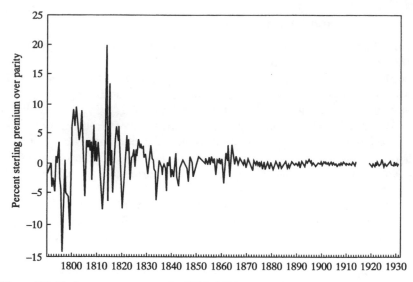

Figure 7.1 Exchange rate, quarterly, 1791–1931

exchange-rate variation is high indeed. Also, the stability of the exchange rate in the years just prior to World War I appears greater than that in 1925–31.

For a fuller data picture to extend the analysis, decadal periods may be used from 1791 to 1910, followed by 1911–14 (terminated by World War I), 1919–25 (floating pound, though adjusted), 1925–31 (interwar gold standard), and 1950–66 (comparison period of Bretton Woods system). Then five alternative measures of variation are utilized, and their values by period presented in table 7.1.

The mean of algebraic values (column two) measures the extent to which deviations from parity compensate for one another. The measure suggests that there were six broad periods of ever-increasing exchange-market integration: 1791 to 1810, 1811 to 1830, 1831 to 1850, 1851 to 1870, 1871 to 1890, and 1891–1914 plus 1950–66, with 1919–31 most comparable to 1871–90. One must be cautious in interpreting this statistic, because in permitting positive and negative deviations from parity to offset each other, the measure understates variation. Consider the maximum divergence from parity (column 6), deemed more meaningful than the range. By this criterion there is a tremendous increase in integration in the 1820s, as well as confirmation of the general trend to enhanced integration thereafter to World War I. From 1881 to 1966 (always allowing for gaps) exchange-market integration is continuously strong, with every quarterly observation

Table 7.1 *Exchange-rate statistics, by period, 1791–1966 (percent sterling premium over parity)*[a]

| Period | Mean | | Standard deviation | | |
	Algebraic values	Absolute values	About mean	About zero	Maximum observation
1791–1800	− 2.70	4.55	5.06	5.75	− 14.58
1801–10	3.46	4.17	3.48	4.93	9.52
1811–20	0.97	4.57	6.19	6.27	19.90
1821–30	1.23	2.01	2.06	2.40	− 5.55
1831–40	− 0.72	1.47	1.87	2.01	− 6.10
1841–50	− 0.73	1.11	1.26	1.46	− 3.60
1851–60	0.42	0.65	0.68	0.80	− 2.24
1861–70	0.32	0.87	1.20	1.25	− 3.13
1871–80	− 0.16	0.37	0.44	0.47	− 1.09
1881–90	− 0.19	0.33	0.36	0.41	− 0.90
1891–1900	0.02	0.25	0.30	0.51	− 0.61
1901–10	− 0.03	0.14	0.19	0.19	− 0.49
1911–14[b]	− 0.04	0.12	0.15	0.15	− 0.28
1919–25[c]	− 0.12	0.24	0.27	0.29	− 0.60
1925–31[d]	− 0.14	0.22	0.20	0.25	− 0.43
1950–66	0.02	0.26	0.32	0.32	0.65

Notes:
[a] A negative sign denotes a sterling discount.
[b] First and second quarter, respectively.
[c] Fourth and second quarter, respectively.
[d] Third and second quarter, respectively.

below 1 percent premium or discount, suggesting a smooth working of the gold standard (to 1931).

Superior statistics are the mean of absolute values and the standard deviation about the mean deviation from parity (the customarily defined standard deviation), shown in columns three and four. The first measure has the advantage that the norm deviation from parity is zero rather than the mean deviation; the second that deviations are squared, thus penalizing observations heavily for being further away from parity. Combining both properties is the standard deviation about zero (essentially the root mean square of the observations), shown in column five.

All three statistics (and the maximum observation) show surprisingly large variability in 1791–1820, with the deviation from parity reaching levels unimaginable under the gold standard in its prime. Also present is the trend of reduced exchange-rate variation, that is, enhanced market integration, all the way to 1914, as well as the profound jump in integration in the 1820s. The measures also exhibit maximum, and truly amazing, tightness of the exchange rate around parity, in 1901–14. The progressive improvement in integration is interrupted in 1811–20 and 1861–70, probably explained by the impact of the War of 1812 and the Civil War.

Associating exchange-market integration with the variability of the exchange rate over time, in particular over decadal or related periods, provides great insight into the rate of development of the foreign-exchange market. The conceptual defects are the heuristic nature of the approach and the lack of a framework to separate and explain the roles of internal and external elements in determining the level of integration. In particular, there is need of a model incorporating specie points and their role in constraining exchange-rate movements. The development and use of this framework and model is the objective of part IV

Part III

Gold points

8 Gold points: theory and practice

1 Gold-point arbitrage versus gold-effected transfer of funds

Both gold-point arbitrage (GPA) and gold-effected transfer of funds (GTF) involve purchasing specie in one country and transporting it across the ocean to be sold in the other country.[1] Under GPA the indirect foreign-exchange transaction via the medium of gold is combined with a direct foreign-exchange transaction in the opposite direction, resulting in a profit. Under GTF the indirect foreign-exchange transaction via gold substitutes for a direct foreign-exchange transaction in the same direction. The gold and foreign-exchange transactions are complements under GPA, substitutes under GTF. The objective under GPA is to make a sure profit, that under GTF is to transfer funds from one country to the other cheaper than via a direct foreign-exchange transaction.

It is ironic that contemporary accounts of such operations almost always pertain to GTF, whereas modern textbooks deal exclusively with GPA. It is not so much that GTF and GPA are confused in authors' minds; rather, the two operations have somehow become merged as one. Only Einzig (1931, p. 18) distinguishes GTF from GPA:

> The terms exchange transaction [GTF] and arbitrage transaction [GPA] are usually used indiscriminately, though there is a considerable difference between them. The object of the exchange transaction is to substitute the shipment of gold for the transfer of funds through the intermediary of the Foreign Exchange Market. The object of the pure arbitrage transaction is the shipment of gold, without any intention of transferring funds, to take advantage of the discrepancy between exchanges and their gold points.

2 Early documented transfer of funds and gold-point arbitrage

For American merchants in colonial times, GTF was much more than an anomalous alternative to transfer of funds abroad by a bill of exchange; it was at least an equal alternative (along with barter). Indeed, as documented by Cole (1929a, pp. 386–9), GTF was the preferred method of making payment to England: "Obviously, not only was there a marked reliance upon specie in foreign dealings, but the exchange transactions were as yet too hazardous to compete on even terms with 'coin and bullion'."

Perkins (1975, pp. 191–5) uses the records of the House of Brown to show that from the early 1820s the House routinely engaged in GTF, comparing the cost of a specie shipment with that of bills. GTF is mentioned by Ingham, Moore, and White in 1829–30 (Secretary of the Treasury, 1830, pp. 6, 49, 68). Detailed cost figures for GTF, called "exchange arbitrations" or "arbitrations of specie," are presented by Reuss (1833, p. 97), *Financial Register of the United States* (1838, p. 288), and Entz (1840, p. 49).

In contrast, I could not find any source documentation of GPA earlier than the 1890s.[2] Yet, given their strong use of GTF, economic agents must have been aware of GPA and undertaken it when the profit opportunity permitted. For example, Temin (1969, p. 67) asserts that a substantial amount of GPA occurred in 1834 via the purchase of 60-day bills on London and the buying of silver (or even gold) and shipping it to the United States.

3   Dominant transferors and arbitrageurs

Sometime between the colonial period and the 1830s, probably around the turn of the century, merchants became more inclined to use bills of exchange than specie to make their payments abroad and by the 1830s had developed "a distinct preference for payment of their foreign obligations by means of bills" rather than by coin (Cole, 1929a, pp. 390, 407–8). From that latter time onward, the dominant transferors and arbitrageurs were the foreign-exchange dealers rather than merchants.

When prior to the 1830s was the time that foreign-exchange dealers became the dominant transferors and arbitrageurs? Perkins (1975, p. 196), referring to the exchange-dealing activity of the House of Brown, observes that "Very few of the firm's customers initiated specie transfers on their own as an alternative to the sterling bill . . . a thorough search of the records over several decades did not reveal a single instance in which a customer threatened to ship gold rather than pay the Browns' rates." The Browns began their exchange brokering in 1803 and exchange dealing in 1811 (Cole, 1929a, p. 390; Perkins, 1975, pp. 20–1); so it may have been in the 1811–20 decade that exchange dealers became virtually the sole arbitrageurs and transferors. As Perkins writes: "The gold points, it seems, had no practical relevance to any group other than the larger foreign exchange dealers like the Browns and the Barings."[3] The House of Barings, a British institution, worked with the Philadelphia-based Second Bank of the United States, which from 1826 to 1841 was the most powerful dealer in the foreign-exchange market (Cole, 1929a, p. 391; Perkins, 1975, pp. 29, 155). Eventually in the nineteenth century, the large New York banks became the preeminent exchange dealers and GTF/GPA gold shippers.[4]

Why did the American foreign-exchange dealers, ultimately the large New York banks, become the dominant transferors and arbitrageurs? First, like their London counterparts, the large American financial houses incurred no commission or brokerage fee in their gold shipments, as they had direct connections with correspondents or agents abroad (Einzig, 1931, p. 82). Second, the House of Brown and Second Bank had "large capital resources and a broad system of branch offices and agents" (Perkins, 1975, p. 7). These institutions, and later the large New York banks, had the "equipment and facilities for handling large transactions" (Cross, 1923, p. 383). Third, they had the staff adept in figuring out profit opportunities through gold flows. Fourth, they had the willingness "both for the sake of advertising and of the sometimes very small profit, to go to the trouble which gold shipments necessarily involve" (Johnson, 1911, p. 510).

But why were the American rather than London houses and banks the dominant participants in GTF and GPA? Prior to World War I, London firms were adversely affected by the existence of markets for sterling bills in the American port cities, with ultimately a flourishing one in New York, but no market for dollar drafts in London. Not only were the American houses and banks located in the foreign-exchange market, but also they were the foreign-exchange dealers. As such, they were the first to notice exchange-rate movements that made GTF and GPA profitable, giving them a timing advantage over London institutions. The continued reluctance of London banks to engage in GTF and GPA in the interwar period, when the cable transfer replaced the bill of exchange as the exchange medium, is not so easily explained (Einzig, 1931, p. 78).

4   Details of transfer and arbitrage operations

4.1   Some conventions

Consider the following notation:

CX = cost of gold-export arbitrage or gold-effected outward transfer of funds, percent

CM = cost of gold-import arbitrage or gold-effected inward transfer of funds, percent

GX = gold-export point, dollars per pound

GM = gold-import point, dollars per pound

M = mint parity, dollars per pound
V = exchange rate, dollars per pound

By definition:

$$GX = M \cdot (1 + CX/100) \tag{8.1}$$

$$GM = M \cdot (1 - CM/100) \tag{8.2}$$

where CX and CM are expressed as a percentage of the amount invested in the operation or, equivalently, of parity. Given positive costs, $GX > GM$. The United States is the domestic country, and the transferors/arbitrageurs are its residents.

It is assumed that transferors and arbitrageurs buy and sell gold proximately at the mint price of the respective authority. The advantage of the assumption is that the gold operation (purchase in one country, shipment across Atlantic, sale in the other country) is equivalent to a foreign-exchange transaction at mint parity. This is without loss of generality, because included in cost (CX or CM) would be any divergence between an actual gold-transactions price and the pertinent mint price (as a percentage of the mint price).[5]

It is also assumed that the direct foreign-exchange transaction undertaken by GPA or forgone by GTF occurs, or would have occurred, proximately at the current market exchange rate defined in V terms as the mid-point of the buying and selling rates.[6] Again there is no loss of generality, because included in cost is any difference between the actual rate at which the foreign-exchange transaction takes place and the hypothetical V.

The exchange-market instrument could be either cable transfer or bill of exchange, the latter represented by the demand bill with no loss of generality.[7] The costs (CX, CM) and therefore gold points (GX, GM), and, of course, the exchange rate (V and the possibly differing actual rate) vary with the instrument. Also, for a given instrument, CX and CM (and therefore GX and GM) differ with the operation (GPA or GTF). In particular, any cost component of CX or CM under GTF is the cost of the gold transfer *minus* the cost of the exchange transaction, because the operations are substitutes. In contrast, a cost component of CX or CM under GPA is the cost of the gold transfer *plus* the cost of the exchange transaction, because the operations are complements. Mint parity (M) is the only fixed parameter throughout the analysis.

4.2   Gold export via cable transfer

Gold-export arbitrage or gold-effected outward transfer of funds is potentially profitable when $V > GX$. Under cable transfer, V is the spot cable rate and GX the cable gold-export point. The arbitrageur or transferor (New York bank) purchases gold from the US Treasury or Federal Reserve Bank of New York, ships it across the Atlantic, and sells it to the Bank of England, obtaining pounds for dollars proximately at M but ultimately at GX, with the incorporation of expenses.[8] For GTF that is the end of it; dollars in the United States have been converted to pounds in England at the rate GX, cheaper than V, a cost-saving proportionate to $(V - GX)$. The interest cost of the gold shipment (that for a one-way Atlantic voyage) remains in GX, because there is zero interest loss in a cable transfer.[9]

Under GPA the situation is more complicated. If the pounds could be sold for dollars at the spot cable rate (the current V), a profit proportionate to $(V - GX)$ would result. The problem is that the pounds are not available until after the gold has been transported from New York to London (so that CX has an interest component, the same as under GTF). No ideal solution existed; but there were three alternatives. The first, selling the pounds after they are obtained, involves a clear exchange risk; for the exchange rate (V) might fall below GX in the interim.

The second option, borrowing pounds in London at the time the gold is purchased in New York, permits the immediate sale of pounds (with the resultant dollars invested in the New York money market), thus eliminating the exchange risk and locking in profit – the proceeds from selling the gold to the Bank of England would be used to repay the loan. However, two components are thereby added to the expense of arbitrage: transactions costs for the money-market operations, and the London–New York interest-rate differential (although if negative the latter is a subtraction from cost).

The third alternative, selling pounds forward (cable) for the number of days equal to the duration between the New York and London gold transactions (essentially the time needed for a one-way Atlantic voyage) eliminates the exchange risk but involves an additional cost, that of forward cover: V minus the forward exchange rate, as a percentage of V (a decrement from CX if negative).[10] Banks preferred to separate their GPA and exchange-rate-speculation activities and through the forward-exchange market rather than the money markets. Therefore "in most cases" and "as a rule" they covered the exchange risk with a forward sale of pounds (Einzig, 1931, pp. 20, 64).

4.3   Gold export via demand bill

The situation is radically different if demand bills are employed as the exchange instrument. Should the sight exchange rate exceed the demand-bill gold-export point $(V > GX)$, the arbitrageur begins his operation by selling demand bills at V, thereby obtaining dollars with which to purchase gold from the US Treasury or commercial banks. Therefore there is no interest cost (nor is there such a cost under GTF).[11] This is not necessarily an advantage, because the price of demand bills would be lower than cables to compensate. The gold is transported to London and sold to the Bank of England, with the pound proceeds used to cover the bills of exchange upon presentation.

The gold transactions effect the transfer of funds abroad at the rate GX rather than the higher rate V, a cost-saving proportionate to $(V - GX)$. For GPA, with the rate for the foreign-exchange transaction determined at the onset of the arbitrage, exchange risk is not present and a profit proportionate to $(V - GX)$ is earned.

4.4   Gold import via cable transfer

Gold-import arbitrage or gold-effected inward transfer of funds occurs when $V < GM$, the spot cable rate below the cable gold-import point. The New York bank buys pounds spot in the foreign-exchange market, uses them to purchase gold from the Bank of England and sells the gold to the US Treasury or Federal Reserve Bank of New York. The gold operation involves an indirect sale of pounds in London for dollars in New York, at a net rate of GM (M plus allowance for expenses), a better price than V, with cost-saving proportionate to $(GM - V)$. With GPA, the profit is proportionate to $(GM - V)$.

Interest cost for the duration of an Atlantic voyage is a component of arbitrage cost, because funds are required for the foreign-exchange transaction initiating the GPA operation. This is also the interest loss under GTF, because the zero interest cost for the alternative foreign-exchange transaction contrasts with the interest loss under the gold shipment.

4.5   Gold import via demand bill

Now let $V < GM$ represent the sight exchange rate below the demand-bill gold-import point. Under GPA, pounds (demand bills) are purchased in New York (or other port city) for dollars at the rate V, shipped to London, and presented to the drawees, with the proceeds used to obtain gold from the Bank of England. The gold is transported to New York for conversion to dollars; so, through gold, pounds are sold for dollars at a proximate rate of M and an expenses-incorporated rate of GM, resulting in profit proportionate to $(GM - V)$. Far from the nil interest cost of gold-export arbitrage, interest is lost for the duration of a *round-trip* Atlantic voyage, since gold is shipped from London only after the bills have arrived from New York.

With GTF, only the gold operation occurs, whereby, through the medium

Table 8.1 *Oceanic-transport interest cost of gold shipment*

	Export		Import	
	Cable	Demand bill	Cable	Demand bill
GPA	one-way	zero	one-way	two-way
GTF	"	"	"	zero

Legend:
GPA = Gold point arbitrage.
GTF = Transfer of funds.
One-way = interest cost of one-way Atlantic voyage.
Two-way = interest cost of two-way Atlantic voyage.
Source: See text.

of gold, pounds in London are converted to dollars in New York at the effective rate GM. The interest cost, that for a one-way Atlantic voyage, would be the same under the alternative (foreign-exchange) operation, sending pounds in London across the ocean to be sold for dollars at the rate V in the New York market. So there is zero interest cost under GTF. The cost-saving is proportionate to $(GM - V)$.

In summary, considering all eight operations (varying with GPA or GTF, export or import, cable or demand bill), the oceanic-transport interest-cost component of GPA and GTF can be that of a one-way Atlantic voyage, a two-way voyage, or zero. The situation is outlined in table 8.1.

5   Dominant exchange-market instrument

Logically, the dominant exchange-market medium used for GPA and considered for GTF was the instrument dominant in the foreign-exchange market – the 60-day bill from colonial times, succeeded by the 3-day bill perhaps in the late 1860s, with the demand bill taking over around 1880 until World War I. After the war, and certainly by 1925 when the dollar–sterling gold standard was restored, the cable transfer must have overtaken the demand bill as the primary exchange medium under GPA and GTF.

That is the logical scenario; but evidence must be assembled to prove its historical accuracy. One reason is that arbitrageurs and transferors need not necessarily have employed the instrument dominant in the foreign-exchange market. Another is that several noteworthy studies of the prewar dollar–sterling gold standard contradict the established pattern by analyzing GPA solely under cable transfer.[12]

The dominance of the 60-day bill for GTF, and presumably GPA, in the antebellum period appears in contemporary gold-point computations, for example, Reuss (1833, p. 97) and Entz (1840, p. 49). The evidence that demand bills became the typical exchange medium for GPA and GTF and remained so to World War I is multifaceted and overwhelming. First, contemporary newspapers cite gold points not for cable transfers but rather for demand bills (or sometimes for 3-day bills, until the early 1880s).[13] Second, in detailed discussions of the components of gold-export arbitrage found in a contemporary newspaper, demand bills are the only exchange instrument.[14] It is with reason that Goodhart (1969, p. 60, n. 46), referring to the 1900–13 period, writes: "the gold points were expressed in terms of the price of sight demand drafts on sterling."

Third, contemporary textbooks to the end of World War I discuss only or primarily demand-bill gold points; barely, if at all, mentioning cable.[15] Patterson (1917, pp. 166–7) expresses the situation well in declaring: "When we say that exchange rates between two countries usually fluctuate between the specie points, we refer only to the rate for demand or sight bills." Fourth, a contemporary lecture (Strauss, 1908, pp. 64–73) presents gold arbitrage via demand bills, adding that "cable transfers require but a word" and suggesting that cable is the preferred medium only in "abnormal times."

Fifth, even post-World War I textbooks pay homage to the primacy of demand bills. Whitaker (1919, pp. 519, 534, 536) writes that "gold movements . . . are governed in the first instance or proximately by the position of the rate for bankers' sight drafts," "an export of gold against a sale of cables should not be considered a standard operation," and "it is generally understood that in practice the greater part of New York's gold imports are provided for by the purchase of demand drafts rather than cables." Cross (1923, p. 386) states that "cables are seldom, if ever, sold against gold exports," though he sees demand bills, long bills, and cables as all legitimate instruments for gold-import arbitrage. Clearly, in concentrating on cable transfers, Morgenstern, Clark, Spiller, and Wood dealt with an instrument that in historical fact was eschewed by arbitrageurs and transferors.

With Britain's return to the gold standard in 1925, cable was the dominant medium for GPA and dominant alternative for GTF. Spalding (1928a, pp. 79–84) mentions both "spot" [cable] and sight exchange in connection with gold points, but in practice treats cable as the alternative to gold shipments. Einzig (1929b, p. 43; 1931, p. 64) states: "The situation in this respect has undergone a considerable change since the war. Gold shipments are no longer covered, as a rule, by means of sight drafts, but by [telegraph-transfer] forward exchange operations." When Dunbar (1929, pp. 110–14) and Whitaker (1933, pp. 360–6) discuss GPA in the context of demand bills with cables mentioned only as an afterward, such passages are vestiges of an earlier edition of their textbooks.

Why the dominance of demand (or 3-days' sight) bills over cables from the inception of the Atlantic cable in 1866 to World War I? For gold-export arbitrage, demand bills eliminate the interest component of cost; but this is not necessarily an advantage – though (Cross, 1923, p. 386) sees it as such – as the price of demand bills would be lower than that of cables to compensate. More important, demand bills automatically remove exchange risk. While borrowing in London can cover exchange risk in a cable transfer, Whitaker (1919, p. 534) mentions it only as something to be avoided, probably because of transactions costs. Neither Cross nor Whitaker even mentions the alternative of a forward-exchange sale, probably because of the high cost of forward cover associated with a wide buying–selling price spread for forward cables on the part of exchange dealers.[16]

For outward GTF and for gold-import arbitrage (involving the actual or potential purchase of pounds in the foreign-exchange market), the primacy of the demand bill (and the 3-days' sight bill to 1879) was initially founded on the discriminatory premium imposed by exchange dealers on the purchase of cable transfers. Further, the relative thinness of the total market for cable transfers compared to that for demand bills made for a wider buying–selling price spread for cables than would otherwise exist, which also discouraged the cable alternative for inward GTF.[17]

6   Stabilization of exchange rate

The gold-point spread is the range of values of the exchange rate from the gold-import point to the gold-export point. It is the set of all V such that $GM \leq V \leq GX$. GPA and GTF act to keep the exchange rate within the spread.

Consider the case of $V > GX$, implying a cost-saving under outward GTF. Whether the alternative exchange-market transaction involves cable transfers or demand bills, the purchase of pounds in the foreign-exchange market is avoided, as is the consequent increase in V. For $V < GM$, there is a cost-saving under inward GTF, which avoids the sale of pounds in the foreign-exchange market and a decrease in V. Therefore GTF prevents an exchange rate outside a gold point from moving even further away from the spread.

Turning to GPA, consider $V > GX$, implying a positive profit from gold-export arbitrage. With the cable medium, pounds are sold forward, depressing the forward exchange rate, increasing CX via the cost of forward cover, and pushing up GX. Thus gold-export arbitrage typically placed V again within the gold-point spread, thereby eliminating arbitrage profit, by widening the spread rather than by lowering the exchange rate. Use of forward cable makes the gold-export point endogenous (dependent on the actions of arbitrageurs).[18]

Sometimes arbitrageurs opted out of forward protection and left the exchange risk uncovered (Einzig, 1931, p. 21). In this situation, spot pounds are sold – but only after they have been obtained via shipping gold from New York to London. As long as gold-export arbitrage is profitable, downward pressure is exerted on V but only with a lag. Therefore there is a delay in returning V to the spread and eliminating arbitrage profit. In summary, the standard description of GPA as an immediate force driving the exchange rate back to an exogenously determined gold-point spread is at variance with the historical reality of the interwar gold standard.

With a demand bill (or under the cable hypothetical situation of borrowing pounds in London), GPA increases the supply of foreign exchange in the standard manner – except for the element of time lag of adjustment – until $V \leq GX$ and arbitrage is no longer profitable.

The textbook story applies to gold-import arbitrage in its entirety, again except for time lag. As long as $V < GM$, pounds (whether cable transfers or demand bills) are purchased, pushing up V – eventually to GM and, with $V \geq GM$, eliminating arbitrage profit. Only when V is within the spread is GPA unprofitable and GTF more expensive than the alternative, exchange-market, transaction. Therefore "efficient" GPA and GTF involve $GM \leq V \leq GX$.

9   Gold-point estimates

1   Techniques of estimation

Absent from the literature is a review of the techniques of obtaining specie points (loosely, "gold" points). Such a survey is provided here, and a surprisingly large number of techniques are delineated. Every known dollar–sterling specie-point estimate, except those for which the source or method is unstated, falls into one of the categories that follow.

Consult an expert: Obvious experts were foreign-exchange dealers, London bullion brokers, and New York bankers. Parliamentary testimony of merchants was a direct way of obtaining gold-point information (House of Commons, 1810, p. 108; 1847–8, part 1, p. 193; part 3, p. 261). Perkins (1975, pp. 192–5) provides specie-point estimates from the records of the House of Brown for several dates over 1823–59, thus "consulting" a foreign-exchange dealer of the past. The *New York Times* (July 7, 1895, p. 17; June 17, 1899, p. 7) presents gold points provided by a "house" and "some dealers." Johnson (1905, pp. 90–1) offers gold-point data "furnished by the representative of one of the largest New York banking houses" and from "another large bullion dealer in New York."

During the 1925–31 gold standard, *The Economist* regularly printed the report of Samuel Montagu and Co., a bullion broker, and on three occasions gold-point estimates were contained therein.[1] Long after the fact, Morgenstern (1959, pp. 188, 191, n. 25) obtained gold points for twenty scattered dates over 1926–33 from a New York banker (obvious, though he does not identify the source).

The advantages of this approach are that data are consistent over time, being from the same source, and presumably have a high degree of reliability, since the source is an expert.[2] The disadvantages are (1) the small number of observations, so that a time series of the gold points cannot readily be constructed, (2) the uncertainty if all components of arbitrage cost are covered in the gold points, as a breakdown of cost is typically not provided, and (3) a possible lack of representativeness, as only one source is used.

Obtain a market consensus: The *New York Times* obtained consensus gold points in the late nineteenth century, and, along with *The Economist*, in the interwar period.[3] The source was described as "the market," "Wall Street," "banks," "bankers," or "shippers." While the third limitation of the previous technique is overcome, the available estimates are for so few dates as to be unusable.

Find the exchange rate at which gold flows: Morgenstern (1959, p. 308) mentions the indirect approach of "taking as gold points those exchange rates at which the gold-export and -import statistics show a specie movement across the border." The technique had been applied by Newcomb (1886, pp. 281–2). There is both a theoretical and a data advantage of obtaining gold points in this way. The theoretical benefit is that attention is devoted exclusively to behavior: gold points are obtained by "revealed preference" alone. On the data side, the technique obviates the need for direct gold-point information and the necessity of selecting among the techniques of obtaining that information, because the indirect approach substitutes.

However, the approach has four difficulties. First, there can be not only individual months or quarters but also long periods of time in which gold is not shipped from one center to the other.[4] Second, even when gold is shipped, it may not be clear whether a commercial or "special" transaction is involved and, if commercial, whether the motivation is GPA or GTF, or some other.[5] Third, even when GPA or GTF can be ascertained, the shipper may be arbitraging or transferring at an unusually low cost, so that drawing an implication for the value of the gold point is unwarranted.[6]

Fourth, the accuracy of bilateral gold-flow data is questionable. In his celebrated study of the issue, Morgenstern (1955, p. 8) concludes that "the statistics of pairwise gold movements, and *a fortiori* those derived from them, are worthless from the point of view of describing the *finer* interdependencies among national economies." Goodhart (1969, pp. 157–81) identifies four sources of error: (1) transport time across the Atlantic, (2) third-country transit, (3) inefficiency of customs in reporting gold flows of travellers, tourists, and immigrants, and (4) clerical mistakes in handling and transcribing basic data. For US–UK monthly gold flows over 1899–1913, Goodhart manages to correct the serious errors and deems the resulting series usable. However, it is doubtful that his careful reconstruction can be applied to earlier decades.

Take the maximum and minimum exchange rate over time: Morgenstern (1955, pp. 304–8) represents the gold-point spread by the range of the observed exchange rate over time. The advantage of this technique is the use of minimal, only exchange-rate, data. One problem is the underlying assumption that the exchange rate can never go beyond the gold points.

Another is the difficulty of determining the time span over which the range is taken. The longer the time span, the greater the exchange-rate experience but also the higher the probability that the true gold points have changed. A sophisticated refinement of the technique is the probabilistic model of Spiller and Wood (1988).

Average estimates across sources and over time: For 1880–1914, Morgenstern (1959, pp. 176–91, 303–8) takes gold-point estimates from diverse contemporary sources (for the years 1894, 1901, 1910, and 1913) and lets the median gold-export and the median gold-import point be the respective gold point for the entire 1880–1914 period. For 1925–31, he averages the estimates of the New York banker (for the gold-export and gold-import point, separately); he also takes the median of the gold points from diverse contemporary sources, including the banker's average. The first is used by Morgenstern, the second by Moggridge (1972, pp. 128, 185) to represent the gold points for the entire 1925–31 period.

While this technique has the virtue of averaging out errors in estimates, it has the disadvantage of imposing invariant gold points over time. Furthermore, the data used to compute the medians are scattered, varying in quality, and inconsistent with one another.

Project an estimate to obtain a time series: From 1877 to 1916, *The Economist* regularly published gold points, but they were invariant over the entire period (except for a change in 1877). While the source is unstated, it is probably Ernest Seyd. Even Morgenstern (1959, pp. 176–82) questions the imposition of a 40-year stability in gold points. Clark (1984) refines the technique by breaking down the cost of shipping gold into two components: interest cost and direct cost. He computes interest cost observation-by-observation from first principles; but imposes a direct cost of 0.3125 percent throughout 1890–1908 (his period of study), then modifies the level by allowing the cost to be 0.5 percent in 1890–1904.

Clark's 0.5-percent figure is pure conjecture on his part. However, the estimate of 0.3125 percent is identified by him as for the year 1906 and ascribed to Myers (1931, p. 343). Actually, the figure ultimately emanates from a contemporary account (*Commercial and Financial Chronicle*, May 12, 1906, p. 1069) and pertains specifically to American gold imports in May 1906. Clark's specification of direct cost is incorrect in three respects: (1) the assumption that costs are constant over time (even allowing for a one-time change), (2) the projection of gold-import onto gold-export cost, and (3) the imposition of an arbitrary figure for 1890–1904. The same technique is used by Giovannini (1993, p. 128), but his 1889–1904 figure is 0.65 percent.[7] A related approach is taken by Brown (1940, p. 708).[8]

Obtain aggregate arbitrage or transfer cost: This technique has the advantage of consistency with the theory of GPA and GTF developed in chapter

8. If the arbitrage or transfer costs of export and import (CX and CM) are known, then they either constitute the gold points in percentage terms or can be plugged into equations (8.1) and (8.2) to produce gold points in dollars per pound. This approach is found in textbooks, scholarly articles, newspaper accounts, and government documents.[9] Its defects are (1) the absence of a check on accuracy of cost – that would require a breakdown of cost, not just a total figure, (2) the inability to generate gold-point time series, because the available estimates come from various sources and are inconsistent, and (3) the lack of a distinction between GPA and GTF costs or gold points.

Sum components of arbitrage or transfer cost: This procedure provides the proper underlay of the previous approach by explicitly building up aggregate arbitrage or transfer cost from component elements. The approach was used in various contemporary publications for over a century beginning in 1830.[10] The advantages of the technique are striking. First, it is methodologically sound, deriving specie points from first principles. Second, it is the way the arbitrageurs and transferors themselves must have calculated specie points. Third, the user is provided with the knowledge of which items are included in aggregate cost. Fourth, it is possible to determine from the cost elements present whether GPA or GTF is under consideration (although omitted components can be due to lack of information or carelessness).

A disadvantage is that the individual observer might not have access to information on all components of GPA or GTF cost, or might use inaccurate data on some components. Further, no guidance is provided on how to construct a time series of gold points. Another problem (common with the preceding approach) is that it may not be clear which arbitrageur/transferor, exchange-rate instrument, or form of specie underlies the specie-point estimate. A component cost may vary with each of these elements, and also with the amount of specie shipped, and with time.

Generate a time series of each cost component and sum the series: The specie-point requirements of this volume are (1) monthly time series for January 1890–December 1906 and May 1925–August 1931 (for comparison with the dollar–sterling "gold points" in 1950–66, under the Bretton Woods system), (2) period averages for the aforementioned 1890–1906 and 1925–31 series, (3) decadal (or related-period) averages from 1791 to 1931, as in table 7.1 but excluding 1801–20 and 1919–25.[11] The technique utilized is to employ all available information to generate a time series of each component of arbitrage or transfer cost. All problems of the preceding approach are overcome.

First, the periods 1890–1906 and 1925–31 have excellent data on cost components, the time series of which are summed to obtain time series of total costs and thence of the gold points. For the decadal periods, only the average cost for each component, and from them only average specie points, need be computed. This limited objective makes data limitations manageable and allows errors in timing of changes of component cost levels to have minimal impact on specie points.

Second, arbitrage versus transfer costs, and thence gold points, are readily distinguished and generated, because of their build-up from individual cost components. Third, the strategy is to develop arbitrage and transfer costs only for the *dominant* arbitrageurs/transferors, the *principal* exchange instrument, and the *primary* form of gold shipped, and to allow for changes in these three qualitative parameters of the gold points. It will also be assumed that the amount of gold shipped is sufficiently high to obtain the lowest level for a given component cost.

Three general rules are followed in generating the time series and decadal average for a given component cost. First, cost is expressed in percentage terms, and can also be interpreted as measured in percent of parity. Second, all consistent data on the cost component are tabulated, with anomalous figures excluded. Third, where two adjacent cost levels are separated by a time span with no information on when the cost change occurred, the change is assumed to have taken place mid-way in that span. This technique ("the mid-point convention") has greater virtue for decadal (or related-period) averages than for monthly series development, because the same impact on the average is obtainable by assuming that the change took the form of a series of steps symmetrical on each side of the span mid-point.

2   Cost components

2.1   Freight, insurance, and handling

These costs were independent of the form of specie (gold or silver, bars or coin). Freight, 1791–1914, and insurance, all years, did not vary with the direction of shipping; but freight, 1925–31, and handling, all years, did so vary. The freight charge could be a two-step rate, with the lower applicable to a shipment exceeding a critical dollar or pound value.

2.1.1   Freight

Table 9.1 presents specie freight-rate data over 1789–1931. Where a source provides two rates, the lower rate is taken, as applicable to the larger amount of shipment. The usual route for transporting specie from New York was to the port of Liverpool, then overland to London – and in reverse for the opposite direction. The freight rate is usually reported as including both the water and land segments of the journey, and this convention is taken as the norm.

Table 9.1 *Freight rate, data, 1789–1931*

Year(s)	Rate (percent)	Source
New York to/from London, 1789–1914		
1789	1	Shepherd and Walton (1972, p. 189)
1827–8	0.50	Secretary of the Treasury (1830, p. 90)
1830, 1833, 1840, 1848, 1851	0.375	Perkins (1975, p. 192), Reuss (1833, p. 97), Entz (1840, p. 49), *Merchants' Magazine* (Sept. 1848, p. 303), *Bankers' Magazine* (Oct. 1851, p. 273)
1859, 1868, 1892, 1896[a]	0.125	Perkins (1975, p. 195), Seyd (1868, pp. 398–400), Clare (1906, p. 130), *New York Times*, May 6, 1896, p. 1.
1896,[b] 1905, 1910, 1911	0.15625	*New York Times*, May 6, 1896, p. 1, Johnson (1905, p. 90; 1911, p.508), Escher (1910, pp. 115, 118)
pre-World War I	0.1875	Whitaker (1919, pp. 524–33), Einzig (1927a, pp. 133–4; 1931, pp. 70, 148–9)
New York to London, 1925–31		
1925[c]	0.25	Spalding (1925, p. 39), Einzig (1929b, p. 95; 1931, p. 149)
1927–31	0.15	*The Economist*, Dec. 3, 1927, p. 1007, Spalding (1928a, pp. 81–4), Swoboda (1928, p. 16), Einzig (1928, p. 663; 1929b, pp. 50, 93, 95; 1931, pp. 71, 148, 150)
London to New York, 1925–31		
1925[c]	0.15	*The Economist*, May 16, 1925, p. 991
1925	0.25	*The Economist*, May 16, 1925, p. 991, Spalding (1928a, p. 81), Einzig (1927a, p. 134; 1931, pp. 70–1)
1927	0.1875[d]	Einzig (1927a, p. 134)
1927–31	0.15	Einzig (1927b, pp. 480–1; 1929b, pp. 93, 95; 1931, pp. 71, 149), Spalding (1928a, p. 84)

Notes:
[a] Last day May 5, 1896.
[b] Effective date May 6, 1896.
[c] In effect on April 28, 1925.
[d] Rate "recently reduced" from 0.25 percent.

Primage was a customary allowance – in Anglo-American trade, 5 percent of the freight charge (North, 1960, p. 609) – paid by the shipper to the master of the vessel for the care of the cargo. Eventually primage became incorporated into the freight rate itself, but when? Reuss (1833, p. 97) and Entz (1840, p. 49) list 5-percent primage as a component cost of shipping specie. North (1960, pp. 607–8) incorporates it in a US freight-rate index for 1820–60. Seyd (1868, pp. 395–401) pointedly excludes primage from his London–New York gold-point estimates by including it for London–California. Therefore, applying the mid-point convention, primage is deemed to have been eliminated in mid-1864.

Period averages and monthly series of the freight rate are determined from table 9.1, external information, and the mid-point convention. This approach will be used also for the other cost components. The average freight rate for the decadal and other periods is shown in table 9.4 for American exports (EXP, New York to London) and imports (IMP, London to New York). From 1791 to 1914 the New York–London freight rate was the same in either direction; for 1925–31, it differed.

1791–1800: Primage is simply added to the 1789 rate. There is no reason to expect a change in rate during this time period. There was no change in technology on the Atlantic run, still regular sailing ships.

1821–30: The reduction in rate from 1 to 0.5 percent probably occurred with innovation and increased competition for specie on the New York–Liverpool run. Packets were sailing vessels organized into liners with regular schedules. The first packet line (Black Ball) began service in 1818 and quickly took over the specie trade from the existing sailing vessels (so-called regular traders – see section 2.4.2), because of the packet speed and punctuality (Albion, 1938, pp. 27–8, 39; Albion and Pope, 1942, pp. 41, 43). The Black Ball line had a monopoly in packet service until 1822, and so the rate probably remained at 1 percent during this time.

The Black Ball first encountered competition on the New York–Liverpool run at the end of January 1822, and its reaction was to double the frequency of its sailings, beginning March 16. This suggests that a decline in the rate from 1 per cent to 0.75 percent may have occurred in mid-March 1822. On September 8, 1822 a third line began service. By autumn 1822 the three lines were operating on a schedule to remain unchanged until 1838.[12] A second decline, from 0.75 to 0.5 percent, therefore, may have occurred around mid-September 1822.

When did the drop from 0.5 to 0.375 percent happen? The earliest source of the lower figure is a House of Brown correspondence of August 30, 1830. The latest date for the rate of 0.5 percent is the year 1828. Therefore the change is deemed to occur mid way between January 1, 1829 and August 30, 1830: November 1, 1829. Weighting the 1, 0.75, 0.5, and

0.375 rates by duration over the total 120-month period, and adding 5-percent primage, the rate of 0.5863 percent is obtained.

1831–50: Primage is added to the 0.375-percent rate. *1851–60*: Sometime between 1851 and 1859, 0.375 fell to 0.125, with the change deemed to have occurred in mid-1855. The duration-weighted average of the two rates is taken and primage is added. *1861–90*: The rate is 0.125 percent, except that for 1861–70 the weighted average of 5-percent primage to mid-1864 and zero thereafter is incorporated.

1901–10: The increase from 0.125 to 0.15625 percent is known to have occurred on May 6, 1896; so the appropriate weighted average of 0.125 and 0.15625 is taken. *1890–1906*: The rate is 0.125 percent for January 1890–April 1896, 0.15625 percent for June 1896–December 1906, and 0.1512 percent (the weighted average of five days at 0.125 and 26 days at 0.15625) for May 1896. For the period average, the monthly weighted average of the three rates is taken.

1911–14: When did 0.15625 percent increase to 0.1875? The various sources state, explicitly or implicitly, that 0.1875 was in effect for several years prior to World War I. The final reference to 0.15625 is for 1911. So 0.1875 is assumed to begin in 1912, and the consequent weighted average of 0.15625 and 0.1875 is computed.

1925–31, New York–London: When did 0.25 percent fall to 0.15? On November 30, 1927, Montagu and Co. reported recent reductions in the rate so it became 0.15 percent (*The Economist*, December 3, 1927, p. 1007). Spalding (1928a, pp. 81–2) notes the cutting of the rate to 0.15 percent in the autumn of 1927. The timing of the Montagu report suggests that the rate reduction occurred in November 1927. So an average rate of 0.20 percent is assumed for that month (average of former and new rates). In summary, the rate is 0.25 percent for May 1925–October 1927, 0.20 for November 1927, and 0.15 for December 1927–August 1931. The 1925–31 period averages are the monthly weighted averages of the three rates for the 72 and 76 months, respectively.

1925–31, London–New York: When in 1925 did the rate increase from 0.15 to 0.25 percent? The Montagu report of May 13 notes the change in the rate, and the previous report was on April 29. So the change is considered to have occurred mid way in this interval, on May 7. When in 1927 did 0.25 fall to 0.1875 percent? Einzig in March 1927 notes that the rate was "reduced recently" from 0.25 to 0.1875 percent; so say it happened at the beginning of March. In September 1927 Einzig observes that the rate of 0.15 percent "eventually resulted." So say it reached that level at the beginning of September. The reduction was in steps ("several reductions"), as noted by Spalding (1928a, p. 84) and implied by Einzig. Successive reduction is also suggested by the reason for the decrease, a freight war. So assume that from

Table 9.2 *Insurance rate, data, 1820–1931, New York to/from London*

Year(s)	Rate (percent)	Source
1827–8, 1830	0.625	Secretary of the Treasury (1830, p. 90), Perkins (1975, p. 192)
1835, 1840, 1845, 1848	0.50	Albion (1939, p. 412), Entz (1840, p. 49), *Merchants' Magazine* (Sept. 1848, p. 302)
1851	0.375	*Bankers' Magazine* (Oct. 1851, p. 273)
1868	0.2625	Seyd (1868, pp. 398–9)
1882	0.1703	*New York Times*, July 2, 1882, p. 9
1892	0.1468	Clare (1906, p. 130)
1896	0.125	*New York Times*, June 28, 1896, p. 2
1905, 1910, 1911, pre-World War I	0.05	Johnson (1905, p. 91; 1911, p. 508), Escher (1910, pp. 115, 118), Whitaker (1919, pp. 524–33), Cross (1923, p. 384)
1925–31	0.05	Swoboda (1928, p. 16), Spalding (1928a, pp. 81–4), Einzig (1927a, p. 134; 1928, p. 663; 1929b, pp. 94–5; 1931, pp. 148–50), Evitt (1936, p. 116), Whitaker (1933, pp. 360–4).

March to September the rate fell in equal steps of 0.00625 percentage points.

In summary, the rate is 0.2306 percent (average of 0.15 and 0.25, weighted by days) for May 1925, 0.25 for June 1925–February 1927, 0.1875 in March 1927 and declining by 0.00625 monthly until September, when it reached 0.15, remaining there through August 1931. The 72-month and 76-month averages are the duration-weighted averages of all these rates.

2.1.2   Insurance

Table 9.2 presents insurance-rate data for specie shipment between New York and London, and table 9.4 the average rate by period. *1791–1800*: There is no known figure prior to 1827, but an estimate for this earliest decade is possible using outside information. There were three things insured: the ship (by the year), prospective freight earnings (by the trip), and specific cargo, such as specie (by the trip). In 1835 the ratio of the specie rate

to the freight-earnings rate (mid-point of range) from New York to Britain
was 0.44 (Albion, 1939, p. 412). The freight-earnings rate is available as a
single figure for 1792 (a peacetime year, with only normal marine risk) and
in annual-range form for 1793, 1796–8, and 1801 (years for which coverage
incorporates both normal marine risks and war risks, the United States
caught in the middle of – and seeking to make profit from – Anglo-French
conflict) (Albion and Pope, 1942, p. 70). Taking the mid-point of the ranges
and linearly interpolating between adjacent figures for missing years, an
annual series of the freight-earnings rate is obtained for 1791–1800, with an
average value of 5.725. The estimated specie rate for the decade is the
product of this rate and 0.44.

1821–30: The 0.625-percent rate is applied to the entire decade. *1831–40*:
The rate of 0.625 percent is assumed to have changed to 0.5 percent mid-way
between 1830 and 1835, at the end of 1832, and the duration-weighted
average of the two rates is taken. *1841–50*: The reduction from 0.5 to 0.375
percent is assumed to have occurred mid-way between 1848 and 1851, and
the weighted average of the rates is taken. *1851–60*: The change from 0.375
to 0.2625 percent "happened" at the end of 1859, by convention, leading to
the usual average.

1861–70: The rate 0.2625 percent applies, but as a peacetime rate. During
the Civil War there was an additional premium, for war risks. War-risk rates
for freight earnings are available only for 1861 (0.5 percent), 1862 (averaging
0.75 percent), and January–August 1863 (3 percent). For the rest of the war
period, the premium must be estimated. "By the time the good news of
Gettysburg and Vicksburg [July 1–4, 1863] had come, the North found that
the worst of its maritime menace had also subsided . . . By late autumn
[1864] all was finally quiet along the [Atlantic] seaboard" (Albion and Pope,
1942, pp. 165–6). This passage suggests a reduced rate of 2 percent for the
rest of 1863, for an annual average of 2.66 percent, followed by 1 percent for
1864. With the maritime menace of Southern raiders over and the war
clearly won by the North, it is reasonable to assume a zero war-risk rate for
1865 and, of course, subsequently.

Albion's specie-rate/freight-earnings-rate ratio for 1845 is 0.4. Applying
this ratio to the war-risk freight-earnings rates and averaging for the decade,
an average war-risk premium for specie of 0.1967 percent is obtained and
added to the basic rate of 0.2625.

1871–80: The rate of 0.2625 percent fell to 0.1703 in mid-1875 by the
usual convention, and the weighted average of the two figures is computed.
1881–90: Similarly, the rate of 0.1703 percent was reduced to 0.1468 percent
in mid-1887, and the average is taken. *1891–1900*: The same procedure is
applied to the rates 0.1468 and 0.125 percent, with the switchover occurring
in mid-1894. *1901–10*: The rate of 0.125 percent is deemed to decline to 0.05

mid-way between 1896 and 1905, at the turn of the century. *1890–1906*: The rate is 0.1468 percent January 1890–June 1894, 0.125 July 1894–December 1900, and 0.05 January 1901–December 1906. The period average is the duration-weighted average of the three rates. *1911–14, 1925–31*: The uniform rate of 0.05 percent is applicable.

2.1.3   Handling

Handling charges were assessable both at the origin and at the destination of a specie shipment. For American exports, the origin rate was for packing and cartage in New York, and the destination rate for landing charges in Liverpool and delivery in London. For American imports, the origin charge was similarly for packing and cartage in London, and there were destination charges (unspecified in the literature) in New York. Table 9.3 lists the handling-rate data for each of the four categories and table 9.4 the period averages derived from them.

(1)   Export: packing and cartage in New York
1791–1800, 1821–30: The earliest known figure, that for 1833, is projected back. *1831–40*: Assume 0.1525 became 0.0714 percent when steamships began to dominate packets as the transport choice for shipment of specie, that is, in May 1838 (Albion, 1938, p. 39). The duration-weighted average of the two rates is taken. *1841–50*: The rate 0.0714 percent is deemed to have fallen to 0.0043 mid-way between 1840 and 1848, in mid-1844, and the appropriate average of the rates is computed. *1851–80*: The rate of 0.0043 percent is applicable.

1881–90: By the usual convention, 0.0043 percent became 0.0050 at the end of 1886. The duration-weighted average of the rates is calculated. *1891–1900*: The rate is 0.0050 percent. *1901–10*: The change from 0.0050 to 0.0055 percent is deemed to have occurred in mid-1908, and the weighted average is taken. *1890–1906*: The figure is 0.0050 percent throughout. *1911–14*: With 0.0060 percent first known for 1913, the switch from 0.0055 happened in mid-1912, and the average is computed.

1925–31 (monthly series and period averages): Gold was first delivered "free on board" by the Federal Reserve Bank of New York in 1928 (Einzig, 1931, p. 150), but when in that year? Einzig (1928, p. 663) has zero charge for May–June and there were no recorded US gold exports to Britain in 1928 until March (*Federal Reserve Bulletin*, May 1928, p. 347). Therefore March 1, 1928, may be assumed as the effective date for a zero rate. Until then, the rate was 0.0126 percent. The period averages are the duration-weighted averages of 0.0126 percent and zero.

Table 9.3 *Handling rates, data, 1821–1930*

Year(s)	Rate (percent)	Source
Export: Packing and cartage in new York		
1833	0.1525	Reuss (1833, p. 97)
1840	0.0714	Entz (1840, p. 49)
1848, 1868	0.0043	*Merchants' Magazine* (Sept. 1848, p. 302), Seyd (1868, p. 399)
1905	0.0050	Johnson (1905, p. 91)
1911	0.0055	Johnson (1911, p. 508)
pre-World War I	0.0060	Whitaker (1919, pp. 524, 529)
1925	0.0126	Spalding (1928a, p. 81)
1928	0	Einzig (1929a, p. 385; 1929b, pp. 51–2, 95–6; 1931, pp. 72, 87, 150)
Export: Landing charges in Liverpool and delivery in London		
1821	0.1416	Secretary of the Treasury (1830, p. 65)
1833	0.0859	Reuss (1833, p. 97)
1840	0.0750	Entz (1840, p. 49)
1851	0.0171	*Bankers' Magazine* (Oct. 1851, p. 274)
1868	0.0014[a]	Seyd (1868, p. 399)
1905	0.0019	Johnson (1905, p. 90)
1911, pre-World War I	0[b]	Johnson (1911, p. 508), Whitaker (1919, pp. 524, 529)
1928, 1929, 1931	0	Einzig (1928, p. 663; 1929b, p. 95; 1931, pp. 149–50), Spalding (1928a, pp. 81, 84), Swoboda (1928, p. 16)
Import: Packing and cartage in London		
1868	0.0085[c]	Seyd (1868, p. 400)
1892	0.0049[c]	Clare (1906, p. 130)
pre-World War I	0.0049	Whitaker (1919, pp. 531, 533)
1925, 1928	0.0030	Spalding (1928a, pp. 81, 84)
Import: Charges in New York		
1868	0.0060	Seyd (1868, p. 400)
pre-World War I	0.0073	Einzig (1931, p. 148)
1925	0.0097	”
1928[d], 1930[d]	0	Einzig (1929b, p. 95; 1931, p. 149)

Notes:
[a] Excludes charges in, and from Liverpool, as included in freight.
[b] Excludes petty charge.
[c] Excludes charges for carriage to Liverpool, as included in freight.
[d] End of year.

Table 9.4 *Freight, insurance, and handling cost, percent, period averages, 1791–1931*

Period	Freight rate		Insurance rate	Handling				Total[a]	
				Exports		Imports			
	EXP	IMP		O	D	O	D	EXP	IMP
1791–1800	1.0500	1.0500	2.5440	0.1525	0.1416	0.8597	0.2128	3.8881	4.6665
1821–30	0.5863	0.5863	0.6250	0.1525	0.1221	0.7413	0.2128	1.4859	2.1654
1831–40	0.3938	0.3938	0.5250	0.1309	0.0830	0.5039	0.1827	1.1327	1.6054
1841–50	0.3938	0.3938	0.4875	0.0278	0.0461	0.2799	0.0388	0.9552	1.2000
1851–60	0.2494	0.2494	0.3638	0.0043	0.0155	0.0941	0.0060	0.6330	0.7133
1861–70	0.1272	0.1272	0.4592	0.0043	0.0014	0.0085	0.0060	0.5921	0.6009
1871–80	0.1250	0.1250	0.2118	0.0043	0.0014	0.0083	0.0060	0.3425	0.3511
1881–90	0.1250	0.1250	0.1621	0.0046	0.0016	0.0049	0.0060	0.2933	0.2980
1891–1900	0.1395	0.1395	0.1326	0.0050	0.0019	0.0049	0.0073	0.2790	0.2843
1901–10	0.1563	0.1563	0.0500	0.0051	0.0014	0.0049	0.0073	0.2128	0.2185
1911–14[b]	0.1786	0.1786	0.0500	0.0058	0	0.0049	0.0073	0.2344	0.2408
1925[c]–31[b]	0.1896	0.1796	0.0500	0.0056	0	0.0030	0.0043	0.2452	0.2369

Notes:
[a] Freight rate + insurance rate + handling (origin + destination).
[b] Second quarter.
[c] Third quarter.
Legend:
EXP = Exports.
IMP = Imports.
  O = Origin.
  D = Destination.
Source: See text.

(2)   Export: landing charges in Liverpool and delivery in London
1791–1800: The 1821 figure, the earliest known, is applied. *1821–30*: The decline from 0.1416 to 0.0859 percent occurred in mid-1827, by the usual rule, and the weighted average is taken. *1831–40*: Similarly, the switch from 0.0859 to 0.0750 percent "happened" in May 1838 and the average is computed. *1841–50*: The same technique is applied to 0.0750 and 0.0171 percent, with the changeover at the end of 1845. *1851–60*: Similarly for 0.0171 and 0.0014 percent, with the switch at the end of 1859. *1861–80*: The rate of 0.0014 percent applies. *1881–90*: At the end of 1886, 0.0014 increased to 0.0019 percent, by the usual convention, and the appropriate average is taken.

1891–1900: The applicable figure is 0.0019 percent. *1901–10*: The change from 0.0019 percent to zero charge (apart from a petty cost, probably a gratuity) occurred in mid-1908, by convention, and the weighted average of 0.0019 and zero is calculated. *1890–1906*: The figure of 0.0019 percent applies. *1911–14, 1925–31*: Zero cost continued.

(3)   Import: packing and cartage in London
1791–1860: The earliest figure is for 1868, too distant for projection back to 1791–1800. "Packing and cartage in London" is a Britain-based expense, as is "landing charges in Liverpool and delivery in London" on the export side. Further, these costs share three similarities: a freight handling charge, specific to specie, and in the same geographic area. Consider the ratio of the "packing and cartage" to "landing charges" rate in 1868: 0.0085/0.0014 = 6.0714. This factor is used to multiply the 1791–1860 averages of "landing charges" to obtain estimated decadal figures for "packing and cartage."

1861–70: The rate of 0.0085 percent is applicable. *1871–80*: By the usual convention, the switch from 0.0085 to 0.0049 percent occurred in mid-1880, and the duration-weighted average of the two figures is computed. *1881–1914*: The rate is 0.0049 percent uniformly. *1925–31*: The applicable figure is 0.0030 percent.

(4)   Import: charges in New York
1791–1860: By the same logic as above, the ratio of the import "charges in New York" to the export "packing and cartage in New York" rate for 1868, 0.0060/0.0043 = 1.3954, multiplies the "packing and cartage" period averages to obtain estimated figures for "charges in New York." *1861–90*: The rate of 0.0060 percent applies. *1891–1914*: The change from 0.0060 to 0.0073 percent occurred at the end of 1890, by convention, and the latter rate is applicable. *1890–1906*: For January–December 1890, 0.0060 percent; for January 1891–December 1906, 0.0073. Each period average is the duration-weighted average of the two rates.

1925–31: The Federal Reserve Bank not only delivered but also picked up gold free of charge in 1928, with the same beginning date of March a reasonable conjecture. So the rate is 0.0097 percent for May 1925–February 1928, zero for March 1928–August 1931, and for the averages the two rates are weighted by duration.

2.2   Transactions cost: components varying with form of specie

2.2.1   *Export: determination of dominant form of specie*

Arbitrageurs and transferors needed to select their specie medium – the form of specie to be shipped. In principle, the alternatives were domestic coin, foreign coin, or bars.

Until July 30, 1834, when the United States was on an effective silver standard, the alternative forms of specie for outward GTF and GPA (logically STF and SPA, "S" for silver) were all coin: the Spanish silver dollar, the American silver dollar, and the American half-dollar. Silver bars are not mentioned in any documents as an export (or import) medium. It is possible that they were not produced in the United States; certainly they were not provided by the US Mint.

From July 31, 1834, with the United States on an effective gold standard, the alternative specie forms were gold bars and American coin, the latter consisting of the $10 eagle, its fractional denominations ($5 half eagle and $2.50 quarter eagle), and the $20 double eagle (from 1850).

Table 9.5 shows the primary specie export by period from 1791 to 1931 (for now, "Assay Bar Premium" may be ignored). There are three methods of determining this dominant specie form. First, contemporary writings (newspapers, magazines, government documents, books) may state the preferred exportable. Second, they may report on what form of specie was actually exported. Third, the marginal costs of the alternative specie forms may be compared, and the one with the lowest cost deemed dominant. This method emanates from first principles and so is preferred on analytical grounds, but it requires detailed cost data for all alternative specie forms, and such data are not generally available.

In practice, therefore, resort must be had to contemporary reporting, that is, the first and second approaches. In table 9.5, such contemporary information is utilized successfully, providing an unambiguous inference regarding the dominant specie form, for all subperiods except May 2, 1897–June 1, 1899. On the assumptions that contemporary reporting is accurate and that there is rational behavior, the three approaches would give identical results.

During 1791–1834, the Spanish silver dollar was the dominant export.

Table 9.5 *Assay bar premium and dominant export, 1791–1931*

| Period | Assay bar premium[a] | | Dominant export |
	Percent	Source	
Jan. 1, 1791–July 30, 1834	—		Spanish silver dollar[b]
July 31, 1834–May 31, 1882	—		US gold coin[c]
June 1, 1882–March 2, 1891	0	HM (1910, p. 586), NYT (July 2, 1882, p. 9)	US Assay bars[d]
March 3–16, 1891	$\frac{1}{25}$	HM (1910, p. 596), NYT (March 18, 1891, p. 8)	"
March 17, 1891–Nov. 21, 1895	—	NYT (March, 18, 1891, p. 8)	US gold coin[e]
Nov. 22, 1895–March 24, 1896	$\frac{1}{16}$	NYT (Nov. 23, 1895, p. 1)	US Assay bars[f]
March, 25–May 28, 1896	$\frac{3}{16}$[g]	Cross (1923, p. 399)	US gold coin[h]
May 29–June 30, 1896	$\frac{1}{8}$[g]	Cross (1923, p. 399), NYT (May 30, 1896, p. 1)	"
July 1, 1896–May 1, 1897	$\frac{1}{10}$	NYT (July 2, 1896, p. 1)	US Assay bars[i]
May 2, 1897–Jan. 31, 1899	"	"	US gold coin[j]
Feb. 1–March 31, 1899	"	"	US Assay bars[j]
April 1–June 1, 1899	"	"	US gold coin[j]
June 2, 1899–June 17, 1900	"	"	US gold coin[k]
June 18, 1900[l]–July 31, 1914	$\frac{1}{25}$	NYT (May 21, 1908, p. 1)[m]	US Assay bars[n]
April, 28, 1925–Feb. 29, 1928	$\frac{1}{20}$	Miller (1925, p. 144), Spalding (1928a, pp. 81, 84)	US Assay bars[o]
March 1, 1928–Sept. 20, 1931	0	Einzig (1928, p. 663), Whitaker (1933, pp. 360, 364	"

Notes:
a A dash indicates that bars were not obtainable for coin from the Treasury.
b Taxay (1966, p. 125), Smith and Cole (1935, pp. 5, 24), Bolles (1894, vol. II, pp. 170–1), Carothers (1930, pp. 75–8), Reuss (1883, p. 97), Kemmerer (1944, pp. 71–2), Laughlin (1900, p. 53), Hepburn (1924, p. 47).
c Perkins (1975, p. 195), NYT (July 2, 1882, p. 9), *Merchants' Magazine* (Sept. 1848, p. 302).
d NYT (June 2, 1882, p. 1; July 2, 1882, p. 9; June 18, 1890, p. 4; March 18, 1891, p. 8; March 19, 1891, p. 3; March 22, 1891, p. 5).
e NYT (March 19, 1891, p. 3; March 21, 1891, p. 3; July 15, 1892, p. 9; January 21, 1893, p. 8; July 12, 1894, p. 6; December 14, 1894, p. 9; December 15, 1894, p. 1; December 16, 1894, p. 9; December 22, 1894, p. 11; January 17, 1895, p. 3; January 19, 1895, p. 9; January 23, 1895, p. 16; January 24, 1895, p. 13; July 7, 1895, p. 17; August 3, 1895, p. 9; August 9, 1895, p. 8).
f NYT (November 23, 1895, p. 1).
g Increase of $\frac{1}{16}$ to $\frac{3}{16}$ percent incorrectly stated as $\frac{1}{8}$ to $\frac{3}{8}$ in NYT (March 27, 1896, p. 1; March 29, 1896, p. 2); but decline from $\frac{3}{16}$ to $\frac{1}{8}$ correctly reported in NYT (May 30, 1896, p. 1; June 27, 1896, p. 1).
h NYT (March 27, 1896, p. 1; March 29, 1896, p. 2; April 21, 1896, p. 1; May 30, 1896, p. 1; June 13, 1896, p. 1; June 27, 1896, p. 1; June 28, 1896, p. 2; June 30, 1896, p. 1; July 2, 1896, p. 1; July 19, 1896, p. 1).
i NYT (July 18, 1896, p. 1; April 27, 1897, p. 12; May 1, 1897, p. 5).
j See text.
k NYT (June 9, 1899, p. 5; June 13, 1899, p. 12; June 17, 1899, p. 7; December 16, 1899, p. 11; *Banker's Magazine* (June 1900, p. 762), Secretary of the Treasury (1901, p. 333).
l Date of June 18 approximate, based on indirect evidence. NYT (June 19, 1900, p. 10) reports large export of bars withdrawn June 18 from Assay Office. Secretary of the Treasury (1901, p. 333) notes change of premium from $\frac{1}{10}$ to $\frac{1}{25}$ percent in fiscal year ending June 30. *Bankers' Magazine* (June 1900, pp. 761–2) observes the "recent removal" of the $\frac{1}{10}$ percent charge.
m Also, Cross (1923, p. 384), Margraff (1904, p. 233), Deutsch (1910, p. 23), Escher (1910, p. 115; 1918, p. 74), Johnson (1905, pp. 90, 91; 1911, p. 508), Strauss (1908, p. 66), Whitaker (1919, pp. 502, 528, 529). Also, see note *l*.
n NYT (March 7, 1909, p. 8). Also, see notes *l* and *m*.
o *The Economist* (May 2, 1925, p. 885; May 16, 1925, p. 991), Spalding (1928a, p. 81), Einzig (1927a, p. 134).
Legend:
HM = Huntington and Mawhinney.
NYT = *New York Times.*

The reason was twofold. It was not only the principal coin in domestic circulation, but also the highest-denomination such coin. The American silver dollar was not a circulatable part of the currency and indeed not even coined from 1806 (see section 3 of chapter 5). The American half-dollar, requiring double the number of coins than the Spanish dollar for a given value shipment, was subject to greater abrasion (wearing out) and therefore would have a lower value in London, where silver was sold by weight (see (3) below).[13]

From July 31, 1834 to May 31, 1882, the dominant exportable was the eagle in its various denominations. Bars were either not readily obtainable or purchasable only at a high premium. However, beginning June 1, 1882, the US Treasury (New York Assay Office) provided gold bars in exchange for US coin. From then on, these "Assay bars" or "Treasury bars" were a viable export alternative to coin. Contemporary information is quite clear as to which specie form was dominant, bars or coin, from June 1, 1882 to September 20, 1931, with the exception of the May 2, 1897–June 1, 1899 time period, as stated above.

In order to determine from first principles the dominant export in the latter time period (via the third method above), the marginal cost of bars and coin, respectively – that is, the components of transactions cost varying with form of specie – must be obtained. For the remaining subperiods of 1882–1931, these costs either for bars or coin, whichever is dominant, are needed to obtain the gold-export point. Of course, they are also required for the primary export during 1791–1882.

(1)   Deviation of purchase price from mint price

For the period of Spanish-dollar dominance, silver coin (the Spanish dollar or American half-dollar) was always obtainable at par (except during the paper standard of 1814–17) by cashing in notes or deposits at commercial banks. The applicable deviation of the purchase price of specie from its mint price was the premium of the Spanish dollar over the American dollar, which reflected the advantage of the heavier Spanish dollar over the abraded American half-dollar equivalent (with coin sold by weight to London brokers). This premium was a (money or opportunity) cost to exporters, because the Spanish dollar was legal tender at par with the American dollar. Data on the Spanish-dollar premium are in table 9.6, and period averages of the components of transactions cost for specie export are in table 9.7.

1791–1800: The two figures for 1792–1811 – the one the mid-point of the range – are averaged. *1821–30*: The mid-point of the range of the 1827–8 figure is taken. By the usual convention, the Spanish-dollar premium became zero mid-way between 1828 and 1833, at the end of 1830.

Table 9.6 *Deviation of transactions purchase price from mint price, exports,*
1792–1882

Year(s)	Rate (percent)	Source
Spanish dollar dominant export: premium of Spanish over US dollar		
1792–1811	¼–1, ½	Taxay (1966, p. 125), Willem (1959, p. 12)
1827–8	½–1 ¼	Secretary of the Treasury (1830, p. 91)
1833	0	Reuss (1833, p. 97)
Eagle dominant export: commission on sale of specie by brokers[a]		
1835	½	Albion (1939, p. 413)
1851	¼	*Bankers' Magazine* (Oct. 1851, p. 273)
1865, 1868	⅛	Cornwallis (1879, p. 12), Perkins (1975, p. 211)
Eagle dominant export: tax on sale of specie by brokers		
June 30, 1864–	⅟₂₀	Sanger (1864, pp. 223, 273)
March 2, 1865		
March 3, 1865–	⅟₁₀	Sanger (1865, pp. 469, 478; 1870, p. 256)
Sept. 30, 1870		

Notes:
[a] Applicable during periods when both New York banks and US Treasury
suspended specie payments.

From July 31, 1834, to May 31, 1882, when eagles were the dominant
export, gold coin was always obtainable from commercial banks on
demand, either directly or via the Treasury – except during periods of a
paper standard. During 1834–61 the banks cashed their notes and deposits
at par directly in coin, and from 1879 onward they cashed them either in
coin or in paper currency redeemable at the Treasury or at a national bank.
In the second half of 1861 and from 1879 onward, coin was always obtainable from the Treasury on demand at par in exchange for redeemable paper
currency. So there was no deviation of the transactions price from mint
price in acquiring coin from commercial banks or the Treasury.

However, during periods when the New York banks suspended specie
payments, there was a cost in purchasing eagles, namely, broker's commission charge, listed in table 9.6. *1831–40*: The commission rate of 0.5 percent
applies for one year (May 10, 1837–May 9, 1838), and the average is taken
with a zero cost for the rest of the decade. *1841–50*: No suspension and
therefore zero cost. *1851–60*: A commission of 0.5 percent was the cost of
purchasing eagles during October 14–December 13, 1857, when the New
York banks suspended specie payments. Again the duration-weighted
average is computed, with zero for the rest of the decade.

Table 9.7 *Transactions cost, exports, percent, period averages, 1791–1931*

Period	Purchase price	Abrasion	Sale price	Mint charges	Currency premium	Exchange-rate cost	Total GPA[a]	Total GTF[b]
1791–1800	0.5625	0	0.2500	0	0	0.6289	1.4414	0.1836
1821–30	0.8750	0.0671	0.2500	0	0	0.3641	1.5562	0.8280
1831–40	0.0500	0.0747	0.1603	0.0586	0	0.2506	0.5942	0.0930
1841–50	0	0.0742	0.1605	0.0913	0	0.2506	0.5766	0.0754
1851–60	0.0042	0.0239	0.2797	0.0137	0	0.2506	0.5721	0.0709
1861–70	0.1717	0.0429	0.3007	0	0	0.2506	0.7659	0.2647
1871–80	0.1000	0.0474	0.3007	0	0.0087	0.2296	0.6864	0.2272
1881–90	0	0.0042	0.1801	0	0	0.1184	0.3027	0.0659
1891–1900	0.0145	0.0800	0.1791	0	0.0178	0.0236	0.3150	0.2678
1901–10	0.0400	0	0.1583	0	0.0218	0.0051	0.2252	0.2150
1911–14[c]	0.0400	0	0.1605	0	0	0.0051	0.2056	0.1954
1925[d]–31[c]	0.0222	0	0.1605	0.0122	0	0.0086	0.2035	0.1884

Notes:

[a] Purchase price + abrasion + sale price + mint charges + currency premium + exchange-rate cost.

[b] Purchase price + abrasion + sale price + mint charges + currency premium–exchange-rate cost (from Table 9.13).

[c] Second quarter.

[d] Third quarter.

Legend: GPA = Gold-point arbitrage.

GTF = Transfer of funds.

Source: See text.

1861–70: The commission to purchase eagles during the greenback period, December 30, 1861–December 31, 1878, was 0.125 percent. There is zero commission for the rest of 1861, and the weighted average is 0.1125 percent for the decade. Another component of purchase cost was a tax on the sale of specie by brokers and bankers – 0.05 percent by the Act of June 30, 1864, increased to 0.1 percent by the Act of March 3, 1865, and repealed as of October 1, 1870, by the Act of July 14, 1870 (see table 9.6). The duration-weighted average of 0.05, 0.1, and zero percent for the 1861–70 decade is 0.0592 percent, which is added to the commission cost. *1871–80*: The commission of 0.125 percent to purchase eagles during the greenback period is averaged with zero afterwards.

From June 1, 1882, when the New York Assay Office first provided an immediate exchange of bars for US coin, these two forms of gold vied for dominance among exporters of specie. There was no purchase cost of coin, but Assay bars were provided only at a premium, this "bar charge" varying over time and ranging from zero to "infinity" (the Treasury refusing to sell bars). This percentage premium, a component of the marginal cost of Assay bars, is shown by subperiod in table 9.5. An obvious rule of thumb is discerned from the table. Depending on whether the bar premium is below or above 0.1 percent, bars (meaning Assay bars) or coin are the dominant export.[14] A bar charge exactly at 0.1 percent generates ambiguity, in particular, for the May 2, 1897–June 1, 1899 period.

From 1881 onward, purchase cost for a given subperiod is either the bar premium or zero, depending on whether bars or coin are dominant.

1881–90: Zero cost, with coin (dominant until June 1, 1882) obtainable at par and bars (dominant from that date) at zero premium. *1890–1906 (monthly series)*: *January 1890–February 1891*: Zero cost, with bars at zero premium. *March 1891*: Average of 0.04 percent premium for 14 days and zero for 17 days. *April 1891–October 1895*: Zero cost, coin dominant. *November 1895*: Average of 0.0625 percent premium for nine days and zero for 21 days. *December 1895–February 1896*: Bar premium of 0.0625 percent. *March 1896*: Average of 0.0625 percent premium for 24 days and zero for six days. *April–June 1896*: Zero cost, coin dominant. *July 1896–April 1897*: Premium of 0.1 percent applicable.

May 1897–June 1899: Cost of 0.1 percent when bars dominant, zero when coin dominant. For month-by-month determination, see (4) below. *July 1899–May 1900*: Zero cost, coin dominant. *June 1900*: Average of 0.04 percent premium for 13 days and zero for 17 days. *July 1900–December 1906*: Bar premium of 0.04 percent. *1901–10, 1911–14*: With bars dominant, its premium of 0.04 percent is applicable.

1925–31: Assay bars were obtained from the Treasury at a premium of 0.05 percent through February 1928, and afterward from the Federal

Reserve Bank of New York at par. The March 1928 date for the switch in source of supply emanates from Einzig's observation that in 1928 the Federal Reserve Bank of New York delivered gold "free on board" (meaning neither bar nor handling charge) combined with no such charge known for May–June and no recorded gold exports to Britain until March (see (1) in section 2.1.3 above). For the period figures, the duration-weighted averages of 0.05 percent and zero are computed.

(2) Abrasion

Abrasion, the reduction in coin weight below the standard for which the mint price is computed, is a component of the marginal cost of coin but not of bars. The act of rubbing together in circulation and even in shipment wears down coin. This depletion may be termed unintended abrasion. In colonial times and even later, the techniques of clipping, filing, and sweating illegally removed some specie content, thus reducing the coin weight, prior to spending the coin. Such intentional abrasion was as prevalent in England (and other countries) as in America.

Abraded coin remains legal tender if above "least current weight" and therefore legally must circulate at par (face value) domestically. Even if below the limit of tolerance – in which case the various Mint Acts set the value in proportion to actual weight – to expect "merchants and ordinary citizens to weigh and calculate the value of every coin they receive" (Taxay, 1966, p. 66) was unrealistic and coins often nevertheless were received at par. However, abroad (in London) the coin was sold by weight – either directly per gross ounce or, treated as bullion, per ounce of fine metal – and therefore was worth less than face value.

Abrasion, therefore, reduces the price per nominal unit of domestic coin corresponding to the London price per ounce (gross or fine) of coin. The percentage abrasion (weight deficiency with respect to standard weight) constitutes an addition to cost for export of domestic coin. To July 30, 1834, this coin was the Spanish dollar; afterward it was the eagle. Data on abrasion from 1791 to 1905 (encompassing all the periods of coin dominance) are in table 9.8.

Abrasion is eliminated by shipping bars; it can be reduced by obtaining high-denomination coin. Double-eagles were preferred over eagles and eagles over half-eagles (the lowest-denomination coin exported) – on the principle that the fewer the coins for a given value shipment, the less the abrasion.[15] Beginning March 1891, however, arbitrageurs and transferors faced a Treasury policy of providing only a mixture of denominations (half-eagle, eagle, and double-eagle) in proportion to the stock at hand.[16]

1791–1800: Abrasion is deemed zero, because the base is the observed average weight of the Spanish dollar in circulation. *1821–30*: The figure of

Table 9.8 *Abrasion of dominant coin export, 1791–1905 (enveloping periods of dominance over bars)*

Month or year(s)	Coin	Rate (percent)	Source
1791	Spanish dollar	0[a]	*International monetary conference* [b] (1879, p. 457)
1821–9[c]	"	0.0671[a]	Secretary of the Treasury (1830, pp. 65–6)
1833	"	0.0769[a]	Reuss (1833, p. 97)
1848	eagle	0.0742[d]	*Merchants' Magazine* (Sept. 1848, p. 303)
1851	"	0.0186	*Bankers' Magazine* (Oct. 1851, p. 274)
1862	"	0.0111[e]	Bolles (1894, vol. III, p. 373)
1868	"	0.0689	Seyd (1868, p. 399)
1882	"	0.0298	NYT (July 2, 1882, p. 9)
March 1891	"	0.08	NYT (March 22, 1891, p. 5)
Dec. 1894	"	0.0930, 0.1674[f]	NYT (Dec. 14, 1894, p. 9)
Jan. 1895	"	0.1651	NYT (Jan. 19, 1895, p. 9)
Aug. 1895	"	0.0930, 0.1860[g]	NYT (Aug. 9, 1895, p. 8)
March 1896	"	0.0514	NYT (March 27, 1896, p. 2)
June 1899	"	0, 0.05–0.15[h]	NYT (June 13, 1899, p. 12)
Dec. 1899	"	0[i]	NYT (Dec. 16, 1899, p. 11)
1905	"	0.07	Johnson (1905, p. 91)

Notes:
[a] With respect to 416-grain standard.
[b] Report of Alexander Hamilton on the establishment of a mint.
[c] Approximate dates.
[d] Includes deficiency in fineness.
[e] Pertains to double-eagle.
[f] Former figure is after sorting and weighing Treasury delivery (latter figure).
[g] Abrasion "often" at latter value; former figure pertains to "recent deliveries."
[h] Gold export described as "practically unabraded" (implicitly an unusual occurrence); so abrasion in range avoided.
[i] Exported coin described as "full weight," implicitly an unusual event.
Legend: NYT = *New York Times*.

0.0671 percent applies. *1831–40*: Abrasion of the Spanish dollar increased from 0.0671 to 0.0769 percent mid-way between 1829 and 1833, in mid-1831, by the usual convention. Beginning July 31, 1834, abrasion of the eagle, at 0.0742 percent, is pertinent. The duration-weighted average of the three figures is computed.

1841–50: The 0.0742-percent rate (for September 1848) pertains to eagles melted down to be sold as bullion to the Bank of England. The 0.0186 figure (for October 1851) and all subsequent numbers pertain solely to abrasion – applicable to eagles sold by weight to the Bank. When did eagles begin to be sold by weight? According to Sayers (1986, p. 48), the Bank first began to deal in foreign gold coin "in 1852 or earlier," and in that year prices for such coin were set according to a specific criterion (see (3) below). It is reasonable to assume that eagles were sold exclusively as bullion until mid-1852. So for 1841–50 abrasion is 0.0742 percent.

1851–60: Abrasion of 0.0742 percent applies to mid-1852, followed by 0.0186, falling to 0.0111 at the beginning of 1857 (by the adopted rule). The duration-weighted average of the three figures is taken. *1861–70*: The increase from 0.0111 to 0.0689 percent happened in mid-1865, by convention, and the appropriate average is computed. *1871–80*: Abrasion is deemed to have changed from 0.0689 to 0.0298 percent in mid-1875, and the weighted average is taken. *1881–90*: With bars dominant (and therefore abrasion zero) from June 1882, the weighted average of 0.0298 percent with zero is calculated.

1890–1906 (monthly series): The basic strategy is to interpolate linearly between dates for which data are available. *January 1890–February 1891*: With bars dominant, abrasion is zero. *March 1891*: Average of zero (bars dominant, 16 days) and 0.08 percent (15 days). *April 1891–November 1894*: Values determined by linear interpolation between 0.08 (March 1891) and 0.1674 percent (December 1894). *December 1894*: 0.0930 percent, because that is the reduced abrasion from 0.1674, after having sorted and weighed coin obtained from the Treasury.

January 1895: 0.1651 percent. *February–July 1895*: Figures result from linear interpolation between 0.1651 (January 1895) and 0.1860 (August 1895). *August 1895*: 0.0930 percent. *September–October 1895*: Values determined by linear interpolation between 0.0930 (August 1895) and 0.0514 (March 1896). *November 1895*: Figure from same interpolation modified by multiplicative factor 0.7 (21/30), because nine days involve bar dominance. *January–February 1896*: Zero, bars dominant. *March 1896*: Average of 0.0514 percent (seven days) and zero (24 days).

April–June 1896: Values obtained by linear interpolation between 0.0514 (March 1896) and 0.075 (June 1899). The latter figure is within the range of 0.05–0.15 percent given for June 1899; but it appears appropriate to reduce the range to 0.05-0.10, to yield a mid-point of 0.075 percent. The reason is the consistency of 0.075 with the closest estimate after June 1899, 0.07 percent in 1905. *July 1896–April 1897*: Zero cost, bars dominant.

May 1897–May 1899: For each month, there are two possibilities: the value obtained by the linear interpolation given above, if coin is dominant; zero, if bars are dominant. For May 1897, the former value is modified by the multiplicative factor 0.9677 (30/31), because for May 1 bars are known to be dominant. The dominance pattern of bars and coin is determined in (4) below. *June 1899*: zero abrasion for entire month, whether bars or coin dominant on June 1. *July 1899–May 1900*: Abrasion of 0.075 percent is assumed. *June 1900*: Average of 0.075 percent (17 days, coin dominant) and zero (13 days, bars dominant). *July 1900–December 1906*: Zero, bars dominant.

1901–14, 1925–31: Zero, bars dominant.

(3)   Deviation of sale price from mint price

Divergence of the sale price for specie in London from the mint price is a component of transactions cost, and is shown by period average in table 9.7. During the period of Spanish-silver-dollar dominance, this dollar was sold in the London market by weight at the market price. The market price of silver with respect to gold is the basis of the definition of parity (see section 3 of chapter 5). Therefore, by construction, silver was sold at par; there is no deviation from the mint price. However, there was a brokerage fee on silver transactions in London – 0.25 percent in 1830 (Perkins, 1975, p. 192) and 0.125 percent in 1833 (Reuss, 1833, p. 97). This fee is indeed a deviation of the sale price from mint price.

1791–1800, 1821–30: The fee of 0.25 percent is projected back to 1791. *1831–40*: By the usual convention, the decline in brokerage from 0.25 to 0.125 percent occurred at the end of 1831. Beginning August (actually July 31) 1834, the dominant exportable was eagles, melted down, formed into bars, and sold as bullion to the Bank of England. At this time and in subsequent decades, the Bank of England was virtually the only destination of gold exported to Britain.[17] The price paid by the Bank was 77s. 9d. per standard ounce (see section 5 of chapter 4), a deviation of 0.1605 percent from the mint price of 77s. 10.5d. The decadal average cost, shown in table 9.7, is the duration-weighted average of 0.25, 0.125, and 0.1605 percent. *1841–50*: With the Bank price continuing to be 77s. 9d., cost of 0.1605 percent applies.

It is reasonable to assume that it was in mid-1852 that direct sale of eagles to the Bank by weight without assay or melting, for immediate payment in pounds, commenced: "the Bank first began (in 1852 or earlier) to deal in foreign gold coin . . . In 1852 the Bank calculated appropriate buying and selling prices for the principal foreign gold coins, which would leave shippers indifferent between handling these or other forms of gold" (Sayers, 1986, p. 48). The history of the Bank purchase price of eagles has a dichotomy. First, there was the normal or usual price, that could remain the same for a substantial period, but was subject to occasional change over time. Second, there were temporary prices, that generally lasted less than a month.

Table 9.9 exhibits both the normal and temporary price, during periods when the eagle was actually or potentially dominant over bars. The purchase cost is the percentage deviation of the actual price from the mint-price equivalent of 76s. 5.50909 . . . d. (5 28/55d.) per ounce. *1851–60*: It appears that 76s. 2.75d. was the price established in mid-1852. So the weighted average of 0.1605 percent (applicable to mid-1852) and 0.3007 percent (reigning thereafter) is taken. *1861–80*: The 0.3007-percent cost continued.[18]

Beginning June 1, 1882, and continuing to 1914, Assay bars vied with eagles as the dominant export. During 1925–31, these bars were the only export. The Bank's purchase price of bars, when it was actually or potentially dominant over eagles during these time periods, is shown in table 9.10. The legal minimum, and the normal, price of bars was 77s. 9d. per standard (11/12th fine) ounce. Temporary prices could last for some months. *1881–90*: Cost is the duration-weighted average of three figures: 0.3007 percent applying to May 31, 1882, coin being still dominant; 0.1605 percent pertaining to the rest of the decade (bars dominant at normal price) except February 1890, for which 0.1605 is averaged with 0.1070 percent. The reason for the latter averaging is the adopted procedure that if information on the duration of a temporary price is unavailable, it is assumed to persist for half a month, followed by return to the normal price.

Before proceeding, two questions require answer. First, did the Bank continue to be the destination of gold shipped from the United States? The answer is that arbitrageurs and shippers did have the option of dealing with the London private (open) gold market, via bullion brokers. It may be that there were occasions when such private sale was of greater volume than that with the Bank.[19] However, the Bank was the primary destination prior to World War I and the sole destination in the interwar period.[20] Arbitrageurs and transferors avoided selling gold to the market, because the Bank provided a perfectly elastic demand at its official buying price, while market demand above that price was unpredictable and usually limited (Einzig, 1931, p. 160).

Second, what were the limits to the Bank purchase prices of bars and coin? The price of bars had a legal minimum of 77s. 9d. per standard ounce, imposed by the Bank Charter Act of 1844. There was no constraint on the maximum price, except that it would have been economically

Table 9.9 *Bank purchase price of eagles by weight, 1868–1914 (periods of actual and potential dominance over bars)*

Date	Per ounce: 76s. and d.	Deviation from mint price[a] (percent)	Source
Normal price			
1868	2¾	0.3007	Seyd (1868, pp. 245, 399)
1892, 1895	3½	0.2190	Clare (1906, pp. 68–9), NYT (Aug. 9, 1895, p. 8), Simon (1968, p. 406)
Pre-World War I	4	0.1645	Whitaker (1919, p. 524), Cross (1923, p. 407)
Temporary prices			
May 1891[b]	4–6½	0.1645, − 0.1080	Clare (1906, p. 69), Cross (1923, p. 407)
June 1891[c]	5	0.0555	Cross (1923, p. 407)
July 1895[d]	3¼	0.2462	Simon (1968, p. 406)
Aug. 1895[e]	3½, 3¾	0.2190, 0.1917	Simon (1968, p. 407)
Sept. 1895	4[f]	0.1645	Simon (1968, p. 408)
April 1898	6[g]	− 0.0535	Sayers (1936, p. 88)
June 1899	"	"	Sayers (1936, p. 90)
Oct. 1899	3½[h]	0.2190	Sayers (1936, p. 91)
Dec. 1899	6[g]	− 0.0535	Sayers (1936, p. 91), NYT (Dec. 16, 1899, p. 11)
Jan. 1900	5[i]	0.0555	Sayers (1936, p. 91)
Feb. 1900	4½[i]	0.1100	"
March 1900	4[i]	0.1645	"
May 1900	6[g]	− 0.0535	Sayers (1936, p. 92)

Notes:
[a] 76 s. 5 ²⁸⁄₅₅d. = 917.50909d.
[b] Price raised to 4d. on May 6, gradually increased until 6½d. in mid-month.
[c] Price reduced to 5d. during first week and shortly after to 3½d.
[d] Price reduced from 3½d. on July 29.
[e] Price raised to 3½d. during week ending August 15 and to 3¾d. in following week.
[f] Increase from 3¾d. in last half of month.
[g] "Higher" or "advanced" price noted by Sayers is assumed to be 6d., as that price is known for December 1899.
[h] Reduced price for eagle assumed to be former normal price.
[i] Stepwise price reductions (at end of January, then February and March) noted by Sayers, assumed to follow pattern of 1d. in first month, ½d. in each subsequent month.
Legend: NYT = *New York Times*.

Table 9.10 *Bank purchase price of bars,*[a] 1882–1931 (periods of actual and potential dominance over eagles)

Period	Price Per standard ounce: 77s. and d.	Deviation from mint price[b] (percent)	Source
1882–1931	9[c]	0.1605	
Feb. 1890[d]	9½	0.1070	Sayers (1936, p. 76)
Oct. 1898[e]	9½[f]	"	Sayers (1936, pp. 89–90)
Feb.– April 1899[g]	9¾[h]	0.0803	Sayers (1936, p. 90)
1901[i]	9¼[f]	0.1338	Sayers (1936, p. 94)
1902[j]	9⅛[f]	0.1471	"

Notes:
[a] Bank bids in London gold market excluded.
[b] 77s. 10½d. = 934.5d.
[c] Normal (and legal minimum) price.
[d] Change from 77s. 9d. made in middle of month.
[e] End of month.
[f] Sayers' vocabulary of "premium," "small premium," "fractional premium" translated into ½d., ¼d., ⅛d., respectively.
[g] All of February and March, early April.
[h] Price ranging up to this level and possibly higher.
[i] Through "greater part" of year.
[j] Frequently during first half of year, ending early-to-mid June.

disadvantageous to the Bank to buy bars at a higher price than its minimum selling price of bars. The latter price was 77s. 10.5d., not so coincidentally the mint price, and in fact this was the Bank's maximum purchase price (Sayers, 1936, p. 82).

The Bank's buying price for foreign coin had an effective minimum, albeit one founded on economics rather than law. The seller of eagles to the Bank always had the option of melting it, refining it from 9/10th to 11/12th fineness, casting it into bars, and selling it at the statutory minimum price for bars. While the price of 77s. 9d. for bars 11/12th fine is equivalent to 76s. 4.03636 . . . d. (4 2/55d.) for gold 9/10th fine, the effective minimum price for eagles was only 76s. 3.5d. in 1891–1914, because of allowances for direct mint expenses and associated interest loss (Whitaker, 1919, pp. 506–7; Sayers, 1936, p. 72). The maximum buying price for American coin again would not long exceed the Bank's minimum selling price of same; the former was 76s. 6.5d. and existed only for parts of May and June 1891 (see below and table 9.9), the latter was 76s. 6d. (see table 9.12).

1890–1906 (monthly series): *January 1890*: Cost is 0.1605 percent. Bars dominant to March 16, 1891. *February 1890*: Average of 0.1070 and 0.1605 percent. *March 1890–February 1891*: 0.1605. *March 1891*: Average of 0.1605 (16 days, bars dominant) and 0.2190 (15 days, coin dominant, new normal price). *April 1891, July 1891–June 1895*: 0.2190 percent. Coin dominant to November 21, 1895. *May 1891*: Average of 3.5d. (0.2190 percent) for five days, average (4d., 6.5d.) = (0.1645, −0.1080) for ten days, 6.5d. (−0.1080) for 16 days. The 76s. component of price is omitted, as in table 9.9. *June 1891*: Average of 6.5d. (−0.1080) for five days, 5d. (0.0555) for five days, and 3.5d. (0.2190) for 20 days.

July 1895: Average of 3.5d. (0.2190) for 28 days and 3.25d. (0.2462) for three days. *August 1895*: Average of 3.25d. for 11 days, 3.5d. for seven days, and 3.75d. for 13 days. *September 1895*: It is assumed that 3.75d. returned to 3.5d. in the last half of the month and in equal durations at 3.75d., 4d. and 3.5d. Therefore average of 20 days at 3.75d., five days at 4d., and five days at 3.5d. *October 1895*: 0.2190 percent, normal price. *November 1895*: average of normal price of coin (0.2190 percent, 21 days) and of bars (0.1605 percent, nine days). Bars dominant from November 22, 1895 to March 24, 1896. *December 1895–February 1896*: 0.1605 percent.

March 1896: Average of normal price of bars (0.1605, 24 days) and new normal price of coin (0.1645, seven days). Coin dominant March 25–June 30, 1896. *April–June 1896*: 0.1645 percent. *July 1896–April 1897*: 0.1605 percent. Bars dominant July 1, 1896–May 1, 1897.

For May 2, 1897–June 1, 1899, the pattern of bars, coin dominance is derived in (4) below. For bars the primary export, sale cost is 0.1605 percent for all months with the following exceptions. *October 1898*: 0.1536 percent, average of 0.1605 (27 days) and 0.1070 (four days). *February–March 1899*: 0.0803 percent. *April 1899*: 0.1418 percent, average of 0.0803 (seven days) and 0.1605 (23 days). For coin dominant, sale cost is 0.1645 percent for all months except the following. *May 1897*: 0.1644 percent, average of 0.1605 (one day, bars dominant) and 0.1645 (30 days, coin dominant). *April 1898*: 0.0555 percent, average of 0.1645 and -0.0535.

From June 2, 1899, dominance is predetermined. *June 1899*: 0.0555 percent, as for April 1898, if coin dominant on June 1; 0.0554 (0.1605 substituting for 0.1645 on June 1), if bars dominant on that date. Coin dominant to June 17, 1900. *July–September, November 1899, April 1900*: 0.1645 percent. *October 1899*: Average of 0.2190 and 0.1645. *December 1899*: Average of 0.1645 and −0.0535, assuming the rise in price occurred in mid-month. *January 1900*: Average of −0.0535 (24 days) and 0.0555 (seven days). *February 1900*: Average of 0.0555 and 0.1100, assuming the price

reduction occurred in mid-month. *March 1900*: Average of 0.1100 and
0.1645, again with the price reduction in mid-month. *May 1900*: Average of
0.1645 and -0.0535.

June 1900: Average of 0.1645 (17 days) and 0.1605 (13 days). Bars dominant from June 18, 1900 onward. *July–December 1900, August–December
1901, July 1902–December 1906*: 0.1605 percent. *January–July 1901*: 0.1338
percent. *January–May 1902*: 0.1471. *June 1902*: Average of 0.1471 (ten
days) and 0.1605 (20 days). *July 1902–December 1906*: 0.1605.

Returning to period averages, *1901–10*: Monthly average, where value for
January 1907–December 1910 is 0.1605. *1911–14, 1925–31*: Cost of 0.1605
percent applies uniformly.

(4)   Determinant of dominant export, 1897–9
The dominant exportable over May 2, 1897–June 1, 1899 can now be determined. The approach is a direct comparison of the marginal cost (MC) of
bars with that of coin. The MC of bars is the sum of the purchase cost,
always 0.1 percent, and the sale cost, 0.1605 percent except for October 1898
(0.1536), February–March 1899 (0.0803), and April 1899 (0.1418).
Therefore bar MC is 0.2605 percent for all months except October 1898
(0.2536), February–March 1899 (0.1803), and April 1899 (0.2418).

Coin MC is the sum of abrasion and sale cost. Sale cost is 0.1645 percent
for all months except April 1898 (0.0555 percent). With the exception of the
four special months, the abrasion value leading to equal MCs is 0.2605 −
0.1645 = 0.0960 percent, which uniformly exceeds the abrasion calculated
in (2) above. For April 1898, the critical value is 0.2605 − 0.0555 percent =
0.2050 percent; for April 1899, it is 0.2418 − 0.1645 = 0.0773 percent – both
again exceeding the computed abrasion. Therefore for all these months coin
is the dominant exportable.

The result is different for February–March 1899. The critical value is
0.1803 − 0.1645 = 0.0158, less than computed abrasion of (2) above. Only
for these two months are bars dominant.

Missing links may now be provided. Table 9.5 is fully justified;, the subperiods May 2, 1897–June 1, 1899 are determined as coin-dominant with
the exception of February–March 1899. The 1890–1906 monthly series for
purchase cost, in (1) above, is completed as follows. *May 1897*: Average of
0.1 percent (1 day, bars dominant) and zero (30 days, coin dominant). *June
1897–January 1899, April 1899–May 1900*: zero (coin dominant).
February–March 1899: 0.1 percent (bars dominant). *June 1900*: Average of
0.04 percent (13 days, bars dominant) and zero (17 days, coin dominant).
Omitted period averages are calculated. *1891–1900 and 1890–1906*: Average
of monthly values for the respective period.

Abrasion, left unfinished in (2) above, has its 1890–1906 monthly series completed as follows. *June 1897–January 1899, April–May 1899*: Value given by linear interpolation between 0.0514 (March 1896) and 0.075 (June 1899). *May 1897*: Average of interpolative value (30 days, coin dominant) and zero (one day, bars dominant). *February–March 1899*: Zero (bars dominant). Period averages, *1890–1906 and 1891–1900*, are again the average of monthly values.

The 1890–1906 monthly series for sale cost, in (3) above, is easily completed. For the dates where alternative values are presented, depending on which specie form is dominant, the bar value pertains to February–March 1899, the coin value for all other months. Period averages, *1890–1906 and 1891–1900*, are again the average of monthly values.

2.2.2 Import: determination of dominant form of specie

Just as for export from the United States, the American importer had to determine the form of specie for GTF or GPA. From 1791 to 1834 (July 30), the United States was on a silver standard and the dominant import was silver dollars, obtained from the London market.[21] In principle, these dollars could be either Spanish or American. However, it is reasonable to take the Spanish dollar as the primary import, because (i) the evidence clearly points to the Spanish dollar as the dominant *export*, and (ii) Spanish dollars arrived in London from various sources, not just the United States.

The Bank of England did not begin selling, as well as buying, foreign coin until (it may be assumed) mid-1852. It is likely that the Bank did not regularly (if at all) sell bars in this period. (By the Act of 1844 it was obliged to buy, but not sell, bars.) So until mid-1852 sovereigns were the only form of gold importable, and from July 31, 1834 they were the primary import.

From mid-1852 to 1914, arbitrageurs and transferors could select their gold-import medium from three alternatives: sovereigns, bars, and eagles. These specie forms differed in their desirability in availability and cost, the latter broken down by component. The cost elements of concern were (i) the deviation of the purchase price from the mint price in London, (ii) abrasion, and (iii) the mint expenses and waiting-time interest-loss in the United States.

Sovereigns had the double advantage over bars and American coin of being always available and at par from the Bank of England (in redemption of its notes). In contrast, bars could be procured only if the Bank was willing to sell them and eagles were obtainable only from about mid-1852 and if in stock. Furthermore, bars and eagles were sold generally at a premium above the mint price or mint-price equivalent.

However, eagles were almost invariably the dominant importable, because of two great advantages over sovereigns and bars. First, at the other side of the Atlantic, the coin could simply be deposited at American banks. Sovereigns and bars had to be taken to the US Mint or New York Assay Office for conversion to coin, and the importer suffered both direct mint expenses and interest loss from waiting time. Second, abrasion (as long as the coin did not fall below least current weight) constituted a subtraction from cost, with the eagles bought by weight in London and circulatable at par in the United States. For bars, the element of abrasion (at zero) neither added to nor subtracted from cost.

For sovereigns, however, abrasion was a positive addition to cost and the amount of abrasion could be relatively substantial compared to American coin. The reason is that the sovereign (at $4.86656), as the highest-denomination British coin, was comparable to the half-eagle ($5.00), the lowest-denomination coin issued to American exporters – who shipped mainly eagles and double-eagles.[22] The rule to be recalled is that the greater the number of coins constituting a given value of shipment, the higher the abrasion.

Under normal conditions from mid-1852 to 1914, therefore, eagles were the preferred form of gold import. Of course, this was because the Bank usually stood ready to provide them at terms that, while varying, were more advantageous to arbitrageurs and transferors than bars and sovereigns. "The Bank . . . would generally prefer to part with foreign coin rather than sovereigns" (Sayers, 1936, p. 72, n. 5). Sovereigns could be needed for note redemption and their minting was costly, whereas eagles at hand did not serve as a legal medium for note redemption and they could be reacquired by offering a sufficiently high purchase price. The same comment as for eagles applies to bars, but "in ordinary times the amount [of bars] sold is small" (Whitaker, 1919, p. 507).

In 1925–31 the situation differed. All the evidence is that bars constituted the sole gold medium for transferors and arbitrageurs (whether for import or export) throughout the period.[23] The authorities provided sufficiently favorable prices for bars so that arbitrageurs did not even need to consider coin as an option.

(1)   Deviation of purchase price from mint price
The purchase cost of specie imports, by period average, is presented in table 9.13. From 1791 to 1834 (July 30), when the Spanish silver dollar was the dominant import, it was bought "at par" in the London market (by construction of parity, as for export). So there was zero deviation from mint price; but brokerage, the same as for sale of silver, constituted a purchase cost. *1791–1800, 1821–30*: 0.25 percent. *1831 40*: Duration-weighted average of 0.25 percent (1831), 0.125 percent (1832–July 30, 1834), and zero (July 31, 1834–40, sovereigns dominant, at zero purchase cost). *1841–50*: zero (sovereigns, zero cost).

Beginning mid-1852, both American gold coin and (it may be assumed) gold bars were available not only from the Bank but also from the London market. It is reasonable to assume that shippers dealt primarily with the Bank, because they thereby avoided brokerage and also had a greater assurance of availability of supply.

The Bank's selling prices of bars and coin, like its buying prices, were subject to upper and lower limits. The upper limit for each form of gold existed because of the legally guaranteed option of private parties to redeem sovereigns with their notes. The maximum recorded price for bars was 78s. 1d. per standard (11/12th fine) ounce, but the binding constraint was probably 78s. 0.5d. It exceeded the mint price, 77s. 10.5d., because of the abrasion of sovereigns obtained by way of redemption (Whitaker, 1919, pp. 559–60; Sayers, 1936, p. 82). For the upper limit to the price of eagles, see (2) below.

The lower limit to the selling price of bars was probably the minimum recorded price, 77s. 10.5d., because (1) this was also the Bank's maximum buying price, and (2) the Bank was required to provide sovereigns at this price (Sayers, 1936, p. 82). The lower limit to the price of eagles may have been the "normal" price, that changed over time (see table 9.11). It would have been economically unwise for the Bank's eagle selling price ever to be below the current buying price (see table 9.9).

From mid-1852 to 1914, eagles were generally the American importer's preferred form of gold. Table 9.11 shows data on the Bank's selling price of eagles during this time period, separated into normal price and temporary prices. In 1852 the Bank set the selling (and buying) price of eagles to leave shippers indifferent between that and other forms of gold. This price was to be altered from time to time to match changes in conditions, for example, in regulations of the foreign (US) mint. Significant changes in US mint charges were (1) the imposition of a charge of 0.5 percent for coining effective June 1, 1853 (Act of February 21, 1853), (2) reduction of the charge to 0.2 percent effective April 1, 1873 (Act of February 12, 1873), and (3) elimination of the charge (Act of January 14, 1875).[24]

The earliest-known price, 76s. 6.5d., reported in 1868, was in effect during the 0.5-percent seigniorage period. On June 1, 1853 – a built-in lag from the February 21 enactment of the 1853 Act – the Bank may be assumed to have increased its selling price of eagles to 76s. 6.5d., from 76s. 6d.

When did the price change back to 76s. 6d., the normal price as of December 1890? This could have been when the charge was reduced (1873) or when eliminated (1875). Assume the latter, as the more-noticeable event, and allow a recognition-and-reaction lag of 2.5 months. So 76s. 6d. is assumed to have become the normal price on April 1, 1875.[25] The next switch in normal price may be assumed to have occurred in mid-1891 (6d. to 6.5d.), followed by mid-1892 (6.5 to 7d.). Normal prices by period are

Table 9.11 *Bank selling price of eagles, 1868–1914*

Date	Price Per ounce: 76s. and d.	Deviation from mint price[a] (percent)	Source
Normal price			
1868	6½	0.1080	Seyd (1868, pp. 245, 400)
Dec. 1890	6	0.0535	Sayers (1936, p. 77)
1892	6½–7	0.1080–0.1625	Clare (1906, pp. 68–9, 130)
Oct. 1897, pre-World War I	7	0.1625	Sayers (1936, p. 87), Whitaker (1919, pp. 507, 533)
Temporary prices			
Oct. 1890	7–8[b]	0.1625–0.2715	Cross (1923, p. 382), Sayers (1936, p. 77)
Dec. 1890,[c] Aug.–Sept. 1906[d]	8½	0.3260	Sayers (1936, pp. 77, 96)
July 1891[e]	—	—	Sayers (1936, p. 78)
Jan. 1893[f]	8	0.2715	"
Aug. 1893,[g] Sept. 1896, Oct. 1897, April 1900,[g] April 1910[g]	7½	0.2170	Sayers (1936, pp. 79, 80, 86, 87)
Aug. 1896[h]	8, 7½. 7	0.2715, 0.2170, 0.1625	Sayers (1936, p. 86)
Sept. 1901	9	0.3805	Sayers (1936, p. 94)
Oct. 1904[i]	9, 8	0.3805, 0.2715	Sayers (1936, p. 95)

Notes:
[a] 76s. 5 28/55d. = 917.50909d.
[b] Considered exorbitant price; Bank refused to sell bars.
[c] Exporters showed a disposition to take sovereigns rather than pay 9d., therefore price reduced to 8½d.
[d] End of August to early September. Subsequently, Bank's stock of eagles became exhausted. Throughout autumn 1906 Bank worked to a special schedule of prices for foreign coin.
[e] Bank placed "difficulties in the way of withdrawing anything but sovereigns."
[f] Foreign coin sold at "advanced prices," assumed to be 1d. over normal price.
[g] Increase in price, assumed ½d. over normal price.
[h] At (presumably) 8d., bars taken. Price reduced twice, to divert demand from bars.
[i] Bank charged such a high price (9d.) for eagles that sovereigns were being taken, though Bank eventually preferred to part with eagles. On Bank's stock of sovereigns being much reduced, it lowered price of eagles to 8d.

Table 9.12 *Bank selling price of US dominant gold importable, 1852–1914*

Period	Dominant importable	Bank price	
		Per ounce:[a] 76s. and d.	Deviation from mint price[b] (percent)
Normal price			
July 1852–May 1853, April 1875–June 1891	eagles	6	0.0535
June 1853–March 1875, July 1891–June 1892	"	6½	0.1080
July 1892–June 1914	"	7	0.1625
Temporary prices[c]			
Oct. 1890, Aug. 1893, Sept. 1896, Oct. 1897, April 1900, April 1910/ Sept.–Dec. 1906[d]	eagles/bars	7½[e]	0.2170
Dec. 1890, Aug.–Sept. 1906[f]	eagles	8½	0.3260
July 1891[g]/Sept. 1901	sovereigns/eagles	9	0.3805
Jan. 1893	eagles	8	0.2715
Aug. 1896	bars/eagles	7⅙[h]	0.1807
Oct. 1904[i]	sovereigns, eagles	8¼	0.2987

Notes:

[a] Eagle-equivalent price for bars and sovereigns.

[b] 76s. 5 ²⁸⁄₅₅d. = 917.50909d.

[c] Half-month duration assumed, except where otherwise noted.

[d] Three-quarters of September, entirety of October–December. At 76s. 8½d., in September, the Bank sold out of eagles. So it raised bar price to 78s. 1d., which suggests that shippers were indifferent between bars and coin at these prices. The maximum price of bars ever recorded was 78s. 1d., on only two isolated occasions (November 1892 and this, September 1906); the Bank's maximum was otherwise 78s., which logically prevailed in this period in light of the exhaustion of eagles and a crisis situation for the Bank's reserves [Sayers (1936, pp. 82, 96)]. If a bar price of 78s. 1d. (937d.) is equivalent to an eagle price of 76s. 8½d. (920.5d.), 78s. (936d.) corresponds to (920.5/937)·936 = 919.5176d., rounding to 919.5d (76s. 7½d.). In the new year (1907) the Bank changed tactic, endeavouring to restore reserves by high bids for bars in the market, suggesting that the normal price for eagles (76s. 7d.) was restored.

[e] Mid-point of range taken.

[f] One-quarter of each month (see note *d* of table 9.11).

[g] Price projected from December 1890 experience (see notes *c* and *e* of Table 7.9).

[h] At 8d. and 7½d., bars taken (at 77s. 10½d.). At 7d., eagles taken [bars at 77s. 11d. – Sayers (1936, p. 86)]. So eagle-equivalent price when bars dominant is 7¼d. Average (7¼, 7¼, 7)d. = 7⅙d.

[i] With eagles at 9d., shippers switched to sovereigns, while at 8d. eagles were taken. This suggests that at 8½d. sovereigns were marginally preferred. Average (8½, 8)d. = 8¼d.

Source: Table 9.11 and see notes.

shown in table 9.12, which exhibits the price of the dominant importable (taken to be eagles uniformly until 1890).

Temporary prices of eagles are in table 9.11 and of the dominant import (not only eagles, sometimes bars or even sovereigns, from 1890) in table 9.12. Temporary prices are assumed to have a half-month duration, unless information is otherwise available. In table 9.12 prices of all specie forms are expressed in eagle-equivalent terms, meaning, for bars and sovereigns, the equivalent price for eagles that would leave shippers indifferent between bars or sovereigns (as the case may be) and eagles. Table 9.11 (and other information) is the source of table 9.12, and the latter table is used to derive the purchase cost for 1851–1914 in table 9.13.

1851–60: Duration-weighted average of zero (1851–mid-1852, sovereigns dominant), 0.0535 percent (July 1852–May 1853, normal price of eagles), and 0.1080 percent (June 1853–60, new normal price of eagles). *1861–70*: 0.1080 percent. *1871–80*: Duration-weighted average of 0.1080 (January 1871–March 1875) and 0.0535 (April 1875–80).

Development of a monthly series, 1881 to 1910, facilitates construction of period averages to the latter date and, of course, incorporates the monthly series for 1890–1906. *January 1881–September 1890, November 1890, January–June 1891*: 0.0535 percent (normal price). *October 1890*: Average of 0.2170 and 0.0535. *December 1890*: Average of 0.3260 and 0.0535. *July 1891*: Average of 0.3805 and 0.1080. *August 1891–June 1892*: 0.1080 percent (normal price). *July–December 1892, February–July 1893, September 1893–July 1896, October 1896–September 1897, November 1897–March 1900, May 1900–August 1901, October 1901–September 1904, November 1904–July 1906, January 1907–March 1910, May–December 1910*: 0.1625 percent (normal price).

January 1893: Average of 0.2715 and 0.1625. *August 1893, September 1896, October 1897, April 1900, April 1910*: Average of 0.2170 and 0.1625. *August 1896*: Average of 0.1807 and 0.1625. *September 1901*: Average of 0.3805 and 0.1625. *October 1904:* Average of 0.2987 and 0.1625. *August 1906*: Average of 0.3260 (0.25 month) and 0.1625 (0.75 month). *September 1906*: Average of 0.3260 (0.25 month) and 0.2170 (0.75 month). *October–December 1906*: 0.2170.

Monthly averages are now computed for the periods *1881–90*, *1891–1900*, *1890–1906*, and *1901–10*. *1911–14*: 0.1625 percent (normal price).

1925–31: Zero purchase cost, as bars were obtained from the Bank of England at the mint price, the Gold Standard Act of 1925 requiring the Bank to provide gold bars at par on demand. It is true that arbitrageurs and transferors had the option of dealing with the London private gold market rather than the Bank. However, in fact, the Bank was their dominant source of

Table 9.13 *Transactions cost, imports, percent, period averages, 1791–1931*

Period	Purchase price	Abrasion	Sale price	Mint charges	Currency premium	Exchange-rate cost	Total	
							GPA[a]	GTF[b]
1791–1800	0.2500	0	0	0	0	0.6289	0.8789	− 0.3789
1821–30	0.2500	0	0	0	0	0.3641	0.6141	− 0.1141
1831–40	0.0573	0.0998	0.3208	0	0	0.2506	0.7285	0.2273
1841–50	0	0.2916	0.4250	0	0	0.2506	0.9672	0.4660
1851–60	0.0868	0.0370	0.0188	0	0	0.2506	0.3932	− 0.1080
1861–70	0.1080	− 0.0334	0	0	0	0.2506	0.3252	− 0.1760
1871–80	0.0767	− 0.0512	0	0	− 0.0087	0.2296	0.2464	− 0.2128
1881–90	0.0553	− 0.0549	0	0	0	0.1184	0.1188	− 0.1180
1891–1900	0.1542	− 0.0614	0	0	− 0.0098	0.0236	0.1066	0.0594
1901–10	0.1666	− 0.0425	0	0	− 0.0218	0.0051	0.1074	0.0972
1911–14[c]	0.1625	− 0.0401	0	0	0	0.0051	0.1275	0.1173
1925[d]–31[c]	0	0	0	0.0188	0	0.0064	0.0252	0.0123

Notes:

[a] Purchase price + abrasion + sale price + mint charges + currency premium + exchange-rate cost.

[b] Purchase price + abrasion + sale price + mint charges + currency premium − exchange-rate cost.

[c] Second quarter.

[d] Third quarter.

Legend: GPA = Gold-point arbitrage.

GTF = Transfer of funds.

Source: See text.

gold.[26] They often were reluctant to purchase gold from the market, even though the price could lie as much as 0.1605 percent below the Bank's selling price (that is, as low as 77s. 9d. instead of 77s. 10.5d.) – and for good reasons.

First, a brokerage charge had to be paid for the market, but not the Bank, transaction. Second, in contrast to the Bank's perfectly elastic supply, the market supply available to American arbitrageurs could be insufficient, because of (1) low gross supply, (2) high demand from non-Bank destinations, or (3) the Bank cornering supply by paying above its statutory buying price of 77s. 9d. In fact, the last sometimes occurred just because the Bank actively bid gold away from American transferors and arbitrageurs. Third, the market supply (principally from South Africa) was concentrated on Tuesday, sometimes Wednesday, and price was essentially nominal on other days – in contrast to the Bank's uniform availability of gold (during its office hours) throughout the week.

Arbitrageurs sought to counter these negative features of market supply by heavy resort to the market only when a "fast boat" to New York (reducing the interest cost of GPA or GTF) coincided with a large market supply. However, the Bank cleverly responded by selling dollars in the foreign-exchange market on those days, forcing the exchange rate above the American gold-import point.[27]

(2)   Abrasion

There are no data on abrasion of the Spanish dollar, the primary import to July 31, 1834. The uncertain condition of such coin, purchased in the London market, suggests that abrasion might be so high that the coin would be weighed in the United States and given a value proportionate to weight, or abrasion might be sufficiently low that the coin would pass at face value and abrasion would be a decrement from cost. A zero value for abrasion is an appropriate compromise in the face of ignorance.

Some data do exist on abrasion of sovereigns, dominant from July 31, 1834 to mid-1852: 0.1556 percent in 1826 (Tucker, 1839, p. 397) and 0.3823 percent in 1863 (Sumner, 1874, p. 112). Period averages of abrasion are in Table 9.13. *1791–1800, 1821–30*: Zero. *1831–40*: Duration-weighted average of zero (1831–July 1834) and 0.1556 (August 1834–40). *1841–50*: By the usual convention, the increase in abrasion occurred at the end of 1844 (mid-way between 1826 and 1863). The duration-weighted average of 0.1556 and 0.3823 is computed.

There are no direct data on the abrasion of eagles supplied by the Bank, but careful estimates can be made for four dates over 1890–1906, based on a cost equivalence with either bars or sovereigns, as shown in table 9.14. In December 1890 the Bank charged 76s. 9d. for eagles, but shippers of specie demanded sovereigns instead; so the Bank reduced the price to 76s. 8.5d.

Table 9.14 *Abrasion of eagles offered for sale by Bank: direct computation*

Item	Dec. 1890	Sept. 1896	Oct. 1904	Sept. 1906
1 Alternative to eagles	sovereigns	bars	sovereigns	bars
2 Abrasion of alternative (percent)	0.25	0	0.25	0
Bank selling price of eagles				
3 Per ounce: 76s. and d.	8¾	7¾	8¼	8½
4 Deviation from mint price (percent)	0.3532	0.2442	0.2987	0.3260
Bank selling price of alternative				
5 Per standard ounce	77s. 10½d.	78s.	77s. 10½d.	78s. 1d.
6 Deviation from mint price (percent)	0	0.1605	0	0.2675
7 Interest rate (percent per year)	5.00	5.45	2.03	9.38
8 Interest loss (percent)	0.0411	0.0045	0.0017	0.0077
Assay office mint charges				
9 Copper (percent)	0.0019	0.0107	0.0019	0.0107
10 Melting (percent)	0.0053	0	0.0053	0
11 Abrasion (percent)	0.0549	0.0685	0.0398	0.0401

Source: See text.

This suggests that at 76s. 8.75d. eagles have a marginal cost equal to that of sovereigns. In October 1904 shippers again switched to sovereigns when the Bank charged 76s. 9d. for eagles. In this instance the Bank reduced its price to 76s. 8d., implying again that at a 0.25d. higher price transferors and arbitrageurs would be indifferent between the two forms of gold.

In September 1896, preferring to lose eagles rather than bars in the face of a gold drain, the Bank raised the price of eagles to 76s. 7.5d. and that of bars to 78s. The implication is that, with eagles 0.25d. higher, shippers would face the same cost with either eagles or bars. At the end of August 1906, the Bank raised its price of eagles to 76s. 8.5d. At that price the Bank sold out of eagles, and in September it raised the bar price to 78s. 1d., which suggests that transferors and arbitrageurs were indifferent between eagles and bars at these respective prices.[28]

Now, the marginal cost (MC) of eagles consists of the deviation from mint price (row 4 of table 9.14) minus abrasion, the value of the latter to be a resultant of this exercise. The MC of sovereigns is the sum of abrasion (row 2), interest loss at the New York Assay Office (row 8), and direct mint charges (rows 9 and 10); while the MC of bars is the sum of the deviation from mint price (row 6), interest loss (row 8), and mint charge (row 9). The (positive) figures in rows 2 and 8–10 require justification.

Row 2: Abrasion of 0.25 percent for sovereigns obtained from the Bank is a conservative estimate that arbitrageurs and transferors probably adopted. The figure is based on experienced abrasion of sovereigns provided by the Bank.[29] *Row 7*: The opportunity cost to GPA or GTF use of funds on the part of New York banks was the renewal rate on New York stock-exchange call loans. This interest rate is in Board of Governors of the Federal Reserve System (1943, pp. 448–9).

Row 8: Computed as $(1 - Q/100)\cdot(L/365)\cdot i$, where i is the interest rate (percent per year); Q the percent of estimated value received upon deposit, 0 in December 1890, 90 on the other dates; and $L = 3$ the time loss (number of days) until the remainder of the payment is received. The 90-percent advance after September 30, 1891 is well documented, and a time loss of three days is a reasonable allowance.[30] The formula involves simple interest, because that is utilized in all contemporary calculations of the interest cost of GPA and GTF.[31]

Rows 9–10: Mint expenses of the New York Assay Office, in Whitaker (1919, pp. 499–501). Mint-fine bars ("gold containing such trifling impurities that the mint does not demand their elimination") were exempt from the melting charge. The Treasury was not empowered to charge for assaying as such.

Equating the MC of eagles to the MC of sovereigns (December 1890, October 1904) or bars (September 1896, September 1906), the unknown abrasion of eagles supplied by the Bank is computed and presented in row 11. Linear interpolation between the adjacent values of row 11 is used to estimate abrasion for the intervening months. Abrasion on American import of eagles is a decrement from cost; so a negative sign is applied to these figures. The December 1890 value is projected back to 1881, and is the average for *1881–90* in table 9.13. The September 1906 estimate is retained to June 1914 and is the value for *1911–14*. The monthly series for 1890–1906 is obtained by the above procedure. Monthly averages provide period values for *1891–1900*, *1901–10*, and *1890–1906*. With bars the specie form in *1925–31*, abrasion is zero.

1851–60: Duration-weighted average of 0.3823 (abrasion of sovereigns), 1851–June 1852, and −0.0239 (from table 9.7, negative of abrasion of exported eagles 1851–60 – representing abrasion of imported eagles, for lack of direct data), July 1852–60. *1861–70*: Average of 1851–60 and 1861–70 abrasion of eagle exports (from table 9.7). *1871–80*: Average of 1871–80 abrasion of eagle exports (taken as negative, from table 9.7) and December 1890 value of abrasion of eagle imports (from table 9.14).

(3)   Deviation of sale price from mint price
1791–1800, 1821–30: Taken as zero, and recorded in table 9.13. For the import of silver, the premium of the Spanish over the American dollar in the United States was inapplicable, with uncertain condition of the coin purchased by weight in the London market.

Sovereigns, dominant from July 31, 1834 to mid-1852, were purchasable by the US Mint at the full mint-price equivalent of $20.6718+ per ounce of fine gold. However, not until the New York Assay Office opened for business in October 1854 was the Mint utilized on a regular basis by gold importers (or any private party), due to delays in coinage and the distance of Philadelphia (location of the US Mint) from New York (see section 5 of chapter 3). Therefore sovereigns had to be sold in the private market for specie. The commission rate on the sale of specie in New York was 0.5 percent in 1835 (Albion, 1939, p. 413).

1831–40: Duration-weighted average of zero (Spanish dollars, 1831–July 1834) and 0.5 percent (sovereigns, August 1834–40). *1841–50*: Duration-weighted average of 0.5 and 0.125 percent, the 0.125 figure from Cornwallis (1879, p. 12) for 1862–78 and the decline in rate assumed to occur at the end of 1848 by convention.

From mid-1852 to 1890, with eagles the dominant import (see table 9.12), there is zero deviation of sale price from mint price. *1851–60*: Weighted average of 0.125 percent (sovereigns, 1851–June 1852) and zero (eagles, July 1852–60). *1861–90*: Zero. From 1890 to 1914, eagles were usually dominant. While there were occasional months in which bars or sovereigns were the primary import, their selling price is expressed in eagle-equivalent terms (table 9.12). So *1890–1914*: again, zero. *1925–31*: Zero. Bars were the only import for GPA and GTF, and they were purchased at par by the Treasury and Federal Reserve Bank of New York.

2.3   Miscellaneous components of transactions cost

A possible cost component is commission paid to an intermediary to carry out the specie transaction on the other side of the Atlantic, meaning in London. In fact, the dominant arbitrageurs and transferors were not subject to this cost. They had offices in London as well as in the American port cities, or had a regular correspondent in London, or co-operated with a London firm on joint account.[32]

Three elements of transactions cost remain: mint charges, currency premium, and exchange-rate cost. The first two always vary with direction of shipment and could differ for the form of specie; exchange-rate cost sometimes depends on the direction of shipment but is invariant to the form of specie. Exchange-rate cost, however, does differ for GPA and GTF. In this respect it differs from all other components of transactions cost and from freight, insurance, and handling. Period averages of the three miscellaneous transactions costs are shown in tables 9.7 and 9.13 for exports and imports, respectively.

2.3.1 Mint charges

Export

For most periods, mint expenses were zero, as shown in table 9.7. During the American silver standard (1791–1834) there were no mint expenses, because exported silver coin was sold by weight in the London market, without melting or assaying. From July 1852 to May 31, 1882, again mint expenses were zero, because the dominant export was eagles, sold by weight to the Bank of England. From June 1, 1882 to June 1914, either eagles or Assay bars were exported. The former were sold by weight to the Bank, the latter accepted by the Bank at the stamped fineness.[33] Therefore, thanks not to statute but to Bank policy, neither eagles nor bars involved the mint expenses of melting and assaying (or the loss of interest during waiting time for these procedures).

For the 1834–52 period, mint expenses were applicable, as eagles were sold to the Bank as bullion. Melting and assaying charges were 0.0546 and 0.0367 percent, respectively (*Merchants' Magazine*, September 1848, p. 303). *1831–40*: Duration–weighted average of zero (Spanish dollar exported, 1831–July 1834) and 0.0913 percent (eagles sold as bullion, August 1834–40). *1841–50*: 0.0913 percent. *1851–60*: Duration-weighted average of 0.0913 (eagles sold as bullion, 1851–June 1852), and zero (eagles sold by weight, July 1852–60).

In 1925–31, with Assay bars the dominant export, there remained no melting charge for these bars (Spalding, 1928a, pp. 78, 86; 1929, p. 25); but the stamped fineness was no longer accepted, resulting in an assaying procedure and related charge. As the bars used for arbitrage were above 0.995 fine (exceeding both the American and British standards), refining (addition of gold to increase the fineness to standard) was never needed. In practice, the Bank did not charge for copper (to reduce the fineness to standard). For assaying (and therefore total mint charges) in 1925–31, Spalding's five-digit figure of 0.01216 percent is taken over his alternative value of 0.0121, obviously a truncation (Spalding, 1928a, pp. 81, 84). *1925–31*: 0.0122 percent.

Import

From 1791 to 1914 mint expenses were nil. In 1791–1834 silver dollars were the primary import. With silver the monetary base of the country, imported coin would be added to general circulation or to reserves rather than brought to the US Mint. In 1834–52 sovereigns were the dominant import. They were sold in the New York private specie market. From mid-1852 to 1914 transferors and arbitrageurs imported either eagles or, on occasion, bars or sovereigns. Prices paid for the latter are expressed in eagle-equivalent form (table 9.12). With eagles returnable either to circulation or reserves, again use of the mint need not be considered.

In 1925–31 gold bars were the import, and they were purchased by the Treasury or Federal Reserve Bank of New York. The fact that the Fed picked up imported gold at zero handling charge from March 1928 did not permit shippers to escape mint expenses.[34] The Treasury (and Fed) did not charge for the very minor expense of copper alloy, or the fee was too insignificant to be noted by contemporary writers. However, by 1925 melting was a charge even for mint-fine bars. Melting charge of 0.01875 percent is stated by Miller (1925, p. 145) and Spalding (1928a, p. 81). *1925–31*: 0.0188 percent.

2.3.2   *Currency premium*

Three times in American monetary history a premium on currency in terms of certified checks occurred (see section 9 and table 3.2 of chapter 3). The premium was an additional cost of specie exports, because bank deposits had to be converted into currency to obtain gold (either eagles directly or eagles to be exchanged for bars at the Assay Office).[35] The premium was a negative cost for imports, because gold obtained from abroad either was currency (eagles) or could be converted to currency at par and thence to deposit balances at the premium.[36]

Data on the currency premium for all three episodes are available in daily form (Sprague, 1910, pp. 57, 187; Andrew, 1908, pp. 292–3). Monthly averages of daily rates are computed and presented in table 9.15. Where the daily figure is a range, the mid-point is taken. Non-market days are excluded from the averages. For 1893, buying and selling rates of brokers are available, the former applicable to importers, the latter to exporters. For 1873 and 1907 the data make no buying/selling distinction, and the same figures are taken for both directions of shipment.

1871–80, 1891–1900, 1890–1906, 1901–10: Period averages are the average value of all the months in the period, incorporating zero values for the months not listed in table 9.15. So the figures for the three affected periods shown in tables 9.7 and 9.13, and for 1890–1906, are much lower than indicated by the values in table 9.15.

Table 9.15 *Currency premium over certified checks, 1873–1907*

Month	Premium (percent)
Sept. 1873	0.5481
Oct. ”	0.4988
Aug. 1893	2.1065, 1.1620[a]
Sept. ”	0.0337, 0.0144[a]
Oct. 1907	0.0926
Nov. ”	2.0417
Dec. ”	0.4875

Note:
[a] Selling rate and buying rate, respectively.
Source: see text.

2.3.3   Exchange-rate cost

Exchange-rate cost is an addition to the cost of GPA but a subtraction from that of GTF. The reason is that the exchange-rate transaction is a constituent element of GPA but the avoided activity under GTF. Indeed, for all cost components, what is included in the cost of GTF is the cost under the gold-effected transfer of funds minus the cost under the alternative, exchange-rate, transaction, the marginal cost of GTF over a foreign-exchange transaction for transfer of funds.

Ideally, exchange transactions would take place at V, the mid-point of the buying and selling prices of pounds in the foreign-exchange market, where V is expressed in dollars per pound (see section 3.6 of chapter 6).[37] Therefore the percentage exchange-rate cost (ERC) is the difference between the market price (MER) of the arbitrageur's actual, or the transferor's potential, foreign-exchange transaction, and the ideal price, taken as a percentage of the ideal price. There are two alternative formulas:

$$ERC = 100 \cdot (V - MER)/V \qquad (9.1)$$

$$ERC = 100 \cdot (MER - V)/V \qquad (9.2)$$

For GTF the computed ERC is made negative, because the exchange-rate transaction is avoided rather than undertaken.

The value of V in any month or quarter over 1791–1931 is in concordance with the long-run exchange-rate series, summarized in table 6.13. The description of GPA and GTF in section 4 of chapter 8 and the discussion in section 3.6 of chapter 6 suggest the following. For specie export over 1791–1914, demand bills are sold by the arbitrageur; formula (9.1) applies with $MER = W$. For specie export, purchase of bills is forgone by the transferor; formula (9.2) pertains with $MER = Z$. For 1925–31, the purchase of spot cable pounds is avoided by the transferor, and formula (9.2) again applies with $MER = Z$. Export GPA in 1925–31 is a special case, discussed below.

For specie import, demand bills (1791–1914) or spot cable pounds (1925–31) are purchased under GPA; so formula (9.2) holds with $MER = Z$. With GTF, the bills or spot cable pounds are avoided sold; so (9.1) applies with $MER = W$.

So, except for export GPA in 1925–31, $ERC = 100 \cdot (V - W)/V = 100 \cdot (0.5 \cdot C)/V = 100 \cdot (Z - V)/V$, where C is broker's commission, dollars per pound. The value of C over 1874–1931 is provided in section 3.6 of chapter 6, permitting computation of ERC via the above formula.

For 1791–1873, commission is available only in the form of percentage of broker's selling price, $100 \cdot k$, where $k = C/Z$. Because $C = k \cdot Z = k \cdot (V + 0.5 \cdot C)$, it follows that $C = k \cdot V/(1 - 0.5 \cdot k)$. Substituting the latter into $ERC = 100 \cdot (0.5 \cdot C)/V$ yields $ERC = 50 \cdot k/(1 - 0.5 \cdot k)$. This formula is used for 1791–1823 and 1824–73, obtaining 0.6289 and 0.2506 percent, respectively.

There remains the case of export GPA in 1925–31. Arbitrageurs covered their exchange risk by selling pounds eight days forward.[38] Exchange-rate cost, then, is given by (9.1) with $MER = RF8$, the eight-day forward cable selling rate. While $RF8$ is unknown, it may be estimated as

$$(V - 0.0003125) + (8/30) \cdot PR$$

where $(V - 0.0003125)$ is the spot selling rate (with broker's commission at 0.000625 dollars per pound – see table 6.4) and PR is the one-month forward premium (negative if a discount).[39] The special case is unique in that ERC is not necessarily positive. A negative exchange-rate cost results from forward pounds at a sufficiently high premium.

A quarterly ERC series for 1791–1931 and a monthly series for 1890–1906 and 1925–31 are thereby obtained for both specie import and export. Now period averages can be computed, and exchange-rate cost is presented as usual, exports in table 9.7, imports in table 9.13. For 1925–31 in table 9.7, exchange-rate cost pertains to GPA (the special case). For GTF, the figure in table 9.13 is applicable. Also, GTF exchange-rate cost has a negative sign in all months and for all period averages.

2.4   Interest cost

2.4.1   Elements in interest-cost computation

Interest cost is computed from the formula

$$IC = m \cdot (T/365) \cdot i \tag{9.3}$$

where IC is interest cost (percent), m is the proportion of the shipment value subject to interest ($0 \leq m \leq 1$), T is the interest duration (number of days), and i is the interest rate (percent per year). There are three types of interest cost: (1) that emanating from the duration of oceanic transportation, (2) that arising prior or subsequent to such transportation, from waiting time at the mint or delay in obtaining or selling specie privately, and (3) the negative cost stemming from interest-free advances offered by the authority of the destination country of the specie shipment.

The value of m, the interest-affected share of the shipment value, is unity with two exceptions. Under (1), $m = 0$ for export GPA and for both export and import GTF during the period of bill dominance, that is, for the time span 1791–1914 (see sections 4.3 and 4.5 of chapter 8). Under (2), m has a positive value below unity for waiting time "at the mint" – though not for private sale of specie – varying by direction of shipment (see section 2.4.3 below).

The value of T, the number of days of interest, varies threefold: with type of interest cost, direction of shipment, and time period. The interest rate, i, is invariant with respect to type of interest cost and direction of shipment. Therefore it warrants detailed discussion at this point.

Interest loss was an opportunity cost for the arbitrageurs/transferors. For the New York banks as dominant arbitrageurs, the pertinent interest rate was that obtainable on loans placed in the New York call-money market – specifically, the renewal rate on New York stock-exchange call loans – because this was the opportunity cost for the use of their funds. These loans were considered by the banks (but not the public) as a conservative investment, the banks giving up higher interest in commercial paper or securities for greater availability of funds (Myers, 1931, pp. 274–5).

A monthly series of the average (renewal) rate on stock-exchange call loans, percent per year, is assembled for 1857–1931. The source is Board of Governors of the Federal Reserve System (1943, pp. 448–51) for 1890–1931, and Macaulay (1938, pp. A142–50) for 1857–89. The two sources provide a consistent series.

The monthly series is continued for 1831–56 by means of the Bigelow (1862, pp. 204–5) series of "street rates" on first-class paper in Boston and New York. Where there are multiple rates for the month, the average is taken. For 1834 and 1835, data are available only for January and December. The January value is repeated for February–June and the December value for July–November.

There is evidence that the Bigelow data are appropriate to continue the interest-rate series. A detailed contemporary account of the cost of GTF (*Financial Register of the United States*, 1838, p. 288), dated February 28, 1838, states loss of interest of 90 days at two to three percent at market rates.[40] Three-percent interest for 90 days corresponds to 12 percent interest for 360 days, and 12 percent per year is Bigelow's rate for February 1838.

Prior to 1831, there are no data on American short-term interest rates. In 1830 the House of Brown in a specie-point computation applied an interest rate of 4 percent, which was Bank Rate at the time. This incident suggests that for the early decades Bank Rate is an acceptable proxy for the opportunity-cost interest rate of arbitrageurs/transferors.

Period averages of the American interest rate, i, presented in tables 9.16 and 9.17, are obtained as follows. *1791–1800*: 5 percent, the unvarying Bank Rate. *1821–30*: Daily-weighted average of the two pertinent levels of Bank Rate, 4 and 5 percent. Bank Rate data are from Clapham (1945, vol. I, p. 299; vol. II, p. 429). *1831–1931*: Period averages constructed as average of monthly series. Monthly series for 1890–1906 and 1925–31 are simply the Board of Governors of the Federal Reserve System data.

2.4.2   Oceanic transportation

From $m = 0$, it follows from equation (9.3) that interest cost from oceanic transportation is zero from 1791 to 1914 for import GTF and for export GPA and GTF. Then, to compute interest cost from transportation duration for 1791–1914 (import GPA) and 1925–31 (export and import GPA and GTF), the value of T by subperiod must be developed. Consider first import GPA over 1791–1914, when the demand bill may be considered the exchange-market instrument (see section 5 of chapter 8). The interest duration pertains to a round-trip Atlantic voyage (see section 4.5 of chapter 8).

Direct data on the time loss involved in a specie-import operation are rare prior to 1925; their entirety follows. In 1823 and 1830 the House of Brown allowed for interest loss of 90 days (Perkins, 1975, p. 192), the same duration independently mentioned in a report in February 1838.[41] A long hiatus follows; then in 1892 time loss of 21 days is stated by Clare (1906, p. 130). Finally, six sources mention 20 days as the time loss over 1900–14. For Escher (1918, p. 80), Whitaker (1919, pp. 532–4), and Cross (1923, p. 390), the 20-day figure applies generally prior to World War I; for Goodhart (1969, p. 8) it pertains to 1900–13; for Johnson (1905, p. 91, n. 1) and Escher (1910, p. 118), it presumably refers to their dates of publication.[42]

To extend information, table 9.18 is useful. It shows the average length of a one-way Atlantic voyage eastbound (New York to Liverpool) and westbound (Liverpool to New York) by dominant specie-carrying vessel type and by period. While Anglo-American oceanic transportation improved in speed, regularity, and reliability during the nineteenth century, the changes occurred much more in discrete jumps than continuously. Four periods are of interest.[43]

Table 9.16 *Elements in interest cost, exports, period averages, 1791–1931*

Period	American interest rate (percent per year)	Transportation duration (days)	Interest cost (percent)			Total	
			From transportation duration	At Mint[a]	Interest-free advances	GPA[b]	GTF[c]
1791–1800	5.00	0	0	0.3288	0	0.3288	0.3288
1821–30	4.30	0	0	0.2827	0	0.2827	0.2827
1831–40	10.42	0	0	0.2484	0	0.2484	0.2484
1841–50	8.14	0	0	0.0033	0	0.0033	0.0033
1851–60	7.95	0	0	0.0005	0	0.0005	0.0005
1861–70	6.50	0	0	0	0	0	0
1871–80	5.65	0	0	0	0	0	0
1881–90	4.08	0	0	0	0	0	0
1891–1900	3.02	0	0	0	− 0.0015	− 0.0015	− 0.0015
1901–10	4.02	0	0	0	− 0.0012	− 0.0012	− 0.0012
1911–14[d]	2.93	0	0	0	0	0	0
1925[e]–31[d]	4.70	8	0.1031	0.0019	0	0.1050	0.1050

Notes:
[a] Or from time needed to transact sale of specie in London market.
[b] Interest cost from transportation duration + interest cost at mint + interest-free advances.
[c] *1791–1914:* Interest cost at mint + interest cost from transportation duration + interest-free advances. *1925–1931:* Interest cost from transportation duration + interest cost at mint + interest-free advances.
[d] Second quarter.
[e] Third quarter.
Legend: GPA = Gold-point arbitrage.
GTF = Transfer of funds.
Source: See text.

Table 9.17 *Elements in interest cost, imports, period averages, 1791–1931*

| Period | American interest rate (percent per year) | Transportation duration (days)[a] | Interest cost (percent) | | | Total | |
			From transportation duration[a]	At Mint	Interest-free advances	GPA[b]	GTF[c]
1791–1800	5.00	150	2.0548	0	0	2.0548	0
1821–30	4.30	90	1.0603	0	0	1.0603	0
1831–40	10.42	78.1	2.2305	0	0	2.2305	0
1841–50	8.14	41.1	0.9163	0	0	0.9163	0
1851–60	7.95	29	0.6316	0	0	0.6316	0
1861–70	6.50	25	0.4451	0	0	0.4451	0
1871–80	5.65	23	0.3557	0	0	0.3557	0
1881–90	4.08	21	0.2348	0	0	0.2348	0
1891–1900	3.02	21	0.1739	0	0	0.1739	0
1901–10	4.02	20	0.2205	0	− 0.0090	0.2115	− 0.0090
1911–14[d]	2.93	20	0.1606	0	0	0.1606	0
1925[e]–31[d]	4.70	8	0.1031	0.0064	0	0.1095	0.1095

Notes:
[a] Plus transaction time in obtaining and selling specie (other than at US Treasury or Federal Reserve Bank of New York).
[b] Interest cost from transporation duration + interest cost at Mint + interest-free advances.
[c] *1791–1914*: Interest cost at mint + interest cost from transportation duration + interest cost at mint + interest-free advances. *1925–31*: Interest cost from transportation duration + interest cost at mint + interest-free advances.
[d] Second quarter.
[e] Third quarter.
Legend: GPA = Gold-point arbitrage.
GTF = Transfer of funds.
Source: See text.

Table 9.18 *Average length of passage, Liverpool–New York, 1791–1890*

Period and transport mode[a]	Passages in average	Average passage (days)		Source
		East-bound	West-bound	
Regular traders: 1791–1800				
pre-1818	unstated	21–8[b]	35–84[b]	Albion and Pope (1942, p. 27)
Packets: 1821–38				
1818–32	521		37.9	Albion (1938, pp. 317, 319)
1818–27	Black Ball line	24	38	Albion (1938, p. 322)
1833–47	835		34.3	Albion (1938, pp. 317, 319)
1838[c]	all	22.0	34.8	*Merchants' Magazine* (July 1839, pp. 85–6)
Steamships: 1838–90				
1839	three ships	15.4	17.0	Bowen (1930, p. 35)
1849	all		13.7	Maginnis (1892, p. 28)
1850	Cunard line	12.7	13.0	Maginnis (1892, pp. 284–5)
1851–56[d]	Cunard, Collins	11.4	12.4	Lindsay (1874, pp. 227, 601), Maginnis (1892, pp. 284–5)
1866	Cunard, Inman[e]	9.8	11.1	Maginnis (1892, pp. 284–5)
1873–80[f]	Cunard, Inman, Guion, White Star[e]	9.2	10.0	”
1881–90[g]	”	8.5	9.0	”

Notes:
[a] Dominant specie-carrying ships.
[b] Passages described as "frequently" within range.
[c] Year or more, beginning Nov. 1, 1837.
[d] Unweighted average of (i) year ending June 30, 1852, (ii) 1855 (Cunard only), (iii) 1856.
[e] Unweighted average of average passages of each line.
[f] Average of 1873, 1875 (westbound only), 1876–80.
[g] Average of all years.

The first period is 1791 to 1817, during which "regular traders" held sway in the two-way specie trade and the transport of bills of exchange to England. These sailing vessels were "regular" only in their limitation of voyages to two (sometimes three) ports. They lacked fixed schedules and announced sailing dates were often disregarded. As the first entry in table 9.18 only partially indicates, there were wide variations in shipping time, due to wartime exigencies (to 1815), vagaries of the weather, and waiting time in port. Also, the Atlantic passage was not only longer westbound than eastbound but also much more variable. The reason is the prevailing westerly winds in the North Atlantic, which are especially stormy in the winter months (Albion, 1938, pp. 9–10, 26; Albion and Pope, 1942, pp. 26–7).

The second period, January 1818–April 1838, involved bill-of-exchange and specie transportation dominated by the packets, sailing vessels unlike regular traders more in operation and organization than in ship design. It is true that the War of 1812 encouraged construction of faster ships, the better for the privateering activities of the Americans. The improvement in speed continued in shipbuilding after the war, but had ended by 1820 (North, 1968, p. 967). Indeed, unlike the "clipper," that was expressly designed for speed and used primarily in the California-to-China run, the packet was built for durability.

The independently operated regular traders gave way to liner service with regular and coordinated sailing schedules that were zealously followed. Captains drove their ships hard, and there is much romanticism about the packets braving the weather while maximizing speed across the Atlantic.[44] The packet reduced the *variation* in transport time (not revealed in table 9.18) much more than the average; but there remained a substantial differential – in both average and variability – between the eastbound and westbound passage.

The third period commences at the end of April 1838, when the steamship replaced the packet as the dominant carrier of specie and bills of exchange. However, for a decade the packet provided good competition to the steamship for this cargo, in part because the steamships on the New York route operated as independent entities rather than liners, in part because a loss at sea and wreck on shore gave these steamships unfavorable publicity and reduced the fleet.

Nevertheless, the benefit of the steamship was readily apparent. The steamship was affected only minimally by the westerly winds on the Atlantic; therefore it reduced not only the average duration of passage but also the variability, especially of the inward (westbound) direction. Also, the time difference between the eastbound and westbound trips was greatly reduced.

The fourth period begins January 1, 1848, with the establishment of regular liner service between New York and Liverpool by Cunard. With the steamships themselves organized in liner service for New York and with an improved steamship record at sea, the packets lost their entire share of the specie and bills-of-exchange trade. From 1848 there was a steady decline in average voyage time and its variability.

The two data sets – (1) time loss in specie-import operations and (2) average and variability of the duration of an Atlantic crossing by direction – are used together to construct transportation duration of the specie-import transaction monthly and by period as required. It should be noted that, for a given time period, the total time (denoted as *TOT*) needed for GPA or GTF includes not only the duration of a round-trip voyage (denoted as *VOY*, with data in table 9.18) but also transaction time in obtaining and selling the specie. So the ratio *TOT/VOY* – a useful parameter in estimating *TOT* for missing periods – exceeds unity, but may be expected to decline over the nineteenth century. Transportation duration for specie import (including transaction time) is shown in table 9.17.

1821–30: 90 days (House of Brown information). *1791–1800*: Taking 90 days, which pertains to the packet as carrier, as the base, extension is made to the regular trader three decades earlier as follows. For a "typical" regular trader, Albion (1938, pp. 16–17) cites an 18-day delay in sailing out of New York as an example of "the annoyances and delays to which the patrons of the regular traders were ordinarily subjected." Doubling the expected sailing delay of the regular traders (for the round trip of a specie-import transaction), an additional five weeks' waiting time must have been allowed in the 1790s.

Further, the average length of the westbound passage was reduced from about 60 days in the 1790s to 38 in the 1820s (see table 9.18). So another three weeks must be added to the time loss. Also, the variability of this voyage fell from a normal range of 35–84 days (table 9.18) to 31–41 days (Albion, 1938, p. 200). Adding about another week to cover the difference in variability (beyond the respective means), the 90 days it took for a specie-import operation in the 1820s expands to about 150 days in the 1790s.

1891–1900: 21 days (Clare's 1892 figure). *1900–14*: 20 days (six sources). *1890–1906*: Change from 21 to 20 days is assumed to have occurred at turn of century. So period average is 20.6 days. *1881–90*: 21 days, projecting Clare's 1892 figure back one decade. *1871–80*: Take as norm the 1880s *TOT/VOY* ratio = 21/17.5 = 1.2 (exact figure). Its product with the 1870s round-trip duration (19.2 days) is 23 days. *1861–70*: The norm ratio applied to the 1866 round-trip length of 20.9 days yields 25 days. *1851–60*: Multiplying the 1850s round-trip figure of 23.8 days by the norm yields 29 days.

1831–40: Consider a new norm *TOT/VOY* ratio, pertaining to packets in 1838: 90/56.8 = 1.6 (rounded). It is reasonable to assume that this ratio fell to 1.2 in two steps: May 1838, when steamships became the primary carrier of specie, and January 1848, when steamship dominance turned into a monopoly. Assuming that half the decline occurred in each step, the ratio for May 1838–December 1847 is 1.4. Applying this ratio to the 1839 round-trip duration (32.4 days), the result is 45.4 days. Then the 1831–40 figure is the average of 90 days for 7.33 . . . years (packet dominance through April 1838) and 45.4 days for 2.66 . . . years (steamship dominance from May 1838): 78.1 days.

1841–50: The round-trip duration for 1848–50 is construed as 26 days, calculated as the sum of 12.7 and average (13.7, 13.0). Applying the norm ratio of 1.2, specie-import time is 31.2 days. The average of 45.4 and 31.2 days for seven and three years, respectively, is 41.1 days.

1925–31: Turning to GPA and GTF import and export for 1925–31, the transportation component of the interest duration is a one-way rather than round-trip voyage, because cable transfer was the exchange medium (see sections 4.2 and 4.4 of chapter 8). The average length of the voyage, with data from all known authorities over 1923–33, is eight (rounded up from 7.77) days.[45] This number is exhibited in tables 9.16 and 9.17 for export and import, respectively. By this time there was no significant difference in duration between the eastbound and westbound voyages.

To obtain the interest cost from transportation (for specie-import, including transaction time), formula (9.3) is applied, both for period averages and the monthly series.[46] Results are shown in tables 9.16 and 9.17.

2.4.3   *Waiting time at mint or for private sale of specie*

Export
1791–1800, 1821–30: The time required to effect the sale of silver coin in London in 1827–8 was 28 days (Secretary of the Treasury, 1830, p. 90). This figure is projected back to the 1790s, and equation (9.3) with $T = 24, m = 1$, and the appropriate period average of i is applied for the two decades. Interest cost is shown in table 9.16.

From July 31, 1834 to June 30, 1852, eagles were sold to the Bank as bullion. The earliest information available on Bank mint charges is provided by Seyd (1868, pp. 170, 244), who observes that 90 to 95 percent of estimated value was paid on deposit, the remainder in two days or "a day or a couple of days." Middling estimates are 92.5 percent and a two-day delay. Therefore interest cost "at the mint" (really the Bank of England acting as a mint) is generated by equation (9.3) with $m = 0.075$ and $T = 2$. The period averages (and monthly series) of i were determined in section 2.4.1.

1831–40: Monthly average of interest cost in the sale of silver in the London market ($T = 24$, $m = 1$), January 1831–July 1834, and in waiting time for mint procedures at the Bank of England ($m = 0.075$, $T = 2$), August 1834–December 1840. Of course, the specific value of i is used in each (monthly) application of formula (9.3). *1841–50*: Result of the formula with $m = 0.075$, $T = 2$, and i the decade average. *1851–60*: The same parameters are applied, but monthly values of i are used. From July 1852 to 1914, $m = 0$, because eagles were sold to the Bank by weight and with immediate payment. The monthly average of interest cost for the entire decade is computed.

1925–31: Spalding (1928a, pp. 78, 86; 1929, p. 26) states that about 95 percent of the value was paid by the Bank on deposit (a conservative estimate, as more than that percentage might be advanced) and that three days was the waiting time for the residual payment. So formula (9.3) is used monthly with $m = 0.05$, $T = 3$, and the specific value of i. Period averages of the monthly interest costs are calculated.

Import

From 1791 to 1914, mint expenses and therefore waiting time at the mint were nil. *1925–31*: The Federal Reserve Bank of New York (or the New York Assay Office of the Treasury) made immediate payment of 95 percent of the estimated value of gold deposits, according to Einzig (1927a, p. 135).[47] Regarding waiting time for residual payment, Whitaker (1933, p. 373) mentions a delay of 7–10 days. The upper limit is taken, as a properly conservative estimate.

Therefore equation (9.3) is applied monthly with $m = 0.05$, $T = 10$, and i the specific interest rate. Period averages of the monthly interest costs are taken. The average for the usual (inner) 1925–31 period is shown in table 9.17.

2.4.4   Interest-free advances

Export

Over 1899–1907 the Bank of England on occasion gave interest-free advances to gold importers on condition the advances be repaid in gold within a fixed number of days, probably nine days for US exports.[48] There were five months in which the policy was applicable to US exports: June 1899, December 1899, August 1900, January 1906, and June 1907.[49] For each of these months, formula (9.3) is applied with a negative sign (because the interest-free advance is a negative cost component), $m = 0.5$ (to impose the half-month duration), $T = 9$, and i is the specific interest rate for the

Table 9.19 *Cost saving from interest-free advances, 1899–1907*

Period	Authority	Intrest rate (percent)	Cost saving (percent)
June 1899[a]	Bank of England	2.63	0.0324
Dec. 1899[a]	"	11.13	0.1372
Aug. 1900[a]	"	1.30	0.0160
Jan. 1906[a]	"	8.65	0.1066
April 14–30, 1906	US Treasury	9.50	0.2950
May 1–29, 1906	"	4.15	0.2127
Sept. 10–30, 1906	"	9.38	0.3598
Oct. 1–23, 1906	"	5.15	0.2094
June 1907[a]	Bank of England	3.13	0.0386

Note:
[a] Half-month duration assumed.
Source: See text.

month. The interest rate and percentage advance for these months are presented in table 9.19.

For all other months, $m = 0$ (no interest-free advance). The monthly series for 1890–1906 is thereby obtained and period averages for 1891–1900, 1901–10, and 1890–1906 are computed as averages of the monthly values. The averages for the two former periods are shown in table 9.16.[50]

Import
Leslie M. Shaw, US Secretary of the Treasury, instituted what became known as the "Shaw Plan" during April 14–May 29 and September 10–October 23, 1906. Shaw deposited government funds in national banks in amounts equal to the value of gold committed to be imported, the deposits to be repaid when the gold arrived.[51] This scheme removed the interest cost from gold imports under GPA and reduced the cost of GTF (always relative to the forgone exchange-market transaction).

For the four months affected, formula (9.3) applies with a negative sign (indicating a negative cost component), m equalling the proportion of the month affected (17/30, 29/31, 21/30, and 23/31, for April, May, September, October), $T = 20$, and i the interest rate for the month. Details for these months are in table 9.19. For all other months, $m = 0$. The monthly series for 1890–1906 is thus developed, and the period averages for 1901–10 (shown in table 9.17) and 1890–1906 are computed as averages of monthly values.

2.5   Risk premium and normal profit

No different from other economic agents, arbitrageurs and transferors required compensation for risk. The uncertainties of GPA and GTF gave rise to a risk premium – what contemporary writers sometimes called "margin of safety" – as an element of cost. Uncertainties could be either one-sided or two-sided. A one-sided risk involved no possibility of gain. The only such risk was that even with insurance, if the specie were lost at sea or stolen, there would be a delay in collecting the insurance claim and recovering the funds. In the early decades, this was considered the greatest risk underlying margin of safety.[52]

Two-sided risk, with the possibility of a gain as well as a loss, had several manifestations. First, there was a residual exchange risk in export GPA in 1925–31, because total duration of interest loss was eleven rather than eight days (the latter the length of the forward contract) for about five percent of the value (see section 2.4.3 above).

Second, interest loss (for specie import in 1791–1914 and for both import and export in 1925–31) varied with the duration of the Atlantic voyage. Also, forward-exchange contracting again was insufficient to remove all exchange risk from GPA export, in the face of uncertain voyage duration.[53]

Third, the price of specie abroad might differ at the time of the transaction from that expected at the initiation of GPA or GTF. In 1829 it was noticed that "silver in England, being a commercial commodity, subject to fluctuation in price, it will not be readily exported, unless with the prospect of a reasonable profit" (Secretary of the Treasury, 1830, p. 91). The risk of an unduly low price was present for exports of silver sold in the London market, and of an unduly high price for specie imports purchased in the market, during 1791–1834. Of course, the opposite movement of price would bring about an unexpected gain.

From mid-1852 to 1914, when the Bank bought and sold eagles by weight and also transacted in bars, profit would be adversely affected by an unexpected reduction in the Bank's purchase price (for specie export) or increase in its selling price (for specie import). Again, profit would be enhanced by price change in the opposite direction.[54]

The fourth two-sided risk was abrasion. Applicable 1834 to 1914, the shipper could not know for certain the amount of abrasion of coin obtained from the US Treasury (eagles) or Bank of England (sovereigns or eagles). An unexpectedly high abrasion of eagles from the Treasury or sovereigns from the Bank, or low abrasion of eagles from the Bank, would reduce profit. The opposite situations could also occur.[55]

A fifth two-sided risk was that bullion could be assayed abroad at a lower (higher) fineness than expected, thus reducing (increasing) profit. This risk applied to the export of eagles 1834–52 and to both the export and import of bars 1925–31.

The amount of risk premium was determined not only by the shipper's subjective probability distribution of uncertain outcomes but also by the shipper's disutility function for unpleasant outcomes (for one-sided risks) and his degree of risk aversion (for two-sided risks). The first determinant suggests a reduction in risk premium over time, because two important elements of uncertainty – the variability of the duration of an Atlantic voyage and the chance of a shipwreck – were substantially reduced with innovations in oceanic transport. There is no information on the second determinant.

In addition to the risk premium, arbitrageurs required a normal profit before they would engage in their operations.[56] Transferors, however, did not require normal profit, because profit was not the motive of their operation. Also, the risk premium applicable to the transferors was the risk premium inherent in the specie shipment minus that of the forgone exchange transaction. However, it is difficult (1) to obtain separate estimates of risk premium and normal profit at the same point of time (usually, either an estimate of joint value is provided, or only normal profit is presented), and (2) to compute the risk-premium differential of the specie shipment over the exchange transaction.[57] Therefore it will be assumed that GTF involved zero normal profit and risk premium.

While some (by no means all) contemporary writers were well aware of the necessity to include normal profit and risk premium in the overall cost of GPA, modern investigators such as Clark (1984) and modern writers of textbooks and treatises generally ignore these items.[58] It should be emphasized that the normal profit (plus risk premium) in GPA was not subsumed in interest cost but rather was computed as a separate item.[59]

Period averages of normal profit plus risk premium are shown in table 9.20. *1821–30*: The earliest estimate, 0.25 percent, is for February 1838, when the packet was still the dominant carrier of specie, and pertains to risk premium alone. Assuming that normal profit was half this premium – a ratio implicit in Spalding (1928a, p. 83) – a figure of 0.375 percent is obtained for this decade of packet supremacy. *1791–1800*: It is appropriate to add 0.125 percent to the 1821–30 estimate. Because the earlier decade was prior to the packet and was replete with war, there was greater variability, less regularity and reliability in shipment.

1831–40: Assume 0.375 fell to 0.25 percent on May 1, 1838, when steamship replaced packet as the dominant carrier, further increasing reliability and regularity. The duration-weighted average of the two estimates is taken. *1841–50*: Assume, similarly, that 0.25 declined to 0.125 percent on January 1, 1848, when regular liner service between New York and Liverpool was

Table 9.20 Direct cost and gold points, percent, period averages, 1791–1931 and 1950–66

Period	Normal profit plus risk premium	Direct cost				Gold points[c]			
		GPA[a]		GTF[b]		GPA		GTF	
		X	M	X	M	X[c]	M[d]	X[c]	M[d]
1791–1800	0.5000	5.8295	6.0454	4.0717	4.2876	6.1583	− 8.1002	4.4005	− 4.2876
1821–30	0.3750	3.4171	3.1545	2.3139	2.0513	3.6998	− 4.2148	2.5967	− 2.0513
1831–40	0.3417	2.0686	2.6756	1.2257	1.8327	2.3170	− 4.9061	1.4741	− 1.8327
1841–50	0.2125	1.7443	2.3797	1.0306	1.6660	1.7476	− 3.2960	1.0339	− 1.6660
1851–60	0.1250	1.3301	1.2315	0.7039	0.6053	1.3306	− 1.8631	0.7044	− 0.6053
1861–70	0.1250	1.4830	1.0511	0.8568	0.4249	1.4830	− 1.4962	0.8568	− 0.4249
1871–80	0.1125	1.1414	0.7100	0.5697	0.1383	1.1414	− 1.0657	0.5697	− 0.1383
1881–90	0.0625	0.6585	0.4793	0.3592	0.1800	0.6585	− 0.7141	0.3592	− 0.1800
1891–1900	0.0625	0.6565	0.4534	0.5468	0.3437	0.6550	− 0.6274	0.5453	− 0.3437
1901–10	0.0625	0.5005	0.3884	0.4278	0.3157	0.4993	− 0.5999	0.4266	− 0.3067
1911–14[e]	0.0625	0.5025	0.4308	0.4298	0.3581	0.5025	− 0.5915	0.4298	− 0.3581
1925[f]–31[e]	0.0750	0.5237	0.3371	0.4336	0.2492	0.6287	− 0.4466	0.5386	− 0.3587
1950–66	—	—	—	—	—	0.6371	− 0.6371	0.6371	− 0.6371

Notes:
[a] Total freight, insurance and handling cost (table 7.15) + total transactions cost (table 7.16 or 7.17) + normal profit plus risk premium.
[b] Total freight, insurance and handling cost (Table 7.15) + total transactions cost (Table 7.16 or 7.17).
[c] 1791–1931: Direct cost + total interest cost (table 7.18). 1950–66: see text.
[d] 1791–1931: − [Direct cost + total interest cost (table 7.19)]. 1950–66: see text.
[e] Second quarter.
[f] Third quarter.
Legend: GPA = Gold-point arbitrage.
GTF = Transfer of funds.
X = Exports.
M = Imports.
Source: Normal profit plus risk premium: see text.

established. Again the appropriate weighted average is computed. *1851–60, 1861–70*: The figure of 0.125 percent remains.

1881–1914: Estimates of 0.03125–0.125 percent and 0.125 percent alone are offered by the *New York Times* (August 9, 1895, p. 8; June 28, 1896, p. 2), 0.04 percent by Escher (1910, p. 117), 0.05 percent by Johnson (1911, p. 509), and 0.03125 percent by Whitaker (1919, pp. 525–6, 530) and Cross (1923, p. 394). All these estimates pertain specifically to normal profit. It is not clear which estimates implicitly include risk premium and which ignore the item. A figure of 0.0625 percent, the mid-point of the *New York Times* range, is a good compromise value among the diverse estimates, higher, as it is, than all the other estimates.

1871–80: Assume 0.125 fell to 0.0625 percent on January 1, 1879, when the United States returned to the gold standard – a significant date both substantially and psychologically. The duration-weighted average of 0.125 and 0.0625 is taken. *1925–31*: The estimate of 0.075 percent, consisting of 0.025 percent normal profit and 0.05 percent risk premium, is suggested by Spalding (1928a, p. 83).[60]

3 Gold-point estimates

Each of the component categories of GPA and GTF expense can be summed in terms of its own elements. The two final columns of table 9.4 are the total freight, insurance, and handling cost for export and import, respectively. These costs apply to both GPA and GTF. The last two columns of tables 9.7 (for export) and 9.13 (for import) provide the sum of transactions cost for GPA and GTF, respectively. There are separate figures for GPA and GTF, because exchange-rate cost (1) is positive for GPA, negative for GTF, and (2) for specie export, differs for the two operations. Freight, insurance and handling cost *plus* total transactions cost *plus* normal profit plus risk premium (applicable to GPA only) yield direct cost, shown in table 9.20 for GPA and GTF, export and import.[61]

Direct cost is distinguished from opportunity cost, the interest foregone on funds allocated to GPA or GTF. Tables 9.16 (for exports) and 9.17 (for imports) sum the three components of interest cost in the final two columns for GPA and GTF, respectively. For exports, the GPA and GTF totals are the same; the difference is that the interest cost from transportation duration for 1791–1914 is excluded from GTF in principle (inapplicable interest expense) and GPA in practice (zero interest expense). For imports, there is positive interest cost from oceanic transportation over 1791–1914; so the difference in total interest cost between GPA (the interest loss of a round-trip Atlantic voyage) and GTF (zero interest loss) is substantive.

Summing direct cost and total interest cost, the gold points, expressed as percent of parity, are obtained (for period averages and monthly series) and shown (for the usual period averages) in table 9.20. The gold-export and gold-import points each differ for GPA and GTF, with the GTF point necessarily lower.

The gold-export point, corresponding to CX in equation (8.1), is considered positive; the gold-import point, corresponding to $-CM$ in equation (8.2), is taken as negative. This convention is logical, because the gold-export point is above parity, the gold-import point below parity.

Although the gold-point estimates are represented in percentage form, or percent of parity, they could just as well be expressed as the number of dollars per pound (see section 4.1 of chapter 8). Irrespective of their form, the gold-point estimates derived here are an improvement over existing figures in at least four respects. First, separate estimates are provided for GPA and GTF. Second, the cost components of these operations are explicitly considered and all such components are incorporated in the derivation. Third, all available information on the components is utilized in the estimation. Fourth, consistent specie-point estimates are provided by period averages over 1791–1931 and as monthly series for 1890–1906 and 1925–31.

What remains is to obtain comparable "gold points" for the 1950–66 period. The intervention points of the Bank of England under the par-value system of the International Monetary Fund are the parameters that correspond to specie points in 1791–1931. From January 1, 1950 to December 16, 1951 the Bank's dollar-buying point (corresponding to the US gold-export point) was $2.80125 per pound and its dollar-selling point (akin to the US gold-import point) $2.79875 per pound. From December 17, 1951 to December 31, 1966 these rates were $2.82 and $2.78 (*The Economist*, December 22, 1951, p. 1538). The critical month, December 1951, had a daily-weighted average export point of $2.8103 and import point of $2.7897.

All these rates can be reexpressed as the percentage deviation from the par value ($2.80 per pound) registered at the International Monetary Fund. The duration-weighted average export and import points for the entire 1950–66 period are listed in the final row of table 9.20. They are symmetrical about parity, because the Bank's intervention points were so constructed. Further, of course, they are "the same for GPA and GTF," although these operations as such no longer occurred.

Part IV

External and internal integration

10 External integration

1 Gold-point spread and asymmetry of gold points

Following chapter 9, the gold-export and gold-import points are, respectively, the cost of specie export (CX) and the negative of the cost of specie import ($-CM$), expressed in percentage terms (percent of parity). Then the gold-point spread (more generally, specie-point spread), also in percentage terms, is the difference of the gold points: $CX - (-CM) = CX + CM$, the sum of the specie-shipment costs. If the gold points are expressed as dollars per pound, GX and GM, then the gold-point spread again is derived as the difference between the gold points, this difference taken as a percentage of (true mint) parity: $100 \cdot [(GX - GM)/M] = CX + CM$ again, following the notation of section 4 of chapter 8. This equivalent formulation of the spread justifies anew the representation of the gold-import point as the *negative* of percentage cost.

Of course, the gold points differ for GPA and GTF, whether for export or import. However, for both operations, the export point always differs in magnitude from the import point. The implication is that the gold points are not equidistant from mint parity. The mid-point of the gold-point spread, then, differs from mint parity. The spread mid-point (SM), expressed as the percentage deviation from parity, is half the sum of the algebraic gold points: $SM = (CX + (-CM))/2 = (CX - CM)/2$. Of course, parity itself in this configuration is zero [$100 \cdot \{(M - M)/M\} = 0$]. Expressed in dollars per pound, the spread mid-point is $RSM = (GX + GM)/2$ and parity M.[1]

The pure value of the spread mid-point, SM, is one thing; its value (RSM) relative to the gold-point spread is another. Consider the measure $RSM = 100 \cdot SM/(SM - CM)$, the deviation of the spread mid-point from parity as a percentage of half the spread itself. This statistic measures the mid-point/parity deviation relative to the width of the spread. It is bounded by zero (for $SM = 0$) and 100 (for $CM = 0$).

Both SM and RSM, each calculated separately for GPA and GTF, of course, are exhibited by period in table 10.1. For GPA, SM (and therefore

Table 10.1 *Mid-point of gold-point spread, period averages, 1791–1931*

| | Mid-point of gold-point spread | | | |
| | Value[a] (percentage deviation from parity) | | Relative value[b] (value as percent of half spread) | |
Period	GPA	GTF	GPA	GTF
1791–1800	− 0.9710	0.0564	− 13.62	1.30
1821–30	− 0.2575	0.2727	− 6.51	11.73
1831–40	− 1.2946	− 0.1793	− 35.85	− 10.84
1841–50	− 0.7742	− 0.3160	− 30.70	− 23.41
1851–60	− 0.2662	0.0495	− 16.67	7.57
1861–70	− 0.0066	0.2160	− 0.44	33.70
1871–80	0.0378	0.2157	3.43	60.93
1881–90	− 0.0278	0.0896	− 4.05	33.23
1891–1900	0.0138	0.1008	2.15	22.68
1901–10	− 0.0503	0.0600	− 9.15	16.36
1911–14[c]	− 0.0445	0.0359	− 8.13	9.10
1925[d]–31[c]	0.0910	0.0900	16.93	20.05

Notes:
[a] Average of gold export point and gold import point.
[b] Ratio of (mid-point value) to (mid-point value − gold import point), percent.
[c] Second quarter.
[d] Fourth quarter.
Legend: GPA = Gold-point arbitrage.
GTF = Transfer of funds.
Source: Gold points: table 7.20.

RSM) is negative in nine of the eleven pre-World War I periods, when the bill of exchange reigned. An important element in this sign configuration is the double interest loss for gold import coupled with zero such charge for export. The positive value of *SM* (and *RSM*) for both GPA and GTF in 1925–31, the period of cable-transfer dominance, is in the face of transportation-interest-loss neutrality. An ingredient here is the zero cost of acquiring and disposing of imported gold, as bars were obtained from the Bank of England and sold to the Treasury (or Federal Reserve Bank of New York) at the respective mint prices. In contrast, exported (Assay) bars were subject to an unfavorable price relative to mint price at both authorities.

The relative value of the spread does not have a discernible pattern. Only in one period (and for GTF alone) is *RSM* above 50 percent. Still, the statistic is trivially low (say, below 5 percent) only in a few cases.

2   Gold-point spread as a measure of integration

In chapter 7 various approaches to exchange-market integration – and associated measures, all involving the exchange rate – were examined. A radically different focus ignores the exchange rate and considers nothing but gold points. Market integration, logically termed "external integration," is represented by the specie-point spread, which in percentage terms is $(CX + CM)$. The narrower the spread, the greater the integration. The spread measures the extent of external integration in the sense of the amount yet to be achieved. Ingredients of the spread, and therefore the proximate determinants of integration, are the component costs of GPA and GTF.

Three authors adopt this technique and put it in practice by collecting data on the movement of specie points over time. Johnson (1905, p. 90, n. 1) comments that during the last quarter of the nineteenth century the gold-export point fell from three to two cents per pound. Cole (1929a, pp. 405–6, 419–20, n. 3) states that the gold-export point fell from over 4 percent in 1760 to 1.25 – 2.25 percent in the 1830s. Taking the dates 1886, 1905, and 1929, he mentions the diminution in the gold-point spread over time. Myers (1931, pp. 74–5, 342–3) observes the specie-export point for 1811, 1829, 1848, 1882, 1906, and 1908; the specie-import point for 1883, 1906, and 1908. Both gold points move closer to parity as time goes on, and she remarks in 1931 that "the drawing together of the gold points is still going on."

In sum, the three authors agree on a narrowing of dollar–sterling specie points in the nineteenth century and beyond. Without displaying data, Einzig (1970, pp. 172–3) discusses the "very gradually . . . narrowing of the spread between specie points" from 1815 over the nineteenth century. He also asserts that "not until the concluding decades of the 19th century and the early years of the 20th century" did the spread narrow to figures comparable to those of the interior period.

There are four deficiencies with how these authors apply the gold-point-spread approach to external integration. First, to the extent they use explicit data (which Einzig fails to do) and that the sources of the data are identified (not done by Johnson), the authors (Cole and Myers) rely on contemporary estimates of specie points. These estimates are inconsistent and of varying quality. Second, the dates of comparison are haphazard rather than systematic, in part because of the scattered nature of the known contemporary specie-point estimates.

Third, the gold-export and -import points are examined separately rather than their spread computed and considered as such. Fourth, no distinction is made between the GPA and the GTF spreads.

Table 10.2 *Gold-point spread, percent, period averages, 1791–1966*

| Period | Gold-point spread[a] | |
	Gold-point arbitrage	Transfer of funds
1791–1800	14.2585	8.6881
1821–30	7.9146	4.6480
1831–40	7.2231	3.3068
1841–50	5.0436	2.6999
1851–60	3.1937	1.3097
1861–70	2.9792	1.2817
1871–80	2.2071	0.7080
1881–90	1.3725	0.5392
1891–1900	1.2824	0.8889
1901–10	1.0993	0.7332
1911–14[b]	1.0940	0.7878
1925[c]–31[b]	1.0752	0.8973
1950–66	1.2742	1.2742

Notes:
[a] Gold export point – gold import point.
[b] Second quarter.
[c] Third quarter.
Source: Gold points: table 9.20.

All four problems are overcome here. First, the gold points exhibited in table 9.20 are derived by generating a time series of each cost component of GPA or GTF using all existing information over 1791–1931, so the gold-point estimates are consistent and of the highest possible quality. Second, the subperiods of 1791–1931 are carefully construed, and comprehensive (except for the omission of 1801–20). Third, the gold-point spread is computed and considered as such, the individual gold points deemed forgettable once they are used for the calculation. Fourth, the spread is separately constructed for GPA and GTF. Table 10.2 exhibits the spread by period for the two operations. For monthly details, figures 10.1, 10.2, and 10.3 show the spread for 1890–1906, 1925–31, and the parity band for 1950–66.

3   Testing of hypotheses of external integration

Hypotheses emanate from conjoining the conclusions of the authors exploring external integration (section 2 above) with the findings of the exchange-rate decadal-variation approach to market integration (section 4

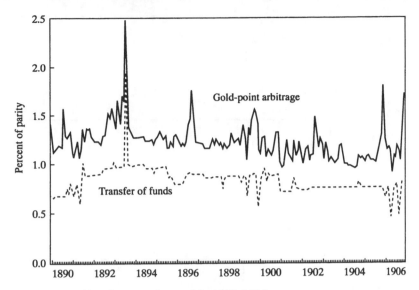

Figure 10.1 Gold-point spread, monthly, 1890–1906

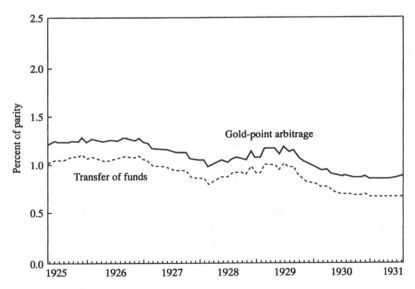

Figure 10.2 Gold-point spread, monthly, 1925–31

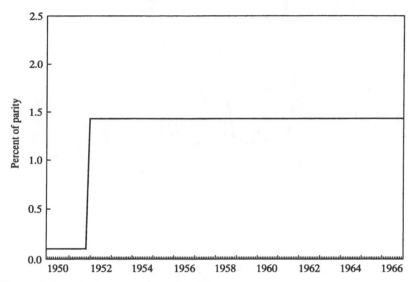

Figure 10.3 Parity band, monthly, 1950–66

of chapter 7). The hypotheses are examined using the specie-point-spread figures in table 10.2.

Hypothesis 1. There is enhanced integration over time. This is true without qualification for the GPA gold-point spread. The spread falls continuously from 1791–1800 to 1925–31. The hypothesis holds for the GTF spread through 1881–90. If the change from the 1790s to World War I, that is, 1791–1800 to 1911–14, is considered, the reduction in the GPA (GTF) spread is 13.16 (7.90) percentage points, or 92 (91) percent.

The proximate elements underlying this phenomenal improvement in external integration are exhibited in tables 9.1 to 9.20. They are declines in the freight, insurance, and handling rates in shipping specie; reductions in transactions costs; improvement in oceanic transportation in speed, regularity and reliability, first with the institution of the packets, then with the development of steamship service, associated with substantial reductions in interest loss; and decrease in normal profit and risk premium.

Hypothesis 2. The progressive improvement in integration is interrupted in the 1811–20 and 1861–70 decades. Specie-point data were not developed for 1811–20. The gold-point spread shows no such interruption for 1861–70, whether under GPA or GTF.

Hypothesis 3. The 1820s decade involved a tremendous increase in integration. Consider the change in external integration among the following three periods: 1791–1800, 1821–30, and 1911–14. From the 1790s to 1820s, the GPA (GTF) spread fell by 6.34 (4.04) percentage points, and from the 1820s to 1911–14 by 6.82 (3.86) percentage points. Therefore by the 1820s about half (48, 51 percent under GPA, GTF) the total improvement in integration to World War I – as measured by the decline in the gold-point spread – had been achieved.

The specie-point spread under GPA (GTF) narrowed from 14.26 (8.69) percent in the 1790s to 7.91 (4.65) percent in the 1820s – a decline of 6.34 (4.04) percentage points, as stated above. How much of this giant improvement in external integration was related to war? Two cost components of GPA and GTF directly and obviously affected by war were insurance and risk premium.

The normal (peacetime) freight-earnings insurance rate, applicable to 1791 and 1792, was 2 percent (Albion, 1942, p. 70). With the actual freight-earnings rate for the 1790s at 5.725 percent and the specie insurance rate for the decade estimated at 2.5440 percent (section 2.1.2 of chapter 9 and table 9.4), the peacetime specie rate would have been the product of 2/5.725 and 2.5440, or 0.8887 percent. The marginal insurance cost due to wartime, therefore, was $2.5440 - 0.8887 = 1.6553$ percent.

Regarding normal profit plus risk premium, the estimate for the 1790s was obtained by adding 0.125 percent to the 1820s figure (see section 2.5 of chapter 9). Assuming that half that augmentation was due to war, the marginal wartime risk premium was 0.0625 percent.

Then the gold-point spread for GPA in 1791–1800 had an extra component totalling double $(1.6553 + 0.0625) = 3.4356$ percent, and that for GTF double $1.6553 = 3.3106$ percent, solely as a consequence of the war characteristic of the decade. Therefore 3.44 (3.31) percentage points of the GPA (GTF) gold-point spread of the 1790s had vanished by the 1820s due merely to the fact that the 1820s were the first full peacetime decade since the 1780s.

In other words, 54 (82) percent of the narrowing of the GPA (GTF) specie-point spread from the 1790s to the 1820s was caused by the differences between war and peace. Not realised in the literature, the enhanced external integration of the 1820s had a powerful component that merely reflected peacetime rather than wartime.

There is some rationale, then, for delineating the trend in external integration from the 1820s, rather from than the 1790s, to 1911–14 (see hypothesis 1). In a relative sense, the improvement in integration remains impressive, with the GPA (GTF) gold-point spread falling by 86 (83) percent.

Hypothesis 4. From 1881 to 1966 (allowing for gaps) integration is at a high level. For the GPA spread, the hypothesis holds to 1925–31, in the sense that, for all periods of that time span, the spread is substantially narrower than in all prior periods. However, the hypothesis is qualified by the continuing decline in the spread to 1925–31. For the GTF spread, the higher level of integration had been reached one decade earlier. From 1871–80 to 1925–31 the gold-point spread is noticeably less than in the prior periods. For both GPA and GTF, the 1950–66 period marks a sharp increase in the spread (decline in integration).

Hypothesis 5. Not until 1881–1910 did the spread narrow to a value comparable to that of 1925–31. This hypothesis is contradicted by the evidence. For GPA, only after the nineteenth century, in 1901–14, was a gold-point spread of the same order of narrowness as that in 1925–31 reached. For GTF, the narrowness of the spread of 1925–31 was surpassed earlier, in 1871–80.

Hypothesis 6. Integration just prior to World War I exceeds that in 1925–31. True for the GTF, not true for the GPA spread.

In the next chapter the external-integration approach, which involves representing exchange-market integration by the gold-point spread, is assessed and reinterpreted in the context of a complete model of integration of the foreign-exchange market.

11 Internal integration

1 The model

In 1929 the greatest historian of the dollar–sterling exchange rate wrote:

Data on the course of exchange on London constitute one of the longest available statistical series on a monthly basis relating to American experience. Figures, most of which have already been tabulated, permit us to carry the study back over a century and a quarter. They are, accordingly, unusually tempting to the investigator who wishes to discover, if he can, by modern statistical analysis, new features of the economic history of the United States.   Cole (1929b, p. 203)

Since that date, the issue on which researchers have concentrated using dollar–sterling exchange-rate data is integration in the foreign-exchange market. This type of analysis was considered in chapter 7. Historians have used gold-point data to explore the same issue, but in a compartmentalized fashion, without reference to the exchange rate. This work was examined and developed in chapter 10.

One problem with the research of previous authors is the use of inappropriate exchange-rate or gold-point data – a defect corrected in chapters 7 and 10 through the employment of the data generated in this study. Other limitations, however, are methodological in nature and retained in the earlier chapters.

First, it is not stated why the gold-point spread itself rather than some transformation is the appropriate measure of external integration. Second, internal integration – the logical complement to external integration – is not even considered conceptually, let alone measured. Third, and consequently, there is the failure to assess quantitatively the relative importance of external and internal forces in fostering integration. Fourth, mint parity is adopted as the exchange-rate norm about which deviations from integration occur. This is in contradiction to the finding of gold-point asymmetry, the divergence of the spread mid-point from parity (see section 1 of chapter 10).

Fifth, the gold-point spread alone provides only a potential envelope for the exchange rate. An alternative interpretation is that the location of the exchange rate itself is viewed as irrelevant. On the other hand, examining exchange-rate variation outside the context of gold points biases measured integration by neglecting the influence of the gold-point spread on the exchange rate.

The basic problem, therefore, is that the exchange-rate-variation approach ignores the gold points, while the gold-point-spread ("external integration") analysis pays no attention to the exchange rate. Exchange-market integration must be examined by means of a model that incorporates both exchange rate and gold points, and that distinguishes between internal and external integration. The following formal model combines the exchange-rate-variation and gold-point-spread approaches, but not in an additive way.

Expressing the gold-export and gold-import points each as a percent of parity (CX and $-CM$), consider external integration (EI) anew. However, let this integration be measured by half the gold-point spread (rather than the full spread, as in chapter 10). Equivalently, external integration is the average of the absolute values of the gold points. Symbolically, $EI = (CX + |-CM|)/2 = (CX + CM)/2$. EI, expressed as a percent of parity, measures the extent of external integration, the amount of integration yet to be achieved. As EI decreases, external integration increases.

The gold points can be redefined as deviations from the spread mid-point (but still expressed as percentage points of parity). Denoting the redefined gold-export and -import points as CX^* and $-CM^*$, respectively, $CX^* = CX - SM = CX - (CX - CM)/2 = (CX + CM)/2 = EI = -(-CM - SM) = -(-CM^*) = CM^*$. Therefore EI can be interpreted as the gold-export point (the negative of the gold-import point) with respect to the spread mid-point rather than with respect to parity.

In a similar vein the long-run exchange-rate (R) series generated in chapter 6 is reexpressed as R^*, the deviation from the spread mid-point (though still expressed as percentage points of parity): $R^* = R - SM = R - (CX - CM)/2$. Of course, the spread mid-point (or gold points) used in the computation is specific to the period to which the exchange-rate values belong. For example, the forty observations of R for the 1791–1800 period are all converted to R^* by means of $SM = -0.9710$ for GPA and $SM = 0.0564$ for GTF (from table 10.1).

Internal integration is concerned with the amount of exchange-rate variation not in and of itself but rather given the gold-point spread or, equivalently, the level of external integration. Should exchange-rate variation decrease for a given level of external integration, internal integration increases. However, a higher level of external integration (a narrower gold-point spread) reduces the internal integration associated with a given amount of exchange-rate variation.

For a given period, consider exchange-rate variation as measured by mean$|R^*|$, the mean of the absolute values of R^*. For a given gold-point spread, or, equivalently, a given value of EI, internal integration varies negatively with mean$|R^*|$. For a given value of mean$|R^*|$, internal integration varies positively with EI.

What is the norm value of mean$|R^*|$, that which involves full internal integration? Perfect internal integration is achieved by $R^* = $ mean$|R^*| = 0$. The exchange rate is always at the mid-point of the gold-point spread. This is a "maximalist" criterion, extreme in its ideal. As an alternative, consider that external integration (EI) is the gold (export or negative import) point; a "minimalist" criterion of internal integration would involve the exchange rate simply respecting the gold point as a limit. While a particular value of R^* might exceed EI, on average it should not do so. Therefore a "minimalist" criterion of internal integration is mean$|R^*| \leq EI$. "Full" or "expected" internal integration is logically a compromise between the "maximalist" and "minimalist" standards; the criterion is mean$|R^*|$ mid-way between zero and EI, that is, mean$|R^*| = EI/2$.

So the expectation of internal integration is that the exchange rate on average be mid-way between the spread mid-point and a gold point. This standard for internal integration can be obtained in another way. Suppose that the exchange rate takes on all values within the spread with equal probability and any value outside the spread with zero probability. Formally, the probability density of $|R^*|$, f($|R^*|$), has zero value beyond EI and is distributed uniformly (rectangularly) between 0 and EI. Therefore the function is described as: (1) f($|R^*|$) $= 0$ for $|R^*| > EI$, (2) f($|R^*|$) $=$ constant $= 1/EI$, for $|R^*| \leq EI$. (The constant is $1/EI$ because the sum of the probabilities of all values must be unity). With equal probability of all values of $|R^*|$ between 0 and EI, the mean (or expected) value of $|R^*|$, which is mean$|R^*|$, is $EI/2$.

How can conditions (1) and (2) be realized? Defining a gold-point "violation" as $|R^*| > EI$, either the absence of such violations ($|R^*| \leq EI$ for all R^*) or "perfect" GPA (instantaneous removal of a violation) yields (1). Within the gold-point spread, there is no reason for the "natural" distribution of the exchange rate to be other than uniform. In fact, a "law of large numbers" might guarantee that over a sufficiently long time period the exchange rate takes on all values within the spread with equal probability. Assuming that the behavior of exchange-market participants (speculators and arbitrageurs) is "neutral" in the sense that it does not disturb the distribution, (2) results. There is an admitted lack of realism in some of these specifications (in particular, perfect GPA and neutral behavior of economic agents within the spread), but the issue is generation of a standard for internal integration rather than a set of realistic conditions under which integration operates.

With full (or expected) internal integration represented by mean$|R^*|$ = $EI/2$, the level of internal integration (II) is the shortfall from full internal integration: II = mean$|R^*|$ − $EI/2$. So, consistent with the interpretation of external integration (EI), II measures the extent of internal integration, the amount of integration yet to be achieved.

Maximum external integration is at $EI = 0$; so $EI \geq 0$, and realistically (because there are positive costs of GPA and GTF) $EI > 0$. Maximum (perfect) internal integration is at $II = -EI/2$, corresponding to mean$|R^*|$ = 0, again unrealistic (on three counts, with R not only constant, not only locked at the spread mid-point of the current period, but also jumping instantaneously to the new spread mid-point in the next period). However, it is certainly possible for $II < 0$ (corresponding to mean$|R^*| < EI/2$). A negative value of II simply means that there is overfull internal integration (II is less than its expected value).

2   Application of the model

The model of exchange-market integration is used to reexamine the integration of the foreign-exchange market from 1791 to 1966. Values for the mean absolute value of the exchange rate (mean$|R^*|$), external integration (EI), and internal integration(II), for both GPA and GTF gold points, are shown by period in table 11.1. The external-integration (EI) values are simply half those of the gold-point spread shown in table 10.2. Therefore the analysis of external integration in chapter 10 stands.

What remains to be done is a corresponding investigation of internal integration. Exchange-rate variation in the form of the mean absolute value of the exchange rate, as a representation of exchange-market integration, was examined in section 4 of chapter 7 and shown by period in table 7.1. How does that concept differ from internal integration (II)? The measure in chapter 7 is mean$|R|$; the one here is mean$|R^*|$ − $EI/2$, denoted as II. Therefore the current measure, II, differs from the former in two respects: (1) divergence from the spread mid-point rather than from parity, that is, the computation of mean$|R^*|$ rather than mean$|R|$ and (2) subtraction of an adjustment factor representing external integration ($EI/2$). Internal integration is exchange-rate variation adjusted for (1) the deviation of the spread mid-point from parity, and (2) external integration.

Hypotheses concerning exchange-market integration were examined for mean$|R|$ and EI, in chapters 7 and 10, respectively. It is natural to investigate

Table 11.1 *Internal and external integration, period averages, 1791–1966 (percentage points of parity)*

Period	Exchange rate[a] Mean of absolute values		External integration gold export point[a]		Internal integration[b]	
	GPA	GTF	GPA	GTF	GPA	GTF
1791–1800	4.1854	4.5699	7.1292	4.3440	0.6208	2.3979
1821–30	2.1443	1.8836	3.9573	2.3240	0.1656	0.7266
1831–40	1.4438	1.4115	3.6115	1.6534	− 0.3619	0.5848
1841–50	1.0414	1.0289	2.5218	1.3500	− 0.2195	0.3539
1851–60	0.8634	0.6106	1.5968	0.6548	0.0650	0.2832
1861–70	0.8703	0.8195	1.4896	0.6409	0.1255	0.4991
1871–80	0.3791	0.4456	1.1036	0.3540	− 0.1727	0.2686
1881–90	0.3207	0.3628	0.6863	0.2696	− 0.0224	0.2280
1891–1900	0.2470	0.2426	0.6412	0.4445	− 0.0736	0.0204
1901–10	0.1466	0.1518	0.5496	0.3666	− 0.1282	− 0.0315
1911–14[c]	0.1167	0.1325	0.5470	0.3939	− 0.1568	− 0.0645
1925[d]–31[c]	0.2764	0.2757	0.5376	0.4487	0.0076	0.0514
1950–66	0.2564	0.2564	0.6371	0.6371	− 0.0622	− 0.0622

Notes:

[a] Expressed as deviation from mid-point of gold-point spread.

[b] Exchange rate minus half gold-export point.

[c] Second quarter.

[d] Third quarter.

Legend: GPA = Gold-point arbitrage.
GTF = Transfer of funds.

Source: See text.

the applicability of these same hypotheses to (mean$|R^*|$ − $EI/2$) = II. The hypotheses are taken from their convenient assembly in chapter 10.

Hypothesis 1. There is enhanced internal integration over time. This hypothesis is true period-by-period from 1791–1800 to 1911–14, except for a temporary reverse movement lasting three periods (1841–70) for GPA and one period (1861–70) for GTF.The figures for GTF, because steadier than those for GPA, appear to be a better measure of internal integration, but subsequent analysis will indicate that this conclusion might be unwarranted (see section 4.4 below).

Considering the change from the 1790s to World War I, the reduction in adjusted exchange-rate variation (improvement in internal integration, ΔII) is 0.7776 (2.4624) percentage points, or 125 (103) percent. The excess over 100 percent reflects overfull internal integration. Amazingly, this happens as early as 1831–40 for GPA.

Hypothesis 2. The progressive improvement in integration is interrupted in the 1811–20 and 1861–70 decades. This holds for 1861–70, but data on EI and therefore II are not available for 1811–20.

Hypothesis 3. The 1820s decade involved a tremendous increase in integration. Indeed, a profound jump in internal integration occurs in the 1820s. From the 1790s to 1820s, II declined by 0.4552 (1.6713) percentage points for GPA (GTF), and from the 1820s to 1911–14 by 0.3224 (0.7911) percentage points. So by the 1820s about 60 percent or more (59, 68 percent under GPA, GTF) of the total improvement in internal integration to World War I had occurred – an even stronger performance than external integration.

Hypothesis 4. From 1881 to 1966 (allowing for gaps) integration is at a high level. The hypothesis holds excellently for GPA, with overfull integration from 1881 (in fact, 1871) to 1914, full integration in 1925–31, and overfull integration again in 1950–66. For GTF, the hypothesis applies with a decade's delay. From the 1880s to 1890s, integration improves by 0.21 percentage points. From 1891 onward, II does not exceed 0.05 percent. Certainly, by 1891–1914 exchange-market integration is unambiguously strong in both external and internal respects.

Hypothesis 5. Not until 1881–1910 does integration reach a value comparable to that of 1925–31. An amended hypothesis is true for GTF; the starting decade is the 1890s rather than 1880s. However, the hypothesis is decidedly rejected by GPA. In the 1830s and 1840s internal integration is not only higher than in 1925–31 but it is also at maximum strength (II at minimum algebraic value). Maximum internal integration in the 1830s and 1840s rather than late in the nineteenth century or close to World War I might suggest that a statistical artifact is at work under GPA. However, a substantive explanation does exist (again see section 4.4 below).

Hypothesis 6. Integration just prior to World War I exceeds that in 1925–31. This statement is true for both GPA and GTF.

3   Elements of internal integration

3.1   Dimensions of internal integration

There are three dimensions to internal integration: integration across space (geographic integration, with reference to the divergence of the exchange rate in the various port cities), across time (temporal integration, pertaining to the variability of the exchange rate), and with respect to the mid-point of the gold-point spread (placement integration, referring to the location of the exchange rate).

Geographic integration is ignored in the model of internal integration. Yet the dispersion of the American foreign-exchange market in the various port cities involved a geographic variation in the exchange rate, the reduction and elimination of which was an inherent part of the integration process (see section 1 of chapter 7).

Temporal integration, incorporated in the model of internal integration via the term $\text{mean}|R^*| = \text{mean}|R - SM|$ for a given value of SM (spread mid-point), has two components: recurring exchange-rate variation (for example, seasonal or cyclical variation) and non-recurring exchange-rate movements (due to exogenous shocks or random events). Improved temporal integration involves dampening or eliminating seasonal and other recurring variation, and moderating the non-recurring movements, thus reducing $\text{mean}|R^*|$ even for a given spread mid-point (SM).

Placement integration is concerned with the location rather than the variation of the exchange rate. The closer the exchange rate is to the mid-point of the gold-point spread, the stronger is internal integration. This dimension of integration is included in the model via the parameter SM in $\text{mean}|R^*| = \text{mean}|R - SM|$.

3.2   Determinants of internal integration

3.2.1   Background to foreign-exchange market

Forces determining the amount of internal integration fall into two categories. First, there are elements that constitute background to the foreign-exchange market. The level of transportation and communication, both international and domestic, clearly relates positively to the extent of internal integration, at the most elemental level as a prerequisite for any foreign-exchange transactions at all, but also in facilitating transactions in sophisticated ways (see sections 4.1–4.3). The state of expectations of participants in the foreign-exchange market is another background element, affecting their desire to hold one or the other currency. Expectations regarding the future value of the exchange rate are the proximate object, but ultimately the expectations are with reference to external events, such as suspension of specie payments. Therefore underlying the expectations is the state of nature, in this example, the stability of the banking system.

Note that the level of transportation and communication either remains the same or improves over time; so decade-by-decade this force can only enhance, never diminish, internal integration. Expectations regarding exchange-rate change and external events are another matter; they can be favorable or unfavorable for internal integration. As for stability of the American banking system, it generally increased over time, although certainly there were fits and starts.

3.2.2   Foreign-exchange market

Participants and operations
The second category is the foreign-exchange market itself, which has several components. One is the nature of the participants in the market. The participants could be either the ultimate buyers and sellers of exchange or they could be intermediaries. If intermediaries, they could be either brokers or dealers in exchange. Brokers bring ultimate buyer and seller together. Dealers may act as brokers, but in addition they perform three other functions. A dealer (1) buys and sells exchange on his own account, (2) acts as a wholesaler in that he buys and sells exchange to institutions (brokers) that deal directly with ultimate buyers and sellers of exchange, and (3) transacts exchange with other dealers. Eventually, the market with dealers alone as participants became what is known as the foreign-exchange market.

Ultimate transactors as the sole market participants are suggestive of a highly imperfect market. Looked at positively, each meeting of buyer and seller enhances geographic and/or temporal integration, albeit internal integration remains at a low level. Brokers are more successful and more efficient at linking buyer and seller than buyer and seller themselves can be; so both geographic and temporal integration is improved by their role. However, because brokers do not take uncovered positions in foreign exchange, there is a limit to the improvement they can achieve in temporal integration, and also in geographic integration where it is conjoined with temporal integration.

Dealers enhance integration by virtue of their special roles. In transacting with other dealers and retail institutions (brokers), they facilitate the operations of these market participants. In transacting on their own account, dealers take uncovered foreign-exchange positions across space, across time, and with respect to the mid-point of the gold-point spread. They also undertake GPA and GTF operations. In so doing, they improve the three dimensions of internal integration.

How so? If the exchange rate differs in two locations at the same time (or, realistically, for the same time period), brokers alone improve geographic integration by spatial arbitrage. If the exchange rate differs in the same location at two points in time (or in two time periods), dealers improve temporal integration by arbitrage over time (if the situation systematically recurs) or exchange-rate speculation (if otherwise). If the exchange rate differs in two locations, each for a different point in time or time period, dealers engage in joint spatial and temporal arbitrage (or speculation), thereby improving both geographic and temporal integration. It is the dealers' undertaking of uncovered positions in foreign exchange that reduces exchange-rate variation over time, thereby enhancing temporal integration (and geographic integration where intertwined with temporal integration).

What about operations that foster placement integration? Two situations should be distinguished. First, the exchange rate is located outside the gold-point spread (beyond a gold point, wherefore a "gold-point violation"). Symbolically, $|R^*| > EI$. GTF and GPA are the operations of relevance. The first prevents the exchange rate from going even further beyond the gold point, that is, from moving even further away from the spread mid-point (SM); the second returns the exchange rate to within the spread, thus bringing it closer to SM (see section 6 of chapter 8). It is recalled that by 1820 the dominant arbitrageurs and transferors performing these operations were foreign-exchange dealers (see section 3 of chapter 8).

Second, the exchange rate is within the spread ($|R^*| \leq EI$), either naturally or by virtue of GPA. In this situation GTF and GPA are inapplicable; for they are cost-effective or profitable, respectively, only when the exchange rate is outside the spread. Rather, a special form of exchange-rate speculation is in order. Such speculation, which operates only within the spread, acts to turn the exchange rate away from the gold points and, ideally, to place the exchange rate right at the spread mid-point ($R = SM$, or $|R^*| = 0$).

The form of speculation of interest emanates from absolute confidence in the gold standard and in the actions of gold-point transferors and arbitrageurs. First, speculators need confidence that, over their time horizon of expected exchange-rate change, the existing gold standard will be maintained, implying confidence in the existing gold points and therefore in the gold-point spread (represented here by EI). There is allowance for period-to-period changes in EI, as components of overall costs of import and/or export GPA might change their values. Second, speculators must have the belief that transferors and arbitrageurs will keep the exchange rate within the spread.

The nature of exchange-rate speculation under these conditions has not been fully explored in the literature, but all the ingredients are contained in White (1963), with double irony an analysis of trader *hedging* via forward cover (rather than exchange-rate speculation) under the *Bretton Woods* system (gold-exchange standard rather than gold standard). White assumes complete confidence on the part of importers and exporters "that, for example, the dollar price of the pound sterling would not move (within the next three months) outside the legal limits of \$2.78 and \$2.82" (White, 1963, p. 487). Conveniently, one can pretend that \$2.78 and \$2.82 are the gold-import and gold-export points, respectively; and White's argument can be applied to speculating rather than hedging and to the gold standard rather than the Bretton Woods system. In symbols, $SM = 0$, $R = R^*$, and $EI = 0.02/2.80 = 0.7143$ percent.

For any analysis of speculation, an assumption about speculators' exchange-rate expectations must be made. White assumes "that the trader [in present context, speculator] normally considers that all spot rates between \$2.78 and \$2.82 have *equal* probabilities of being realized in three months [in present context, over the speculators' time horizon of expected exchange-rate change]" (White, 1963, p. 489, italics in original). With the probability of an exchange rate outside the gold-point spread deemed zero, the probability density function $f(|R^*|)$ is exactly as in section 1: $f(|R^*|) = 0$ for $|R^*| > EI$, $1/EI$ for $|R^*| \leq EI$.

Now consider the spread mid-point, \$2.80 in White, $SM = 0$ here. The speculator engaging in numerous, repeated transactions will expect to realize positive profits, on average, by (1) buying pounds in the \$2.78 to \$2.80 range ($-EI \leq R^* < 0$), for the probability that the pound will appreciate exceeds 50 percent, and (2) selling pounds in the \$2.80 to \$2.82 range ($0 < R^* \leq EI$), for the probability that the pound will depreciate exceeds 50 percent.[1]

The amount of funds that speculators commit to their operations depends on the profit potential of an exchange-rate change. At the gold points themselves, \$2.78 and \$2.82 ($-EI$ and EI), there is a maximum profit of four cents per pound ($2 \cdot EI$ percent) and an average expected profit of 2 cents per pound (EI percent), which is the highest average profit. Therefore speculators will buy and sell the maximum amount of pounds at the respective rates. At the spread mid-point, \$2.80 (zero), expected average profit is zero and no speculative funds will be committed.[2] At the intermediate exchange rates, \$2.79 and \$2.81 ($-EI/2$ and $EI/2$), there is a maximum profit of three cents per pound ($1.5 \cdot EI$ percent) and an average expected profit of 1 cent per pound ($0.5 \cdot EI$ percent); an intermediate amount of pounds will be bought and sold, respectively. "Given the uncertainties of his assumed probability distribution at any particular time," as White states, the speculator will gradually increase his purchases of pounds as the rate falls from \$2.80 to \$2.78 (R^* falls from 0 to $-EI$) and gradually increase his sales of pounds as the rate rises from \$2.80 to \$2.82 (R^* rises from 0 to EI).[3]

The resulting effect of this speculation, then, is to put increasing pressure on the exchange rate to turn away from either gold point and back toward the spread mid-point, the closer the exchange rate is to a gold point, because the speculative demand for (supply of) foreign exchange increases, the closer the exchange rate is to the gold-import (export) point.

It is noted that the critical exchange rate at which there is zero speculative demand and supply of foreign exchange is the mid-point of the spread, not the mint parity. Therefore this type of exchange-rate speculation, under ideal assumptions, would always return the exchange rate to the mid-point of the gold-point spread ($R = SM$ or $R^* = 0$), with the force to do so strengthening, the further the exchange rate is from the mid-point. Thus placement integration is achieved. Absent ideal assumptions, this speculation improves placement integration but does not make it complete.[4]

Market structure
The second component of the foreign-exchange market is the market structure. Is the market purely competitive, controlled by a monopolist, strongly influenced by a price leader, or subject to intense competition among oligopolists? A market with strong competition – whether purely competitive or oligopolistic – enhances internal integration by driving down profit margins in arbitrage and speculation activities. However, one dominant market participant, in the form of a giant exchange dealer, can have a much more beneficial effect on integration. Such a dealer would possess financial strength and economies of scale, both of which would foster the arbitrage and speculation operations required for improved internal integration.

Indeed, it is arguable that the principal force that fostered internal integration in the nineteenth century was the growth and operations of two giant American foreign-exchange dealers. One was a chartered bank, the Second Bank of the United States under the presidency of Nicholas Biddle; the other a private banker, the House of Brown. If not monopolists, they certainly were effective price leaders – the Second Bank in 1826–36, the House of Brown in the fifteen years before the hegemony of the Second Bank and in the period from the demise of Biddle's successor bank in 1841 to the resumption of specie payments in 1879.

A careful consideration of the determinants of internal integration (introduced above) is indicated, with reference to their roles in the pattern of integration over time (hypotheses in section 2, as applicable, for the internal-integration series in table 11.1).

4   Background forces

4.1   International transportation

Oceanic transportation improved in speed, regularity, and reliability during the nineteenth century, first with the introduction of the packets, then with the development of steamship service. The beneficial effect on external integration is obvious; but there was also a positive impact on internal integration. The level and variability of the interest discount in the demand component ($t = 0$) of time bills of exchange was reduced. This pushed up the bill price closer to a spot-rate (cable) equivalent and reduced the variation in the bill and in the derived exchange rate.[5] Certainly this element played a role both in the long-run upward trend in internal integration and in the sharp jump in the 1820s (with the advent of the packets).

4.2   International communication

Transatlantic communication, as well as transportation, improved over the nineteenth century. In part, this was a consequence of the aforementioned gains in shipping speed, regularity, and reliability. In part, it was due to the availability of cable communication in the final third of the century and its enhanced use in the last two decades. Better communications improved exchange dealers' projections of the "arrival rate" for bills, that is, the rate at which bills would be rediscounted in London. With more accurate information, the risks dealers took were alleviated and exchange-rate variability was reduced.[6] Again there is explanation of the progressive improvement in integration over time and the great advancement in the 1820s.

In addition, the intense use of cable communication from 1882 onward integrated the stock and bond markets of New York and London to such an extent that changes in the exchange rate evoked substantial volumes of international capital movements, and that acted to stabilize the rate. Also, when the exchange rate went beyond a gold point, movement of securities rather than gold could return the rate to within the gold-point spread. Such international flow of securities constituted a substitute for, and an additional force to, GTF and GPA.[7] These forces help explain the high level of integration from 1881–90 to 1950–66.

4.3   Domestic transportation and communication

Improvement in domestic transportation and communication obviously fostered geographic integration. Davis and Hughes (1960, p. 59) present this element well: "as communication and transportation facilities improved, the US financial market became better integrated; and thus internal exchange rates disappeared and rates in any city were conditioned by rates in contiguous areas. This widening of the 'extent' of the exchange market also tended to damp the amplitude of the fluctuations."[8]

The authors are wise in noting the connection between geographic and temporal integration. Enhanced geographic integration by definition reduced exchange-rate variation among port cities at a point in time; that very effect also dampened the variation in any one port city over time. The trend of progressive improvement in internal integration is thereby supported. Also, the interruption of this process in 1861–70 receives explanation: "secession drastically reduced the 'extent of the market.'"

4.4   Expectations and underlying state of nature

Expectations of exchange-market participants concerning external events affected their exchange-rate expectations and their operations and activities, and thereby exchange-rate variability. Expectations regarding the occurrence, extent, severity, and duration of suspension of specie payments were potentially important for internal integration in any period in which the local (later the entire American) banking system was viewed as unstable. What is relevant here is not the observed amount of depreciation of paper currency (that being accounted for by adjustment of the exchange rate) but rather expectations regarding suspension or restoration of specie payments and the financial impact of same.

The unusually high internal integration in 1831–50 under GPA might reflect (1) expectation of more-rapid resumption of specie payments than in fact took place during the suspensions of 1837–42, (2) expectation of less currency depreciation under these suspensions than in fact occurred, and (3) lower subjective probability of suspension of specie payments during subperiods when specie payments were made than the customary assigned probability.

Expectations of the opposite nature from (1) and (2) might help explain the deterioration in internal integration, for both GPA and GTF, in the first decade of the greenback period (1861–70). In the next decade (1871–80) internal integration recovered, and again resort can be had to expectations (1) and (2).

After the Civil War, the American banking system became more stable. Davis and Hughes (1960, p. 62) observe that, as a result, the bank suspensions of 1873 and 1893, as well as the Baring Crisis of 1890, did not substantially affect the exchange rate. Certainly, the decadal values of internal integration covering these years (as well as 1907, another important episode

of suspension) show no interruption to the trend of progressive improvement. However, the enhanced stability of the banking system was relevant
not only in and of itself but also for its effect on expectations. Points (1) – (3)
above became stronger as the banking system achieved greater stability. Of
course, the reverse causation was also operative.

Expectations of war versus peace and (in wartime) victory versus defeat
also affect internal integration. The former played a role in the high value
of *II* in 1791–1800, the latter in the relatively high value in 1861–70, and
both would have been seen to be influential in 1801–20, if only (gold-point)
data were available to compute *II*. The steady improvement in internal
integration from the 1870s to World War I is in part explained by the
absence of any war between the United States and Britain and the absence
of major war between any one of these countries and other powers.
Expectations of peace were favorable and internal integration thereby fostered.

5   Exchange-market participants prior to the rise of the Second Bank

5.1   Individual merchants

The problem with the American foreign-exchange market since its inception in colonial times and continuing to the end of the eighteenth century
was that it was naturally imperfect. This poor internal integration, exhibited in the high *II* value for 1791–1800, had several causes.

First, all bills of exchange were sterling drafts, drawn on London; none
were dollar drafts, drawn on the American port cities. This characteristic
made the foreign-exchange market inherently one-sided, as noted by Myers
(1931, p. 76). A low (high) supply of sterling bills in the port city necessarily
resulted in a higher (lower) exchange rate [or export (import) of gold] rather
than a purchase (sale) of dollar drafts in London.

Second, the demand for and supply of bills by merchants were split both
geographically and temporally. The supply of bills, generated primarily by
exporters of cotton and tobacco, was in the South and concentrated in the
winter. The demand for bills, principally by importers of commodities, was
in the North and in the late summer and autumn. So, as Perkins (1975, p. 7)
concludes: "Because the supply of bills and the demand for them were
separated so widely in time and place, the early exchange markets did not
function smoothly; exchange rates, meaning prices, were subject to sharp
ups and downs rather than gradual movements."[9]

Third, the "trading class" was small in number in colonial times and so
developed the habit of "pass[ing] their bills from hand to hand" (Cole,

1929a, p. 388). With brokers not involved, the ultimate transactors (merchants) constituted the participants in the foreign-exchange market.

Fourth, existing technology for perfecting the market, in particular, newspaper advertising, went unutilized. "Bills were not offered in this manner [via newspaper advertisements] until the close of the eighteenth and the beginning of the nineteenth century" (Cole, 1929a, p. 388).[10]

Fifth, the supply of bills was subject to sharp fluctuations, in part because of the lack of diversification in American exports, with cotton and tobacco constituting about two thirds of domestic exports.[11]

Sixth, capital transactions did not play a stabilizing role in the exchange rate and balance of payments, because capital flows were small. "Neither long nor short-term lending and borrowing was of particular importance at the turn of the century." In particular, merchants rarely invested in foreign currencies: "it appears that there was then little short-time lending and borrowing through the exchanges" (Smith and Cole, 1935, p. 24).

5.2   Stock and exchange brokers

It is possible that the earliest brokers in the foreign-exchange market were "stock and exchange brokers." Though their primary transactions lay elsewhere – in banknotes, domestic exchange, collection of interest, transfer of stocks, etc. – they stood ready to "purchase and sell on commission . . . bills of exchange," so advertising as early as 1801 (Cole, 1929a, p. 392).

5.3   Merchant houses and banks

Early in the nineteenth century some merchants in the port cities began to expand their horizons beyond commodity trade and engage in monetary transactions, in particular, the buying and selling of sterling bills of exchange. From merchants, they became merchant-bankers and were on the way to becoming private, meaning unincorporated, banks. Though not chartered by state or federal government, they were the dominant banks in the foreign-exchange market. Beginning as brokers, they evolved into dealers.[12]

Commercial (chartered) banks "did not buy and sell bills as intermediaries among merchants" (Cole, 1929a, p. 393). While some such banks engaged in foreign-exchange transactions on behalf of the US Treasury, they were not "active factors in the exchange market as a whole" (Cole, 1929a, pp. 393–4). In fact, "dealing in foreign exchanges was considered the domain of merchants and not that of chartered banks" (Redlich, 1951, p. 130). In 1817, a year after the Second Bank of the United States was federally chartered, a committee of the directors was appointed to examine whether the bank should have a foreign-exchange business at all! "At the time . . . apparently foreign-exchange transactions were still not accepted as assuredly the proper province of such an institution" (Cole, 1929a, p. 394).

5.4   House of Brown

Of all the merchants that became merchant-bankers and then private banks, the House of Brown had the most clearly defined such process. It was also the most prestigious and had the greatest influence on the foreign-exchange market.[13] The House of Brown provided leadership in exchange-market integration from about 1810 to the ascendancy of the Second Bank of the United States in 1826 under the presidency of Nicholas Biddle. It resumed this dominance after the demise of Nicholas' Biddle's successor bank in 1841 and retained it until after specie payments resumed in 1879 (see section 7.1 below). The current section is concerned with the role of the House of Brown in the exchange market prior to Second Bank dominance.[14]

At the end of 1800, Alexander Brown became a linen importer in Baltimore. By 1803 he had become a foreign-exchange broker, purchasing sterling bills from exporters in Maryland and Virginia, selling them to importers in Baltimore. In 1810 a branch was established in Liverpool, permitting the firm, by drawing on the branch, to supply sterling bills on demand in exact amount to fit the purchaser's needs. (The bills were accepted in Liverpool but paid in London.) The firm became the price leader in the market. "There are no indications that the Browns deferred to any other firm in pricing their bills" (Perkins, 1975, p. 21). It helped that the Browns established a Philadelphia branch in 1818 and a New York branch in 1825.

By the early 1820s the House of Brown was running an uncovered foreign-exchange account, with temporary excesses of sales over purchases of sterling bills. This activity played a major role in the improved internal integration in the 1820s. The exchange-market leadership of the House of Brown would be seen also in enhanced integration in the previous decade, were data only available. The volume of their exchange-rate transactions was growing steadily. In the 1820s the Browns had only one failure in perfecting the market: "they did not maintain a permanent and continuous market for bills of exchange. In the 1820s the partners were not willing to buy or to sell sterling at all times. Rather, they reserved the right to decline service to customers and the general public" (Perkins, 1975, p. 6).

6 Exchange-market participants during Second Bank hegemony

6.1 Second Bank of the United States

In 1823 Nicholas Biddle became president of the Second Bank of the United States, a position he was to hold throughout the Bank's existence. In 1826 the Bank began the extensive foreign-exchange operations that led even Edwin Perkins, the historian most perceptive of the contributions of the House of Brown in integrating the foreign-exchange market, to observe that "the organization that contributed most to the maturation of the American foreign exchange market was the Second Bank of the United States under the leadership of Nicholas Biddle" (Perkins, 1975, p. 154).

Why was internal integration fostered more by the Second Bank than by the House of Brown, the leader in the foreign-exchange market prior to 1826? First, the Second Bank, based in Philadelphia, had actual branches in all the major American foreign-exchange centers (the port cities) and not just agents, with which the House of Brown made do elsewhere than in Baltimore, New York, and Philadelphia. The Second Bank opened eighteen branches shortly after it began operations and eight more later, though one was abandoned (Wright, 1949, p. 368). The total number of 25 branches plus one main office contrasts sharply with the three cities in which the House of Brown was located.

The branch-banking system gave a threefold advantage to the Second Bank. (1) A strong information network provided market data to the decision-maker (Nicholas Biddle) in Philadelphia. (2) The branches were ideal for carrying out transactions in the localities in which they resided. (3) The branches presumably were loyal and reliable, whereas the House of Brown experienced difficulties in obtaining suitable representatives in the South (Perkins, 1975, p. 24).

Second, "the Second Bank also possessed far greater capital resources than any of its competitors in the foreign exchange field" (Perkins, 1975, p. 154). Third, it was allied with a powerful merchant-banking firm in London, Baring Brothers and Company, whereas the House of Brown had only its branch in Liverpool. The House of Baring granted the Second Bank a running credit originally of £100,000, from 1829 £250,000. This was the amount by which bills drawn in advance on Baring Brothers could exceed remittances of bills or specie or other coverage. A credit this large for foreign-exchange operations was unprecedented in Baring history. It was also the case that Biddle made aggressive use of this financial arrangement, causing grief for the Barings both because the Second Bank's account with the Barings fluctuated to the Barings' disadvantage and because the Barings (as well as the Bank of England) viewed Biddle's foreign-exchange operations as overly large and speculative.[15]

Nevertheless, the combined financial strength of the Second Bank and House of Baring gave the Bank substantial economies of scale in foreign-exchange transactions, encouraging a large volume of operations, and also permitted it to take risks in the form of open foreign-exchange positions. Thus in both its volume and nature of transactions, the Second Bank enhanced internal integration.

Fourth, while for the House of Brown any improvement in internal integration that resulted from its profit-making activities was a byproduct rather than an objective, Biddle acted on a belief that he had a mission to provide the United States with both a national and a stable foreign-exchange market. His concern was no less than to integrate the market in all three dimensions. (1) *Geographic integration*: "Biddle . . . viewed the greater coordination of the southern and northern markets as one of his primary responsibilities" (Perkins, 1975, p. 7). (2) *Temporal integration*: Stability in the exchange rate was also an important objective for Biddle. In particular, he was determined to rid the country of the seasonal pattern of the dollar–sterling exchange rate (Perkins, 1975, pp. 154–5). (3) *Placement integration*: Biddle was concerned whenever the exchange rate went beyond the gold-point spread, not only because of the large movement in the exchange rate that brought it there but also because the money market was affected by the resulting flow of specie. In such a circumstance he would take steps to return the exchange rate to within the spread, either through direct exchange-rate transactions or through GTF/GPA (Redlich, 1951, p. 131; Myers, 1970, p. 88).

What were Biddle's principal accomplishments in internally integrating the American foreign-exchange market? First, he actively united the geographically split, Northern and Southern, markets.[16] The southern branches of the Bank specialized in purchasing bills of exchange, while the northern branches specialized in selling them. Geographic integration received a powerful boost, the Bank earned handsome profits, and the resulting price movements in the two regions were to the advantage of both southern exporters and northern importers.

Second, Biddle reduced the natural seasonality in the exchange rate, because geographic integration of the market involved purchase of bills during the seasons when the exchange rate was low (winter and spring) and sale of bills when the rate was seasonally high (summer and fall).[17] "The Second Bank was an innovator when it came to buying and selling foreign exchange according to a seasonal pattern" (Perkins, 1975, p. 155). Amazingly, both the House of Baring and American observers considered this technique to be speculative in nature. Of course, temporal integration benefited enormously from Biddle's counterseasonal operations.

Third, the Second Bank stood always ready to buy or sell sterling bills.[18] In thus maintaining a continuous market for foreign exchange, Biddle fostered both geographic and temporal integration.

Some assert that the Second Bank was so strong in its 1826–36 heyday as to constitute a monopoly in the foreign-exchange market. The Bank is said to have "virtually controlled" the market (Catterall, 1902, p. 112) and to have "secured a virtual monopoly of foreign exchange dealings" (Myers, 1931, p. 69). Cole (1929a, p. 394) disagrees, stating that "nowhere does the power of the institution seem to have approached a monopoly." Rather, most writers view the Second Bank as the dominant participant in the foreign-exchange market, with substantial market power, and functioning as the price leader, having taken over that role from the House of Brown in 1826.[19] Certainly, the substantial increases in internal integration in the 1820s and 1830s owe much to the Second Bank from the second half of the 1820s, although, as Perkins (1975, p. 29) warns, one must not neglect the role of the House of Brown in the first half of that decade.

6.2   Other commercial banks

Because of the example and leadership set by the Second Bank, other commercial banks began substantial dealing in foreign exchange. This did not happen until the 1830s.[20]

6.3   House of Brown

During the period of Second Bank dominance, the House of Brown was "one of the two or three houses who represented something of a second tier of bill sellers between the Second Bank and ordinary endorsers" (Perkins, 1975, p. 30). Its role in integrating the market was now a clearly subsidiary one.

7   Exchange-market participants after the Second Bank

7.1   House of Brown

At the end of 1836 the Second Bank of the United States came to an end, not because of business failure but because (due to political opposition, principally on the part of President Andrew Jackson) its charter was not renewed upon expiration. A successor bank chartered by the state of Pennsylvania and initially under Biddle's management "was able to exert some influence over exchange rates," but encountered great financial difficulties and failed in 1841 (Perkins, 1975, p. 155). The House of Brown proceeded to reclaim the market leadership role it had enjoyed in the fifteen years prior to the Second Bank's hegemony.[21]

There are several reasons why the House of Brown was able to regain market dominance. First, it had been the principal competitor of the Second Bank during 1826–36. Second, it emulated Biddle by establishing offices in all the port cities. The existing branches in New York and Philadelphia were complemented by new branches in Mobile and New Orleans in 1838 and Boston in 1844, and there were agencies in Charleston and Savannah.[22]

Third, the Liverpool branch continued to play the role of a Baring, providing an office on which sterling could be drawn and credit obtained. Though lacking the financial strength of the House of Baring, the Liverpool branch was an integral part of the entire House of Brown. The resulting "unity of purpose" (Perkins' terminology) provided an advantage over competing firms that dealt with independent firms in England, as indeed it did over the Second Bank (but probably not enough to compensate for the great financial strength and prestige of Baring Brothers).

Fourth, potential competitors did not build up their foreign-exchange business, because of the pessimism associated with the bank suspensions and failures over 1837–41 and the poor state of the economy – factors that did not dissuade the House of Brown.

Fifth, the Browns divided operational responsibilities between their main offices, New York and Liverpool, according to comparative advantage (Perkins, 1975, p. 197).

Sixth, beginning in 1832 (when President Jackson vetoed a Congressional bill to renew the Second Bank's charter, suggesting the Bank might come to an end in four years) the House of Brown imitated the Second Bank by engaging heavily in the geographic and seasonal operations that were the Bank's forte, thereby preempting the void that would occur with the demise of the Second Bank and its successor institution. In so doing the Bank enhanced internal integration in the 1840s and 1850s (until the end of the antebellum period).

An important contribution of the House of Brown to internal integration in the 1840s and 1850s was its technological innovation of utilizing the domestic telegraph system. The telegraph enabled completion of the geographic integration of the foreign-exchange market by providing virtually instantaneous dissemination of information and communication of instructions, and by greatly enhancing the speed of transactions. The Browns used the telegraph to maintain a uniform exchange rate in all the major port cities and to change that rate with ever greater frequency over time.

Thanks in part to their "superior, more centralized information system," the House of Brown became the price leader in the foreign-exchange market in the 1850s and continued to have this status in the 1880s.[23] However, the firm did not have market influence to the same extent as the Second Bank had enjoyed. The reason was twofold. First, the House was not as strong relative to the rest of the market as the Bank had been. Second, in contrast to Nicholas Biddle, the House did not seek to integrate and control the foreign-exchange market as such. As stated by Perkins (1975, p. 186):

Aside from the partially seasonal aspect of their operations, the Browns' main function was that of a broker, or middleman, between the current sellers and buyers of exchange. And from that standpoint, the absolute level of rates, except for exceptionally high premiums or low discounts, was not a matter of crucial importance. Their primary concern was the maintenance of a sufficient margin between any given selling rate and the price simultaneously paid for covering bills of exchange.

In contrast to the Second Bank, the internal integration that resulted from the Browns' exchange-market leadership and operations was not one of their objectives.

7.2   Other private banks

The main participants in the foreign-exchange market from the 1840s to the 1890s were the large private bankers of New York. Brown Brothers was the most important, as discussed in the previous section. After the fall of the Second Bank, the Browns' chief competitors were the few other active private bankers, especially Prime, Ward, and King, and Fitch Brothers and Company (Myers, 1931, pp. 69–70). In 1871 the newly merged Drexel, Morgan and Company became the Browns' chief competitor (Perkins, 1975, p. 209). Even by the 1880s the number of market participants was very small: "Though other [than Brown Brothers] private bankers shared in the business, they numbered scarcely half a dozen; and these half-dozen, with their attendant brokers, composed the foreign-exchange market of the 'eighties, purveying to most incorporated banks of the whole country as well as to commercial houses" (Cole, 1929a, p. 408).

As it was observed in the early 1920s: "Two or three decades ago private bankers enjoyed a practical monopoly of the country's foreign exchange business" (York, 1923, p. 415). Led by the House of Brown, these houses were involved in the improvement in internal integration to the end of the century.

7.3   Incorporated banks

Incorporated banks as distinct from private banks did little foreign-exchange business in the antebellum period. "In fact, after the fall of the

Second United States Bank – and perhaps in part because of that fall – the rôle of commercial banks as a whole in foreign-exchange dealings appears to have been much less important than before" (Cole, 1929a, p. 395). After the Second Bank, the incorporated institutions were only state banks and state-chartered trust companies; in the 1860s they were joined by national banks. These institutions persisted in little interest in foreign exchange until the turn of the century (Myers, 1931, p. 348).[24]

This situation did not change until around 1900. Myers (1931, p. 348) writes: "It was not until the turn of the century that it became common for national banks to undertake a foreign exchange business." Escher (1933, p. 94) states that incorporated institutions were "far less of a factor [in the foreign-exchange market] at the beginning of the present century than were the privately owned banking houses." In 1911 it was observed: "For a national bank to have a foreign department was, until only a few years ago, an unusual thing, the business being concentrated almost entirely in the hands of the private bankers" (Johnson, 1911, p. 512).

The relative importance of incorporated and private banks shifted rapidly. Again it was written in 1911: "Recent years have, however, seen a great change in this regard. Where it was the exception for the big bank or trust company to do a regular foreign exchange business only a comparatively short time ago, it is now the rule. . . . In the city of New York the past decade has seen two institutions, one a national bank and the other a trust company, come to take a commanding position in the foreign exchange field" (Johnson, 1911, pp. 512–13).

Probably it was during World War I that the private banks gave way to incorporated institutions as the principal group in the foreign-exchange market: "among the changes in the last forty years are the following: a decline in the importance of the merchant-bankers, accompanied by the elevation in significance of the incorporated banks and trust companies – a movement which received acceleration in the recent war years" (Cole, 1929a, p. 419).

By the early 1920s the incorporated institutions were clearly dominant. In 1923 it was said: "In New York practically all the large banks and trust companies are engaged in this branch of banking as well as a number of private banking firms. . . . At present by far the greater part is transacted by incorporated banks, three or four of which are reputed to do a good deal more than half of the total trading in the open market" (York, 1923, pp. 414–15). A decade later the statement was at least as strong: "these [incorporated] institutions, especially since the War, have built up their foreign departments to a point where it can safely be said that by them there is today being handled the great bulk of the country's foreign exchange business." The private international banking houses remained in the market, but with a much reduced market share due to "the huge additional volume of business developed by the national and state banks" (Escher, 1933, pp. 94–5).

In the 1960s the foreign-exchange market consisted of 20–5 American banks, mostly in New York, with less than half of them doing the bulk of the business. Also trading actively in foreign exchange were about twenty branches or agencies of foreign banks.[25]

In the decades when the status of the dominant exchange-market participant was switching from private to incorporated banks (1901–14), internal integration was greater than in the decades before or after. Though internal integration remained at a high level, it ceased to be overfull in 1925–31 (but returned to that status in 1950–66). The explanation of this pattern might lie in market structure.

8   Market structure

The varying market structure of the American foreign-exchange market definitely affected the level of internal integration and its movement over time. In colonial times and to the end of the eighteenth century, the ultimate transactors – exporters and importers – were also the proximate transactors and the only participants in the market. There was free entry into the market, but with ambiguous implication for integration. Each entrant, after all, carried with him nothing but one side of a transaction for which the other side had to be found. If the new entrant readily completed a "double coincidence of barter," integration was enhanced; if not, integration was diminished. It is not surprising that in the 1790s integration was low indeed (II extremely high – see table 11.1).

The early brokers and exchange dealers, those in the first quarter of the nineteenth century, found entry easy, notwithstanding the market dominance of the House of Brown in the 1811–25 period. Such free entry certainly fostered internal integration; for the would-be market participants were brokers and dealers, ready to intermediate in transactions.

The market structure changed radically when the Second Bank became dominant. "The Second Bank . . . drove profit margins down so much that many firms left the field entirely. . . . The dominant position of the Second Bank discouraged new entries into the exchange field" (Perkins, 1975, p. 225). In 1811–25 both the leadership of the House of Brown and free entry had enhanced integration. In 1826–36 the Second Bank through its policies and operations improved integration but through its effect on market structure worsened integration.

A few merchants who had been more firmly entrenched in the market, but who were by no means specialists, stayed in the field to cover some of the gaps left by the Second Bank . . . the market became increasingly concentrated with only one dealer that could be clearly identified as a genuine specialist in handling foreign exchange transactions exercising leadership   (Perkins, 1975, p. 225).

From 1837 to 1842 only the House of Brown expanded foreign-exchange operations to take over the vacuum left by the Second Bank and that Biddle's successor bank could not successfully fill. The market remained concentrated, perhaps a duopoly but with the House of Brown ever stronger and the Biddle bank ever weaker. Nevertheless, with two large market participants engaged in competition throughout the 1830s, the foreign-exchange market enjoyed substantial internal integration, seen clearly in the GPA figure (table 11.1).

In 1841, with Biddle in retirement, his bank failed and the Browns were supreme, except for the House of Baring in conjunction with its American agents (now, of course, excluding the Second Bank). The Barings actually took steps to reduce their foreign-exchange business over time (Perkins, 1975, pp. 155, 165). However, the Browns did not long enjoy limited competition. "After 1843 economic conditions improved and a host of new firms gradually entered the market. . . . The advances in communications which followed the spread of the telegraph lines reduced risks substantially and led brokers and dealers alike to increase their activities" (Perkins, 1975, p. 225).

So again, as in the 1811–25 period, free-entry competition complemented the market leadership of the House of Brown. "Although the Browns were formidable competitors, they did not have the market power to restrict entry into the field" (Perkins, 1975, p. 225). Therefore their response was to increase their volume of transactions in an effort to increase market share. However, the market flexibility afforded the Browns was too low for the strategy to work. The result was that their profit margin fell even more and the competition was not driven out.[26] This outcome was bad for the House of Brown but good for the market's internal integration in the 1840s and 1850s. The Browns' profit margin on foreign-exchange transactions fell from 1–1.5 percent in the early 1820s to 0.5 percent in the 1840s and 0.125–0.25 percent in the late 1850s (Perkins, 1975, pp. 26–7, 160–1, 206). Correspondingly, internal integration under GTF continued to improve to the end of the antebellum period.

The Civil War, the suspension of specie payments, and new complexities in handling bills of exchange permanently destroyed free entry into the foreign-exchange market. In fact, many firms left the market. The House of Brown enjoyed an increased profit margin of almost 0.375 percent on foreign-exchange transactions in the late 1860s (Perkins, 1975, pp. 206–7).

The market became oligopolistic, with only large and specialized dealers as participants. Cole (1929a, p. 408) notes that "By the decade of the 'eighties . . . The business [of the foreign-exchange market] had been transferred wholly to professional hands." In fact the change had occurred two decades earlier. "An irreversible trend toward greater specialization and concentration emerged in the 1860s. Whereas the firm [House of Brown] previously had been the market leader among a diverse group of exchange dealers, it now held the same position of leadership within a market that was becoming increasingly oligopolistic" (Perkins, 1975, p. 206). In 1868 the market consisted of about a dozen participants (Perkins, 1975, p. 209). By the 1880s this number had been halved (Cole, 1929a, p. 408).

On the return to the gold standard in 1879, an intense price competition emerged among these specialized dealers, helping to explain the increasingly tight internal integration in the final two decades of the century.[27] Integration became even stronger, in fact overfull, in 1901–14, but faltered to underfull levels in 1925–31. A reason for the higher integration in the early twentieth century is probably the existence of not one but two strong groups – private banking houses and incorporated banks and trust companies – in the foreign-exchange market, albeit the relative importance of the groups was in the process of change (see section 7.3).

In 1950–66 integration became overfull again. The larger number of effective players in the market compared to the 1920s may be part of the explanation.

9   Importance of internal versus external integration

In explaining the dampening of exchange-rate variation over the nineteenth century, Davis and Hughes (1960, pp. 58–9) contrast "factors external to the American economy," that is, "reduced ocean-transport cost coupled with the increased speed and reliability of transport and communications and the development of adequate ocean insurance," with "fundamental changes within the US economy," such as reduced frequency of bank specie suspensions and improved communication and transportation facilities in the US financial market.

Davis and Hughes describe the external factors as "important," but they are said to be "powerfully reinforced" by the internal developments. In fact, from 1791–1800 to 1911–14, $\Delta EI/\Delta II = 8.46\ (1.60)$ under GPA (GTF). The external factors in the form of EI had about 8.5 (1.5) times the impact of the internal forces, represented by II. Narrowing of the specie points dominated developments internal to the American foreign-exchange market in enhancing integration, a result that contradicts Davis and Hughes and those who cite their view with implicit approval.[28]

It must be acknowledged that external versus internal integration is not the same as external versus internal factors. Some external factors impinge causally on internal integration. Examples are international transportation and communication and the alliance of British firms (House of Baring, Liverpool branch of House of Brown) with American foreign-exchange dealers. Correspondingly, internal factors play a role in determining external integration. For example, government policy sets the prices at which specie is transacted by arbitrageurs and transferors. In sum, there are relationships between internal and external integration beyond the identity that relates internal integration, external integration, and exchange-rate variation: $II = \text{mean}|R^*| - EI/2$.

Nevertheless, the analysis is continued. As discussed above (section 3 of chapter 10), there is some rationale for delineating the trend in exchange-market integration from the 1820s (rather than 1790s) to World War I. Now $\Delta EI/\Delta II = 10.58$ (2.44) under GPA (GTF). The improvement in external relative to internal integration, a multiple of about 10.5 (2.5), is even greater than with the 1790s starting period.

Internal integration is an important concept and its enhancement over time was fundamental to the development of the American foreign-exchange market. However, the improvement in external integration, meaning narrowing of the gold-point spread, was the much more important element in the process of perfecting the market.

Part V

Market efficiency

12 Theory of market efficiency

1 Definition of exchange-market efficiency under a gold standard

1.1 Isolation of existing literature

A vast literature on the efficiency of the foreign-exchange market under a floating exchange rate exists, and the many empirical investigations are readily organized under the rubric of the theory of efficient asset markets.[1] In contrast, studies of the efficiency of a gold standard differ radically among themselves in the very criterion of efficiency.

Interestingly, the exchange-market-efficiency literature makes no allusion to the literature on gold-standard efficiency. The reason is fourfold. First, the research on gold-standard efficiency has been neither reported nor interpreted in the context of the theory of asset-market efficiency, though it is implicitly in that tradition.[2] Second, the gold-standard studies, unlike those in the efficient-asset-market mainstream, devote minimal attention to explicit model-building.

Third, studies of floating-rate efficiency concentrate on the current floating-rate period that began in the 1970s, whereas the literature on gold-standard efficiency is historical in nature, pertaining almost entirely to the pre-World War I dollar–sterling gold standard.[3] Fourth, conventional wisdom holds that a necessary condition for efficiency is a free market or, at most, government intervention lightly superimposed on a market dominated by private transactors, wherefore a gold standard is by nature inefficient.[4]

1.2 Efficient asset market

"A market in which prices always 'fully reflect' available information is called efficient" (Fama, 1970, p. 383).[5] In the foreign-exchange market, the price is the exchange rate or a configuration of exchange rates. Consider the

215

profit – defined in the usual way as revenue minus overall cost – from any given arbitrage or speculation activity in the foreign-exchange market. Letting overall cost be the sum of direct cost (freight, insurance, handling, and transactions cost), interest (or opportunity) cost, risk premium, and normal profit, the residual revenue becomes pure economic profit. All variables are expressed as a percentage of the amount invested and for a given time period. Of course, for the specified activity, one or more components or subcomponents of cost could be zero.

1.3   Equilibrium expected profit

Equilibrium expected profit *in the current period* is defined as the profit level that is expected to result, on average, when all information available to arbitrageurs and speculators *in the previous period* is fully reflected *in the previous period's* exchange rate or, correspondingly, fully utilized in determining the *previous period's* profit. Of course, it is the actions of arbitrageurs and speculators that would bring about the "full reflection" and "full utilization." Included in the information so reflected and utilized would be knowledge about the previous period's values of exchange rates, profits, revenues, and the four cost components of the various arbitrage and speculation operations, their past behavior over time, as well as their determinants and interrelations and the history of same, and whatever is knowable about the implication of the information for future exchange rates and future speculative and arbitrage profits.

Certain conditions – presumed satisfied in the dollar–sterling foreign-exchange market in the late nineteenth and the twentieth centuries – make this equilibrium profit from arbitrage or speculative activity *zero*. First, either there are many arbitrageurs and speculators, no one of whom acting alone can affect the exchange rate (pure competition), or there is unrestrained competition among a small number of arbitrageurs and speculators (vigorously competitive oligopoly).[6] Second, knowledge about the revenue and cost components of arbitrage or speculation profit is substantial (though not necessarily perfect or complete). Third, arbitrageurs and speculators are rational expected-profit maximizers, trading as long as expected profit exceeds zero, thereby driving it to zero, at least "on average" (sufficient for a zero level of expected profit).[7]

1.4   Equilibrium exchange rate

Corresponding to equilibrium (zero) profit is the "equilibrium" exchange rate, but this rate may differ from the usual concepts of exchange-rate equilibrium, because the market-efficiency definition of equilibrium specifies a relatively restricted duration of the unit time period. On the one hand, there must be sufficient time in the unit period to complete in the current period all arbitrage and speculation activities potentially profitable on the basis of any information available and fully utilized in the previous period. Lacking time in the current period to adjust profit and the exchange rate to the posited equilibrium (based on information available at the beginning of the period), the "equilibrium" could be non-realizable. On the other hand, the unit period must not be much longer than that minimum duration: the longer the period, the greater the potential number and magnitude of changes in the revenue and cost parameters that give rise to arbitrage and speculation profits, and therefore the lower the expectation that this period's profit – given the information available and fully utilized last period – will be zero "on average."

While the "equilibrium" exchange rate that results from a unit period so delimited is not long-run in nature, therefore, neither is it "immediate-run." Instantaneous adjustment of the exchange rate involves too short a unit period for the market-efficiency equilibrium concept applied to a gold standard. A substantial time period is required to effect gold-arbitrage operations, or exchange-rate speculation combined with money-market transactions, much longer than is involved in pure spatial arbitrage or quick-reversal speculation in the foreign-exchange market.[8]

1.5   Exchange-market efficiency

The general definition of exchange-market efficiency is that the actual profit in a given (current) time period from any arbitrage or speculation activity equal, on average, the equilibrium expected profit for that time period (or, equivalently, that the actual exchange rate equal, on average, the equilibrium exchange rate). With equilibrium expected profit zero for all time periods, the definition becomes that actual profit in a time period be zero, on average.

Market efficiency requires that the current-period *expected* profit from any arbitrage or speculation activity – and, correspondingly, the current-period exchange rate – adjust fully to all the information available in the *previous* period. Because new information (for example, changes in the revenue or cost parameters of arbitrage or speculation profit) can become available during the current period, *actual* profit can be non-zero, but only as a matter of luck.[9] Market efficiency is consistent with positive or negative profits for arbitrageurs and speculators, even as a group, but not earned persistently or predictably. If, for simplicity, one omits consideration of the unit period, market efficiency has the usual definition of a situation in which private market participants (arbitrageurs and speculators) cannot earn a predictable or persistent economic profit on the basis of publicly available information.

The special concept of "perfect" market efficiency is a useful limiting case. It involves *zero* actual profit for *all* time periods, and requires the additional assumption of *perfect* competition. In a frictionless world of perfect knowledge, information is always correct and complete; arbitrage and speculation take an infinitesimal amount of time; the exchange rate always reflects all information; and, in particular, the rate adjusts instantaneously to any new information. Thus any positive or negative profit opportunities are immediately eliminated. Perfect market efficiency may be said to result from "perfect arbitrage" and "perfect speculation."

2   Tests of exchange-market efficiency

One dimension of tests of exchange-market efficiency is whether they involve (1) pure arbitrage, (2) pure speculation, or (3) a combination of arbitrage and speculation. A second dimension hinges on the fact that a gold standard possesses two properties not present in a floating exchange rate: (1) a gold-point spread and (2) an exchange-rate norm value, which could be either mint parity or the mid-point of the gold-point spread. Tests of exchange-market efficiency fall into four categories, depending on whether one, the other, both, or neither of these properties are recognized. This, second, dimension is used to group the tests formally.

2.1   Tests that ignore both spread and norm value

Tests that ignore the two characteristics of a gold standard fall into three subgroups. First, some tests of exchange-market efficiency are inapplicable to a gold standard because of unsuitable methodology. Testing for certain results of pure speculation, in particular, the randomness of exchange-rate changes and the profitability of filter rules (buying [selling] whenever a currency's value is a predetermined percent above [below] its most recent trough [peak]), makes sense only for floating exchange rates.[10] Market efficiency is deemed to increase with enhanced randomness of exchange-rate changes or reduced profitability of following filter rules. Under a gold standard, exchange-rate changes are decidedly *non*-random in the vicinity of a gold point, and filter rules that breach a gold point ridiculously bet on a greater violation of the gold point rather than a return to the spread.

Second, there are tests of gold-standard exchange-market efficiency that pertain to a gold standard but could just as well be used for a floating exchange rate. Examples are comparisons of forward and futures rates, the spot and lagged forward rates, the actual forward rate with professional forecasts, or the actual forward rate with the theoretical rate predicted by interest-rate parity, all of which are done in the floating-rate literature.[11] The

first correspondence relates to arbitrage, the second and third to speculation, and the last to covered interest arbitrage. Market efficiency is judged to
increase with the closeness of each correspondence. These tests cannot be
applied to the pre-World War I dollar–sterling exchange market, because
forward-rate data are unavailable.

Third, some tests, though disregarding the unique characteristics of a
specie standard and as applicable to a floating rate as a specie standard, are
substantially warranted in the early, decentralized, American foreign-
exchange market. These are investigations of spatial arbitrage and
exchange-rate seasonality (the latter giving rise to profit opportunity
exploitable by covered and uncovered interest arbitrage). Spatial arbitrage
and exchange-rate seasonality are the market-efficiency analogues to geographic integration and seasonal variation under market integration (discussed in sections 1 and 2 of chapter 7). Market efficiency (as well as
exchange-market integration) may be deemed to increase with a decrease in
geographical price dispersion or seasonal variation.

Another test that might be in this subgroup is triangular arbitrage.[12] The
closer are direct and indirect (third-currency intermediated) exchange rates,
the stronger is market efficiency. Morgenstern (1959, pp. 223–41, 567)
examines monthly direct franc/dollar and mark/dollar exchange rates and
their cross rates via the pound sterling (among other three-currency rela-
tionships) over 1878–1914 and 1925–31 and concludes that "the cross rates
of exchange behave 'irrationally' in that there are neither zero, nor small,
nor clearly constant differences between them and the direct rates." His
work is criticized by Borts (1960, pp. 224–5) for ignoring the buying–selling
spread in the foreign-exchange market. In effect, apparent systematic profit
could readily be eliminated by transactions cost.

Another problem is that the exchange-rate data in the three markets may
not be strictly synchronized over time. McCormick (1979, pp. 411–15)
shows that even *hours* of non-simultaneity substantially widen the measured difference between the direct and indirect exchange rate. In sum,
Morgenstern's results exhibit apparent, but misleading, persistent profit
opportunities.

2.2   Tests that incorporate norm value

Market efficiency under a specie standard can be measured negatively with
the variation of the exchange rate about the exchange-rate norm of mint
parity. Such tests ignore the specie-point spread and so pertain at least as
much to a paper as a gold standard. Intra-annual movement and decadal
variation of the exchange rate provide two tests in this vein, and they are discussed under the market-integration rubric in sections 3 and 4 of chapter 7.

To the extent that this movement and variation are systematic, they offer profit opportunities via pure exchange-rate speculation or covered/uncovered interest arbitrage. The smaller the intra-annual movement or decadal variation, the greater the market efficiency (and, of course, the stronger the market integration).

2.3   Tests that incorporate spread

Some tests of market efficiency relate the exchange rate to the gold-point spread. One technique, applied to the dollar–sterling gold standard by Morgenstern (1959) and Clark (1984), checks the magnitude, frequency, and persistence of gold-point violations (implying profitable GPA). Perfectly efficient GPA would involve no gold-point violations. Another approach examines the consistency of gold-point violations with the direction of the corresponding gold flow. These tests have the methodological advantage of focusing on the particular profit opportunity (GPA) offered by a specie standard.

Both tests suffer from the stringent data requirement of gold points specific to individual exchange-rate observations rather than simply averages over time. Spiller and Wood (1988) "solve" the problem of obtaining reliable gold-point data by using no gold-point information at all! Arbitrage costs and opportunities are estimated by fitting probabilistic functions to the exchange rate.

The gold-flow approach has deficiencies of its own. First, there is the additional data problem that it may be unclear which gold-flow figure to use: the net gold flow to all countries or the bilateral gold flow between the two countries whose currencies constitute the exchange rate under examination. The bilateral flow is methodologically correct, the multilateral flow statistically of higher quality.[13] Second, banks may not import gold even though the exchange rate is beyond the gold-import point. An example is during a financial crisis, when banks may sell foreign exchange for immediate cash, avoiding the delay in gold import but worsening – if not actually bringing about – the gold-point violation (see section 3.2.2 of chapter 13). Third, gold may be imported at a loss for several reasons: to influence the stock market, to expand bank cash reserves for the purpose of credit creation, and to obtain a "window-dressing" effect (Cross, 1923, pp. 395–6).

2.4   Tests that incorporate spread and norm value

Given a gold standard, uncovered interest arbitrage and forward speculation, under reasonable assumptions, involve consideration of both (1) the gold-point spread and (2) the exchange-rate norm value in the form of the spread mid-point. The same comment applies to forward speculation combined with covered interest arbitrage. Under perfect market efficiency these operations, discussed in sections 5 – 7 below, would yield zero profit.

3   Selection of arbitrage and speculation operations

In the remainder of this chapter a theory of gold-standard market efficiency is presented incorporating the types of arbitrage and speculation oriented to a gold standard: gold-point arbitrage (GPA), uncovered interest arbitrage (UIA), covered interest arbitrage (CIA), and forward speculation (FS). GPA, UIA, and FS are analyzed because they are either specific to a gold standard (GPA) or follow a particular pattern under that regime (UIA and FS). Gold-flow analysis is not studied, because its problems prevent it from being amenable to empirical testing. CIA is selected for two reasons: (1) it is intertwined with UIA and FS, and (2) combined with FS, it also takes a specific form under a gold standard.

Innovations are (1) joint consideration of GPA, UIA, CIA, and FS, and (2) careful attention to transactions cost, risk premium, and taxation. The institutional framework of the 1925–31 dollar–sterling gold standard is imposed, because it will be the main testing ground of the theory (see chapter 13).

4   Gold-point arbitrage

4.1   In favor of the pound

An operation in favor of the pound involves an immediate purchase of pounds (either spot or forward, depending on the operation), thus increasing the exchange value of the pound (in one or the other market). In the case of gold-point arbitrage (GPA), gold-import arbitrage is the direction that favors the pound. Let RS (symbolized by V, the mid-point of the buying and selling rates, in section 3.6 of chapter 6) denote the spot exchange rate and GM the US gold-import point, both expressed in dollars per pound. For $RS < GM$, there is a positive profit from the gold-import form of GPA. Spot pounds are purchased, pushing up RS to GM, where arbitrage profit is eliminated. Therefore efficient gold-import arbitrage involves the spot exchange rate no lower than the gold-import point: $GM \leq RS$.[14]

It is sometimes convenient to redefine the exchange rate from $RS = V$ (number of dollars per pound) to $RS = S$ (percentage deviation from parity), done in section 3.7 of chapter 6. Then efficient GPA yields $-CM \leq S$.

Arbitrage profit is of the nature of a capital gain, and in 1925–31 the dominant gold-point arbitrageurs were the large New York banks (see section 3 of chapter 8). During this period the United States treated capital gains and losses as ordinary income for corporate-tax purposes, while the United Kingdom did not tax capital gains (Blakey and Blakey, 1940, p. 588; Spaulding, 1927, p. 127). Therefore after-tax profit under GPA is the product of $(1 - t_{US})$ and pretax profit, where t_{US} is the US *ad valorem* (one-hundredth the percentage) corporate tax rate. The value of GM (and, later, of GX, the gold-export point) and the existence of GPA profit is independent of taxation; only, the amount of profit is reduced proportionately.

4.2   In favor of the dollar

An operation in favor of the dollar entails an immediate sale of pounds (either spot or forward, depending on the operation), thereby reducing the exchange value of the pound (in one or the other market). Gold-export arbitrage is the direction of GPA in favor of the dollar. Letting GX denote the US gold-export point (expressed in dollars per pound), for $RS > GX$ there is a positive profit from the gold-export form of GPA. Either spot or forward pounds are sold, depending on whether the arbitrageur bears the exchange risk or covers it. Correspondingly, RS decreases to GX or the short-term forward rate decreases, the latter increasing the cost of forward cover and pushing GX up to RS. Either way, the arbitrage profit is eliminated. Therefore efficient gold-export arbitrage involves the spot exchange rate no higher than the gold-export point: $RS \leq GX$.[15] In terms of percentage deviation from parity, the condition is $S \leq CX$. The comments on taxation in section 4.1 apply here as well.

4.3   Efficiency band

The gold-import and export points are the lower and upper critical value of the exchange rate for GPA in the following sense. Below (above) the gold-import (export) point, there is a positive profit and efficient GPA would bid up (down) the exchange rate until the exchange rate is above (below) the gold-import (export) point and the profit opportunity from GPA is eliminated. Therefore $[GM, GX]$, meaning the set of all RS such that $GM \leq RS \leq GX$, is the GPA efficiency band, commonly called the gold-point spread. The gold-import (export) point could be termed the lower (upper) GPA efficiency point or limit. In terms of percentage deviations from parity, the efficiency band or spread is the set of all S such that $-CM \leq S \leq CX$.

Perfect GPA would result in the exchange rate located *always* within the spread. The term "gold-point violation" was coined by Morgenstern (1959,

p. 241) to describe an exchange rate outside the spread (the GPA efficiency band): $RS < GM$ or $RS > GX$. Under perfect arbitrage, by definition, there are no gold-point violations.

5   Uncovered interest arbitrage

5.1   Institutional environment

As a form of exchange-rate speculation, albeit combined with money-market activity, uncovered interest arbitrage (UIA) can be either stabilizing or destabilizing for the foreign-exchange market. The UIA of interest involves stabilizing speculation and emanates from absolute confidence of the arbitrageurs that, over their horizon (say, N months), (1) the existing gold standard will be maintained, (2) the gold points will be subject only to normal period-by-period variation as arbitrage-cost components change their values, and (3) efficient GPA will exist. The principal interest arbitrageurs (covered or uncovered) were the large New York banks for arbitrage in favor of the pound and the large London banks for arbitrage in favor of the dollar (Einzig, 1937, p. 172).

The interwar arbitrageur had his profits potentially affected by both US and UK taxes. Unlike the United States, which had simple corporate taxation, so that an *ad valorem* (one-hundredth the percentage) tax rate of t_{US} applied, the United Kingdom had an integrated system of personal and corporate taxation. Corporations paid the standard income-tax rate, but were allowed to deduct the tax paid on dividends distributed. Foreign corporations, such as a New York bank, though subject to tax on their UK-source income, were also allowed to make this deduction.[16] Letting t_{UK}^n denote the UK *ad valorem* income-tax rate, and p the taxed firm's dividend–payout ratio (ratio of dividends to gross profit), the effective UK tax rate (t_{UK}) is the nominal tax rate (t_{UK}^n) reduced by the ratio of undistributed to gross profit $(1 - p)$: $t_{UK} = (1 - p) \cdot t_{UK}^n$, where $0 \le p \le 1$.

The arbitrageur was affected by US and UK taxes on the two components of his income: capital gain (or loss) and interest. In 1925–31 the United States treated capital gains and losses as ordinary income for corporate-tax purposes. Britain did not tax capital gains, but then capital losses were not deductible from income. At least proximately, there was double taxation of international investment income. The banks had to pay income tax to their respective government on their entire income from all sources, therefore including interest income abroad. Also, each domestic government imposed its income tax on non-resident income earned in the domestic country. Therefore New York (London) banks were subject to both countries' tax on interest income earned in London (New York).

However, special rules applied to moderate the double taxation (see sections 5.2 and 5.3).

Allowing for the taxation environment, the interwar arbitrageur thought in terms of a strict separation of exchange-rate and interest gains. Direct evidence is provided in a contemporary description of the arbitrageurs' behavior centered on this separation (Einzig, 1937, pp. 242–3). Indirect evidence is the fact that an analogous approximation was long used in the related, but more highly developed, literature on interest-rate parity (efficient covered interest arbitrage). In fact, it was not until 1953 that the exact formula for interest-rate parity appeared in print (Spraos, 1953, pp. 87–9).

Actually, it is mathematically impossible to separate the exchange-rate and interest gains. What the arbitrageur ignored was the fact that there is an exchange-rate gain on the interest return.[17] The error in ignoring this interaction is likely to be very small, and the approximation simplifies the mathematics of efficiency and enhances intuition. So the analytical compromise in deferring to the historical reality of a subjective approximate gain for the arbitrageur is at an acceptable level.

5.2   In favor of the pound

For UIA in favor of the pound, the underlying assumption is that efficient gold-import arbitrage will govern; so the expected spot exchange rate is no lower than the gold-import point: $RS^e \geq GM$, where RS^e is the spot rate expected to prevail N months in the future. In principle, RS^e may lie anywhere within the gold-point spread, but not outside it; for, by assumption, arbitrageurs have a zero subjective probability of a gold-point violation.

The arbitrageur (New York bank) purchases pounds at the current spot rate (RS), planning to reverse his transaction after N months, that is, to sell pounds at the expected spot rate(RS^e). In the interim the funds are invested in the London rather than the New York money market.

The United States taxed the entirety of the New York bank's arbitrage income, while the United Kingdom taxed the investment income earned in London. However, the United States permitted in effect an *ad valorem* tax credit on foreign taxes up to the US tax rate, with any excess foreign taxes deductible from taxable income.

Exchange-rate gain is a capital gain (if positive) or a capital loss (if negative), treated as ordinary income under US corporate taxation. Therefore expected after-tax exchange-rate gain is $E_L^{uia} = [(RS^e - RS)/RS] \cdot (1 - t_{US})$. However, net interest return depends on the relationship of t_{US} to t_{UK}, the US and UK effective tax rates. Let I_{UK} denote the London and I_{US} the New York interest rate, each expressed (as is inherently the exchange-rate gain) in *ad valorem* terms per N-month period. For $t_{US} < t_{UK}$ (case a), the interest return is $I_{La} = I_{UK} \cdot [1 - t_{UK} + t_{US} \cdot (t_{UK} - t_{US})] - I_{US} \cdot (1 - t_{US})$, while for $t_{US} > t_{UK}$ (case b) the return is $I_{Lb} = (I_{UK} - I_{US}) \cdot (1 - t_{US})$. The subscript "L" is used for operations in favor of the pound, because *lower* exchange-rate bounds are determined by market efficiency.

There are two components of cost. First is transactions cost, TC, expressed in *ad valorem* terms as a proportion of the amount invested. It is assumed that the entirety of TC is deductible from taxable income, although in reality only the monetary costs of exchange-market and money-market transactions have this property.[18] It is also assumed that the deduction is taken totally on taxable income for the home country (the United States, for operations in favor of the pound) and none for the foreign country.

The second cost component is a risk premium for exchange-rate risk. A reasonable specification of this risk premium is that it is proportional to the maximum *ad valorem* exchange-rate loss. In the present case, the risk premium is $R_L^{uia} = r \cdot (RS - GM)/RS$, where $0 \le r \le 1$ and r may be called the risk-premium parameter. A zero value of r involves risk neutrality, while a value of unity implies extreme risk aversion: arbitrageurs require full compensation for the maximum possible exchange-rate loss, given their absolute confidence that the future spot exchange rate will not be below the gold-import point: $RS^e \ge GM$. Risk premium is a deduction from economic but not accounting (taxable) profit.

Expected economic profit (on an *ad valorem* basis per N-month period) is the exchange-rate gain plus the interest return minus transactions cost minus risk premium: $\pi_{Lx}^{uia} = E_L^{uia} + I_{Lx} - TC \cdot (1 - t_{US}) - R_L^{uia}$, for $x = a, b$. Solving $\pi_{Lx}^{uia} = 0$ for RS yields $RS_{Lx}^{uia} = [RS^e \cdot (1 - t_{US}) + r \cdot GM]/[(1 - t_{US}) \cdot (1 + TC) - I_{Lx} + r]$, for $x = a, b$. If and only if the exchange rate falls below this critical value, $RS < RS_{Lx}^{uia}$, does UIA in favor of the pound yield a positive profit.

5.3   In favor of the dollar

Underlying uncovered interest arbitrage (UIA) in favor of the dollar is full confidence that efficient gold-export arbitrage will exist in the next N months, so the expected spot rate is no higher than the gold-export point: $RS^e \le GX$. The interest arbitrageur (typically, a large London bank) sells pounds at RS, planning to purchase pounds at RS^e in N months. In the meantime the funds are invested in the New York rather than the London money market. For uncovered arbitrage, with capital gains excepted from taxable income under UK law, expected exchange-rate gain is untaxed at $E_U^{uia} = (RS - RS^e)/RS$. Just as for UIA in favor of the pound, interest income abroad (now in New York) was taxed in both countries. However, UK tax law did not permit a tax credit for taxes paid abroad; rather, such taxes were deductible from taxable income. Therefore interest return is the negative of $I_U = I_{UK}\cdot(1 - t_{UK}) - I_{US}\cdot[1 - t_{US} - t_{UK}\cdot(1 - t_{US})]$. Symmetrical to UIA in favor of the pound, risk premium is $R_U^{uia} = r\cdot(GX - RS)/RS$. Expected economic profit is exchange-rate gain plus interest return minus transactions cost minus risk premium: $\pi_U^{uia} = E_U^{uia} - I_U - TC\cdot(1 - t_{UK}) - R_U^{uia}$. Solving $\pi_U^{uia} = 0$ yields $RS_U^{uia} = [RS^e + r\cdot GX]/[1 - I_U - TC\cdot(1 - t_{UK}) + r]$. UIA generates a positive profit if and only if the exchange rate exceeds this critical value: $RS > RS_U^{uia}$. The subscript "U" is used for operations in favor of the dollar, because *upper* exchange-rate bounds are determined by market efficiency.

5.4   Efficiency band

If the exchange rate is below the lower critical value, $RS < RS_{Lx}^{uia}$ for $x = a, b$, then there is a positive profit, $\pi_{Lx}^{uia} > 0$, and efficient UIA would bid up RS, as pounds are purchased to take advantage of profit opportunity, reducing the exchange-rate gain, E_L^{uia}, and increasing the risk premium, R_L^{uia}. The process continues until profit is zero, $\pi_{Lx}^{uia} = 0$, and the exchange rate ceases to be below the lower critical value, $RS \geq RS_{Lx}^{uia}$. If the exchange rate is above the upper critical value, $RS > RS_U^{uia}$, a similar mechanism wipes out profit opportunity and makes the exchange rate no greater than that value, $RS \leq RS_U^{uia}$. Therefore $[RS_{Lx}^{uia}, RS_U^{uia}]$, meaning the set of all RS such that $RS_{Lx}^{uia} \leq RS \leq RS_U^{uia}$, is the UIA efficiency band, and RS_{Lx}^{uia} (RS_U^{uia}) is the lower (upper) UIA efficiency point or limit.[19]

As a special case, consider the model of exchange-rate speculation developed in section 3.2.2 of chapter 11. That model is a special case of the UIA theory developed here. In its general form, the model of chapter 11 has risk neutrality ($r = 0$), no taxation ($t_{US} = t_{UK} = 0$), and zero international interest-rate differential ($I_L = I_{UK} - I_{US} = 0$). Also, most fundamentally, the expected exchange rate is equal to the mean of the imposed (uniform) probability distribution of the exchange rate, which is the mid-point of the gold-point spread ($RS^e = RM$), recalling that $RM = (GX + GM)/2$. The efficiency band is $[RS_L^{uia}, RS_U^{uia}] = [RM/(1 + TC), RM/(1 - TC)]$, a non-symmetrical band centered around the spread mid-point and the width of which varies positively with transactions cost. In its specific form, the model has zero transactions cost ($TC = 0$), and $RS_L^{uia} = RS_U^{uia} = RM$, so the efficiency band reduces to the mid-point of the gold-point spread.

6   Covered interest arbitrage

6.1   In favor of the pound

The New York bank can cover the exchange-rate risk, by selling pounds N months forward, resulting in covered interest arbitrage (CIA). Then the risk-premium parameter, r, is zero and the expected spot rate, RS^e, is replaced by the N-month forward rate, RF. After-tax exchange-rate gain is now $E_L^{cia} = [(RF - RS)/RS] \cdot (1 - t_{US})$. Economic profit is exchange-rate gain plus interest return minus transactions cost: $\pi_{Lx}^{cia} = E_L^{cia} + I_{Lx} - TC \cdot (1 - t_{US})$, for $x = a, b$. Solving $\pi_{Lx}^{cia} = 0$ for RS yields

$$RS_{La}^{cia} = [RF \cdot (1 - t_{US})]/[(1 + TC) \cdot (1 - t_{US}) - I_{La}]$$
$$RS_{Lb}^{cia} = RF/[(1 + TC) - (I_{UK} - I_{US})]$$

In case b, the taxation element behaves the same way as for GPA. The UK tax is irrelevant and the US tax rate affects profit proportionally via the factor $(1 - t_{US})$; RS_{Lb}^{cia} is the same as if $t_{UK} = t_{US} = 0$. Again, if and only if the exchange rate falls below the critical value, $RS < RS_{Lx}^{cia}$ for $x = a, b$, does CIA in favor of the pound involve a positive profit.

6.2   In favor of the dollar

Under covered interest arbitrage (CIA), the London bank buys N-month forward pounds at RF. exchange-rate gain is $E_U^{cia} = (RS - RF)/RS$, and economic profit – exchange-rate gain plus interest return minus transactions cost – becomes $\pi_U^{cia} = E_U^{cia} - I_U - TC \cdot (1 - t_{UK})$. Setting $\pi_U^{cia} = 0$ yields $RS_U^{cia} = RF/[1 - I_U - TC \cdot (1 - t_{UK})]$. CIA results in a positive profit if and only if the exchange rate exceeds this critical value: $RS > RS_U^{cia}$.

6.3   Efficiency band

If the exchange rate is below the lower critical value, $RS < RS_{Lx}^{cia}$ for $x = a, b$, then there is a positive profit, $\pi_{Lx}^{cia} > 0$, and efficient CIA would bid up RS, as pounds are purchased to take advantage of profit opportunity, reducing the exchange-rate gain, E_L^{cia}. The process continues until profit is zero, $\pi_{Lx}^{cia} = 0$, and the exchange rate ceases to be below the lower critical value, $RS \geq RS_{Lx}^{cia}$. If the exchange rate is above the upper critical value, $RS > RS_U^{cia}$, a similar mechanism wipes out profit opportunity and makes the exchange rate no greater than that value, $RS \leq RS_U^{cia}$. Therefore $[RS_{Lx}^{cia}, RS_U^{cia}]$ is the CIA efficiency band.[20]

7   Forward speculation

7.1   In favor of the pound

The type of forward speculation (FS) of interest, in favor of the pound – as the type of UIA – is stabilizing, and so likewise involves, with full confidence, the expected spot rate no lower than the gold-import point:

$RS^e \geq GM$. The forward speculator purchases forward pounds at RF, planning to sell them spot in N months at RS^e. For FS compared to UIA, RF replaces RS and $I_{UK} = I_{US} = 0$. Expected after-tax exchange-rate gain is $E_L^{fs} = [(RS^e - RF)/RF]\cdot(1 - t_{US})$ and risk premium is $R_L^{fs} = r\cdot(RF - GM)/RF$. Expected economic profit is the exchange-rate gain minus transactions cost minus risk premium: $\pi_L^{fs} = E_L^{fs} - TC\cdot(1 - t_{US}) - R_L^{fs}$, which, equated to zero, generates $RF_L^{fs} = [RS^e\cdot(1 - t_{US}) + r\cdot GM]/[(1 + TC)\cdot(1 - t_{US}) + r]$. With no interest investment, t_{UK} does not enter the formula for RF_L^{fs}. If and only if the forward rate is below this critical value, $RF < RF_L^{fs}$, does FS in favor of the pound produce a positive profit.

7.2   In favor of the dollar

The forward speculator of interest, like the uncovered interest arbitrageur, has, with complete confidence, the expected exchange rate no higher than the gold-export point: $RS^e \leq GX$. The speculator sells forward pounds at RF, planning to buy pounds spot at RS^e in N months. Expected exchange-rate gain, again untaxed, is $E_U^{fs} = (RF - RS^e)/RF$ and risk premium is $R_U^{fs} = r\cdot(GX - RF)/RF$. Expected economic profit is exchange-rate gain minus transactions cost minus risk premium: $\pi_U^{fs} = E_U^{fs} - TC\cdot(1 - t_{UK}) - R_U^{fs}$, which, equated to zero, yields $RF_U^{fs} = [RS^e + r\cdot GX]/[1 - TC\cdot(1 - t_{UK}) + r]$. A positive profit is generated if and only if the forward rate exceeds the critical value: $RF > RF_U^{fs}$.

7.3   Efficiency band

An argument parallel to that for uncovered or covered interest arbitrage (UIA or CIA) shows that $[RF_L^{fs}, RF_U^{fs}]$ is the forward-speculation (FS) efficiency band; but this band pertains to RF rather than RS.[21] To obtain a corresponding band for RS, FS may be combined with CIA. For operations in favor of the pound (dollar), the interest arbitrageur not only buys (sells) spot pounds but also sells (buys) forward pounds, while the forward speculator buys (sells) these forward pounds. The result is a roundabout reduction to UIA, and may be called the joint operation of FS with CIA, or indirect UIA. The lower (upper) efficiency point, RS_{Lx}^j (RS_U^j) is obtained by substituting RF_L^{fs} (RF_U^{fs}) into RS_{Lx}^{cia} (RS_U^{cia}), and the "FS with CIA" (also called "joint" or "indirect UIA") efficiency band is $[RS_{Lx}^j, RS_U^j]$ for $x = a, b$. The efficiency limits are:

$$RS_{La}^j = \{(1 - t_{US})\cdot[RS^e\cdot(1 - t_{US}) + r\cdot GM]\}/\{[(1 + TC)\cdot(1 - t_{US}) + r]\cdot[(1 + TC)\cdot(1 - t_{US}) - I_{La}]\}$$
$$RS_{Lb}^j = \{RS^e\cdot(1 - t_{US}) + r\cdot GM\}/\{[(1 + TC)\cdot(1 - t_{US}) + r]\cdot [1 - (I_{UK} - I_{US}) + TC]\}$$

$$RS_U^j = \{RS^e + r.GX\}/\{[1 - TC\cdot(1 - t_{UK}) + r]\cdot$$
$$[1 - TC\cdot(1 - t_{UK}) - I_U]\}$$

The derivation of the "FS with CIA" efficiency limits requires the assumption that the horizon (N) and transactions cost (TC) are the same for the forward speculators and the interest arbitrageurs.[22] If the resulting efficiency bands are to be compared with corresponding UIA bands, it must also be assumed that TC has the same value for UIA and CIA.[23] More pointedly, it would be absurd for an economic agent to pursue UIA indirectly and thereby add unnecessarily to transactions cost. Rather, the joint FS with CIA operation is better viewed as undertaken by different agents, resulting in the joint efficiency limits. It may be noted that the corresponding direct and indirect UIA efficiency limits – RS_{La}^{uia} versus RS_{La}^j, RS_{Lb}^{uia} versus RS_{Lb}^j, and RS_U^{uia} versus RS_U^j – are not identical, with more-complex formulas for the indirect limits. Contrary to intuition, setting $TC = 0$ would not make the corresponding limits equal.

13 Empirical testing of market efficiency

1   Unit of observation

A perfectly efficient operation involves the pertinent exchange rate always within the efficiency band of that operation. Perfectly efficient gold-point arbitrage (GPA) requires absolute confidence in the maintenance of the gold standard over the time needed for the operation to be completed, specifically, in being able to transact in gold with both authorities. In turn, perfectly efficient uncovered interest arbitrage (UIA) and forward speculation (FS) (and in fact the applicability of the UIA, FS model) require full confidence in perfectly efficient GPA over the agent's horizon. Covered interest arbitrage (CIA) has no such condition for its efficiency, because that operation behaves the same way under a gold standard as under a flexible exchange-rate system.

For perfect efficiency, (1) perfect knowledge of the relevant parameters in the efficiency band (or, equivalently, in the associated profit formulas) and (2) instantaneous adjustment are also needed. Otherwise, only what may be called general efficiency – but not perfect efficiency – is attainable. General efficiency incorporates "inefficiencies" (violations of efficiency points) that are of small magnitude and non-persistent.

To test for the market efficiency of GPA, UIA, CIA, and FS, monthly data are used. So efficiency is tested only in the general sense. This means that measured efficiency is consistent with inefficiencies in the form of intra-month profit opportunities that average out for the month. While, for a given operation (GPA, UIA, CIA, FS), violations of efficiency points for isolated months indicate some inefficiency (even in the general sense), especially serious would be their persistence over several months.

2   Sample periods

The interwar dollar–sterling gold standard provides the basic sample period: May 1925–August 1931, the 76 full months for which the standard

230

applied. This experience is selected because it alone has the data and information to test all the operations for market efficiency. For comparison purposes, two other sample periods are adopted, one from the pre-World War I gold standard, the other from the post-World War II Bretton Woods system (gold-exchange standard).

The Bretton Woods experience is of interest because it possessed the two defining characteristics of a gold standard specified in section 2 of chapter 12. Currencies (except the US dollar) had a declared par value, quite analogous to mint parity. There was a band of 1 percent around the par value within which the member government – acting through an agency, such as its Treasury or central bank – was required to maintain spot exchange-rate transactions. This "parity band" corresponds to the gold-point spread. Indeed, the term "gold points" was used synonymously for the parity points or limits.

Britain was on the Bretton Woods system continuously from December 1946 to August 1971. The pound's par value was altered, however, by the depreciations of September 1949 and November 1967. So the maximum period encompassing full years of an unchanged par value is the seventeen-year period from 1950 to 1966. This is the period outside the span of the gold or specie standard, that was examined in the context of exchange-market integration in chapters 10 and 11. It will play a similar comparison role under the rubric of GPA in this chapter.

For the pre-World War I era, a sample period of the same length is appropriate, and 1890 to 1906 is selected. This period is close to 1890–1908, which is adopted by Clark (1984) for his study of GPA.

The recurring lack of confidence in Britain's maintenance of the pound's current par value during the Bretton Woods system is ably documented.[1] Depreciations comparable in magnitude to those of 1949 and 1967 could have occurred without surprise on several occasions between 1950 and 1966, because changes in the par value were institutionalized in the Articles of Agreement of the International Monetary Fund and because of Britain's repeated foreign-exchange crises. During periods of sterling crisis – parts of 1951–2, 1955–6, 1957, 1961, and 1964–5, involving eight years of the seventeen-year period – speculators did not necessarily have confidence in the maintenance of the pound's par value and hence the parity band, and therefore could not be expected to provide the stabilizing speculation of UIA. Indeed, they probably engaged in the opposite behavior (destabilizing speculation).

One implication is that the UIA and FS models cannot be applied to the 1950–66 period. These exclusions make the CIA model uninteresting, leaving only the analogy of GPA to be investigated. Another implication is even more serious. Does the tendency to destabilizing speculation as a characteristic of the Bretton Woods system bias the results for the remaining operation, GPA (or GPA analogue), toward market inefficiency compared to the 1890–1906 period?

The answer is negative, because during the eighteen-year period from 1890 to 1907 there was, similarly, an acute lack of confidence in the ability of the United States to remain on the gold standard, leading to similar episodes of destabilizing speculation. So again the UIA and FS models are inapplicable. There were recurrent runs on banks and bank failures, and for a one-month period in 1893 banks refused to provide cash for their deposits or even to honor certified checks (see section 9 of chapter 3). Coupled with the runs on banks were runs on the Treasury's gold reserves. A $100-million gold reserve had a profound psychological impact as the "apprehension minimum" (quoting Bagehot) as well as a "legal minimum."[2] At the end of 1893 the reserve was below $70 million and by February 1895 it had fallen to $41 million. The gold standard was on the verge of collapse at that point and was saved only by the cooperative action of the Treasury and a bankers' syndicate.

Both contemporary observers and later historians agree that there was a fluctuating, and at times acute, lack of confidence in US maintenance of the gold standard on the part of both Americans and foreigners in the early and mid-1890s.[3] In respect to lack of confidence, the British Bretton Woods experience is strikingly comparable:

The US experience in 1891–1897 was similar to British post-World War II exchange crises. In both cases, a government was seeking to maintain a fixed exchange parity. In both cases, it was uncertain whether the government would succeed. In both cases, it was clear that, if there were any change, it would be a depreciation of the relevant currency. Hence, in both cases, there was an incentive to reduce the balances held of the currency in question, and this incentive varied in intensity as the chances of the maintenance of fixed parity varied" (Friedman and Schwartz, 1963, p. 105).

Of course, the actions of a banking syndicate in "saving" the gold standard in 1895 (and again in 1896, when gold exports were blocked) have no analogue under the Bretton Woods System.[4] Rather, the similarity is that exchange-rate speculation occurred against a background of periodic expectations of a change in the dollar/sterling parity for about the same aggregate time during each sample period. Therefore there is no clear sample bias of exchange-rate expectations on the empirical results to come.

It is also arguable that there could not possibly be gold-point violations in 1950–66, as the United Kingdom, through its agent, the Bank of England, was under the international legal obligation to maintain the exchange rate within 1 percent of parity. However, the "gold points" of interest are not the legal maxima of 1 percent but rather the inner points, that were the announced intervention limits of the Bank of England and that were well under 1 percent (see section 3 of chapter 9).

3   Gold-point arbitrage

3.1   Conventional wisdom and empirical studies

The quick working of gold-point arbitrage under the gold standard in the late nineteenth and early twentieth centuries, especially for the dollar–sterling foreign-exchange market, has long been part of the conventional wisdom of economic historians. The greatest historian of this market, referring to the period 1897–1913, wrote: "the foreign-exchange market in New York was given a steadiness theretofore unknown. . . . Any appreciable deviation of exchange rates from parity tended to provoke a movement of gold into and out of the country" (Cole, 1929b, p. 213). The foremost historian of foreign-exchange in general, stated: "But on the whole the behaviour of the sterling–dollar rate conformed to the 'rules of the game' and kept within gold points for some thirty-five years prior to 1914" (Einzig, 1970, p. 195).

Contradicting this conventional wisdom, the empirical studies of Morgenstern (1959) and Clark (1984), supported by the incidental finding of Moggridge (1972), call into question the celebrated GPA efficiency of the US–UK gold standard. Coining the term "violations of gold points" for observations of the exchange rate outside the gold-point spread and hence profitable opportunities for GPA, Morgenstern (1959; pp. 246–8, 252–3) finds 45 months of such violations in 1880–1914 and eleven months in 1925–31. Moggridge (1972, pp. 128, 185) discovers ten months of GPA inefficiency in 1925–31. The results of Clark (1984, pp. 800–3) are strongest, with GPA inefficiency occurring in 47 months in 1890–8 and 51 weeks in 1899–1908 – a total of 98 instances. Perhaps most disturbing to believers in market efficiency is that the gold-point violations are often consecutive over several periods.

These authors have cause to trumpet their findings. Morgenstern (1959, p. 276) highlights "the incredible phenomenon of exchange rates often and persistently beyond the gold points." Clark (1984, p. 818) comments: "It was found that gold point violations often persisted for several successive months. This suggests that the gold standard system did not always eliminate profit opportunities quickly. . . . These findings are inconsistent with the view that the gold standard system functioned efficiently."

3.2   Empirical testing

3.2.1 Data and results

To test for GPA efficiency – the exchange rate between the gold points, $GM \leq RS \leq GX$ or, equivalently, $-CM \leq S \leq CX$ – monthly values are needed for the spot exchange rate (RS or S) and gold points (GX and GM, or CX and $-CM$) for 1890–1906, 1925–31, and 1950–66. It is convenient to consider the variables in the form of percentage deviation from parity: S, $-CM$, and CX. Their time series are developed in chapters 6 and 9.

GPA inefficiencies are listed in part I of table 13.1. The charge that the gold standard at the turn of the century was beset by GPA inefficiencies is found to be false. There are only three, isolated, months of a gold-point violation in 1890–1906. Also, in the interwar period GPA was uniformly efficient on a monthly average basis. For comparison, there was one violation of a "gold point" in 1950–66.

The magnitude of a gold-point violation can reasonably be defined as the deviation of the exchange rate from the violated gold point as a percentage of the gold point: $100 \cdot [(S + CM)/(-CM)]$ and $100 \cdot [(S - CX)/CX]$ for an import and export-point violation, respectively. All four GPA inefficiencies are with respect to the US gold-import point. Only for August 1893 is the inefficiency large.

It might be mentioned that the taxation element turns out to be irrelevant for GPA efficiency, and not only because of its proportional effect on GPA profit. While the US had a corporate income tax in 1925–31, there were no gold-point violations during that period. The gold-point violations in 1890–1906 occurred when there was no US income tax.[5]

3.2.2   Explanations of gold-point violations

The differential pattern of GPA inefficiency in the Morgenstern–Moggridge–Clark studies versus the present findings requires explanation. Also, there must be an accounting of the (albeit only four) gold-point violations discovered here. Any test of market inefficiency is a joint test of several hypotheses. In particular, the hypotheses are (1) the specified values of the variables and parameters of the model of GPA equilibrium, (2) the validity of the model itself, and (3) GPA efficiency. Each hypothesis is considered in turn, with applicability as warranted to the three existing and the current findings of gold-point violations.

Values of variables and parameters
Exchange rate: Morgenstern, Moggridge, and Clark employ the cable-transfer exchange rate throughout their time periods, with the exception of Morgenstern for 1880 to August 1886. In the interwar period cable was certainly the medium for GPA, but decidedly the bill of exchange was dominant prior to World War I, and in the form of the demand bill from about 1880 (see section 5 of chapter 8). In adopting the cable transfer for the pre-World War I period, Morgenstern and Clark dealt with an instrument that typically was eschewed by gold-point arbitrageurs.

Table 13.1 *Gold-point violations, 1890–1906, 1925–31, 1950–66*

Month	Exchange rate (percentage deviation from parity)	Gold point (percentage deviation from parity)	Magnitude of violation[a] (percent)
I Gold-point arbitrage			
A Violations of gold-import point			
1891: Oct.	− 0.6898	− 0.6680	3.27
1893: Aug.	− 0.1258	0.3447	136.50
1906: Sept.	− 0.6476	− 0.6445	0.48
1951: Sept.	− 0.0464	− 0.0446	4.01
B Violations of gold-export point			
None			
II Transfer of funds			
A Violations of gold-import point			
1890: March	− 0.2673	− 0.2555	4.61
Sept.	− 0.4109	− 0.2555	60.81
Dec.	− 0.5381	− 0.3918	37.34
1891: Sept.	− 0.5852	− 0.3095	89.10
Oct.	− 0.6898	− 0.3092	123.07
Nov.	− 0.6283	− 0.3091	103.29
Dec.	− 0.5175	− 0.3090	67.50
1892: Jan.	− 0.3330	− 0.3087	7.85
1893: July	− 0.5750	− 0.3597	59.86
Aug.	− 0.1258	0.7751	116.23
Oct.	− 0.4642	− 0.3591	29.27
Nov.	− 0.4129	− 0.3589	15.05
1896: Sept.	− 0.5695	− 0.3889	46.43
Oct.	− 0.5140	− 0.3619	42.01
1897: Oct.	− 0.4051	− 0.3928	3.14
1898: Jan.	− 0.3948	− 0.3664	7.76
Mar.	− 0.5839	− 0.3669	59.13
April	− 0.6352	− 0.3672	72.99
Sept.	− 0.5181	− 0.3687	40.51
Oct.	− 0.4236	− 0.3691	14.77
Dec.	− 0.4565	− 0.3696	23.48
1899: Jan.	− 0.4236	− 0.3700	14.49
1900: Oct.	− 0.4996	− 0.3968	25.91
Nov.	− 0.4174	− 0.3971	5.12
1903: Nov.	− 0.5900	− 0.3327	77.35
Dec.	− 0.5962	− 0.3330	79.04
1906: April	− 0.4133	− 0.0408	913.20
May	− 0.3393	− 0.1231	175.67
July	− 0.4010	− 0.3357	19.45
Aug.	− 0.4195	− 0.3766	11.39
Sept.	− 0.6476	− 0.0577	1022.68
Oct:	− 0.3743	− 0.1808	107.01
Dec.	− 0.6208	− 0.3902	59.12
1925: Oct.	− 0.4947	− 0.4384	12.85
1951: Sept.	− 0.0464	− 0.0446	4.01
B Violations of gold-export point			
1895: Aug.	0.6351	0.5416	17.26
Dec.	0.4833	0.4543	6.37
1896: Jan.	0.4641	0.4543	2.15

Note:
[a] Deviation of exchange rate from gold point as percentage of gold point, absolute value.
Source: See text.

The way the cable exchange rate may have led to greater measured inefficiency than if the, correct, demand-bill rate had been used is as follows. The cable rate exceeds the bill rate, because the latter incorporates an interest component emanating from the duration of a New York to London Atlantic voyage (see section 2 of chapter 6). The cable rate, being too high, could lead to measured inefficiencies under gold-export arbitrage. It is also true that it could enhance measured efficiency under gold-import arbitrage.

Gold points: There are several reasons why the gold points of Morgenstern, Moggridge, and Clark are probably narrower than the true gold points, leading to spurious cases of GPA inefficiency. First, unlike the present writer, these authors do not explicitly respect the difference between GPA and GTF gold points. Except for Clark's development of the interest-cost component of arbitrage cost, none of the previous authors (Morgenstern, Moggridge, and Clark) generates gold-point data from first principles (see section 1 of chapter 9). The outcome is uncertainty as to whether the gold points that they use pertain to GPA, GTF, or some mix.

The issue is relevant because GTF points are inherently smaller in magnitude (see section 3 of chapter 9). To the extent that the gold-point data utilized apply to GTF rather than GPA, the gold-point violations of the three authors may be spurious. To illustrate the quantitative impact of this element, consider part II of table 13.1, which exhibits GPA inefficiencies for GTF. The three gold-point violations under GPA in 1890–1906 become 33 under GTF!

Second, Clark (1984, pp. 798–9) substitutes the product of the spot exchange rate and the US/UK interest–cost ratio for the forward exchange rate in his export-arbitrage profit formulas. This substitution ignores transactions costs in the countries' money markets, a deficiency recognized by Clark (1984, p. 804) as overestimating his arbitrage profitability figures, that is, GPA inefficiencies.

Third, the gold points of all three authors, like most estimates extant, are probably unduly small in magnitude, because of the omission of direct mint expenses, interest forgone in waiting time for mint procedures in selling gold, exchange-rate cost (recognized only in principle by Clark), risk premium, and normal profit. The use of existing estimates rather than construction of gold points from first principles, the latter done only by the present author, gives scope for such omissions.

Fourth, the technique of imposing invariant gold points over time, utilized by the three authors, ignores the trend of smaller gold points over time, especially for 1890–1906. When Clark allows for a higher cost in the early part of the period, the number of GPA inefficiencies drops from 98 to 23.

Validity of model of equilibrium
Assumption of confidence in the gold standard: If gold-point arbitrageurs
lack confidence that the gold standard will be maintained by one of the
countries, then the model of GPA equilibrium – involving gold flows (dis-
equilibrium) when the exchange rate is outside the gold-point spread – may
become inapplicable. During the 1890s, the view that the United States
might abandon the gold standard is well documented (see section 2). How
would this belief affect the behavior of gold-point arbitrageurs? These
agents would have had a positive subjective probability of a dollar depreciation in terms of gold and the pound, either because the US mint price would
be increased or because the US would go on a paper standard. The resulting
incentive would be to import and not to export gold. However, not to
engage in gold-export arbitrage involves the surrender of an immediate
profitable opportunity.

What is the evidence regarding arbitrageur's balancing of these
considerations? The present study finds no export-point violation during
1891–96, and only two months of import-point violation. It appears that
arbitrageurs had a sufficiently short time horizon and/or a sufficiently low
probability of a dollar depreciation in the near term, that they typically took
advantage of GPA profit opportunities, whatever the direction of the gold-
point violation.

Assumption of authorities transacting in gold with private parties: In
1950–66 the US and UK authorities did not pursue a policy of transacting
in gold in both directions with all comers. The countries were not on the
gold standard, and GPA could not be consummated. The so-called GPA
inefficiency in September 1951 reflects the Bank of England not respecting
its self-imposed lower intervention point, allowing the pound to depreciate
against the dollar beyond the announced limit (but still well within the 1-
percent parity band mandated by the International Monetary Fund).

Efficiency
Intra-monthly observations: Clark's exchange-rate observations pertain to
specific days (one per month or week) and the interest-rate component of
his gold-point figures is computed from weekly interest-rate data. In contrast, the exchange-rate and gold-point data of the present study are (actually or essentially) monthly averages of daily observations. It is possible that
some of the inefficiencies found by Clark are genuine but of the intra-month
variety, that would be eliminated on a monthly average basis. However, this
explanation is of small importance, because the preponderance of Clark's
gold-point violations are consecutive for two or more time periods.

Gold-point manipulation: Clark's principal explanation of gold-standard
inefficiencies in 1890–1908 is direct manipulation of gold points by the

Bank of England and US Treasury. However, his discussion of the policies employed is incomplete, reveals an awareness of neither Sayers' (1936) definitive work on the Bank's gold-market operations nor the existence of the Treasury's bar premium, and offers no specific dates beyond the Treasury's well-known actions under Secretary Shaw in 1906 (Clark, 1984, pp. 816–17). While the policies are discussed in detail in chapters 3, 4, and 9, an outline of their effects on the gold points follows.

Bank actions that lowered the American gold-export point, thereby enhancing a gold inflow into Britain, consisted of raising its purchase prices for bars and foreign coin above normal levels and making interest-free loans to gold importers. Bank policies that lowered the American gold-import point, discouraging gold outflow from Britain, involved raising selling prices for bars and foreign coin above normal levels, refusing to sell bars, and redeeming its notes in deliberately underweight sovereigns.

Treasury actions that raised the gold-export point, discouraging a gold outflow, were raising the bar premium above the normal rate (0.04 percent – see table 9.5) and refusing to sell bars outright. The Treasury's policy of refusing to provide double eagles exclusively but paying out coin in proportion to the various denominations in stock cannot logically be considered a gold-point manipulation. Finally, in making interest-free loans to gold importers, the Treasury raised the gold-import point, fostering a gold inflow.

Clark (1984, pp. 791, 814–19) gives as the reason for the Bank and Treasury gold-point manipulation their desire to delay the workings of the gold standard insofar as it imposed limits on discretionary monetary policy, in particular, the intent to circumvent the obligation to reduce the money supply when gold reserves fell.[6] Sayers (1936, pp. 71–101), in contrast, developed a full history of the Bank's gold-point manipulation based on the view that changing the gold points was an alternative to increasing the Bank's rediscount rate (Bank Rate) when imbalance was external and it was desired not to upset internal balance to stem a gold outflow or encourage an inflow. Also, the Bank's gold-point intervention complemented a Bank-Rate change when the latter was ineffective either in the sense of not governing the market rate or in the sense of not affecting gold flows sufficiently.[7]

The difference between the Clark and Sayers interpretations is substantive, even though both view gold-point manipulation as an alternative to monetary policy. For Clark, that monetary policy is passive, the money supply changing with gold reserves in accordance with the "rules of the game" of the gold standard. For Sayers, it is active, with gold-market policy used in place of, or in conjunction with, Bank-rate policy aggressively designed to foster a net capital inflow and improve gold reserves. Sayers explanation is supported by (1) a detailed description and analysis of the

Bank's interest-rate and gold-market policies in the 1890–1914 period and (2) reference to contemporary newspaper reports and commentaries that stated, and encouraged, the relationship between Bank-rate and gold-point policies. In contrast, Clark's argument for his position is founded entirely on his incorrect cost estimates of shipping gold.

The Treasury's motivations for gold-point operations were quite different from those of the Bank, but again were incorrectly described by Clark. Secretary Shaw's interest-free advances in 1906 were unrelated to the state of the Treasury's gold reserves; the objective was to provide extra funds for commercial banks, thereby easing seasonal or cyclical pressure in the money market.[8] As for the Treasury's bar embargo and high premium in the 1890s, these were part of "a sequence of short-sighted expedients to obtain and retain gold" in the face of a lack of confidence in US maintenance of the gold standard and "a series of flights and returns [from/to the dollar] as views altered" (Friedman and Schwartz, 1963, pp. 106, 104).

Irrespective of the motivation for gold-point manipulation, examination is required of Clark's judgment that such policies constituted "interference in the workings of the gold standard system," even stating that the Bank and Treasury "tampered with the free workings of the gold market" (Clark, 1984, pp. 792, 818).[9] On the contrary, the Bank and Treasury always adhered to the basic statutes that placed their respective countries on the gold standard. For the Bank, the Resumption Act of 1819 required it to cash its notes in sovereigns at the mint price, while the Bank Charter Act of 1844 mandated that it purchase gold bars at 77s. 9d. per standard ounce (see sections 4 and 5 of chapter 4). For the Treasury, the Resumption Act of 1875 stipulated gratuitous coinage of standard gold bullion (meaning that only the expenses of converting bars and foreign coin into US coin would be assessed and not the additional charge of 0.2 percent specified in the Mint Act of 1873). Also, the Treasury was required to redeem US notes, Treasury gold certificates, and Treasury notes in coin by the acts of 1875, 1882, and 1890 (see sections 4 and 5 of chapter 3).

These obligations, always followed in the 1890–1914 period, placed outer limits on the dollar-sterling gold points, given (1) freight, insurance, and handling costs, (2) other transactions costs (abrasion, mint charges, currency premium, and exchange-rate cost), (3) interest cost, and (4) normal profit and risk premium. In offering to buy or sell foreign coin and to sell bars, at any price for which there were takers, and in making interest-free advances, the Bank went beyond statutory requirements and narrowed the gold-point spread, thus enhancing external integration but in no way impairing GPA efficiency. In supplying bars, at any premium for which takers existed, and in making interest-free advances, the Treasury did the same.

As the gold-market policies of the Bank and Treasury varied over time, the gold-point spread would narrow or widen, but it would never go beyond the outer limits emanating from obligations under the basic statutes. Arbitrageurs responded to the altered cost of receiving or selling gold as they would to a change in transport charge, insurance rate, interest cost, or any other component of arbitrage cost. There was no hindrance to GPA efficiency. In sum, gold-point manipulation did nothing more than alter the costs of gold shipments, but with the costs always remaining less than in the absence of such manipulation and in the presence of statutory observance by the Bank of England and the US Treasury.

Banking syndicates: Clark (1984, p. 817) puts forward another cause of gold-standard inefficiencies: the activities of banking syndicates in preventing gold exports. He discusses two such syndicates, the Morgan–Belmont group, operating in February–September 1895, and a similar syndicate functioning in July–August 1896.[10] Clark's results show that all ten months exhibit gold-export point violation.

To the extent that these syndicates succeeded in putting pressure on gold exporters to act against their economic interest via threats or bribes, then gold-point violations could occur. However, the present study shows no GPA inefficiencies during the periods when the syndicates functioned (and in fact not one gold-export violation on a monthly average basis during 1890–1906). So while in principle banking syndicates could have induced arbitrageurs to desist from profitable activity, the evidence is that they did not have this effect in a measurable monthly way.

Need for liquidity: When New York bankers, who were the gold-point arbitrageurs, desired quick liquidity, they could sell sterling bills for immediate domestic currency, and were especially likely to do so during a financial crisis. The increased supply of bills could push the exchange rate below the gold-import point. There was no immediate correction via GTF or GPA, because of the delay in obtaining funds via gold import. Ironically, the gold-point arbitrageurs (the New York banks) bring about the gold-point violation, rather than correct an exogenously imposed one (from their standpoint).[11] This is almost certainly the explanation of the only substantial GPA inefficiency in table 13.1, that of August 1893. The financial crisis of 1893 was most severe in that month, when a premium on currency occurred (see section 9 of chapter 3).

4   Interest arbitrage and forward speculation

4.1   Existing empirical studies

The efficiency of CIA or FS is nowhere examined for the 1925–31 dollar–sterling gold standard. Although Morgenstern (1959, pp. 168–9,

n. 3) acknowledges predecessors who investigated UIA efficiency under a gold standard, he was the only author until Giovannini (1993) to have done so using gold-point data and is still the only author to have examined the interwar experience. While Morgenstern does not provide monthly results (unlike the case for GPA), it is clear that he finds substantial UIA inefficiency for the interwar dollar–sterling gold standard. The mean interest-rate differential plus one standard deviation is high relative to maximum exchange-rate risk – 12 percent below or 42 percent above the risk, depending on the gold-point figures used to measure maximum risk.[12] Morgenstern's findings of UIA inefficiencies might again be spurious, not only because invariant gold points are assumed (as for GPA) but also because his model is misspecified (see note 19 to chapter 12).

There exists a voluminous literature on empirically testing the efficiency of UIA under a floating exchange rate, but it provides no guidance for a gold standard.[13] When the exchange rate is confined within the gold-point spread, it cannot display non-stationarity or heteroscedasticity, econometric problems that dominate the literature on floating rates. Also, modeling of the risk premium for UIA – a complicated task under a floating exchange rate – takes an obvious form (outlined in section 5.2 of chapter 12) under a functioning gold standard.

4.2   Empirical testing

4.2.1   Confidence in efficient gold-point arbitrage

To engage in the stabilizing kind of UIA and FS, so that these activities have the efficiency bands derived in sections 5.4 and 7.3 of chapter 12, arbitrageurs and speculators require full confidence, at least over their horizon, in the maintenance of the gold standard and in the efficiency of GPA. In sum, they must have absolute confidence that the exchange rate will remain within the gold-point spread.

Two tests of this confidence may be made. First, is the spot exchange rate within the gold-point spread ($GM \le RS \le GX$): is GPA currently efficient? This test is passed for all 76 months of May 1925–August 1931 (see section 3.2.1 above). While GPA was found efficient only in terms of monthly averages, this result is consistent with examination of UIA and FS, too, on a monthly average basis.

However, expectations are by nature prospective rather than retrospective. Therefore, second, is the expected spot rate within the spread ($GM \le RS^e \le GX$)? For any months for which the answer is negative, there is a lack of confidence that the gold standard will be maintained or that efficient GPA will occur. The UIA and FS models become inapplicable, and such months must be dropped from the sample.

4.2.2   Data and values of parameters

To test for the confidence in future GPA efficiency that underlies UIA and FS, data on the expected exchange rate (RS^e) and gold points (GX and GM) must be obtained and the length of horizon (value of N, recalling that RS^e is N months ahead) discerned. To compute the UIA and FS efficiency limits, the value of the risk-premium parameter (r) is needed. The interest-arbitrage (UIA and CIA) efficiency bands involve interest rates in London and New York (I_{UK} and I_{US}). Transactions cost (TC) and the values of taxation parameters over time (t_{US}, t_{UK}^n, p) must be obtained to compute the efficiency limits for all three operations (UIA, CIA, and FS). Of course, time series of the spot exchange rate (RS) and forward exchange rate (RF) are needed as the subject of interest-arbitrage (UIA, CIA) and forward-speculation (FS) efficiency, respectively.

Length of horizon: A horizon of three months ($N = 3$) is assumed, because a shorter horizon (say, one month) can allow a small adverse exchange-rate movement to wipe out the interest gain of UIA – a factor apparently taken into account by interest arbitrageurs in 1925–31 (Einzig, 1937, p. 244). Therefore *ad valorem* profit of UIA, CIA, and FS is measured per three-month period.

Experienced exchange rates: The spot exchange rate (RS) and the one-month and three-month forward exchange rates (RF) are mid-points of the buying price and selling price – that is, buying price plus the spread – of the pound, and so are expressed as the number of dollars per pound. The variable RS, developed as V in chapter 6, corresponds to the variable S (percentage deviation from parity) used in section 3.2.1 (see sections 3.6 and 3.7 of chapter 6). The three-month RF is constructed as $RS + PR$, where PR is the forward premium (negative if a discount).[14]

Risk-premium parameter: Einzig (1937, pp. 243) observes: "All but the most speculative amongst them [the interest arbitrageurs] allowed for the possibility of maximum depreciation, and did not undertake uncovered interest arbitrage unless the difference between interest rates was in excess of the possible extent of depreciation to gold point." In terms of the developed model of UIA, the London and New York banks operated on an r of unity, a value projected to the forward speculators. (Einzig is ignoring the expected exchange-rate gain and transactions cost, elements incorporated in the present model.)

Expected spot rate: Recalling that the arbitrageurs, both covered and uncovered, in the interwar period were the large London and New York banks, the value of their expected spot rate (RS^e) is unknown. Two alternative representations are considered: (i) the three-month forward rate (RF) and (ii) the mid-point (RM) of the gold-point spread, obtained as $RM = (GX + GM)/2$.

The justification for RM is twofold. First, unlike in the immediate prewar period, the banks did not discern a regular pattern in movements of the dollar–sterling exchange rate. Einzig (1937, p. 243) writes: "During the period of stability between 1925 and 1931, seasonal movements were much less regular than before the war and fluctuations within the gold points were apt to be much wider. Many disturbing factors which did not exist before the war assumed considerable importance from time to time. It was therefore no longer safe for arbitrageurs to take it for granted that the exchange would not depreciate to gold point."

The banks' subjective probability distribution of the exchange rate was apparently nearly uniform, assigning virtually equal probability to values of the exchange rate within the gold-point spread (with zero probability assigned to the exchange rate outside the spread). If the banks engage in repeated transactions, the appropriate RS^e is the mean value of their subjective probability distribution, and in this case the mean value is RM. Second, RM is a good approximation to RS^e for the class of probability distributions that are either close to uniform or relatively symmetrical about RM or any value in its neighborhood.

In favor of the forward exchange rate (RF) as the representation of the expected spot rate (RS^e) is the fact that it is indeed the conventional proxy. The justification is the generally accepted theory that, under market efficiency, the expected spot rate and the forward rate can differ only by a, presumed small, risk premium.

However, under a gold standard the equating of RS^e to the forward rate is not so readily based on efficient forward speculation; for all that such efficiency establishes is the forward-speculation efficiency band, $[RF_L^{fs}, RF_U^{fs}]$ (see section 7 of chapter 12). The risk premium is not small, as the value of unity for r is as applicable to forward speculation as to UIA, and transactions cost is also present. The positive risk premium, transactions cost, and tax-rate parameters all act to widen the band. Only if these elements were all zero ($r = TC = t_{US} = t_{UK}$) would the band reduce to $[RS^e, RS^e]$ so that $RF = RS^e$.

Also, the forward-rate proxy for RS^e, unlike RM, suffers from the deficiency that it does not emanate from constructing the arbitrageur's subjective probability distribution of the exchange rate on the basis of the perceived size and regularity of exchange-rate movements.

Transactions cost: A transactions cost of 0.5 percent per annum, implying *ad valorem TC* of 0.00125 per three-month period, was a "standing rule" of covered interest arbitrageurs in the interwar period (Einzig, 1937, pp. 25, 172–3) and is assigned also to forward speculation.

Interest rates: The dominant money-market instruments for three-month investment were bankers' bills and treasury bills in London, bankers' bills and stock-exchange time loans in New York.[15] Therefore I_{UK} (I_{US}) is the

Table 13.2 *Corporate tax rates, May 1925–June 1931*

Period	Critical dividend-payout ratio (p_c)	UK for dividend-payout ratio of (percent)			US (percent)
		0	$p_c/2$	$(1 + p_c)/2$	
May 1925–Dec. 1925	0.3500	20.00	16.50	6.50	13.00
Jan. 1926–Dec. 1927	0.3250	20.00	16.75	6.75	13.50
Jan. 1928–Dec. 1928	0.4000	20.00	16.00	6.00	12.00
Jan. 1929–Dec. 1929	0.4500	20.00	15.50	5.50	11.00
Jan. 1930–March 1930	0.4000	20.00	16.00	6.00	12.00
April 1930	0.4565	22.08	17.04	6.00	12.00
May 1930–March 1931	0.4667	22.50	17.25	6.00	12.00
April 1931	0.5118	24.58	18.29	6.00	12.00
May 1931–June 1931	0.5200	25.00	18.50	6.00	12.00

Source: See text.

average of the three-month rates on bankers' acceptances and treasury bills (stock-exchange time loans), converted from percent per annum to *ad valorem* per three-month period.[16]

Taxation parameters: Values of taxation parameters over time are presented in table 13.2. The US corporate tax rate, $100 \cdot t_{US}$, obtained from Blakey and Blakey (1940, p. 524) is shown in the final column. The UK nominal tax rate, $100 \cdot t_{UK}^n$, from Mitchell (1988, p. 645), is in the third column. The lower efficiency limits for UIA and CIA each have two alternative formulas, depending on whether case a ($t_{US} < t_{UK}$) or case b ($t_{US} > t_{UK}$) is applicable. Recalling that $t_{UK} = (1 - p) \cdot t_{UK}^n$, for $p < (>) p_c$, case a (b) applies, where $p_c = 1 - t_{US}/t_{UK}^n$. The value of the dividend–payout ratio (p) is unknown; but three alternative values of p centered around p_c and bounded by [0, 1] are 0, $p_c/2$, and $(1 + p_c)/2$. Corresponding values of t_{UK} are t_{UK}^n, $(1 - p_c/2) \cdot t_{UK}^n$, and $(1 - p_c) \cdot t_{UK}^n/2$; and their values over time are shown in table 13.2. Note that $p = 0$ and $p = p_c/2$ involve case a, and $p = (1 + p_c)/2$ case b.

4.2.3   Results

Confidence in future GPA efficiency, mandated for stabilizing UIA and FS, is justified by the expected spot rate within the spread: fulfillment of $GM \leq RS^e \leq GX$. For the expected rate at the spread mid-point ($RS^e = RM$), this relationship holds of necessity, by virtue of the definition of RM.

However, for the expected rate equal to the forward rate ($RS^e = RF$), the relationship is violated in July and August 1931, the last two full months of the gold standard, when $RF < GM$. As the US gold-import point (GM) is the UK gold-export point, lack of confidence in Britain's adherence to the gold standard is indicated, and these months are deleted from the sample, leaving the 74 months May 1925–June 1931.

For RS^e proxied by RF, there are no violations of UIA or FS efficiency, and so this representation is dropped from further consideration as uninteresting.[17] For RS^e proxied by RM, the months of UIA, CIA, and FS inefficiencies are shown in the first column of table 13.3. Consider first violations of the lower efficiency limit. There are 15–20 months (the number varying with the value of p) for which $RS < RS_{Lx}^{uia}$, one month for which $RS < RS_{Lx}^{cia}$, and 29 months for which $RF < RF_L^{fs}$. The only upper-limit violations of efficiency pertain to CIA, with 4–5 months (the number dependent on p) for which $RS > RS_U^{cia}$. With a total of 74 months for which the model is applicable, the number of market inefficiencies is not small. Even more serious than the existence and number of inefficiencies is their persistence – with a three-month, four-month, and two six-month periods of consecutive violations of RS_{Lx}^{uia} and a two, three, four, five, and thirteen-month successive violation of RF_L^{fs}.

However, the magnitude of the violations is less striking than their number and persistence. Table 13.3 presents two measures of magnitude: (1) unexploited profit on a percentage-per-annum basis (obtained as $400 \cdot \pi_{Lx}^{uia}$ for the UIA lower-limit violations, and similarly for the other violations) and (2) the distance of RS (RF, for FS) from the violated efficiency point as a percentage of the full distance of the nearer gold point (GM for a lower-limit violation, GX for an upper-limit violation) from the efficiency point. For the UIA violations, for example, (2) is $100 \cdot [(RS_{Lx}^{uia} - RS)/(RS_{Lx}^{uia} - GM)]$. For uncovered and covered interest arbitrage (UIA and CIA), results are shown for three alternative values of p (one of which is the range, $[p_c, 1]$, for which case b applies, for the lower-point violations).[18]

Given efficient GPA, the distance measure is bounded by [0, 100] percent. In contrast, the upper bound of profit is not so intuitive. Let a "serious" inefficiency be defined as the distance exceeding 50 percent. Then there are only five instances of serious inefficiencies: two for UIA, three for FS. Four of these are in 1925, the first year of the gold standard.

4.2.4   Explanations of inefficiencies

What could explain the totality of UIA, CIA, and FS inefficiencies and their concentration on the lower efficiency limits? Just as for GPA, answers fall into three categories, corresponding to the hypotheses that are tested

Table 13.3 *Violations of market efficiency, May 1925–June 1931*

Month	Profit (percent per annum)	Distance to gold point[a] (percent)
Lower efficiency point violated[b]		
Uncovered interest arbitrage (for p: 0, $p_c/2$, [p_c, 1])		
1925: May	0.46, 0.59, 0.73	21, 25, 29
Sept.	0.46, 0.57, 0.68	39, 44, 48
Oct.	0.89, 1.00, 1.11	79, 81, 82
Nov.	0.53, 0.65, 0.76	43, 48, 53
Dec.	0.58, 0.73, 0.87	29, 34, 38
1926: Oct.	0.36, 0.50, 0.63	21, 27, 31
Nov.	0.72, 0.85, 0.98	40, 44, 47
Dec.	0.16, 0.29, 0.42	9, 15, 21
1927: Jan.	——, ——, 0.10	——, ——, 6
Feb.	0.36, 0.48, 0.60	23, 28, 33
March	0.23, 0.35, 0.47	14, 20, 26
June	——, 0.10, 0.22	——, 6, 12
July	0.22, 0.34, 0.46	14, 20, 26
Aug.	——, ——, 0.07	——, ——, 4
1930: Nov.	——, 0.03, 0.13	——, 3, 12
Dec.	——, 0.08, 0.19	——, 7, 15
1931: Jan.	0.45, 0.56, 0.66	40, 45, 49
Feb.	0.28, 0.39, 0.51	18, 24, 29
March	0.26, 0.38, 0.50	17, 23, 29
April	0.01, 0.15, 0.29	1, 9, 17
Covered interest arbitrage (for p: 0, $p_c/2$, [p_c, 1])		
1925: Dec.	——, 0.02, 0.19	——, 3, 20
Forward speculation		
1925: May	1.25	75
June	0.46	27
July	0.18	10
Sept.	1.01	59
Oct.	0.75	43
Nov.	0.72	42
Dec.	0.15	9
1926: May	0.49	29
Sept.	0.26	15
Oct.	0.55	31
Nov.	0.68	39
Dec.	0.20	11
1927: Jan.	0.07	4
Feb.	0.48	29

Table 13.3 (*cont.*)

Month		Profit (percentage per annum)	Distance to gold point[a] (percent)
	Mar.	0.51	33
	April	0.20	13
	May	0.09	5
	June	0.28	18
	July	0.53	35
	Aug.	0.38	25
	Sept.	0.06	4
1929:	Aug.	0.01	1
	Sept.	0.15	10
1930:	Dec.	0.17	16
1931:	Jan.	0.50	48
	Feb.	0.75	72
	March	0.50	48
	April	0.19	18
	June	0.01	1

Upper efficiency point violated[b]

Covered interest arbitrage (for p: $0, p_c/2, (1 + p_c)/2$)

1928:	June	0, 0, 0[c]	0, 0, 0[d]
1929:	April	0.21, 0.24, 0.31	5, 6, 8
	May	0.12, 0.15, 0.22	3, 4, 5
1930:	March	0.05, 0.06, 0.07	2, 2, 3
	April	——, ——, 0[c]	–, –, 0[d]

Notes:
[a] Distance of exchange rate from violated speculation point as percentage of distance of nearer gold point from speculation point.
[b] A dash indicates no violation for the specified dividend-payout ratio (p).
[c] Less than 0.005 percent.
[d] Less than 0.5 percent.
Source: See text.

jointly: (1) the specified values of the variables and parameters of the model of UIA, CIA, or FS equilibrium, (2) the validity of the model, and (3) market efficiency of the operation.

Values of variables and parameters
The observed occurrences of UIA, CIA, and FS inefficiency could be spurious, hinging on incorrect values of the parameters or variables entering the

respective efficiency bands, so that hypothesis (1) rather than (3) should be rejected. The various variables and parameters are considered from this standpoint. Changes in their values such that the efficiency band is widened would reduce the scope for efficiency-band violations.

Gold points: A wider gold-point spread (lower GM and higher GX) would widen the UIA and FS efficiency bands, because the numerator of the lower efficiency point would decrease and of the upper efficiency point increase (see sections 5 and 7 of chapter 12). The gold-point figures derived here involve a wider spread than most estimates, because all cost components of arbitrage are incorporated. Also, the gold points are carefully constructed using all available information on these cost components. So it is unlikely that too narrow a gold-point spread is a source of UIA and FS inefficiencies.

Length of horizon: Suppose that the dominant horizon of speculators is one month rather than three. Then the call-money rate (on stock-exchange loans) would be the pertinent New York interest rate. During the final and frenetic period of the New York stock-exchange boom, from July 1928 to October 1929, the call-money rate was dominant for international investment (Einzig, 1937, p. 269; 1962, p. 315; Sayers, 1976, p. 219). Yet this is a period during which there were no UIA, and only two FS, efficiency-band violations even for a three-month horizon. Assuming a one-month horizon could lead to no greater UIA, and hardly more FS, efficiency.

Transactions cost: The estimate of 0.5 percent per annum, adopted here, has been uniformly accepted by researchers for the interwar period and even into the postwar period.[19] While higher transactions cost would widen the efficiency band of every operation (see sections 5–7 of chapter 12), empirically 0.5 percent is an upper limit of estimates occurring over time.[20]

Interest rates: An obvious alternative to the dual interest-rate variables (I_{UK} and I_{US}) selected is the interest rate on bankers' acceptances alone. It happens that the bankers'-bill interest-rate differential is uniformly greater than ($I_{UK} - I_{US}$). Now, almost certainly, the greater is the UK–US interest-rate differential, the higher are both lower and upper efficiency limits for UIA and CIA (see sections 5 and 6 of chapter 12).[21] Therefore the scope for violations of the lower (upper) speculation point would increase (decrease) were the interest rate on bankers' acceptances alone used. Because of the concentration of inefficiencies on the lower limit (under the dual interest-rate variables), the number and magnitude of inefficiencies would surely increase on balance (under bankers' acceptances alone). So the measured inefficiencies do not reflect selection of the interest-rate variables.[22]

Expected exchange rate: Because using the forward rate (RF) to proxy the expected exchange rate (RS^e) yields no violations of the UIA and FS efficiency bands, representation of RS^e by an average of the spread mid-point

(RM) and RF would surely reduce the number and magnitude of inefficiencies. The possibly spurious nature of the uniform efficiency under RF (see note 17) mitigates against this approach.

Risk-premium parameter: The value of unity for the risk-premium parameter (r) is at the upper limit consistent with the UIA and FS models. Any lower value would only narrow the efficiency band. For simplicity, assume that $I_{UK} - I_{US} = t_{UK} = t_{US} = TC = 0$. Then, with $r = 1$, the lower (upper) efficiency points of UIA and FS [RS_{Lx}^{uia} and RF_{L}^{fs} (RS_{U}^{uia} and RF_{U}^{fs})] are simply the average of the spread mid-point and the gold-import (export) point [RM and GM (GX)]. The efficiency bands are half the gold-point spread, symmetrical about RM.

Suppose that, rather than being at extreme risk aversion, speculators are risk neutral ($r = 0$). Then $RS_{Lx}^{uia} = RF_{L}^{fs} = RS_{U}^{uia} = RF_{U}^{fs} = RS^{e} (= RM)$. The UIA and FS efficiency bands degenerate to a point, and maximum scope for inefficiencies results. If $r = 0.5$, $RS_{Lx}^{uia} = RF_{L}^{fs} = (2 \cdot RM + GM)/3$ and $RS_{U}^{uia} = RF_{U}^{fs} = (2 \cdot RM + GX)/3$. The bands are only one-third the gold-point spread, symmetrical about RM, compared to one-half the spread for $r = 1$. The unitary value of r, along with Einzig's other information on UIA in the interwar period, may be accepted with confidence, because of their foundation on "daily contact with bankers" (Einzig, 1937, p. vii).

Validity of models of equilibrium
Assumption of confidence in the gold standard: Underlying the UIA and FS models is the basic assumption of confidence in maintenance of the gold standard on the part of the interest arbitrageurs and speculators. The absence of gold-point violations by spot and forward exchange rates justifies this assumption through June 1931.[23] Nevertheless, some episodes of efficiency-band violations may be interpreted as emanating from a temporary lack of confidence in Britain's ability or willingness to maintain the gold standard, that is, a temporary positive probability that the pound would be devalued. In effect, r would exceed unity, because arbitrageurs and speculators operating in favor of the pound currently believe that the exchange rate can fall below the US gold-import point. A sufficiently high r can make profit from UIA or FS zero, thus wiping out the UIA and FS inefficiencies, but the model as such becomes invalid. Because the episodic loss of confidence was asymmetrical, regarding UK and not US maintenance of the gold standard, the concentration of inefficiencies on the lower efficiency points can also be explained in this way.[24]

In May 1927 the Bank of France withdrew a demand for gold from the Bank of England, for fear of forcing Britain off gold. "This episode had demonstrated sterling's susceptibility to external pressure and revealed the Bank of England's reluctance to defend the exchange rate at any cost"

(Cairncross and Eichengreen, 1983, p. 46). Even though pressure on the pound was relieved, expectations of devaluation may have become positive and remained there over the next several months, increasing r beyond unity and thus explaining the UIA and FS efficiency-band violations of June–September 1927.

In 1928, in contrast, there was "speculators' confidence that these pressures [on the pound] were largely seasonal and that the Bank of England remained committed to the defence of the existing parity." So, having returned to unity, r remained there, and no UIA inefficiencies occurred (even in spite of the New York stock-market boom and crash) until the end of 1930, though there were two months of FS inefficiency (one of trivial magnitude) during that time.

Williams (1963, p. 523) states that the Bank of England's policy of allowing interest rates to fall during the course of 1930, combined with other factors, "importantly weakened foreign confidence in London . . . reflected in the continued weakness of sterling throughout 1930 and especially from October onwards." Clay (1957, p. 369) observes that "the first reports began to reach the Bank of distrust in sterling" shortly after October 10, 1930. So the UIA and FS efficiency-band violations of November 1930–April 1931 may likewise be explained by r exceeding unity. Why there was a respite in May and June is puzzling (the FS violation in June is of trivial magnitude). Perhaps a diversion was created by the European financial crises, which did not spread to the pound until mid-July. As Williams (1963, p. 524) comments: "When confidence [in sterling] did finally break (15/16 July) it came as a surprise. A crisis stemming from lack of confidence in London as a banking centre was not expected by the authorities."

In sum, all the UIA and virtually all the FS lower-point violations from June 1927 onward *may* be explainable by rejecting the models of UIA and FS equilibrium. A reason against this line of argument is that the interest arbitrageurs involved and the gold-point arbitrageurs were the same economic agents, the New York banks, and the gold-import point was not violated. Somehow the banks' lack of confidence in the pound (positive probability of a pound devaluation) had to be sufficient for UIA efficiency-band violations but insufficient for gold-point violations. So r could not have been much above unity.

Efficiency
Institutional limits on interest arbitrage: An alternative explanation, for UIA and CIA inefficiencies, is institutional limits imposed by banks on the volume of their international interest arbitrage, emanating from a desire to have sufficient liquid funds to satisfy regular customers (Einzig, 1937, pp. 171–2, 180–1). The concentration of inefficiencies at the lower limit could

be due to a relatively greater concern of New York banks for their domestic customers, in light of the city's recent rise as an international financial center. The stigma attached to forward speculation at the time (Einzig, 1937, pp. 143–5) may similarly explain the FS inefficiencies, although not their concentration at the lower point.

Part VI

Regime efficiency

14 Market forces

1 Definition of regime efficiency

Two concepts of gold-standard efficiency are explored in this study. Market efficiency, involving the behavior of private parties in response to the profit opportunities afforded by the gold standard, was the topic of part V. Gold-point arbitrage (GPA) market efficiency was tested empirically for three time periods: 1890–1906, 1925–31, and 1950–66. Uncovered and covered interest arbitrage (UIA, CIA) and forward speculation (FS) efficiency were tested only for 1925–31.

Related to market efficiency but distinct is regime efficiency, pertaining to the probability of maintenance of the gold standard with the existing mint parity. This type of efficiency will be studied empirically in detail only for 1925–31 but as a general phenomenon for all periods over 1791–1931, 1950–66.

The criterion of regime efficiency is that private participants and central banks behave in such a way that the probability of maintenance of the gold standard is, ideally, maximized, or at least enhanced. The regime efficiency considered is short run in nature, encompassing only the horizon of the interest arbitrageurs and forward speculators. It is certainly true that long-run regime efficiency of the dollar–sterling gold standard in 1925–31 was low – because of (1) Britain's overvalued currency relative not just to the dollar but also to the undervalued currencies of Britain's trading competitors (France and Belgium), (2) Britain's downwardly rigid wages, unfavorable shifts in comparative advantage, and capital-account weakness, and (3) the precariousness of short-term foreign funds in London. However, these unstable elements may not have been noticed by arbitrageurs and speculators, or the connection to confidence in Britain's adherence to the gold standard not made, or the elements may have been viewed by these economic agents as not applicable to their, short-run, horizon.

To develop the criterion of perfect regime efficiency, consider the importance of efficient gold-point arbitrage (GPA) for regime efficiency.

Maintenance of the gold standard is enhanced by the absence of gold-point violations, because such violations contain the danger of turning the stabilizing speculation of uncovered interest arbitrage (UIA) and forward speculation (FS) into destabilizing speculation. Gold-point violations can directly destroy the subjective probability distribution that underlies stabilizing UIA and FS (in particular, that there is a zero probability of the exchange rate violating a gold point within the agent's horizon). They also involve gold flows, implying a reserves decline for one of the countries, the continuance of which can lead to a general loss of confidence in that country's ability to maintain the gold standard, whence destabilizing speculation.[1]

This argument suggests the desirability of a given exchange-rate change having a minimum probability of leading to a gold-point violation. The implication is that the distance of the exchange rate (RS) from a gold point should be maximized; equivalently, the distance of the rate (RS) from the spread mid-point (RM) should be minimized. The ideal value of RS, therefore, from the standpoint of short-run regime efficiency, is RM. Perfect regime efficiency would locate the exchange rate always at the spread mid-point: $RS = RM$.

2   Regime efficiency under market efficiency

Notwithstanding the inefficiencies discerned empirically in chapter 13, in this section universal market efficiency is assumed and the implications for regime efficiency are explored. The theoretical argument applies to either general or perfect market efficiency; the empirical results pertain to general efficiency and to 1925–31.

The importance of efficient GPA for regime efficiency was discussed in section 1. For GPA, the assumption of market efficiency is justified empirically for 1925–31 (see section 3.2.1 of chapter 13). Clearly, the general market efficiency of GPA that existed throughout May 1925–June 1931 was a strong positive force for regime efficiency. Given efficient GPA, the narrower the gold-point spread (the higher GM and the lower GX), the stronger the regime efficiency. The average gold-point spread over May 1925–June 1931 was 1.0791 (0.9007) percent under GPA (GTF). Of course, the maximum distance of RS from RM under efficient GPA is half the gold-point spread.

To the extent that the direct UIA, indirect UIA, or covered interest arbitrage (CIA) efficiency bands are within the GPA efficiency band (gold-point spread), under market efficiency they enhance regime efficiency by reducing the maximum distance of RS from RM beyond that fixed by GPA in at least one direction.

Table 14.1 *Asymmetries in efficiency bands, May 1925–June 1931*

Dividend–payout ratio (p)	Number of observations			
	Beyond gold point		Beyond spread mid-point[a]	
	Lower[b]	Upper[c]	Lower[d]	Upper[e]
Uncovered interest arbitrage				
0	11	0	0	0
$p_c/2$	7	0	0	0
$(1 + p_c)/2$	3[f]	0	0[f]	0
Covered interest arbitrage				
0	28	0	0	57
$p_c/2$	22	0	0	55
$(1 + p_c)/2$	20[f]	0	2[f]	51
Forward speculation with covered interest arbitrage				
0	35	0	0	12
$p_c/2$	31	0	0	12
$(1 + p_c)/2$	28[f]	44	0[f]	0

Notes:
[a] Spread mid-point outside efficiency band.
[b] Lower limit of efficiency band below gold-import point.
[c] Upper limit of efficiency band above gold-export point.
[d] Lower limit of efficiency band above spread mid-point.
[e] Upper limit of efficiency band below spread mid-point.
[f] For lower limit, $p_c \le p \le 1$.

Table 14.1 shows the number of months for which an efficiency limit falls outside a gold point. Let RS_L denote a given lower efficiency limit for a given operation and RS_U the corresponding upper efficiency limit. The second column of the table lists the number of months (out of 74) for which $RS_L < GM$ (for example, for $p = 0$, there are 11 occurrences of the lower UIA efficiency limit below the gold-import point, $RS_{La}^{uia} < GM$) and the third column the number of observations for which $RS_U > GX$. Define RSM_L = maximum (RS_L, GM) and RSM_U = minimum (RS_U, GX). Then $(RSM_U - RSM_L)$ may be called the "band width relative to the band mid-point," and the impact of market efficiency on the range of RS beyond that of efficient GPA is measured by $BW1 = 100 \cdot [(RSM_U - RSM_L)/(GX - GM)]$, where the percentage improvement in regime efficiency is $100 - BW1$.

What is the theoretically expected value of $BW1$? For simplicity, assume that transactions cost, tax rates, and differential interest return are all zero:

$TC = t_{UK} = t_{US} = I_{UK} - I_{US} = 0$. Then $RS_{La}^{uia} = RS_{Lb}^{uia} = RS_{La}^{j} = RS_{Lb}^{j} = (RM + GM)/2$ and $RS_{U}^{uia} = RS_{U}^{j} = (RM + GX)/2$, while $RS_{La}^{cia} = RS_{Lb}^{cia} = RS_{U}^{cia} = RF$. Both the direct and indirect UIA efficiency bands are half the width of the gold-point spread $(GX - GM)$, symmetrical about RM; so $BW1 = 50$ percent, and the impact of market efficiency (beyond GPA) on regime efficiency is also 50 percent.

The proxy of the expected exchange rate (RS^e) by the spread mid-point (RM) rather than any other value enhances regime efficiency, because it makes for a symmetrical efficiency band, thus acting to minimize the maximum distance between the exchange rate (RS) and RM. Generally, regime efficiency is fostered by low values of transactions cost (TC) and the risk-premium parameter (r). Suppose $t_{UK} = t_{US} = I_{UK} - I_{US} = 0.^2$ Then $r = TC = 0$ implies $RS_{La}^{uia} = RS_{Lb}^{uia} = RS_{La}^{j} = RS_{Lb}^{j} = RS_{U}^{uia} = RS_{U}^{j} = RM = RSM_{L} = RSM_{U}$, and $BW1 = 0$. Under market efficiency, regime efficiency becomes perfect $(RS = RM)$.

Table 14.2 (second column) shows mean($BW1$) (over the 74 observations) for UIA, CIA, and "FS with CIA" (indirect UIA) under the various alternative values of the dividend–payout ratio (p), with the coefficient of variation of $BW1$ (standard deviation as a percent of mean) in parentheses. The empirical impact of market efficiency on regime efficiency is less than the 50-percent improvement suggested by the above analysis. Direct UIA efficiency reduces the range of RS, on average, by about thirty percent relative to the gold-point spread. Indirect UIA efficiency can reduce it even more – by over 40 percent on average for case a $(p = 0$ and $p = p_c/2$, see section 4.2.2 of chapter 13) – but the variation of this reduction is much greater than that for direct UIA. It should be noted that the mean band width is defined as a percent of the width of the gold-point spread, which itself is variable: the coefficient of variation of $(GX - GM)$ is 13.16 percent.

To demonstrate definitively that direct UIA is more conducive to regime efficiency than is indirect UIA, consider the "band width relative to the spread mid-point" (as a percentage of the width of the gold-point spread): $BW2 = 100 \cdot [(|RSM_{U} - RM| + |RM - RSM_{L}|)/2 \cdot (GX - GM)]$. The percentage increase in regime efficiency from pure efficient GPA (RS at GX or GM), for which $BW2 = 50$, is $50 - BW2$. The measure $BW2$ is motivated by the asymmetry of the empirical efficiency bands relative to RM. In fact, there are instances in which $RS_{L} > RM$ or $RS_{U} < RM$ (see columns four and five of table 14.1), so that the efficiency band is entirely on one side of RM. $BW2$ is the average distance of the efficiency-band points from RM (with the end points not permitted to exceed the gold points), as a percent of the width of the gold-point spread. For direct and indirect UIA, the theoretically expected value of $BW2$, under the simplifying assumption $TC = t_{UK} = t_{US} = I_{UK} - I_{US} = 0$, is 25 percent.

Table 14.2 *Band width delimited by market efficiency, May 1925–June 1931*

Dividend–payout ratio (p)	Mean band width relative to:	
	Band mid-point[a]	Spread mid-point[b]
	(percent of gold-point spread)	
Uncovered interest arbitrage		
0	69.72 (3.47)	37.28
$p_c/2$	68.71 (3.24)	36.58
$(1 + p_c)/2$	68.15[c] (2.13)	35.52[c]
Covered interest arbitrage		
0	31.74 (25.26)	44.74
$p_c/2$	30.23 (23.84)	44.81
$(1 + p_c)/2$	29.76[c] (22.78)	44.36[c]
Forward speculation with covered interest arbitrage		
0	58.46 (32.75)	47.74
$p_c/2$	56.08 (38.08)	48.34
$(1 + p_c)/2$	83.55[c] (10.28)	50.36[c]

Notes:
[a] Coefficient of variation in parentheses.
[b] Mean plus two standard deviations.
[c] For lower limit of band, $p_c \leq p \leq 1$.

In light of the variability of the efficiency bands, table 14.2 (third column) exhibits the value of the mean plus two standard deviations of $BW2$. Efficient direct UIA has the greatest impact, with a 13–14 percent improvement in regime efficiency from pure efficient GPA on average *plus* allowing for two standard deviations from the mean – an excellent performance relative to the 25-percent theoretical improvement in regime efficiency. Efficient indirect UIA (joint "FS with CIA") has the least effect, with efficient CIA in the middle.

3   Role of market forces

With RM – by definition the mid-point of the gold-point spread – the ideal value of RS for regime efficiency, it is doubly natural to define the pound "weak" as the spot exchange rate below the spread mid-point ($RS < RM$) and "strong" as the rate above the spread mid-point ($RS > RM$). When the pound is weak (strong), one wants uncovered and covered interest arbitrage

(UIA and CIA) to operate in favor of the pound (dollar), thereby moving RS closer to RM. Should the operation take place in the opposite direction, the effect is to move RS further from RM, perverse for regime efficiency. Therefore, for $RS < (>) RM$, it is desirable that profit from the operation in favor of the pound (dollar) exceed zero: π_{Lx}^{uia}, $\pi_{Lx}^{cia} > 0$ (π_{U}^{uia}, $\pi_{U}^{cia} > 0$). In terms of market (as distinct from policy) variables, the corresponding necessary condition is (1) a positive exchange-rate gain: $RM - RS > (<) 0$ for UIA, $RF - RS > (<) 0$ for CIA, and/or (2) a positive interest return: the interest-rate differential $I_{UK} - I_{US} > (<) 0$ for both UIA and CIA. In percentage terms, the market (pretax) exchange-rate-gain term is $100 \cdot [(RM - RS)/RS]$ for UIA, $100 \cdot [(RF - RS)/RS]$ for CIA, and the market interest-return term in percent per annum is $400 \cdot (I_{UK} - I_{US})$. Interestingly, condition (1) is automatically fulfilled for UIA.

Further, if one were to choose among UIA, CIA, and joint "FS with CIA" (indirect UIA) as alternative operations for the support of regime efficiency, on the assumption of perfect market efficiency the empirical results of section 2 show that UIA should be selected. So UIA may be set against CIA and FS in turn.

Consider first UIA versus CIA. For $RS < RM$, it is desired that $\pi_{Lx}^{uia} - \pi_{Lx}^{cia} = (1 - t_{US}) \cdot (RM - RF) - (RS - GM) > 0$, a necessary condition for which is $RM - RF > 0$. Similarly, for $RS > RM$, one wants $\pi_{U}^{uia} - \pi_{U}^{cia} = (RF - RM) - (GX - RS) > 0$, with the necessary condition $RM - RF < 0$. In percent, the conditional term is $100 \cdot [(RM - RF)/RM]$. By a similar argument, for $RS < (>) RM$, it is desired that $\pi_{Lx}^{uia} - \pi_{L}^{fs} > 0$ ($\pi_{U}^{uia} - \pi_{U}^{fs} > 0$), with the necessary condition $RF - RS > (<) 0$ and/or $I_{UK} - I_{US} > (<) 0$, which is consistent with conditions previously delineated.

In sum, the fulfillment of any of four market conditions (inequality in the "correct" direction) – involving $100 \cdot [(RM - RS)/RS]$, $100 \cdot [(RF - RS)/RS]$, $100 \cdot [(RM - RF)/RM]$, and $400 \cdot (I_{UK} - I_{US})$ – is conducive to regime efficiency. Furthermore, the non-fulfillment of a condition (inequality in the "incorrect" direction) is unfavorable to regime efficiency. Table 14.3 summarizes the influence of the critical market variables on regime efficiency.[3] There are 64 observations for which the pound is weak ($RS < RM$) and 10 for which the pound is strong ($RS > RM$). As a continuous measure of the strength of the pound, take the deviation of the exchange rate from the gold-import point (which is the UK gold-export point) as a percent of the width of the gold-point spread: $STRP = 100 \cdot (RS - GM)/(GX - GM)$, which, under gold-point arbitrage (GPA) efficiency, is zero for RS at the pound's lowest value (GM) and 100 at its highest value (GX). So a "weak" ("strong") pound is defined as $RS < (>) RM$ or $STRP < (>) 50$. $STRP$ has a mean value of 22.92 for $RS < RM$ and 65.41 for $RS > RM$.

Table 14.3 *Influences on regime efficiency, May 1925–June 1931*

Variable	Percent of observations conducive to efficiency		Mean of variable		Correlation coeff.[c]
	Pound weak[a]	Pound strong[b]	Pound weak[a]	Pound strong[b]	
Spread mid-point *minus* spot rate (percent)	100	100	0.30	− 0.16	− 0.98
Forward rate *minus* spot rate (percent)	38	100	− 0.02	− 0.11	− 0.54
Spread mid-point *minus* forward rate (percent)	98	60	0.32	− 0.05	− 0.80
London *minus* New York interest rate (percent per year)					
Market rate	53	30	− 0.20	0.05	0.24
Central bank rate	83	0	0.64	0.66	0.13
Exchange-market intervention ($ million)	55	90	0.78	− 3.92	− 0.18

Notes:
[a] Spot rate below mid-point of gold-point spread (strength of pound below 50 percent), 64 observations. Positive value of variable is conducive to efficiency.
[b] Spot rate above mid-point of gold-point spread (strength of pound above 50 percent), ten observations. Negative value of variable is conducive to efficiency.
[c] With strength of pound, 74 observations. A negative sign is conducive to efficiency.
Source: See text.

When the pound is weak, a positive (negative) value of a market variable enhances (detracts from) regime efficiency. The opposite is true for a strong pound. The table shows, for the months under which the pound is weak and strong alternatively, (1) the percent of observations for which efficiency is enhanced by the market variable and (2) the mean value of the variable. Also, (3) as a continuous measure of the impact of a market variable on regime efficiency, the correlation of the variable with $STRP$ is presented: a negative (positive) correlation enhances (diminishes) efficiency.

The $(RM − RS)/RS$ and $(RM − RF)/RM$ variables are most conducive to regime efficiency, especially when the pound is weak. Of course, the former variable can only enhance regime efficiency. When the pound is weak, this variable provides a pretax exchange-rate gain of 0.30 percent for UIA. In contrast, the market interest-rate differential $(I_{UK} - I_{US})$ is arguably more unfavorable than favorable for regime efficiency. When the pound is weak, this variable is positive barely more often than negative and its mean value is actually negative; furthermore, its correlation with $STRP$ is perverse. The remaining variable, $(RF - RS)/RS$, is also, on balance, unfavorable to regime efficiency, when the pound is weak.

15 Policy variables

1 The role of policy variables

Policy variables have a dual impact on regime efficiency. First, market variables are themselves influenced by policy variables. Second, policy variables can also have a direct influence on regime efficiency. Because only short-run regime efficiency is studied, basic policies (such as the mint value of a country's currency and sterilization of reserves flows) are not considered. Two short-term policies of interest are discount-rate policy and exchange-market intervention.

2 Discount-rate policy

It was found in section 3 of chapter 14 that market interest rates were not favorable for regime efficiency. Why was this so? Underlying the market rates in London and New York were Bank Rate (the Bank of England's discount rate) and the Federal Reserve Bank of New York discount rate, respectively. Monthly series of these central-bank rates are constructed as averages of daily observations.[1] As shown in table 14.3, the Bank Rate – Federal Reserve Bank of New York discount-rate differential, denoted as $I_{BR} - I_{DR}$, comparable to the market-rate differential $(I_{UK} - I_{US})$, is positive for 83 percent of the months (53 out of 64) when the pound is weak (and, perversely, for all ten months when the pound is strong). Also, for $RS < RM$, the mean value of $(I_{BR} - I_{DR})$ is over three-fifths of a percentage point per year – ostensibly quite conducive to regime efficiency.

However, the average magnitude of the market-rate differential, $I_{UK} - I_{US}$, is minus one-fifth of a percentage point per year under a weak pound, a full four-fifths of a percentage point below the central-bank rate differential. Also, the correlation of $(I_{BR} - I_{DR})$ with $STRP$ is, like that of $(I_{UK} - I_{US})$, positive (albeit low), which acts against regime efficiency. Therefore, although $I_{BR} - I_{DR}$ often operated in the right direction, (1) its magnitude was, on balance, too low to affect $I_{UK} - I_{US}$ sufficiently to

263

enhance regime efficiency, and (2) it was not calibrated to the weakness of the pound.

The explanation is that each central bank had its discount rate as a single instrument with which to achieve several policy goals. The Federal Reserve had three targets for its discount rate, emanating, respectively, from the desires "to help the hapless British" (external balance, or the strength of the pound), "to combat speculation in the New York stock market," and of "not depressing the economy" (internal balance) (Temin, 1989, pp. 20–3). There were two policy objectives for Bank Rate: internal and external balance (Cairncross and Eichengreen, 1983, pp. 38–9).

For $I_{BR} - I_{DR}$ strongly conducive to regime efficiency, international cooperation was of paramount importance. This meant the subordination of other targets to external balance, specifically, the strength of the pound. The Federal Reserve was generally unwilling to do this, notwithstanding statements to the contrary.[2] In contrast, the Bank of England often, though not always, kept Bank Rate higher than internal considerations would dictate, for the sake of external balance.[3] However, with minimal Federal Reserve cooperation and a reluctance on the part of the Bank to abdicate Bank Rate policy to the London–New York market interest-rate differential ($I_{UK} - I_{US}$ in the present chapter), $I_{BR} - I_{DR}$ was of insufficient magnitude and flexibility to improve regime efficiency markedly.[4]

So discount-rate policy was of little help to regime efficiency. While it often involved a higher Bank Rate than the Federal Reserve discount rate (generally desirable for efficiency, given the pound's chronic weakness), the differential was insufficient in magnitude to widen the market-rate differential substantially and indeed even to make it generally in favor of London under a weak pound.

3   Exchange-market intervention

Both the Bank of England and the Federal Reserve banks intervened in the foreign-exchange market. Their joint net purchase (sale) of pounds for dollars acted to increase (decrease) RS. This joint exchange-market-intervention variable, denoted as $EMINT$ and measured in millions of dollars, is the subject of the last row entry in table 14.3.[5] For $RS < (>) RM$, regime efficiency dictates that intervention be in favor of the pound (dollar), that is, $EMINT > (<) 0$.

Regime efficiency benefited minimally from this policy variable. True, $EMINT$ is negatively correlated with $STRP$, but the correlation is low. Also, $EMINT$ is positive only in a slight majority of months when the pound is weak. Finally, and devastatingly, the (monthly) average value of $EMINT$ under a weak pound is a paltry $0.78 million – insufficient to affect the value of RS measurably.

Why was exchange-market intervention in favor of the pound so little when regime efficiency often warranted a lot of it? Five reasons may be suggested. First, the Bank itself discouraged too much intervention by the Federal Reserve, because of the fear that financing would delay adjustment (Clarke, 1967, pp. 43–4). Second, after 1927, with the decline in central-bank cooperation (see note 4), the Federal Reserve attitude toward sterling support hardened and the feeling grew that such support should be limited (Moggridge, 1972, pp. 192–3). Third, the amounts of foreign bills held by the Federal Reserve banks traditionally were "very small in proportion to the size of the markets which they were supposed to influence" (Hardy, 1932, pp. 101, 116).

Fourth, there was an ongoing technical dispute between the Bank and the Federal Reserve over the medium of Fed intervention to support the pound (Beckhart, 1932, p. 458; Clarke, 1967, pp. 161–2, 175). The Fed wanted its sterling in the form of bills, implying direct market intervention, whereas the Bank preferred support via Fed dollar deposits at the Bank, thus giving the Bank itself the wherewithal to intervene in the market. This dispute at times adversely affected the timing, if not the amount, of market intervention. Fifth, there was the problem of the Fed desire to liquidate acquired foreign-bill holdings quickly (Beckhart, 1932, p. 158; Clarke, 1967, pp. 162, 176). Often the effect on regime efficiency was perverse.

4   Appendix: data on exchange-market intervention

EMINT, the Bank–Fed joint exchange-market-intervention variable, is constructed as $\Delta FRHP - \Delta BHD$, where *FRHP (BHD)* is end-of-month Federal Reserve (Bank of England) holdings of pounds (dollars), with corrections to $\Delta FRHP$ or ΔBHD to exclude direct central-bank transactions, to the extent such transactions are identifiable. Federal Reserve purchases of sterling bills from the Bank obtained by increasing Bank deposits at a Reserve Bank are not so excluded, but net out to zero because of the joint nature of the *EMINT* variable.

Federal Reserve holdings of pounds (FRHP): The basic series is "bills payable in foreign currencies," found in Federal Reserve Board (1926–32). There are no data prior to September 30, 1925; it is assumed bill holdings are unchanged from April 30 to September 30 – a reasonable assumption because until mid-1926 month-to-month changes are very small. For June 1931, $\Delta FRHP$ is assumed zero, because the data are contaminated by international credit agreements, which account for the bulk of the holdings. For all months, the series in principle is inclusive of non-sterling bills; however, there is good evidence that virtually all bills (until June 1931) are sterling, with the exception of an operation in Hungarian pengos in July–August

266   Regime efficiency

Table 15.1 *Exchange-market intervention in favor of pound, May 1925–June 1931 (millions of dollars)*

Month	1925	1926	1927	1928	1929	1930	1931
Jan.		− 4.77	− 0.14	− 4.98	19.47	14.01	0.14
Feb.		− 19.69	− 0.15	− 9.42	0.01	4.87	− 26.76
March		0.34	0.14	0.66	− 4.82	4.87	− 43.83
April		0.08	− 0.70	− 0.55	0	4.88	14.61
May	0	− 0.01	0.05	− 0.73	− 14.60	− 4.86	4.87
June	0	0.44	11.10	− 0.16	− 9.73	− 19.46	0
July	0	− 0.61	0.91	14.60	− 9.72	− 29.20	
Aug.	0	0.01	− 4.99	14.60	30.75	0.01	
Sept.	0	5.33	− 15.19	14.60	− 5.12	4.87	
Oct.	− 0.36	0.12	− 15.95	25.08	5.71	15.64	
Nov.	− 0.27	0.10	− 10.85	43.81	− 12.44	10.00	
Dec.	0.27	0.47	− 0.33	9.73	− 0.36	4.40	

Source: See text.

1929 (Beckhart, 1932, pp. 457–60; Hardy, 1932, pp. 101–3). To correct for that operation, the amount of $1 million is subtracted from $\Delta FRHP$ in July and added to it in August.

Bank holdings of dollars (BHD): The basic data are dollar holdings of the Bank of England (Sayers, 1976, pp. 349–55). From information in Moggridge (1972, pp. 135, 181–8) and the *Federal Reserve Bulletin* (September 1929, p. 124), known or estimated direct central bank transactions are excluded. The resulting series is converted to dollars by multiplication by 4.86656. *EMINT* is listed in table 15.1.

16 Net outcome

1 Methodology of measuring regime efficiency

1.1 Determinants of regime efficiency

The efficiency bands of the various operations – gold-point arbitrage, uncovered interest arbitrage, covered interest arbitrage, and joint "forward speculation with covered interest arbitrage" – the extent to which the operations are efficient (within the respective bands), and the influences of the various market and policy variables combine with the determinants of external and internal integration to generate a certain level of regime efficiency. So interest now extends beyond 1925–31 to 1791–1931, 1950–66 – the entire time span of the study. What is the appropriate measure of the extent of regime efficiency?

1.2 A simple measure of efficiency

Perfect regime efficiency is defined as the exchange rate at the mid-point of the gold-point spread. At this point it is convenient to revert to expressing the exchange rate in percentage points of parity and as the deviation from the spread mid-point: R^*, as developed in section 1 of chapter 11. So perfect regime efficiency is given by $R^* = 0$. A simple measure of the amount of regime inefficiency is then $|R^*|$. This is the experienced (observed) deviation of the exchange rate from the spread mid-point. For a given period of time with a time series of $|R^*|$, the average of the deviations may be taken; so the measure of inefficiency becomes mean $|R^*|$.

  The lower bound of mean $|R^*|$ is zero, for the exchange rate (in dollars per pound) uniformly at the spread mid-point (RS at RM), where there is perfect regime efficiency. There is not an unconstrained upper bound. However, under perfect GPA, there is an upper bound (minimum regime efficiency or maximum inefficiency) of half the gold-point spread in percentage terms, given by CX^*, the gold-export point expressed in percentage points of parity and as the deviation from the spread mid-point (the notation again from section 1 of chapter 11). The upper bound is reached for the exchange rate at either gold point (RS at GM or GX, in dollars per pound), where there is maximum regime inefficiency given efficient GPA.

There are several problems with mean$|R^*|$ as the measure of regime efficiency. First, it provides a biased representation of regime efficiency, because there is likely to be a positive correlation between mean$|R^*|$ and the width of the gold-point spread. After all, under efficient GPA the gold-point spread constrains the exchange rate to be within it. Second, the measure is not explicitly derived from a loss function. Third, it is not developed as a special case of a class of measures emanating from a general loss function. Fourth, there is no standard of attainable (rather than perfect) regime efficiency, comparable to the concept of general market efficiency. An explicit modelling approach to measuring regime efficiency corrects these problems.

1.3   A model of measurement of efficiency

1.3.1   Loss function

Logical properties of the loss function relating the disutility from regime inefficiency to the deviation of the exchange rate from the spread mid-point are as follows. (1) Disutility is zero at the spread mid-point. (2) At other exchange rates disutility is positive. (3) The loss increases with the distance of the exchange rate from the spread mid-point. (4) The loss depends on only the absolute deviation of the exchange rate from the mid-point and not whether the deviation is positive or negative.

Two fundamental loss functions with these properties are the identity function (disutility equals deviation itself) and square function (disutility equals square of deviation). The square function especially penalizes exchange-rate deviations the further they are from the spread mid-point. Disutility increases at a higher rate than for the identity function.[1]

1.3.2   Experienced versus hypothetical loss

Experienced loss: Given any sample period of a gold (in general, specie) standard, the deviation of the exchange rate from the spread mid-point – this deviation expressed as a percentage of parity, taken as positive, and denoted as $|R^*|$ – can be constructed for all observations. Then the experienced average loss from regime inefficiency is the average deviation, mean$|R^*|$, or the average of the squared deviations, mean$(|R^*|^2)$, depending on the specific loss function. These are the observed average disutilities relative to the (zero) loss under perfect regime efficiency ($R^* = 0$ for all observations).[2]

Hypothetical loss: Consider the case of R^* a continuous random variable with density (probability distribution function) $f(R^*)$. Assuming perfect GPA efficiency, $f(R^*) = 0$ for $|R^*| > CX^*$. With positive GPA cost, $CX^* > 0$. Assume that UIA and CIA are "neutral" in the sense that, combined with non-arbitrage and non-speculation market forces, they distribute the exchange rate along all points within the spread with equal probability. Then, recalling (from section 1 of chapter 11) that $-CM^*$ denotes the gold-import point and that $CX^* = CM^*$, R^* has the uniform (rectangular) distribution

$$f(R^*) = 1/(CX^* - (-CM^*)) = 1/(CX^* + CM^*) = 1/(2 \cdot CX^*)$$
$$\text{for } |R^*| \leq CX^*$$
$$= 0 \text{ for } |R^*| > CX^*$$

Hypothetical average disutility emanates from this distribution, and depends only (and positively) on the gold point, CX^*. Therefore average disutility is positively correlated with the width of the gold-point spread. The hypothetical average loss from regime inefficiency is again the average exchange-rate deviation or average squared exchange-rate deviation (depending on the specific loss function), but the exchange-rate function follows the assigned uniform distribution. The deviation is on average half the magnitude of a gold point ($CX^*/2$), and this is the average hypothetical disutility under the identity loss function. For the square loss function, average hypothetical disutility is $(CX^*)^2/3$, though intuition must give way to mathematics for the derivation.[3]

Efficiency ratio: With both the actual and hypothetical average losses measured relative to the zero disutility of perfect regime efficiency (and, of course, calculated for the same sample period), the ratio of the average actual to the average hypothetical disutility measures actual loss from regime inefficiency relative to the loss emanating from a hypothetical situation of perfect GPA and a uniform exchange-rate distribution within the gold-point spread.[4] Multiplication by 100 expresses the ratio in percentage terms. Insofar as the ratio is below (above) 100, regime efficiency may be accepted (rejected) for the sample period. A ratio of 100 is the criterion of attainable regime efficiency.

The efficiency ratio is $200 \cdot [\text{mean} |R^*|/CX^*]$ for the identity loss function and $300 \cdot [\text{mean}(|R^*|^2)/(CX^*)^2]$ for the square function.[5]

The lower bound of the efficiency ratio is zero, which occurs under perfect efficiency ($R^* = 0$ for all observations): the exchange rate is always at the spread mid-point. Under perfect GPA, the upper bound (minimum regime efficiency or maximum inefficiency) is reached when the exchange rate is always at a gold point ($|R^*| = CX^*$). Then mean$|R^*| = CX^*$, mean$|R^*|^2 = (CX^*)^2$; the efficiency ratio is 200 for the identity loss function and 300 for the square function.

1.3.3   Relaxation of assumptions

Uniform distribution function: The analysis could proceed just as well with the exchange rate having a hypothetical non-uniform distribution about the gold-point spread. If the exchange rate has a greater probability the closer it is to the spread mid-point, then the efficiency standard becomes tougher; whereas if the rate has higher probability as it approaches a gold point, then the standard is easier. At one extreme, hypothesized perfect efficiency places the exchange rate always at the mid-point, and efficiency for the given sample period can never be accepted. At the other extreme, perfect GPA but perverse behavior of other economic agents can be assumed such that the exchange rate is always at one or the other gold point. Now efficiency would be easy to accept. A uniform distribution appears to yield a good compromise standard.

Loss function: The model requires only that disutility be related to the deviation of the exchange rate from some norm value. Any of the four properties of the loss function can be dropped. The function can be discontinuous. For example, disutility can be made zero for the exchange rate within the spread and positive outside the spread. The function can be asymmetrical, as would occur, for example, by substituting mint parity for the spread mid-point as the norm value of the exchange rate.

Exchange-rate system: The model can be applied to any exchange-rate system involving a band of floating-rate activity with the band delimited by some effective force. For the gold standard, that force was private arbitrage and speculation, underlain by the willingness and ability of domestic authorities to transact in gold with the agents of these operations. Under the Bretton Woods system, the force was exchange-rate setting by domestic authorities. The model is equally applicable to either system.

1.3.4   Relationship to internal integration

On the surface, the regime-efficiency ratio appears to be simply another way of measuring internal integration. By definition, as presented in section 1 of chapter 11, $II = $ mean$|R^*| - EI/2$, where $EI = CX^*$; so $II = $ mean$|R^*| - CX^*/2$. This formula may be compared to the efficiency ratio for the identity loss function: $200 \cdot ($mean$|R^*|/CX^*)$. Apart from the constants, the only difference is that internal integration is of the form $A - B$ and the efficiency ratio the form A/B. Is this an essential difference and do the concepts differ in any other respects?

In fact, internal integration and regime efficiency, though related, are distinct in both concept and measurement. First, internal integration pertains to the perfection of the foreign-exchange market, whereas regime efficiency is concerned with the stability of the monetary standard. Second, the statistic mean$|R^*|$ is in part an indicator of *variation* of the exchange rate under exchange-market integration, gauging temporal as well as placement integration (see section 3.1 of chapter 11), but is purely a measure of *central tendency* for regime efficiency. Third, internal integration was developed under a specific (linear) formula, while regime efficiency is consistent not only with nonlinear formulas but also with entire families of alternative measures.

Fourth, regime efficiency is a stricter concept than internal integration. Stability of the monetary system (say, a gold standard) might be dependent strongly on the location of the exchange rate. Efficient GPA definitely keeps the exchange rate within its (the GPA) gold-point spread; the same cannot be said for "efficient" GTF in relation to its spread. GTF only plays a role in preventing a gold-point violation from worsening in frequency and magnitude (see section 6 of chapter 8). Therefore only the GPA spread and mid-point are used to construct R^* and CX^*, the ingredients in the numerator and denominator of the regime efficiency ratio. In contrast, internal and external integration were legitimately computed alternatively under GPA and GTF (see table 11.1). External integration is a dimension of market integration but not of regime stability; so the role of GTF can be considered alternative to GPA only for integration.

2 Empirical results

Table 16.1 presents the average experienced exchange-rate deviation from the spread mid-point, the average hypothetical deviation, and the corresponding efficiency ratio for both the identity and square loss functions by period. The statistics are calculated for two sets of periods: (1) the usual periods spanning 1791–1800 to 1950–66 and based on quarterly exchange-rate observations, (2) the periods for which monthly exchange-rate observations have been developed (1890–1906, 1925–31, 1950–66). The figures in table 16.1 pertain entirely to the GPA gold-point spread, and it is no coincidence that the average experienced and hypothetical deviations for the identity function are identical (except for fewer significant digits) to the exchange rate and half the gold-export point in table 11.1 (columns two and four in each table). Figures 16.1, 16.2, and 16.3 plot gold points, spread mid-point or parity, and the exchange rate monthly for 1890–1906, 1925–31, and 1950–66.

Table 16.1 *Exchange-rate deviation from spread mid-point, gold-point arbitrage, 1791–1966*

Period	Mean experienced deviation[a]		Mean hypothetical deviation[a]		Efficiency ratio[b]	
	Identity function	Square function	Identity function	Square function	Identity function	Square function
Quarterly observations						
1791–1800	4.19	27.97	3.56	16.94	117.42	165.10
1821–30	2.14	6.33	1.98	5.22	108.37	121.24
1831–40	1.44	3.74	1.81	4.35	79.96	86.07
1841–50	1.04	1.54	1.26	2.12	82.59	72.88
1851–60	0.86	0.92	0.80	0.85	108.14	108.51
1861–70	0.87	1.52	0.74	0.74	116.85	205.40
1871–80	0.38	0.23	0.55	0.41	68.70	56.37
1881–90	0.32	0.15	0.34	0.16	93.46	97.74
1891–1900	0.25	0.08	0.32	0.14	77.03	61.98
1901–10	0.15	0.04	0.27	0.10	53.34	35.15
1911–14[c]	0.12	0.02	0.27	0.10	42.66	20.59
1925[d]–31[c]	0.28	0.09	0.27	0.10	102.83	95.44
1950–66	0.26	0.10	0.32	0.14	80.48	75.57
Monthly observations						
1890–1906	0.24	0.09	0.30	0.13	78.37, 77.62[g]	71.88, 64.90[g]
1925[e]–31[f]	0.28	0.10	0.27	0.10	104.01, 102.97[g]	97.24, 94.21[g]
1950–66	0.27	0.11	0.32	0.15	85.21, 87.18[g]	76.38, 78.16[g]

Notes:
[a] Percentage points of parity.
[b] Ratio of mean experienced to mean hypothetical deviation, percent, except where note g.
[c] Second quarter.
[d] Third quarter.
[e] May.
[f] August.
[g] Mean of monthly ratios of experienced to hypothetical deviation.

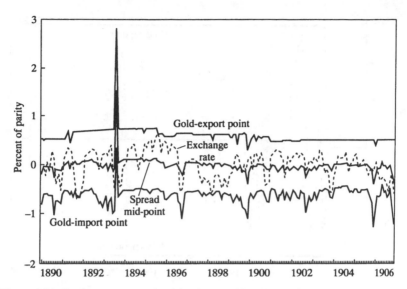

Figure 16.1 Exchange rate and gold points, gold-point arbitrage, monthly, 1890–1906

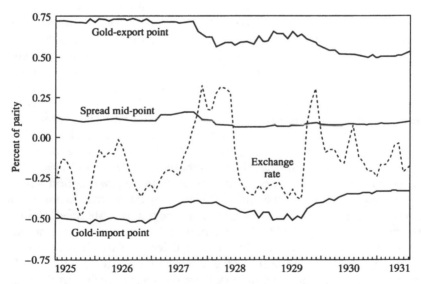

Figure 16.2 Exchange rate and gold points, gold-point arbitrage, monthly, 1925–31

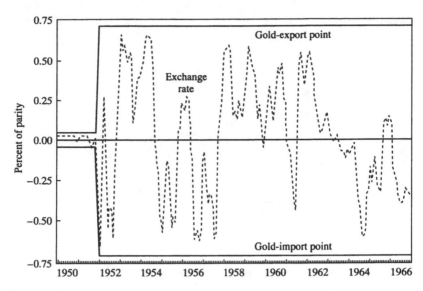

Figure 16.3 Exchange rate and gold points, monthly, 1950–31

Considering first the results based on quarterly observations, the tremendous decline in the average experienced exchange-rate deviation in the 1820s compared to the 1790s is even more apparent with the square than the identity function, because of the existence of extreme observations in the 1790s. In the 1860s, the decade incorporating the Civil War, the identity function shows average deviation hardly above that of the 1850s, but the square function exhibits a substantial increase. Thereafter, to World War I, the average deviation of the exchange rate from the spread mid-point falls steadily to the amazingly low figures of 0.12 and 0.02 percent of parity under the identity and square functions, respectively. In 1925–31 average deviation increases to levels intermediate between those of the 1880s and 1890s. The deviations for 1950–66 are about the same as for the interwar period.

Dividing the average experienced deviation by the average hypothetical deviation and multiplying by 100, the efficiency ratio is obtained. Results are most interesting. Unlike for external and internal exchange-market integration, the improvement in regime efficiency in the 1820s is by no means overwhelming. Indeed, for the identity function (comparable to II, the measure of internal integration), there is a greater decline in the ratio (and therefore increase in regime efficiency) from the 1820s to the 1830s than from the 1790s to the 1820s.

The criterion of attainable regime efficiency (a 100-percent ratio) is accomplished by the 1830s, lost in the 1850s and 1860s, but then regained uniformly except (almost but not quite) for the identity function in 1925–31.[6] Again, in 1911–14 regime efficiency is at a remarkably high level: 43 percent for the identity function and 21 percent for the square function. The regime-efficiency ratio suggests that World War I marked a watershed in gold-standard stability. Regime efficiency in the interwar period worsened noticeably. For the identity function, the efficiency ratio more than doubled so that regime efficiency was no longer attained. For the square function, the ratio more than quadrupled. In contrast, in 1950–66 regime efficiency is attained, with the ratios again between the levels for the 1880s and 1890s.

Turning to the monthly observations, they show that there is little precision forgone when quarterly observations are used to compute the average experienced deviation of the exchange rate. Values are about the same for corresponding time periods irrespective of unit of observation (month or quarter). Also, in five of six cases (the square function for 1890–1906 the only exception), the difference between computing the efficiency ratio as the ratio of the monthly average experienced to the monthly average hypothetical deviation or as the average of the monthly experienced/hypothetical ratios is fairly small.

Returning to the interwar period, regime efficiency is worse than for the other monthly periods, 1890–1906 and 1950–66. Yet, whether monthly or quarterly exchange-rate observations are used, regime efficiency is accepted for the square loss function and barely rejected for the identity function. In either situation the ratio is in the neighborhood of 100. This means that regime efficiency in 1925–31 was about the same as that emanating from efficient GPA and a uniform distribution of the exchange rate within the gold-point spread. This is perhaps a surprising result, in view of the long–run regime inefficiency of the interwar gold standard. However, long-run does not necessarily translate into short-run regime inefficiency (see section 1 of chapter 14), and the latter is what the efficiency ratio measures.

The important conclusion is that the short-run regime efficiency of the 1925–31 dollar–sterling gold standard was far greater than the conventional wisdom concedes. In this the role of private market participants was positive if not paramount, as shown in the results of chapters 13–14. Until confidence in the gold standard collapsed in July 1931, GPA exhibited complete market efficiency (on a monthly unit of observation). Further, from May 1925 through June 1931, speculators and arbitrageurs in the foreign-exchange and money markets behaved as if any lack of confidence that they had in the gold standard and in efficient GPA was episodic rather than systemic. Also, the likelihood of the expected exchange rate being close to the spread mid-point and the location of the UIA and CIA bands in relation to the gold-point spread enhanced regime efficiency.

However, market forces were not uniformly conducive to regime efficiency. The extreme risk aversion of exchange-rate speculators and interest arbitrageurs and the non-negative correlation of the London – New York market interest-rate differential with the strength of the pound detracted from efficiency. Further, the interest-rate differential often had the sign opposite of that mandated for regime efficiency.

Short-run policy on the part of the monetary authorities of the United Kingdom and United States offered precious little assistance to regime efficiency, as found in chapter 15. The international discount-rate differential (Bank Rate minus Federal Reserve Bank of New York rediscount rate) was generally too low to affect the market interest-rate differential significantly and further was not oriented to the weakness of the pound. Exchange-market intervention acted to weaken the pound in a large minority of months, and, when supportive, was of low magnitude on average.

On balance, it was the operations of private participants rather than of monetary authorities that gave regime efficiency the strength that it had in the interwar period.

Part VII

Conclusions

17 Summary and conclusions

1 Institutions

1 A country's domestic and international monetary standards – be they metallic (gold, silver, or bimetallic) or paper – can differ, as can its effective and legal domestic standard (sections 1 and 4 of chapter 2).

2 A gold (or other metallic) standard involves both domestic and international conditions (sections 2 and 3 of chapter 2).

3 The monetary system of colonial times continued to exist in the United States to the mid-1790s, with no effective American mint until 1794 (sections 1 and 2 of chapter 3).

4 The gold value of the dollar was unchanged from 1837 to 1934 (section 2 of chapter 3).

5 The United States was formally bimetallic until 1873–1874, when silver was legally demonetized (section 3 of chapter 3).

6 Several kinds of US government or central bank paper currency convertible into coin on demand were authorized, between 1861 and 1913 (section 4 of chapter 3).

7 The important US Mint Acts, that determined coinage of private bullion and provision of gold bars, were in 1792, 1834, 1837, 1853, and 1882 (sections 5 and 6 of chapter 3).

8 Banks were a late development in American history, and were of four types: federal, private, state, and national (section 7 of chapter 3).

9 Disregarding paper standards, the United States was on an effective silver standard to 1834 and a gold standard thereafter (section 8 of chapter 3).

10 The American metallic standard was interrupted by a number of paper standards, some of which noticeably disturbed the foreign-exchange market

and only the last two of which (1917–22 and 1933–) involved not only "suspension of specie payments" but also divergences from an international gold standard (section 9 of chapter 3).

11   The British unit of account is unchanged from the Anglo-Saxon period (section 1 of chapter 4).

12   There has been minting of coins in Britain more or less continuously since Roman times (section 2 of chapter 4).

13   Important changes in the silver weight of the pound occurred in 1601 and 1816, in its gold weight in 1601, 1663, 1696, 1699, and 1717 (section 2 of chapter 4).

14   Britain was legally on a silver standard until the mid-thirteenth century, on a bimetallic standard to 1774, 1798, or 1816, depending on one's point of view, and then on a gold standard (sections 3 and 8 of chapter 4).

15   From its inception in 1694, the Bank of England issued banknotes, convertible into coin; but government paper money, redeemable in gold coin, was not authorized until 1914 (section 4 of chapter 4).

16   In 1666 Britain became the first country to have both free (open to all) and gratuitous (free of seigniorage) coinage (section 5 of chapter 4).

17   From the mid-eighteenth century, with rare exception, the Bank of England rather than the mint was the preferred destination for the sale of gold by private parties (section 5 of chapter 4).

18   Banking developed in England since the mid-seventeenth century, with the Bank of England, private banks in London, country banks, and (by legislation of 1826 and 1833) joint-stock banks (section 7 of chapter 4).

19   Britain was effectively on a silver standard to the turn of the eighteenth century, when a bimetallic standard ruled, and on a gold standard thereafter (section 8 of chapter 4).

20   Unlike the United States, Britain had only one paper-standard episode prior to World War I, but then a permanent domestic paper standard (section 9 of chapter 4).

21   Deviations from an international metallic standard go back to the turn of the thirteenth century in England, but laws were often evaded, and the divergences stemming from World War I were greater than for the United States (section 9 of chapter 4).

22   The American foreign-exchange market centered in the dominant port city, eventually New York (section 1 of chapter 6).

23   The dominant exchange-market instrument was the sterling bill of exchange to World War I – with the sixty-day bill giving way to the three-day bill after the Civil War and the demand bill from 1879 – and the cable transfer after World War I (section 2 of chapter 6).

24   Gold-point arbitrage is distinguished from gold-effected transfer of funds (sections 1 and 2 of chapter 8).

25   In the 1811–20 decade merchants gave way to foreign-exchange dealers, ultimately the large New York banks, as the dominant transferors and arbitrageurs (section 3 of chapter 8).

26   Gold-effected transfer of funds and gold-point arbitrage were dependent in their details on the exchange-market instrument and the direction of gold shipment (section 4 of chapter 8).

27   The dominant exchange-market medium for gold-effected transfer of funds and gold-point arbitrage was the 60-day bill to the later 1860s, the 3-day bill to about 1880, the demand bill to World War I, and the cable transfer in 1925–31 (section 5 of chapter 8).

2   Theory

1   Gold-effected transfer of funds prevents an exchange rate outside a gold point from moving further away from the spread, while gold-point arbitrage returns it to the spread (section 6 of chapter 8).

2   To analyze gold-point arbitrage as an immediate force returning the exchange rate to an exogenously determined gold-point spread ignores adjustment lag in general and the special features of cable transfer in particular (section 6 of chapter 8).

3   The dimensions of internal integration are geographic (integration across space), temporal (variability of the exchange rate), and placement (location of the exchange rate with respect to the mid-point of the gold-point spread) (section 3 of chapter 11).

4   Determinants of internal integration include background to the foreign-exchange market (transportation and communication, expectations, stability of the banking system) and the foreign-exchange market itself (participants, operations, and market structure) (section 3 of chapter 11).

5   Exchange-rate speculation emanating from absolute confidence in the gold standard and in the operations of gold-point arbitrageurs is a powerful force making for placement integration (section 3 of chapter 11).

6   Exchange-market efficiency under a gold standard is exposited by defining profit as true economic profit, making explicit the roles of arbitrageurs and speculators as the earners of this profit, and incorporating the duration of the unit time period (section 1 of chapter 12).

7   Tests of exchange-market efficiency are categorized by (i) whether they involve arbitrage, speculation, or a combination, and (ii) whether they incorporate the gold-point spread, an exchange-rate norm value (either mint parity or the spread mid-point), neither, or both (section 2 of chapter 12).

8   A model of gold-point arbitrage, covered and uncovered interest arbitrage, and forward speculation is developed that involves (i) joint consideration of the operations and (ii) careful consideration of transactions cost, risk premium, and taxation (section 4 of chapter 12).

9   The ideal value of the exchange rate from the standpoint of regime efficiency (short-run maintenance of the gold standard) is the mid-point of the gold-point spread (section 1 of chapter 14).

3   Measurement

1   Metallic (mint) parity is distinguished from legal parity (section 1 of chapter 5).

2   A path breaking report on the measurement of dollar–sterling parity was provided by John Quincy Adams in 1821 (section 2 of chapter 5)

3   Not until 1873 was legal dollar–sterling parity and the expression of the exchange rate made consistent with true mint parity (sections 4 and 5 of chapter 5).

4   There are many techniques of gold-point estimation, but the best involves generation of time series of cost components of gold-effected transfer of funds or gold-point arbitrage, and summing of the series as appropriate (section 1 of chapter 9).

5   Representing exchange-market integration by the gold-point spread (external integration) has specific problems that can be overcome but methodological problems than cannot (sections 2 of chapter 10 and 1 of chapter 11).

6   Representing exchange-market integration by exchange-rate variation has methodological problems, and internal integration is appropriately measured by a model combining the gold-point spread and exchange-rate variation approaches (section 1 of chapter 11).

7   A model of measurement of regime efficiency is offered, involving a dis-utility function and a probability distribution function of the exchange rate about the gold-point spread (section 1 of chapter 16).

4   Data

1   True mint parity is computed for 1791–1834, even though Britain and the United States were on different effective metallic standards (section 3 of chapter 5).

2   A quarterly exchange-rate series for 1791–1931, 1950–66 – and monthly series for 1890–1906, 1925–31, 1950–66 – are generated to satisfy a set of specified criteria (section 3 of chapter 6).

3   Gold points are developed in the form of decadal (or related period) averages for 1791–1931 and as monthly time series for 1890–1906, 1925–31, and 1950–66 (sections 2 and 3 of chapter 9).

5   Empirical results

1   Geographic integration demonstrates a strong movement to exchange-market integration in the 1820s (section 1 of chapter 7).

2   Seasonality analysis and intra-annual movement of the exchange rate, conducted by other authors, indicate weak exchange-market integration until the second half of the nineteenth century (sections 2 and 3 of chapter 7).

3   Exchange-rate variation shows a jump in exchange-market integration in the 1820s and a long-run improvement in integration (section 4 of chapter 7).

4   The mid-point of the gold-point spread differs from mint parity (section 1 of chapter 10).

5   Both external and internal integration show tremendous increase in integration in the 1820s and enhanced integration over time (sections 3 of chapter 10 and 2 of chapter 11).

6   Improvements in transportation and communication (both interna-tional and domestic) enhanced internal integration over the nineteenth century (section 4 of chapter 11).

7   Internal integration was also affected by expectations regarding suspen-sion or restoration of specie payments, currency depreciation under such suspension, war versus peace, and victory versus defeat in wartime (section 4 of chapter 11).

8   The identity of the dominant participants in the foreign-exchange market and the nature of the market structure played a profound role in the determination of the level of internal integration (sections 5–8 of chapter 11).

9   Improvement in external rather than internal integration was the more-important element in the process of perfecting the American foreign-exchange market (section 9 of chapter 11).

10   The 1890–1906 and 1925–31 sample periods for testing market efficiency exhibit comparable characteristics (section 2 of chapter 13).

11   There are only three months of a gold-point violation in 1890–1906 and none in 1925–31 (section 3 of chapter 13).

12   The measured gold-point inefficiencies of other authors probably emanate from incorrect gold-point data (section 3 of chapter 13).

13   There are a substantial number of inefficiencies of uncovered interest arbitrage and forward speculation in 1925–31, though their magnitude is less striking than their number and persistence (section 4 of chapter 13).

14   The principal explanation of exchange-market inefficiencies is episodic loss of confidence in the gold standard (section 4 of chapter 13).

15   Efficient uncovered interest arbitrage enhances regime efficiency in 1925–31 by about thirty percent relative to the gold-point spread (section 2 of chapter 14).

16   While two of three exchange-rate conditions are conducive to regime efficiency, the UK–US interest-rate differential has a net unfavorable effect (section 3 of chapter 14).

17   Discount-rate policy in the two countries was minimally helpful to regime efficiency (section 2 of chapter 15).

18   Exchange-market intervention on the part of the Bank of England and the Federal Reserve banks was too weak to enhance regime efficiency (section 3 of chapter 15).

19   The improvement in regime efficiency in the 1820s is not overwhelming (section 2 of chapter 16).

20   Regime efficiency in 1925–31 is less than before World War I, but nevertheless about the same as that arising from hypothctical efficient gold-point arbitrage and uniform distribution of the exchange rate within the gold-point spread (section 2 of chapter 16).

Notes

1 Introduction

1 Recently, a body of literature has developed that is concerned with the value of the exchange rate within a "target zone" set by monetary authorities. This "target-zone theory" began with an unpublished manuscript of Paul Krugman in 1987, which developed into a seminal paper, Krugman (1991). The theory has been applied empirically to gold-standard experience, for example, by Hallwood, MacDonald, and Marsh (1995).

The target-zone model has limitations that are not shared in this volume. First, the model is all-inclusive, applicable to any exchange-rate zone the end-points of which are defended by the authorities. A gold-point spread is treated simply as a special case of a target zone. The institutional features of a gold standard in general or in a specific experience, and the cumulative history of a country's monetary standard, are ignored. Second, the model is much more concerned with the behavior of the exchange rate inside the band (the preferred term, more-general than "spread") than outside it. Third, the model assumes rational expectations, perfect knowledge of present values of variables and parameters, and instantaneous adjustment – elements that perhaps pertain to the present-day foreign-exchange market but that may be contrary to historical experience. Fourth, the model does not propel its proponents to any special data generation. Existing gold-point estimates and exchange-rate series are deemed appropriate for empirical application. Fifth, the model imposes a rigorous framework so that the only manifestation of an exchange-rate regime that is of interest is the credibility, and therefore viability, of the target zone. Other issues of importance under historical gold or silver standards – for example, exchange-market integration and the efficiency of arbitrage and speculation operations – are ignored.

2 The most comprehensive such study is Eichengreen (1992). An important exception is Hallwood, MacDonald, and Marsh (1995), who make use of target-zone theory and data in Officer (1993).

3 The upheaval created by World War I forces the gap 1914–19.

2 Monetary standards

1 "In specie" is Latin for "in kind," meaning, in this context, money in the form of minted metal.

2 As noted by Whitaker (1933, p. 319), this minimum can be large, as long as it is reasonable.
3 The meaning of "inconvertibility" was quite different in the 1791–1931 period from what it subsequently became. The former meaning of inconvertibility was "the currency non-exchangeable for specie at the established price," resulting in a floating exchange rate. The current definition is "far-reaching controls on trade and payments." "'Convertibility' as an objective of monetary policy before 1914 meant, not, as it does today, the avoidance of exchange and direct trade controls (which were then virtually unknown), but rather the avoidance of fluctuating exchange rates that would result from severing the fixed link between the national currency and gold." (Bloomfield, 1959, p. 23). See also Friedman and Schwartz (1963, p. 7), Temin (1969, pp. 114–18), and Triffin (1960, pp. 21–30).

3   American monetary standard

1 Later, the Reich (Holy Roman Empire) coined the "Reichsthaler," in English "rix–dollar," which in size and silver content was close to the peso. Therefore it was natural for the latter currency to be called the "Spanish dollar," originally by the London dealers in foreign exchange. See Nussbaum (1957, p. 10) and Carothers (1930, pp. 21–2).
2 The real was termed a "bit" by the colonists, a name they used for any small silver coin. The Spanish dollar was also divided into half–dollars and quarters, the latter known as "two bits." See Carothers (1930, pp. 34–5). Subsequently, the American (and Canadian) quarter–dollars were also colloquially called "two bits," a usage extending into the second half of the twentieth century.
3 The Morris report is in *International Monetary Conference* (1879, pp. 425–32) and is discussed by Carothers (1930, pp. 46–9) and Taxay (1966, pp. 15–16).
4 The Jefferson plan is reprinted in *International Monetary Conference* (1879, pp. 437–43) and discussed by Carothers (1930, pp. 50–1) and Taxay (1966, pp. 20–1).
5 The Congressional report and legislation, including a mint bill that followed in October 1786, are in *International Monetary Conference* (1879, pp. 445–51). For commentary, see Carothers (1930, pp. 51–6), Taxay (1966, pp. 22–5), and Watson (1899, pp. 19–25).
6 Hamilton's report is printed in *International Monetary Conference* (1879, pp. 454–84) and discussed by Carothers (1930, pp. 62–5) and Taxay (1966, pp. 44–51).
7 The Act is in Huntington and Mawhinney (1910, pp. 474–9), with good summaries provided by Carothers (1930, pp. 62–5) and Taxay (1966, pp. 65–7).
8 See Stewart (1924, pp. 18–19) and Carothers (1930, pp. 81–2). The individual states took their time in formally adopting the new federal unit of account – for example, Massachusetts in 1794, New York in 1797, Maryland in 1812, and, incredibly, New Hampshire not until 1948 and by popular referendum changing its constitution that established the shilling as the monetary unit. See Nussbaum (1957, p. 56).

9 On this differential treatment of gold and silver coins, see Alexander Hamilton's report, in *International Monetary Conference* (1879, p. 456).

10 These comments are not to be interpreted as strictures against the colonial monetary system. Indeed, as Sylla (1982, p. 23) writes: "One would be hard pressed to find a place and time in which there was more monetary innovation than in the British North American colonies in the century and a half before the American Revolution." To the accomplishments mentioned by Sylla one might add, for the Revolutionary Period, the joint Congressional-state refunding plan of 1780 for the redemption of Continental bills. This was historically the first contractionary monetary reform of a paper currency. For the basic literature on the colonial monetary system, see the bibliographical essay prepared by Perkins (1980, pp. 121–2). The paper-money experience of the Revolutionary Period is described by Carothers (1930, pp. 37–41), Dewey (1934, pp. 34–41), Nussbaum (1957, pp. 35–9), Studenski and Krooss (1963, pp. 25–9), Nettles (1962, pp. 24–31), Hepburn (1924, pp. 13–19), Sumner (1874, pp. 43–9), and Del Mar (1899, pp. 93–116). As Sylla points out, it was the reaction to the inflationary paper-money experience of the Revolution (rather than the mixed history of colonial paper money) that led to a specie standard for the federal United States. The Continental bills ("old tenor") depreciated to one-thousandth of face value, becoming worthless by 1780. Sumner (1874, pp. 46–7) writes: "A barber's shop in Philadelphia was papered with it, and a dog, coated with tar, and the bills stuck all over him, was paraded in the streets." Even the reform currency ("new tenor") depreciated to one-sixth of its silver value.

11 Whether under troy weight, used for precious metals, or the common avoirdupois weight, a grain is identical. Under troy weight, there are 24 grains in a pennyweight, 480 in an ounce, and 5760 in a pound. In contrast, there are 437.5 grains in an avoirdupois ounce and 7000 in a pound.

12 The reports are reprinted and discussed in Watson (1899, pp. 21–2, 243–55).

13 Hamilton's report is impressive in its basis on economic argument. One can agree with Watson (1899, p. 33) that: "It is difficult to pay to this report that tribute which it deserves. It was so exhaustive in its analysis, so profound in its reasoning, so comprehensive and logical in every position taken, that to this day it is regarded as an authority on money and coinage."

14 For the explanation of why the unwieldy fineness was adopted, see Carothers (1930, pp. 62–3), Willem (1959, pp. 4–6), and Kemmerer (1944, p. 66, n. 3). The legislations are in Huntington and Mawhinney (1910, pp. 473–9).

15 The date traditionally ascribed to this emission is October 1792 (see, for example, Watson, 1899, p. 64; Hepburn, 1924, p. 45); but Taxay (1966, pp. 71–2) provides evidence that it was no later than July.

16 The letter, dated December 30, 1893, is printed in Lowrie and Clarke (1832, pp. 270–1). The legislation is in Peters (1748, p. 341). For a description of this episode, see Taxay (1966, pp. 120–1). Until 1873 the Mint was attached to the Department of State rather than the Treasury.

17 The first gold deposit occurred on February 12, 1795, with its coinage done July 31. For a list and description of the early deposits at the Mint, see Stewart (1924, pp. 44–50).

18 The Mint officials involved in the overfineness of the silver dollar were not pun-
ished – not even reprimanded – for their behavior. Depositors, of course,
received less coined money for their silver bullion than the law specified. One
such depositor received reimbursement from Congress. Discussions of the over-
fine silver-dollar episode are presented by Bolles (1894, vol. II, pp. 161–3),
Taxay (1966, pp. 89–90), Watson (1899, pp. 229–31), and Willem (1959, pp.
1–9). Strangely, Taxay and Willem state that the 1794–5 dollar consisted of
374.75 grains of fine silver (rather than the true 374.4). The source documents –
printed in Lowrie and Clarke (1832, pp. 352–8, 588), Congress of the United
States (1851, pp. 3667–71), and Select Committee on Coins (1832, pp. 17–20) –
clearly show 374.4 to be the correct number. Hepburn (1924, p. 44, n. 1) explicitly states the correct figure, while Watson quotes a source document containing
it.

19 The Acts are in Huntington and Mawhinney (1910, pp. 496–7, 500–8) and discussed in Carothers (1930, pp. 91–5), Taxay (1966, p. 200), and Watson (1899,
pp. 85–7, 97–9).

20 The acts mentioned in this paragraph are in Huntington and Mawhinney (1910,
pp. 508–9, 511–13, 530–50, 593, 610–14). Time series of gold and silver coinage
are in Director of the Mint (1942, pp. 68–71). On the one-dollar piece, see
Carothers (1930, p. 135).

21 The legislation and proclamation are in Krooss (1969, vol. IV, pp. 2793–805).

22 For the text of some of these Acts, see Huntington and Mawhinney (1910, pp.
481–91, 497–8). A summary and critique is provided by Carothers (1930, pp.
66–7, 78–9, 101–2). See also Hepburn (1924, pp. 46–7, 60).

23 For the act, see Huntington and Mawhinney (1910, pp. 517–18); for the history
of withdrawing the foreign coin, Carothers (1930, pp. 138–48).

24 The Act is in Huntington and Mawhinney (1910, pp. 511–13).

25 See Huntington and Mawhinney (1910, p. 568) and Laughlin (1900, p. 305).

26 See, for example, Carothers (1930, p. 233), and Friedman (1990b, p. 1165).

27 "According to bimetallists, the Coinage Act of 1873, which discontinued the
silver dollar as a monetary standard, passed Congress through the corrupt
influence of a cabal of powerful government bondholders who conspired with
treasury officials and influential congressmen. By establishing a single gold unit
of account, the cabal presumably hoped to raise the market value of its public
securities" (Weinstein, 1967, p. 307). Histories of "silver politics" are provided
by Friedman and Schwartz (1963, pp. 113–19), Hepburn (1924, pp. 268–304),
Laughlin (1900, pp. 92–105, 211–17, 259–61), and Myers (1970, pp. 197–222).

28 The silver legislations are in Huntington and Mawhinney (1910, pp. 689–90,
579–81, 589–91, 599–600).

29 For all the above legislation, see Huntington and Mawhinney (1910, pp. 634–45)
and Sanger (1863, p. 338).

30 There is evidence that certificate issuance had always been of this nature. See
Friedman and Schwartz (1963, p. 25, n. 11).

31 These Acts pertaining to gold certificates are in Huntington and Mawhinney
(1910, pp. 175–9, 693–6, 704–10) and *Statutes at Large of the United States of
America* (1911, p. 965; 1921, p. 370).

32 The Federal Reserve Act and the Act of June 5, 1933 are in Krooss (1969, vol. IV, pp. 2436–70, 2723–4).
33 Morris' money unit was 0.25 grain of silver; therefore one pound (5760 grains) of silver would coin 23,040 units. The mint price, however, would be 22,237 units per pound. Mint charges, therefore, would be $(23,040 - 22,237)/23,040 = 3.49$ percent. Under the 1786 Acts, a silver (gold) dollar would have a zero-charge mint price of 5760/409.7891 (5760/26.8656) dollars per pound Troy, equalling $14.0560 ($214.4006), versus an actual mint price of $13.777 ($209.77), involving mint charges of $(14.0560 - 13.777)/14.0560 = 1.98$ percent for silver and $(214.4006 - 209.77)/214.4006 = 2.16$ percent for gold.
34 The logical interpretation, given by Bolles (1894, vol. II, pp. 512–13), that payment in coin is to be provided within 40 days of the deposit of bullion and within five days for the 0.5-percent charge, is not the letter of the statute.
35 However, the Act of March 31, 1795 did assess charges by weight for deposits of bullion below US standard. See Huntington and Mawhinney (1910, pp. 483–5).
36 Coinage itself actually occurred at the Mint, not at the Assay Office. All other Mint functions were performed on the premises of the Assay Office. For discussion of the Assay Office at New York, see Watson (1926, pp. 10–12, 19, 32–3).
37 For these Acts, see Huntington and Mawhinney (1910, pp. 586, 596, 616).
38 For the early history of banking in the United States, see Hammond (1957, pp. 40–88). The statistics are from Hammond (1957, pp. 144–6).
39 See Huntington and Mawhinney (1910, pp. 327–9, 330–62) for these Acts, and Friedman and Schwartz (1963, pp. 16–23) for discussion of the formative years of the national banking system.
40 The Bland–Allison Act of February 28, 1878 authorized issuance of silver certificates by the Treasury in return for deposits of silver dollars.
41 See Nussbaum (1950, pp. 596–7). The Act of June 12, 1945 is in Krooss (1969, vol. IV, pp. 2875–6).
42 There are two cases in which legal bimetallism can be effective. First, if the country happens to select a mint ratio close to the world gold/silver price ratio, bimetallism results as long as the divergence of the ratios is within limits (set by arbitrage costs and market imperfections). Friedman (1990a, p. 90) notes that "these costs define upper and lower 'gold–silver price ratio points' between which the market ratio can vary without producing the complete replacement of one metal by the other [in the domestic country]." Such a situation could likely exist only temporarily. England had effective bimetallism for a few years at the turn of the eighteenth century, in the process of switching from an effective silver to an effective gold standard (see section 8 of chapter 4).

Second, a lasting bimetallism can happen if the country possesses a sufficient stock of gold and silver coin and is important enough in the international economy to dominate the world gold/silver price ratio. France, with a mint ratio of 15.5, was in a position of dominance from 1803 to 1850 (Yeager, 1976, p. 296). Friedman (1990a, p. 89) points out that what gave France preponderant influence on the world price ratio (although he exaggerates in describing France's ability to "peg" the ratio) was not only France's economic importance relative to the rest of the world but also the country's high propensity to use specie as money, both directly as coins and indirectly as reserves for paper currency and bank deposits.

43 The market series, compiled by Soetbeer (1879, pp. 130–1), is of much higher quality than alternative data. The Soetbeer series is an annual average of twice-weekly official market quotations in Hamburg to 1832 and uses generally accepted London data thereafter. In contrast, alternative series (based on the London market) exhibit neither their data source nor their method of construction and furthermore suffer from obvious errors, both in the level of some observations and in their year-to-year movement. See S. Dana Horton, various appendices, in *International Monetary Conference* (1879, pp. 649, 701, 708–9) and Laughlin (1896, pp. 288–91). The French mint ratio of 15.5 is not used in place of the Soetbeer data because, while the world price ratio may have been principally determined by the French ratio, deviations did occur and in fact were the norm. Indeed, for a minority view claiming that the reach of French bimetallism has been exaggerated, see Shaw (1896a, pp. 178–80).

44 His average computed market ratio in the United States was 14.99, the world ratio in 1791 was 15.05, and the recommended and adopted ratio 15.

45 Again the Soetbeer data are used for the 1834–73 market rate. The two episodes (1792–1834 and 1834–73) of the divergence between legal and market rates are described by Carothers (1930, pp. 75, 81–101), Hepburn (1924, pp. 47–61), and Watson (1899, pp. 71–3, 78–96).

46 Actually, termination of coinage of the silver dollar in 1873 and its demonetization in 1874 merely reflected long-standing reality. As Carothers (1930, p. 235) states: "Exported before 1806, not coined from 1806 to 1836, and not in circulation from 1836 to 1873, the [silver] dollar was an unknown coin." (On this history of the silver dollar, see note 10 to chapter 5.) So the elimination of the silver dollar by the 1873–4 legislation was in the nature of modifying the coinage law to accord with actuality. However, it is argued by Friedman (1990b) that the economic consequences of abandoning legal bimetallism, which meant alternating effective monometallism, were harmful for the United States. In particular, an effective silver standard would have avoided the 1891–7 crisis (see section 2 of chapter 13).

47 For discussion of the meaning and mechanism of suspension of specie payments, see Temin (1969, pp. 114–18) and Triffin (1960, p. 22). This phenomenon was also part of the colonial experience with paper money. The colonies did not set fixed rates between paper currency and coin, and markets existed in which the two types of money traded for each other. Perkins (1980, p. 111) writes of "the market value of the paper relative to specie and foreign exchange" in the colonial period. He notes that in situations in which paper had depreciated, creditors would accept either specie or paper money at its current market value. In contrast, during the Continental-money experience of the Revolutionary Period, Gresham's Law operated in full force and coin disappeared from circulation. The reason is that the states legislated strict parity of the paper with coined money. The penalties for not respecting the face value of Continental currency were severe. "The notes were made full legal tender and refusal to accept them forfeited the debt and incurred other money penalties, pillory,

imprisonment, loss of ears even, and being outlawed as enemies of their country" (Hepburn, 1924, p. 17).

48 "Each of the antebellum financial panics had been marked by a rush on diverse state-chartered banks by holders of banknotes who wanted to convert their holdings into specie . . . after the Civil War the public did not exhibit doubts about the safety of national banknotes. The postbellum panics were instead marked by rushes of bank depositors to convert their deposits into currency, which included national banknotes and federal government issues as well as specie." – Sylla (1972, p. 233)

49 For histories of these suspensions, see (1) *for 1814–17*, Bolles (1894, vol. II, pp. 261–83, 317–29), Hammond (1957, pp. 227–50), Secretary of the Treasury (1838, p. 5), Smith (1953, pp. 110–15), Smith and Cole (1935, pp. 25–9), and Sumner (1874, pp. 64–75); (2) *for 1837–42*, Davis and Hughes (1960, pp. 57, 61), Hammond (1957, pp. 465–501), Hepburn (1924, pp. 132–8), Knox (1900, pp. 76–7, 502–5), Martin (1898, pp. 30–3), Myers (1931, pp. 64–8), Smith (1953, pp. 190–227), Sumner (1874, pp. 132–54), and Temin (1969, pp. 113–71); (3) *for 1857*, Dunbar (1904, pp. 266–93), Hammond (1957, pp. 710–13), Knox (1900, pp. 512–13), and Sumner (1874, pp. 180–7); (4) *for 1860–61*, Dunbar(1904, pp. 309–10) and Knox (1900, pp. 513–14); (5) *for 1861–78*, Officer (1981) and the references cited there.

50 On June 17, 1864 Congress legislated the prohibition of the gold market (though allowing brokers to transact in gold within their offices), but the bill was repealed on July 2 (Huntington and Mawhinney, 1910, pp. 182–3). The intent was to reduce the premium on gold, but the law was ineffective, with the premium actually increasing.

51 On the 1873, 1893, and 1907 currency premia, see Andrew (1908, pp. 290–3), Clark (1984, pp. 819–20), Cross (1923, pp. 397–9), Friedman and Schwartz (1963, pp. 110, 161–2), and Sprague (1910, pp. 56–61, 186–95, 280–6).

52 See Chandler (1958, pp. 103–4), Secretary of the Treasury (1920, pp. 181–2; 1922, p. 72), Brown (1940, p. 37), and Beckhart (1924, p. 267).

53 Excellent histories of the 1933–4 events are provided by Friedman and Schwartz (1963, pp. 462–74) and Yeager (1976, pp. 346–50).

54 The last explanation is stated by Davis and Hughes (1960, p. 62) and Perkins (1975, pp. 155–6).

55 See Taus (1943, p. 153), Cross (1923, p. 377), Brown (1929, pp. 18, 26; 1940, pp. 34, 37), and Beckhart (1924, pp. 268–73).

56 The latter was by proclamation under the Act of October 6, 1917, as amended by the Act of March 9, 1933. The proclamation is in Krooss (1969, vol. 4, pp. 2717–18).

57 For details, see Beckhart (1924, pp. 252–67), Taus (1943, pp. 157, 178), Chandler (1958, pp. 102–3), Brown (1940, p. 43), and Cross (1923, p. 377).

58 The proclamation is in Krooss (1969, vol. IV, pp. 2714–16).

4   British monetary standard

1 Discussion of the British unit of account is based on the excellent presentation in Feavearyear (1963, pp. 6–9).

2 The term "pound sterling" emanates from the fact that in the twelfth century the penny was called a "sterling," possibly emanating from *steorra* (Latin for "star"), some of the early coins having been adorned with a star. For alternative speculation, see Craig (1953, p. 6).

3 Useful histories of the British monetary standard are provided by Feavearyear (1963), Craig (1953), and, though with limited time spans, Ashton (1955, pp. 167–77), Horsefield (1960), Horton (1887), and Li (1963).

4 These Acts are in *International Monetary Conference* (1879, pp. 345–7, 373–8).

5 The order and Royal Proclamation for coinage of the guinea and sovereign, respectively, are in Horton (1887, pp. 229–30, 282–3).

6 The Order is in Horton (1887, pp. 229–30).

7 The relevant sections of the Acts are in Horton (1887, pp. 243–6).

8 The Treasury order and the report adopted by Parliament are in Horton (1887, pp. 250–4).

9 The Proclamation is in *International Monetary Conference* (1879, p. 316).

10 For the Proclamation, see Horton (1887, pp. 282–3).

11 The Act is in *Public General Statutes* (1870, pp. 153-62).

12 See Horton's excellent discussion in *International Monetary Conference* (1879, pp. 373–4).

13 These Acts are in *International Monetary Conference* (1879, pp. 332–49).

14 The Resumption Act is fully described in Feavearyear (1963, p. 221). The relevant section of the Bank of England Act, 1833, and the Currency and Bank Notes Acts are in Shrigley (1935, pp. 40, 62–5, 79–85).

15 The 1666 and 1768 Acts are in *International Monetary Conference* (1879, pp. 309–14).

16 See the tables in Feavearyear (1963, pp. 435–6).

17 For the relevant parts of these documents, see Shrigley (1935, pp. 1, 27).

18 For the relevant section of the Bank Charter Act, see Shrigley (1935, pp. 43–4).

19 Of course, the Bank coined its bullion at the Mint as the Mint's only customer. It would even do so at a loss, to preserve the gold–convertibility of its notes.

20 The relevant portion of the Budget Speech and the entire Gold Standard Act are in Sayers (1976, pp. 80–6).

21 For the early history of banking in Britain, see Cameron (1967, pp. 15–99), Clapham (1945, vol. 1, pp. 156–72), and Kindleberger (1993, pp. 53–6, 77–96).

22 These foreign ratios were stated by Isaac Newton, Master of the mint, in a report of September 21, 1717. The report is in *International Monetary Conference*, pp. 317–18, and the ratios are conveniently summarized in Li (1963, pp. 151–2).

23 Annual data on coinage of gold and silver are in Craig (1953, pp. 410–21).

24 Good discussions of the Bank Restriction Period are in Cannan (1925, pp. vii–xlvi) and Kindleberger (1993, pp. 63–6).

25 See Cross (1923, p. 377), Brown (1929, p. 6; 1940, pp. 34–5), and Fraser (1933, pp. 32–3).

26 The decision to end legal redemption was due to a breakdown of the moral suasion of private bankers to deny gold to their customers. See Sayers (1986, pp. 147–8).

27 The press notice announcing the order is in Sayers (1976, pp. 264–5) and the Act is in Shrigley (1935, p. 86).
28 For a history of the Moratorium and texts of the documents, see Kirkaldy (1921, pp. 1–14, 405–9).
29 See Beckhart (1924, p. 252), Shrigley (1935, p. 63, n. 1), and Brown (1940, p. 42).

5   Parity

1 The section on dollar–sterling parity, entitled "Note, on the proportional value of the pound sterling and the dollar," is in *International Monetary Conference* (1879, pp. 490–501). Hepburn (1924, p. 48) writes: "Adams's paper shows great labor and research upon a subject concerning which at that time very little material was available to the student."
2 Among such contemporary writers are Samuel Moore, Director of the United States Mint, and John White, Cashier of the Second Bank of the United States (Secretary of the Treasury, 1830, pp. 49, 67). Later authors who adopt the gold par include Hepburn (1924, p. 61) and Macesich (1960, pp. 414–16, n. 21). Adams himself is skeptical of all parity measures: "It is, perhaps, of as little importance what the conventional par of exchange is, as whether a piece of linen or of broadcloth should be measured by a yard or an ell. The actual exchange is never regulated by the medium or any other par . . . ." (*International Monetary Conference*, 1879, p. 492).
3 Adams comments: "It is contended by some writers upon the commercial branch of political economy, that this medium is the only equitable par of exchange; but this is believed to be an error" (*International Monetary Conference*, 1879, p. 492).
4 The Proclamation is in Brigham (1911, pp. 161–3). The mint finding, a report submitted on May 18, 1704, is consistent with Isaac Newton's Mint Report of July 17, 1702, in which the valuation of the Spanish dollar ("Piastre of Spain or Sevil piece of 8 Reaus") is 53.88, rounded up to 54, pence (Shaw, 1896b, p. 140). The Proclamation was in response to the differential rating of the Spanish dollar in the American colonies. Supported by a subsequent Act of Parliament, it permitted an overvaluation of the Spanish dollar or other foreign coin by up to one third (to the level of 6s., for the Spanish dollar) in local shillings. Both the proclamation and the law were widely evaded in the colonies. For complete histories, see Brock (1975, pp. 130–67) and Nettles (1934, pp. 229–49). A good summary is in Nussbaum (1950, p. 558).
5 See, for example, Gallatin and White, in Secretary of the Treasury (1830, pp. 39, 67) and Cole (1929a, pp. 406–7, n. 1).
6 By Nussbaum (1950, p. 334; 1957, p. 32) and Davis and Hughes (1960, p. 55).
7 The Acts are in Peters (1848, vol. I, pp. 41, 167, 673).
8 The Acts are in Peters (1848, vol. I, p. 680; vol. II, pp. 374–5; 1846, vol. III, pp. 322, 525, 779).
9 For example, the Act of March 3, 1873 (Huntington and Mawhinney, 1910, p. 209), Davis and Hughes (1960, p. 55), Cole (1929a, p. 407, n. 1), Sumner (1874, p. 112), Myers (1931, p. 72), Clark (1984, p. 797), and Perkins (1978, p. 410).

294   Notes to pages 51–58

Yeager (1976, p. 310) is a rare exception, stating the parity correctly as $4.86656. Myers (1931, p. 72) errs more seriously in declaring that "a rate of $4.8665 to the pound, which after 1834 was just par." Davis and Hughes (1960, p. 55) make the same mistake and worse, in not only stating "the exchange par after 1834 was $4.8665" but also using that parity in computations from the beginning of 1835 instead of only after January 17, 1837. In their errors they are followed by Perkins (1978, p. 410).

10   While the Spanish dollar contained more silver, the American dollar was better designed and brighter. Clever American traders exported American dollars to the West Indies in return for Spanish dollars, and either deposited these at the United States Mint for coinage or put them into circulation after removing some of the silver content. At the direction of President Jefferson, who was aware of the problem, the Mint suspended coinage of silver dollars in 1805, not to be resumed until 1840 (apart from nominal amounts produced in 1836 and 1839). Accounts of the dollar coinage suspension are provided by Carothers (1930, pp. 75–6), Watson (1899, pp. 73–5), Taxay (1966, pp. 125–6), and Hepburn (1924, pp. 47–8).

11   Annual data on mint production by coinage denomination are found in Director of the Mint (1942, pp. 68–73).

12   The legislative activity that led to the gold-dollar (and double-eagle) coinage and the aftermath at the Mint are described by Taxay (1966, pp. 201–10). Interestingly, what was supposed to be the predominant gold piece, the $10 eagle, was not coined in the period 1805–37; rather, half- and quarter-eagles were produced.

13   The principal gold coin over the preceding century was the guinea, worth 1.05 (21/20) pounds sterling from 1717. See section 2 of chapter 4.

14   This procedure is performed for the various paper standards in section 3.8 of chapter 6.

15   As early as 1829, Albert Gallatin used the same technique to compute parity for various gold/silver price ratios, including 15.8080, the "aver. ratio silver bullion to gold coin," and a preferred ratio of 15.6069 (Secretary of the Treasury, 1830, pp. 36, 43). The former ratio is close to the Soetbeer value of 15.78 for 1829. In 1830 S. D. Ingham, Secretary of the Treasury, corrected "real par" (gold par) for the divergence between the American mint ratio (15) and the average price ratio of gold to silver bullion in England over 1820–9 (15.8), thus obtaining "real par at the true ratio" (Secretary of the Treasury, 1830, p. 6). In 1838 Levi Woodbury, then Secretary of the Treasury, referred to the Gallatin preferred estimate and pointed out that: "The true par varied as the market value of gold varied, when compared with silver" (Secretary of the Treasury, 1838, p. 3). Sumner (1874, pp. 104–5) mentions the same Gallatin estimate and notes "the difference between the coinage rating and the true value of the metals."

16   The Act is in Peters (1846, vol. IV, p. 700).

17   See Hepburn (1924, p. 62) and Nussbaum (1950, p. 334, n. 8; 1957, p. 32). The Acts cited are in Peters (1860, vol. IV, p. 593; vol. 5, p. 496).

18   See Nussbaum (1950, p. 334). The Act of 1873 is in Huntington and Mawhinney (1910, p. 209); the relevant sections of the Acts of 1894 and 1921 are in *Statutes at Large of the United States of America* (1895, p. 552; 1923, p. 17).

19 It has been suggested that the reason for this unique treatment in dollar exchange-rate quotations, the opposite of that for all other currencies, "was probably that the pound sterling was the only unit which was larger than the dollar." See Myers (1931, p. 347). An alternative explanation was the overriding importance of sterling in the American foreign-exchange market and in world trade and capital flows generally.

20 See, for example, Secretary of the Treasury (1830, p. 67).

21 See, for example, Myers (1931, p. 72), Macesich (1960, p. 416, n. 21), and Hepburn (1924, pp. 61–2).

22 See Sumner (1874, p. 112), Cole (1929a, p. 407, n. 1), and Myers (1931, p. 73).

6   Exchange rate

1 See Einzig (1970, p. 178) and Perkins (1975, pp. 4, 11).

2 The relative rise and fall of individual port cities is discussed in Cutler (1961, pp. 24–76), Myers (1931, pp. 3–5), and Albion (1938, pp. 1–3).

3 Remnants of direct dealings between importers and exporters remained as late as the 1830s. See note 10 to chapter 11. It is also true that in the colonial period, and continuing to some extent thereafter, the bill of exchange was only one way of making payment to London; barter trade and specie shipments were alternatives of equal importance. On all this, see Cole (1929a, pp. 386–91, 395–7), Einzig (1970, p. 178), and Perkins (1975, p. 5).

4 See Perkins (1975, p. 184), Patterson (1917, pp. 90, 96–7), and Spalding (1928a, p. 170).

5 Modern historians have forgotten the element of days of grace and assert or assume that a 60-day bill is cashable 60 days (rather than 63 days) after presentation. The false statement is explicitly made by Perkins (1975, p. 6) and the error of using a duration of t rather than $t + 3$ days for t (> 3)-day bills mars the empirical work of both Davis and Hughes (1960) and Perkins (1978). Contemporary writers are clear on the British law on days of grace and, specifically, on the 63-day effective maturity of a 60-day bill. See Entz (1840, p. 49), Clare (1906, p. 120, n. 1), Spalding (1928b, pp. 70–1; 1929, p. 31), Whitaker (1919, pp. 85, 260), Patterson (1917, pp. 90, 98, 167), Deutsch (1914, p. 130), and Cross (1923, pp. 137–8).

6 See Einzig (1970, pp. 178–9) and Perkins (1975, pp. 6–7). The stage was set in the colonial period, as bills were drawn in British pounds sterling and not the local currency.

7 See also Davis and Hughes (1960, p. 53).

8 Cole (1929a, p. 404; 1929b, p. 204, n. 3) and Perkins (1975, p. 184) may be consulted. Again, the 60-day bill was a holdover from colonial times, the duration resting on mere custom.

9 See Cole (1929a, p. 414; 1929b, pp. 213–14) and Perkins (1978, p. 396).

10 See Cole (1929a, pp. 414–15), Davis and Hughes (1960, p. 59), and Perkins (1975, pp. 184, 291, n. 24).

11 Writers in the immediate prewar period make this point. Strauss (1908, p. 64) states: "By foreign exchange, we mean bills of exchange . . . although sometimes

money is paid on cabled orders, known as cable transfers." He discusses demand exchange and then observes that "cable transfers require but a word" (p. 73). Johnson (1911, p. 511) discusses the relative size of New York and other markets for foreign exchange exclusively in terms of bills transacted.

12 "The rate for cable transfers is the basic spot rate in the market" (Holmes and Schott, 1965, p. 34). "The Bank of England, as agent for Her Majesty's Treasury, fulfills its IMF obligation on exchange rate fluctuations by being committed to deal in spot telegraphic transfers for US dollars at the limits of 2.78 and 2.82, respectively" (Bank of England, 1969, p. 90).

13 See Patterson (1917, p. 44), Escher (1918, pp. 12–13), Whitaker (1919, pp. 626–8), Cross (1923, pp. 126–7), and Einzig (1970, pp. 178–9, 243–4).

14 See Myers (1931, pp. 349–50) and Brown (1940, p. 147).

15 For selection of these periods, see section 2 of chapter 13.

16 This is Perkins' (1978, p. 393) interpretation, which I accept. Other authors dispute that there is a change in maturity in the bills underlying the *Chronicle* series, and consider the exchange rate to be "sight" throughout. See Cole (1929b, p. 214) and Persons, Tuttle, and Frickey (1920, p. 54). Their argument is unconvincing, because it rests on post-1878 statements in the *Chronicle*, whereas the contemporaneous descriptions explicitly stated in the *Chronicle* and *Financial Review* indicate the maturity change and are consistent with Perkins' empirical findings on discriminatory pricing (see section 2).

17 Perkins does not mention this second characteristic of his data.

18 For a biography of Nathan Trotter, see Tooker (1955).

19 The series is in Davis and Hughes (1960, pp. 70–2).

20 Joseph G. Martin was a Boston stockbroker, who collected a large quantity of statistical material relating to stock and money markets. See Macaulay (1938, p. A341, n. 13).

21 From 1862 onward, the highest and lowest rates for the month are shown. In using the series, the mid-point of the range is taken.

22 Tooker (1955, p. 99) notes that "often Trotter, particularly in the early years, purchased bills in a casual fashion." Davis and Hughes (1960, p. 68) state that "in the early days, unfamiliar names [of drawees] predominated." The year 1834 is apparently the watershed between bills of generally low and generally high quality. Davis and Hughes note that over the full 1803–95 period Trotter's bills had a total of 295 acceptors, but only thirteen, all well-known, from 1834.

23 Originally published in Secretary of the Treasury (1830, pp. 78–85), the series is reprinted in *International Monetary Conference* (1879, pp. 634–41). Though not stated explicitly in the tabulation of the series, the 60-day maturity of the underlying bills is the only one mentioned in White's accompanying letter and documentation. Neglected by modern economic historians (Davis and Hughes, Perkins), the White series is mentioned by Hepburn (1924, p. 55) and Myers (1931, p. 69), and I claim rediscovery.

24 It is true that the data are only allegedly market transactions, based on White's once-removed report. One might even surmise that the series represents merely quotations from the leading Baltimore dealers, but this would imply that White

was lying in describing the data as compiled from "average monthly sales" and "actual sales" of the dealers. As he was an official of the Second Bank of the United States responding to a set of queries from the Secretary of the Treasury, he would have no incentive to describe information incorrectly. As for the possibility that the dealers themselves misinformed White as to the nature of the data they were providing, again what would have been the advantage for them to do so? Further, the dealers are described as "of high standing" and "highly respectable" – unlikely sources of misinformation. Although definitive proof is lacking, it is reasonable to conclude that the data are indeed market transactions, as White asserts.

25 Actually, the series is used here in the form of percent premium over nominal parity, because that was the original expression and has greater accuracy.

26 Smith and Cole lack two observations, but they are readily estimated. The February value is repeated for the missing March 1823, because the Martin series (slightly higher in value) has this property. The January 1815 figure (missing from both series) is obtained by averaging those in the two adjacent months.

27 Note that, in spite of the almost contrary statement of Davis and Hughes (1960, pp. 52, 56) and Perkins (1978, p. 392), the interest component is not eliminated. What remains in the demand bill, and is absent from a cable transfer, is the interest loss during the projected elapsed time between the purchase of a bill in the American port city and its presentation in England. So the Davis and Hughes (1960, p. 52) and Perkins (1978, pp. 393–4) description of the resulting series as a "pure" exchange rate is inappropriate, if "pure" is taken to mean "devoid of the interest element."

28 This formula is equivalent to that presented in complex form in Davis and Hughes (1960, p. 56).

29 Perkins mentions three authors, writing no earlier than 1933. His case is even stronger, because contemporary writers when time bills were dominant confirm his thesis of the primacy of the London over any American interest rate. Cole (1929a, p. 414, n. 1) quotes the *Financial Register* of 1837 as follows: "A bill at sight *would* command about ½ per cent more [than a 60-day bill], equal to the interest in London for 60 days." Seyd (1868, p. 400) refers to "quoted in New York . . . 60 days' Exchange on London, to which London interest must be added for short." See also Johnson (1911, p. 516), Brown (1914, pp. 131–3), Patterson (1917, p. 167), and Escher (1918, p. 50). Authors in the 1920s also support Perkins' position: Cole (1929b, p. 204, n. 3), Spalding (1928a, p. 125; 1928b, pp. 69, 91), and Dunbar (1929, pp. 114–15).

30 Perkins relies entirely on Cross (1923, pp. 352–8) for the analytical argument. Cross criticizes the slightly different discussions of Pierson (1913, pp. 527–9) and Whitaker (1919, pp. 598–601). A later author, Southard (1940, pp. 84–5), resurrects Whitaker's analysis.

31 Source data for Perkins' empirical finding are from the House of Brown banking firm and the *Financial Review*. Impressive for his time, Cross (1923, pp. 359–65) performs an empirical analysis for 1907–8 and 1913 that is only slightly less sophisticated than that of Perkins and reaches a supportive conclusion: "as

the foreign [London] open market discount rate rises there is a tendency for the spread between sight bills and long bills to become greater, but by no means proportionately greater" (Cross, 1923, p. 364).

32 The original monthly series is averaged to convert to a quarterly series. The Overend–Gurney series has been exhibited once before in quarterly form, by Silberling (1923, p. 257). The Silberling presentation suffers from four incorrect data observations. It has not been previously noted in the literature that the Overend–Gurney series, which ends in May 1857, is extendible to December 1858 via a consistent other source, Bigelow (1862, p. 205). See table 6.1. For January and February, 1858, multiple observations are averaged.

33 See King (1936, pp. 12, 14–15, 27). Silberling (1923, p. 241) writes: "The Usury Laws fixed the maximum rate of interest and discount at 5 per cent, and contemporary literature indicates that this rate was, at least from 1790 to 1822, the prevailing and unvarying rate of discount throughout the country." The principal exception is from 1817 to mid-1818, when evidence suggests that the market rate dipped below Bank rate. See King (1936, pp. 27–9).

34 In most cases I was able to reconcile the Davis–Hughes annual table with the original records; in a few years there remain slight discrepancies. I am grateful to Marjorie A. Kierstead of the Manuscripts and Archives Department of Baker Library at Harvard University for making available the records of the Trotter bills of exchange.

35 For quarterly Z series, M is from table 5.2, For annual Z series, M is obtained as annual averages of the quarterly M series. For monthly Z series, M = 4.8665635.

36 Of course, there was also demand-note, followed by greenback, depreciation in 1862–78.

37 The authors use the same data source as for table 6.7.

38 Davis and Hughes (1960, p. 54) comment (incorrectly) that lack of data prevents correction for the Bank Restriction Period and the American 1814–17 paper standard; they make no mention about the necessity of adjusting for the other currency-depreciation episodes in the nineteenth century.

39 The Trotter-versus-Martin comparison performed by Davis and Hughes (1960, pp. 56–8) is flawed by not correcting the series for their time-bill form or for paper standards earlier than the greenback period.

40 Supporting this counter-argument are the counts that in non-common quarters, Trotter exceeds 10 percent of parity three times (all in 1834) and White five times (over 1796–1814).

7   Exchange–market integration

1 On domestic exchange rates, see Smith and Cole (1935, p. 26) and Perkins (1975, pp. 186–7).

2 The values are much too low for this measure to be the variance as ordinarily defined.

3 In fact, Davis and Hughes recompute their variance for those quarters excluding periods of paper standards.

8   Gold points: theory and practice

1   Strictly speaking, "specie-point arbitrage" and "specie-effected transfer of funds" are the correct terms, and the specie transported was either gold or silver, depending on the American effective standard. Consistent with customary usage, however, the terms "gold" and "specie" will often be used synonymously here and in the rest of the volume.

2   Writing in 1892, Clare (1906, pp. 129–30) describes GPA in cost detail. The *New York Times* (December 18, 1892, p.5; December 16, 1894, p. 9; November 10, 1895, p. 1) alludes to GPA by linking bills sold and gold shipped. A detailed computation of profit from GPA is presented in *New York Times*, August 9, 1895, p. 8.

3   When the exchange rate (sterling premium) became so high that it would have been profitable for merchants to substitute specie for bills, the banks had already suspended payments. Ironically, "an extremely high premium inevitably led to suspension and a reversion to the bill of exchange" (Perkins, 1975, p. 196). The demise of the merchant as direct transferor/arbitrageur continued to the end of the interwar gold standard. See Whitaker (1919, pp. 518–19), Spalding (1928a, p. 82), and Einzig (1931, pp. 18–19). A detailed history of foreign-exchange market participants is in sections 5–8 of chapter 11.

4   That the New York banks were the foreign-exchange dealers is stated by Cole (1929a, pp. 408, 420–1), Johnson (1905, pp. 88–91), and Strauss (1908, pp. 64–5). Statements that the transferors/arbitrageurs were the New York banks, qualified to be "large," "big," or "few," are in Newcomb (1886, pp. 281–2), Johnson (1905, pp. 90–1; 1911, p. 510), Strauss (1908, pp. 65–7), Escher (1910, pp. 115, 117; 1918, pp. 75–6, 79), Spalding (1915, pp. 30–2; 1928a, p. 82; 1928b, pp. 41–3), Whitaker (1919, pp. 519–37; 1933, pp. 362–5), Cross (1923, pp. 383, 389), and York (1923, pp. 46, 49).

5   There could be two such divergences, because the gold operation in GTF or GPA involves two transactions.

6   See section 3.6 of chapter 6. If there is paper-currency depreciation to be corrected, then V would have to be replaced by, say, E, the dollars-per-pound equivalent of R (see sections 3.8–3.9 of chapter 6): $E = M \cdot (1 + R/100)$.

7   The lower price of a 60-day bill is compensated by the longer time, and therefore higher interest loss (if the bill is purchased) or gain (if the bill is sold), until the bill is cashable.

8   When the United States was on a silver standard, silver would be obtained from US banks and sold in the London market.

9   Only the interest cost from oceanic transportation requires special consideration here. For other components of interest cost, see sections 2.4.3–2.4.4 of chapter 9.

10 The "ideal" price at which to sell pounds is V; there is a loss in selling at a lower forward rate. This exchange-rate cost is not applicable to GTF, because the alternative exchange operation is a straightforward spot transaction.

11 If funds are transferred via a demand bill, pounds are purchased in New York and not usable until arrival in London. So there is an interest loss for the

duration of an Atlantic voyage. This is also the loss with the gold export. Therefore there is zero interest cost under GTF.

12 The studies are Morgenstern (1959), Clark (1984), and Spiller and Wood (1988).

13 For example, for gold-export points: *Financial Review*, 1875, p. 5; *Commercial and Financial Chronicle*, January 28, 1882, p. 108; *New York Times*, July 2, 1882, p. 9; December 27, 1885, p. 7; March 27, 1896, p. 2; April 21, 1896, p. 1; June 28, 1896, p. 2; April 27, 1897, p. 12; June 2, 1899, p. 14; June 9, 1899, p. 5; June 13, 1899, p. 12; June 17, 1899, p. 7; December 16, 1899, p. 11; March 7, 1909, p. 8. For gold import points: *Commercial and Financial Chronicle*, April 2, 1881, p. 358; March 3, 1883, p. 232; May 12, 1906, p. 1069; *New York Times*, December 1, 1898, p. 4. In several other articles in the *New York Times*, a stated gold point, though unidentified, clearly is for demand bills, shown by comparison with the explicit demand-bill gold-point citations above. In contrast, I could find only one reference to a cable gold point: *New York Times*, November 27, 1892, p. 5.

14 *New York Times*, August 9, 1895, p. 8; June 28, 1896, p. 2.

15 For example, Johnson (1905, pp. 88–91), Clare (1906, pp. 129–30), Escher (1910, pp. 114–18; 1918, pp. 77–80), Brown (1914, pp. 106–13).

16 There are three reasons for a wide spread. First, even though Goodhart (1969, p. 57), citing several authorities, asserts that "New York had a flourishing market, both in forward cable transfers . . . and in forward exchange bills," he is forced to admit that "there are no statistics on forward exchange rates extant." Contemporary newspapers regularly published quotations on sight, 60-day, and (spot) cable rates. Omission of forward rates indicates that the prewar foreign-exchange market might have had a less active market for forward exchange than some authors suppose. Second, the 10-day forward contract (essentially the duration of an Atlantic voyage) required for GPA was quite distinct from the normal thirty, sixty and ninety-day maturities of forward transactions of other market participants, suggesting a thin market for a 10-day contract. Third, the intermittent nature of gold arbitrage itself made for an often inactive market.

17 "Before the war . . . there was no difficulty in getting a fair exchange rate for the sight draft, as . . . even large amounts could easily be absorbed without unduly affecting the exchange rate" (Einzig, 1931, p. 64). The perception of a relatively thin cable market continued into the early 1920s: "The cable market is less active as a rule than the demand market" (York, 1923, p. 105).

18 The reason for this unusual situation is that the *spot* cable gold point is the focus. Were the forward cable gold point considered instead, the gold point would indeed be exogenous.

9   Gold-point estimates

1 On one other occasion, the expert is unidentified. See *The Economist*, May 2, 1925, p. 885; May 16, 1925, p. 991; December 3, 1927, p. 1007; June 22, 1929, p. 1382.

2 However, Morgenstern's data are suspect, because there are several instances of recurring values, even though figures are to five decimal places.

3 *New York Times*, July 2, 1882, p. 9; March 27, 1896, p. 2; March 29, 1896, p. 2; April 21, 1896, p. 1; November 17, 1927, p. 1; December 5, 1927, p. 36; December 14, 1927, p. 43; March 22, 1928, p. 31; *The Economist*, January 9, 1926, p. 52; March 9, 1929, p. 486. Cross (1923, pp. 388, 391) offers consensus gold points of "authors and bankers."

4 For example, the *New York Times* (December 14, 1927, p. 43) reported no gold exports at all from New York to London between 1914 and the end of 1927.

5 See Einzig (1931, pp. 12–21, 29, 76–7).

6 See *New York Times*, December 14, 1927, p. 43; March 22, 1928, p. 31; Einzig (1931, pp. 76–7).

7 Giovannini takes average monthly direct cost for US exports 1890–1904 and for US imports 1905–8 (both from Officer, 1986, p. 1056) and projects each figure onto the other direction.

8 Brown uses an Einzig 1925 gold-point estimate for 1925–7 and an Einzig 1928 estimate for 1928–31. The "series" is consistent; but the variability of the gold points is only superficially recognized and the data quality is dependent entirely on Einzig.

9 For example, Secretary of the Treasury (1830, pp. 6, 49, 63), Haupt (1894, pp. 485–6), Spalding (1915, pp. 28–9), Einzig (1929a, p. 381), *New York Times*, June 28, 1896, p. 2; *The Economist*, May 2, 1925, p. 885; May 16, 1925, p. 991; October 3, 1925, p. 522.

10 For example, Secretary of the Treasury (1830, pp. 68, 90–1), Reuss (1833, p. 97), Seyd (1868, pp. 398–400), Johnson (1911, pp. 507–8), Spalding (1928a, pp. 81–4), Einzig (1931, pp. 148–50). There is also the hypothetical calculation of the House of Brown for 1830 in Perkins (1975, p. 192).

11 Construction of the monthly component series, under (1), and of their averages, under (2), is described in detail in section 2, but the series and averages are not tabulated. The interesting component-cost averages are under (3), as almost the entire 1791–1931 time period is covered; and so both construction is described and the averages listed in tables in section 2. The 1925–31 average under (2) is May 1925–August 1931 (76 months), and under (3) is July 1925–June 1931 (72 months) or, equivalently, 1925 (third quarter)–1931 (second quarter). The 1890–1906 average, under (2), is 204 months.

The 1801–10 and 1811–20 decades are excluded from (3) for two reasons. First, they embody periods of American trade embargoes against Britain (intermittently from 1807), as the United States was caught in the middle of Anglo-French wars, and the American–British war of 1812–15. Anglo-American specie flows under these circumstances were subject to great difficulty not reflected in arbitrage/transfer costs. Second, data on such costs are virtually nonexistent for these decades, as they are for 1919–25 (until Britain returned to the gold standard).

12 On this liner history, see Albion (1938, pp. 20–31; 1939, pp. 38–45).

13 There is a reference in the contemporary literature to half-dollars exported "direct from the US Mint" (Secretary of the Treasury, 1830, p. 65), which would eliminate the abrasion from circulation, though not from shipment; but this had

to be a rare and serendipitous occurrence, because of the delay in coining bullion at the Mint (see section 5 of chapter 3).

14 On occasion, private bars were exported, especially during March 1891–November 1895, when the Treasury placed an embargo on its sale of bars. Private bars were obtainable only at a premium. Even when otherwise dominant over coin, they constituted only a small proportion of gold shipments, presumably due to limited availability. See *New York Times*, January 17, 1895, p. 3; January 19, 1895, p. 9; January 23, 1895, p. 16; January 24, 1895, p. 13; August 3, 1895, p. 9; May 1, 1897, p. 5.

15 See *New York Times*, July 2, 1882, p. 9; March 19, 1891, p. 3; December 20, 1892, p. 1.

16 See *New York Times*, March 19, 1891, p. 3; March 20, 1891, p. 8.

17 "The British imports of gold and silver came to the Bank almost without exception" (Clapham, 1945, vol. II, p. 279). In 1869 a Bank official wrote that the Bank's bullion office was "used precisely as if it were a dock warehouse."

18 The Bank adhered to its 1852 buying schedule for foreign coin until 1890, although it may have paid higher prices on occasion during that time span (Sayers, 1986, p. 49).

19 The only contemporary statement that I could find to this effect is *New York Times*, July 2, 1882, p. 9.

20 The weekly reports of the London bullion-brokerage firm of Samuel Montagu (printed in *The Economist*) never mention GPA or GTF as a source of market supply.

21 The only direct evidence on the form of import is the House of Brown importing silver of unspecified form in 1823 and silver dollars in 1830 (Perkins, 1975, p. 192).

22 This point is made in *New York Times*, March 22, 1891, p. 9.

23 See table 9.5 and *The Economist*, May 2, 1925, p. 885; May 16, 1925, p. 991; Einzig (1927a, p. 134), Escher (1933, pp. 62–3), Whitaker (1933, pp. 360–4), Evitt (1936, p. 115).

24 See section 5 of chapter 3. For the effective date of (2), see Director of the Mint (1874, p. 1).

25 Changes of 0.5d. involve a price change of under 0.06 percent, barely 10 percent of the 0.5-percent seigniorage charge. The Bank's "indifference" criterion could not have been satisfied for all three eagle prices. Nevertheless, except for possible timing, there is no error in the cost computation. The Bank did not follow its own pricing rule!

26 The weekly reports of Samuel Montagu rarely describe American demand for open-market gold as dominant over its demand for Bank gold.

27 On the London gold market during 1925–31 and these issues, see Anderson (1949, p. 201), Bareau (1947, pp. 213–14, 217–18), Brown (1929, pp. 280–5), Einzig (1931, pp. 111–22, 160–1), Evitt (1936, p. 115), Moggridge (1972, pp. 171–6, 185–6), Spalding (1928a, pp. 77–9; 1929, pp. 639–42), and Whitaker (1933, pp. 370–1).

28 For full histories of these episodes, see Sayers (1936, pp. 77, 86, 95, 96).

29 See Whitaker (1919, pp. 480, n. 2, 496, 559) and Cross (1923, p. 382).

30 See *New York Times*, October 1, 1891, p. 9; Deutsch (1910, pp. 22–3), Patterson (1917, pp. 175–6), Whitaker (1919, pp. 501–2), Cross (1923, p. 382), and York (1923, pp. 15–16).

31 However, Clark (1984, p. 797) computes compound interest for his gold-point estimates.

32 See Secretary of the Treasury (1830, p. 49), Entz (1840, p. 49), *Bankers' Magazine* (October 1851, p. 273), *Commercial and Financial Chronicle*, March 3, 1883, p. 232; Whitaker (1919, p. 524), Cross (1923, p. 387), and Einzig (1931, pp. 82, 147).

33 On this acceptance, see *New York Times*, March 18, 1891, p. 8; January 17, 1895, p. 3; January 19, 1895, p. 9; November 23, 1895, p. 1; Whitaker (1919, p. 505). The contrary statement in *New York Times*, January 24, 1895, p. 9, was corrected on November 23; or, in its referral to "Europe," Britain is excluded.

34 That inference can be made from the comment of Brown (1932, p. 217): "The fact that there is only one scale for weighing imported gold, the assay office scale, is still a limiting factor on the amount of gold that can be imported into New York in a given shipment."

35 If the banker began with currency, the cost was an opportunity one, as he gave up the alternative of exchanging the currency for deposits at a premium.

36 Clark (1984, pp. 819–20) explains well the effect of currency premium on the gold points.

37 The caveat of note 6 to chapter 8 applies.

38 The eight-day figure is specified by Einzig (1929b, p. 43; 1931, p. 64) and is consistent with the average length of an Atlantic voyage.

39 Einzig (1937, pp. 449, 458–71) presents weekly series of the one-month pound-forward-rate discount (in cents). The data are multiplied by minus one (to obtain a positive premium, negative discount), divided by 100 (to convert to dollars), and averaged by month.

40 While 60 to 90 days are stated, 90 days alone are repeated.

41 *Financial Register of the United States* (1838, p. 288). The House of Brown stated five months' interest loss, but for a 60-day bill. The equivalent elapsed time for a demand bill would be three months.

42 Johnson, Escher (1910), and Goodhart state a 10-day duration on a cable-transfer basis. The time is doubled for a demand bill, following Whitaker.

43 References for what follows are Albion (1938, 1939), Bowen (1930), Clark (1920), Lindsay (1874), Maginnis (1892), Taylor (1951), and Tyler (1939).

44 For example, Clark (1920, p. 39) writes: "these little ships, with their full-bodied, able hulls, and their stout spars, sails, and rigging, were driven outward and homeward across the Atlantic, through the fogs and ice of summer and the snow, sleet and gales of winter, for all the speed that was in them."

45 The sources are: *The Economist*, December 3, 1927, p. 1007, Dunbar (1929, p. 113), Cross (1923, p. 386), Swoboda (1928, p. 16), Spalding (1928a, pp. 81–4; 1928b, p. 69), Einzig (1927a, pp. 134–5; 1928, p. 663; 1929b, pp. 94–6; 1931, pp. 148–50), Whitaker (1933, p. 364). Where a range is given, the mid-point is taken. Where several values are presented, the average is taken. Whitaker is unique in incorporating the demand bill rather than cable transfer as the exchange instrument; so his 16-day time loss is halved to eight.

46 The 1890–1906 monthly series involves a one-time decline in T, the 1925–31 series a constant T. Both series have the value of i varying monthly.

47 Spalding (1928a, p. 81) states a figure of 94.5 percent, Whitaker (1933, p. 373) 95–8 percent. There is agreement on 95 percent, or close to it, by the three authorities.

48 A range of six to nine days is mentioned by Sayers (1936, p. 92), and nine days was the approximate duration of a one-way voyage between New York and London.

49 See Sayers (1936, pp. 83–96) and also *New York Times*, June 9, 1899, p. 5; December 16, 1899, p. 11.

50 Just as for the currency premium (section 2.3.2 above), the period averages are necessarily much smaller than the affected monthly figures.

51 For details on the Shaw plan, see Andrew (1907, pp. 543–8), Strauss (1908, pp. 83–4), Cross (1923, pp. 396–7), Myers (1931, p. 343), Friedman and Schwartz (1963, pp. 155–6), Goodhart (1969, pp. 111–13), Timberlake (1993, pp. 186–95), and *Commercial and Financial Chronicle*, April 21, 1906, p. 893; May 12, 1906, p. 1069; October 27, 1906, p. 1002.

52 See *Financial Register of the United States* (1838, p. 288) which provides the earliest estimate of risk premium.

53 The nature of the residual exposure to exchange risk is discussed well by Clark (1984, p. 795).

54 On the possibility of the Bank's purchase price of gold differing on arrival from that prevailing at the initiation of GPA or GTF, see Brown (1914, pp. 110–11).

55 For example, a contemporary account of specie export states that "shippers had to take chances also on coin more or less abraded" (*New York Times*, December 14, 1894, p. 9).

56 As Spalding (1928a, p. 83) writes: "in actual business transactions no firm, or two firms, will incur the risks incidental to a gold shipment, simply to have the satisfaction of saying that they have procured their dollars as cheaply as if they had purchased, say, cable transfers on New York. The operation in practice must obviously hold out a prospect of a small profit."

57 It can be said that the differential risk premium was much smaller when the exchange transaction involved demand bills (1791–1914) than cable transfers (1925–31), as bills required transportation across the Atlantic.

58 An admirable exception is Yeager (1976, p. 20). Clark (1984, pp. 797, 805) recognizes the variability of transport time as a risky element, but his treatment does not involve recognition of risk premium as an element in cost. He assumes a ten-day interest loss, this being the average duration of a gold shipment, and then indicates how his results vary for shipping time ranging between seven and 14 days. This procedure misses the point of margin of safety. Taking only the average as the expected duration of the voyage is entirely appropriate, provided a risk premium for the variability of shipping time (and other uncertainties) is included in cost.

59 Whitaker (1919, p. 530) states: "We should assume that banks must ordinarily obtain a profit of 1/32 of 1% before they will undertake specie shipments, and therefore *without regard to possible interest charges* we should add 15/100 of 1¢ to each of the above rates to find the actual rates at which export may be expected to take place" (italics added).

60 Spalding's (1928a, p. 84) computed gold-point calculation allows only 0.05 percent for normal profit plus risk premium; but his textual discussion, because of its detail, is given priority.

61 All summations in this section are performed for both period averages and monthly values (1890–1906, 1925–31), but shown only for the usual period averages.

10   External integration

1 Note that $SM = 100 \cdot [(RM - M)/M] = (CX - CM)/2$ after substitution of $RM = (GX + GM)/2$, $GX = M \cdot (1 + CX/100)$, and $GM = M \cdot (1 - CM/100)$. The last equations are (8.1) and (8.2).

11   Internal integration

1 White's analogue is that importers from the United Kingdom will gain, on average, by hedging (buying forward pounds) for a $2.78 to $2.80 forward rate and rejecting hedging in the $2.80 to $2.82 range, while exporters to the United Kingdom will gain, on average, by hedging (selling forward pounds) for a $2.80 to $2.82 forward rate and rejecting hedging in the $2.78 to $2.80 range (White, 1963, p. 489).

2 Because exchange-rate speculation entails transactions cost, no funds would be committed not just at $2.80 ($R^* = 0$) but also within a narrow band around $2.80.

3 In considering the demand for forward pounds by importers from the United Kingdom and the supply of forward pounds by exporters to the United Kingdom, White (1963, pp. 489–91) assumes that the demand and supply curves are mirror images of each other (resulting from balanced trade and identical hedging behavior by the importers and exporters). In fact, he graphs the case of linear curves with slopes of the same magnitude, whereupon the curves intersect – meaning zero net demand for forward pounds – at the mid-point rate, $2.80.

4 Among the ideal assumptions are zero transactions cost, zero interest-rate differential between the two countries, no taxation in the two countries, and risk neutrality on the part of the speculators. For a model that drops these assumptions, see section 5 of chapter 12.

5 The point is well made by Perkins (1975, p. 46).

6 See Cole (1929a, p. 415) and Whitaker (1919, pp. 255–6).

7 See Cole (1929a, p. 416).

8 See also Davis and Hughes (1960, p. 61) and Perkins (1975, pp. 155–6).

9 See also Cole (1929b, pp. 208–11) and Myers (1931, p. 75).

10 As late as the 1830s, it appears that "a substantial part of foreign-exchange transactions still took place directly between the exporter and importer of goods." The "appreciable continuance among merchants themselves of direct trading in bills of exchange" is explained by the fact that such transactions were "facilitated by the newspapers of the day which, with little cost, could perform

the service of bringing buyers and sellers together" (Cole, 1929a, pp. 396–7, 420).

11 See Myers (1931, p. 75) and Smith and Cole (1935, p. 24).

12 On the merchant houses, see Cole (1929a, pp. 392, 403), Myers (1931, p. 69; 1970, p. 73), and Smith and Cole (1935, p. 6).

13 Cole (1929a, p. 392) writes: "no other house [than the Brown concerns] in this country presents so clearly a case of evolution from commodity to 'paper' business, and no other private enterprise rivalled these associated firms in the field of international finance."

14 The standard reference on the House of Brown is Perkins (1975), who provides a bibliography on pp. 302–3. For the present section, heavy reliance is on Perkins (1975, pp. 20–1, 26–8, 150–3). See also Cole (1929a, pp. 390–2).

15 On the relationship of the Second Bank and the House of Baring, see Hidy (1944), Smith (1953, pp. 44–6), Hammond (1957, pp. 318–19), and Perkins (1975, pp. 154, 156).

16 On this role of the Second Bank, see Catterall (1902, p. 111), Hidy (1944, p. 270), Hammond (1957, p. 318), and Perkins (1975, p. 154).

17 See Redlich (1951, p. 131) and Perkins (1975, p. 154).

18 See Redlich (1951, p. 133) and Perkins (1975, p. 29).

19 The authors with this opinion are Hidy (1944, p. 270), Wright (1949, p. 369), Smith (1953, p. 46), and Perkins (1975, pp. 29, 154).

20 See Cole (1929a, p. 404) and Myers (1970, p. 73).

21 Virtually the entirety of this section is based on Perkins (1975, pp. 45–6, 147–8, 156–9, 182–6, 197, 204–5).

22 After the Civil War, agencies were utilized in all four Southern cities (Charleston, Savannah, New Orleans, and Mobile).

23 See Cole (1929a, p. 408) and Perkins (1975, pp. 182–6).

24 According to Cole (1929a, pp. 420–1), reasons for the absence of incorporated banks from the foreign-exchange field may be found "in the need for rapid, unhampered, and frequent decisions in trading, in the utility of intimate personal contacts with a large body of merchants, and in the necessity of reliance by English houses upon the strict personal integrity of their American correspondents in many of their operations."

25 See Holmes and Schott (1965, pp. 11–12) and Federal Reserve Bank of New York (1969, pp. 98–9).

26 See Perkins (1975, pp. 161–2, 165–6, 225).

27 In response to the competition, within the first seven months of 1879 the differential between the rate for buying and selling foreign exchange at the House of Brown fell from 0.5 percent, the rate for over half a century, to 0.25 percent for large transactions (Perkins, 1975, pp. 220, 270, n. 37).

28 Perkins (1975, pp. 155–6) and Officer (1983, p. 607). The latter author has since changed his view.

12   Theory of market efficiency

1 See, for example, the review of Levich (1985, pp. 1020–36).

2 Some investigators of gold-standard efficiency are blameless, because they wrote before Benoit Mandelbrot and Paul Samuelson developed the theory of asset-market efficiency in the mid-1960s, which Fama (1970, pp. 383–417) formalized more generally in 1970.

3 There are exceptions. Poole (1967) investigates the efficiency of earlier twentieth-century floating-rate experiences, while Morgenstern (1959) studies gold-standard efficiency in the interwar period as well as prior to World War I, and for France and Germany as well as for Britain and the United States.

4 Thus Levich (1985, pp. 1020, 1024, n. 39) notes: "With the establishment of floating exchange rates in the early 1970s (presumably dominated by free-market behavior), it was natural to begin the investigation of foreign exchange market efficiency." To his credit, he goes on to write: "It is important to note that government intervention per se does not imply exchange market inefficiency." However, he does not state that a gold standard can be efficient; nor does he acknowledge the literature on gold-standard efficiency.

5 The best exposition of the theory of asset-market efficiency remains Fama (1970, pp. 384–8); a formulation in terms of the foreign-exchange market is provided by Levich (1985, pp. 1022–5). Though technically correct, these treatments are too general and too mathematical to be fully understood by the non-specialist. I hope to make the theory clear to the general reader by defining profit as true economic profit, making explicit the roles of arbitrageurs and speculators as the earners of this profit, and paying attention to the duration of the unit time period.

6 It is the latter alternative that pertained to the exchange market from 1879 onward. See section 8 of chapter 11. Note that what is being considered is the foreign-exchange market among the dealers themselves, the interbank market after World War I. Certainly the ultimate transactors behaved as pure competitors, leaving only a certain leeway (the dealers' buying-selling price margin) to be determined in the interbank market per se.

7 Inclusion of risk premium and/or normal profit in cost is convenient pedagogically and does not detract from generality. Were one or both items excluded from cost, equilibrium profit would equal the risk premium and/or normal profit rather than zero.

8 This statement has the proviso of fast communication of information and instruction, such as that offered by a telegraphic network for the domestic foreign-exchange market (utilized substantially in the United States by the late 1870s) and by oceanic cable for the international market (employed fully in the dollar–sterling market by the later 1880s). See Cole (1929a, pp. 414–16) and Perkins (1975, pp. 182–3).

9 In the case of activities that take less than the unit period to complete and in particular those (such as spatial arbitrage and quick-reversal speculation) that can be done in a fraction of the period, repetitive operations occur to adjust to new information all during one period.

10 For a review and critique of these tests, see Levich (1985, pp. 1023–5, 1028–31).

11 For a survey, see Levich (1985, pp. 1025–35).

12 Spatial and triangular arbitrage are discussed in Levich (1985, pp. 1025–6).

13 Clark (1984, pp. 820–2) justifies theoretically use of the multilateral flow by proving that under certain assumptions the only gold flow in a multicountry world would be between the two countries with the greatest arbitrage profitability. However, his proof is flawed by two unrealistic assumptions. First, a three-country model is considered. It is not clear that the proof is extendable to a larger number of countries. Second, the price of gold in each country and the costs of shipping gold between countries are assumed to be known with certainty. The existence of a positive variance in expected profit would surely lead to country diversification in arbitrage operations, to reduce risk.

14 The argument to this point corresponds to that in sections 4.4–4.5 of chapter 8 (for the cable and bill exchange medium, respectively) and to section 6 of that chapter.

15 The argument is consistent with that in sections 4.2–4.3 and 6 of chapter 8.

16 For institutional information on US and UK taxation in 1925–31, see Spaulding (1927), Herndon (1932), Blakey and Blakey (1940), and Richman (1963).

17 It may be noted that the exchange-rate and interest gain could each be either negative or positive. See section 5.2.

18 Also included in TC are normal profit and a risk premium reflecting the "political" risks of foreign investment.

19 Two alternative models of UIA efficiency under an absolutely credible gold standard are found in the literature. Morgenstern (1959, pp. 166–8, 302–3) and Giovannini (1993, pp. 130–4). Both abstract from exchange-rate gain and transactions cost. Giovannini also assumes in effect that $r = 0$. While Morgenstern recognizes this risk element, his modelling is imprecise, lacking reference to the nature of the arbitrageur's risk aversion. Morgenstern simply defines inefficiency as the short-term international interest-rate differential exceeding the maximum exchange-rate risk, the latter measured as the difference between the gold-export and gold-import points as a percentage of parity. Giovannini goes beyond Morgenstern in recognizing the concept of an efficiency band, but he derives an interest-rate rather than exchange-rate band. Neither author incorporates taxation, a defect of virtually all studies of interest arbitrage irrespective of period [with Levi (1977) and Kupferman and Levi (1978) the conspicuous exceptions], and only Morgenstern applies the model to the interwar experience. A model similar to that of Giovannini is in Svensson (1991).

20 Neither Morgenstern nor Giovannini relates his model of UIA efficiency to CIA or forward speculation (FS). To the best of my knowledge, only Clarke (1967), who ignores transactions cost and taxation, studies CIA efficiency during the interwar gold standard.

21 I am not aware of any other study of FS efficiency under a credible gold standard.

22 That N is the same is unlikely, because the primary forward speculators were decidedly not the large London and New York banks and therefore not the same agents as the dominant interest arbitrageurs (Einzig, 1937, p. 144). The assumption of a common TC is questionable, because FS saved the cost of money-market transactions.

23 The transactions cost of CIA might include a risk premium to compensate for exchange-rate risk not fully covered in a forward contract – the risk of exchange–rate loss due to premature repatriation. So TC for CIA in reality might be slightly greater than for UIA. However, the interest arbitrageur, in making the decision whether to cover exchange risk in the forward market, does not change his horizon. So UIA and CIA inherently have the same N.

13   Empirical testing of market efficiency

1 For an excellent account, with extensive references to the literature, see Yeager (1976, pp. 441–72).
2 "So long as the Treasury's surplus gold fund has held above $100,000,000, the public mind has been generally easy; when the gold has fallen below that level, misgivings and market disturbances have at once begun" Noyes (1895, p. 575). The "legal minimum" refers to the provision in the Act of July 12, 1882 suspending the Treasury's issuance of gold certificates in exchange for coin deposit when the Treasury's reserves to redeem US notes fell below $100 million. This provision was repeated and extended in the Gold Standard Act of 1900. The redemption obligation covered both US notes and Treasury notes, and the Treasury was to have a reserve fund of $150 million for their redemption. When the fund fell below $100 million, the Treasury was to borrow to restore the Fund to the $150-million level. See Huntington and Mawhinney (1910, pp. 586–7, 610–14).
3 See Noyes (1895, pp. 588, 592; 1909, pp. 162, 232–33), Sprague (1910, pp. 141–2, 158, 179), Myers (1931, p. 378), Fels (1959, pp. 167, 185–6, 191–5), Simon (1960, pp. 32–3; 1968, p. 386), Friedman and Schwartz (1963, pp. 104–13), and Garber and Grilli (1986, p. 649). Also, using "target-zone" theory, Hallwood, MacDonald, and Marsh (1995) find that there were "large [dollar] devaluation expectations" during the 1890–7 period.
4 In the 1890s, however, the bankers were no public-spirited agents, but rather were motivated by self-interest. Their provision of gold to the Treasury in 1895 involved the purchase of government bonds at 104½ (4.5 percent above face value) at a time when comparable bonds were being transacted at 113½, and the bonds were marketed by the syndicate at 112¼ eleven days after the purchase. In four days of bargaining (in writing, by dispatch), the syndicate maintained a tough bargaining stance and won its terms. Either the bankers were prepared to see the gold standard fall, or they were confident that the government would not let it fall (that is, would accept the terms of the syndicate). As Noyes (1895, p. 592) notes: "It was, however, perfectly plain that the administration had no choice but to accept the syndicate's proposition or suspend government specie payments."
5 The Act of August 27, 1894 imposed a tax of two percent on the "net profits or income" of corporations effective January 1, 1895, but in May 1895 the Supreme Court found the law to be unconstitutional. See Seidman (1938, pp. 1016–20) and Stanley (1993, pp. 136, 299, n.2).
6 Dutton (1984, p. 192) concludes from an econometric analysis that the Bank did not follow the "rules of the game" in its monetary policy. "Whether passive or

active in the process, the Bank apparently acted as a buffer between reserve movements and money-supply changes. The rules would demand that it be an amplifier." However, the study deals only with policies other than gold-point manipulation.

7　As Dutton (1984, p. 178) notes, "They [the Bank's 'gold devices'] were usually used to retain or attract gold without resorting to extreme Bank-rate changes that would otherwise be necessary."

8　See Friedman and Schwartz (1963, pp. 154–6) and Goodhart (1969, pp. 111–14).

9　In a similar but milder vein, Dutton (1984, p. 178) states: "Their use was in a sense a violation of the rules, since the devices interfered with the free convertibility of gold at clearly specified rates of exchange."

10　For histories of these syndicates, see Noyes (1895, pp. 591–602; 1909, pp. 234–49), Simon (1960, 1968), and Friedman and Schwartz (1963, pp. 111–13).

11　See Brown (1914, pp. 113–14) and Cross (1923, p. 395).

12　These results are computed from Morgenstern (1959, pp. 184, 306–9, 318), after correcting an arithmetic mistake. While Morgenstern also errs in applying a time dimension to the exchange-rate risk, making it vary with the maturity of the investment (noted by Borts, 1960, p. 227), his "360-day" results are methodologically correct.

13　For surveys of the literature and recent testing, see Cumby (1988), Hodrick (1987), Kaminsky and Peruga (1990), and Taylor (1987).

14　The technique is consistent with estimation of the eight-day forward selling rate in section 2.3.3 of chapter 9. Einzig (1937, pp. 449, 458–71) presents weekly series of the three-month pound-forward-rate discount (in cents). The data are multiplied by minus one (to obtain a positive premium, negative discount), divided by 100 (to convert to dollars), and averaged by month.

15　See Brown (1940, pp. 651–4), Einzig (1937, pp. 23, 162, 265–6; 1962, pp. 49–50, 312), and Moggridge (1972, pp. 34–6). The dominance of the UK treasury bill in the London money market involved a major change from the prewar period. In contrast, US treasury bills were not issued until December 1929, were offered irregularly until 1931, and even then remained of minor interest to international investors. Ironically, there was no London equivalent of stock-exchange time loans (loans to brokers covered by stocks and bonds as collateral).

16　For example, a 4-percent annual rate translates to 0.01 for the three-month horizon. The data source is Board of Governors of the Federal Reserve System (1943, pp. 454–7, 656, 658). The London data are monthly averages of daily or weekly rates. For New York, the data are weekly and are averaged to obtain monthly observations.

17　However, it is possible that the uniform general efficiency of UIA and FS under RF has a strong spurious component. Suppose that the forward rate (RF) is close to the current spot rate (RS). Substituting RS for RS^e places it in the UIA and FS efficiency bands by mathematical necessity, rather than by force of UIA or FS, for all reasonable values of I_{UK}, I_{US}, t_{UK}, t_{US}, and TC. For example, this result easily occurs for $I_{UK} - I_{US} = t_{UK} = t_{US} = TC = 0$. The closer RS^e is to RS, the less the scope for UIA and FS inefficiencies. On average, over all 74 months, the forward rate is only one-third as far from RS as is RM. So it is not surprising that using the forward rate for RS^e results in no UIA or FS inefficiencies.

18 The third alternative value of p, $(1 + p_c)/2$, in table 13.2 and section 4.2.2 above is contained in $[p_c, 1]$.

19 See Bloomfield (1950, p. 52) and Spraos (1953, p. 95).

20 See Officer and Willett (1970, p. 251).

21 There is a slight uncertainty to the statement, because the individual interest rates in the differential are weighted by taxation parameters.

22 Furthermore, because of their popularity with arbitrageurs, it would be a mistake to exclude the UK treasury-bill rate and the New York time-loan rate from the interest-rate variables. See Brown (1940, pp. 651–2) and Einzig (1937, p. 265).

23 Also, using "target-zone" theory, Hallwood, MacDonald, and Marsh (1995) demonstrate that "the sterling–dollar exchange rate was almost fully credible during the interwar gold standard," except for a significantly positive expected devaluation of the pound in the last few months of the gold standard.

24 In addition, the relatively small number of CIA inefficiencies could be due to the fact that, unlike UIA and FS, CIA could be carried on under the gold standard without extra risk compared to a flexible exchange-rate system.

14   Market forces

1 It is true that the adjustment mechanism of a gold standard is itself dependent on gold flows and their nonsterilization by the monetary authorities. However, this consideration is long-run in nature, in contrast to the short-run focus of regime efficiency. It is also true that GPA can return the exchange rate rapidly to the gold-point spread; but prudence demands that reliance on such arbitrage be a last resort.

2 The role of a nonzero $(I_{UK} - I_{US})$ is explored in section 3.

3 The last two rows of the table pertain to chapter 15.

15   Policy variables

1 The source data are Sayers (1976, p. 347) and Board of Governors of the Federal Reserve System (1943, pp. 440–1).

2 As Friedman and Schwartz (1963, p. 269) write: "foreign considerations were seldom important in determining the [Federal Reserve] policies followed but were cited as additional justification for policies adopted primarily on domestic grounds whenever foreign and domestic considerations happened to coincide."

3 The traditional view of economic historians is that Bank Rate was geared overwhelmingly, if not exclusively, to maintenance of the gold standard, to the neglect of the domestic economy. Temin (1989, p. 31) notes: "Interest rates were kept high to attract short-term capital and to stabilize the pound." Cairncross and Eichengreen (1983, p. 38) comment: "Maintenance of a high Bank rate . . . was relied upon to attract capital inflows whenever the exchange

rate weakened." However, an econometric study of the goals of Bank Rate policy finds "a sensitivity to domestic conditions when formulating Bank Rate policy" (Eichengreen, Watson, and Grossman, 1985, p. 741).

4 Such central-bank cooperation as there was broke down in 1928. This is the story told by Clarke (1967) and generally accepted by economic historians (see Eichengreen, 1984, p. 66). Eichengreen presents a model of central-bank inter-action in the interwar gold standard incorporating discount rates as the policy instrument, but ignores the existence of a gold-point spread. He shows that cooperation can lead to improved internal balance for both countries. Elsewhere, Eichengreen, Watson, and Grossman (1985, p. 739) demonstrate econometrically that Bank Rate was not sensitive to the London–New York market interest-rate differential.

5 This variable has not been examined systematically in other studies of the dollar–sterling interwar gold standard, perhaps because of the difficulty of dis-entangling direct central-bank transactions from exchange-market interven-tion. The method of constructing $EMINT$ is described, and the variable tabulated, in section 4.

16   Net outcome

1 Mathematically, let $u(R^*)$ denote the loss function relating u, the disutility from regime inefficiency, to R^*, the deviation of the exchange rate from the mid-point of the gold-point spread. Logical properties of the u function are (1) $u(0) = 0$; (2) $u(R^*) > 0$, R^* 0; (3) assuming u is continuously differentiable, $u' \gtreqqless 0$ for $R^* \gtreqqless 0$; (4) $u(R^*) = u(-R^*)$. Two fundamental u functions with these properties are the identity ($u = |R^*|$) and square ($u = |R^*|^2$). These loss functions involve disutility increasing at the rate of 1 and $2|R^*|$, respectively, as $|R^*|$ increases.

2 Suppose a given sample period of N observations. Then the experienced average (mean) loss from regime inefficiency is mean$(u) = (\Sigma u)/N$, which specifically is mean$|R^*|$ and mean$(|R^*|^2)$ for the two u functions adopted.

3 Conjoining the assumptions regarding f(R^*) and $u(R^*)$, the hypothetical average (expected) loss from regime inefficiency given the gold-point parameter CX^* is:

$$E(u|CX^*) = (1/CX^*)\int_0^{CX^*} u(R^*)\mathrm{d}R^* = [U(CX^*) - U(0)]/CX^*$$

where U is a particular integral of u. Intuitively, the first equality defines the expected value of u as the sum (integral) of all values of u in the interval $[0, CX^*]$, that is, all positive values of u, divided by the width of the interval $(CX^* - 0)$. Because the function u is symmetrical, only the interval $[0, CX^*]$ need be consid-ered.) The second equality provides the formula to calculate $E(u|CX^*)$.

For the identity and square functions, the respective U functions are $(R^*)^2/2$ and $(R^*)^3/3$, and computed values of $E(u|CX^*)$ ("integration formulas") are $CX^*/2$ and $(CX^*)^2/3$. Intuitively, the average value of $u(R^*)$ over $[0, CX^*]$ may be approximated by $u(CX^*/2)$, which correctly yields $CX^*/2$ for the identity loss function. For the square function, however, this approximation is an understatement, $(CX^*)^2/4$ rather than $(CX^*)^2/3$, because the function increases at an increasing rate.

4 Because the denominator of the ratio is positively correlated with the width of the gold-point spread, the bias inherent in mean$|R^*|$ (and in the mean of any monotonic function of $|R^*|$) as a measure of efficiency – arising from neglect of the influence of the spread in constraining $|R^*|$ – is corrected.

5 For the identity function, the efficiency ratio is
   $100 \cdot [\text{mean}|R^*|/(CX^*/2)] = 200 \cdot [\text{mean}|R^*|/CX^*]$.
   For the square function, the ratio is
   $100 \cdot [\text{mean}(|R^*|^2)/\{(CX^*)^2/3\}] = 300 \cdot [\text{mean}(|R^*|^2)/(CX^*)^2]$.

6 In Officer (1993, p. 118) this efficiency ratio for 1925–31 is mistakenly halved – my error. The analysis that follows there is too strong.

References

Albion, Robert Greenhalgh, *Square-Riggers on Schedule.* Princeton, NJ: Princeton University Press, 1938.
  The Rise of New York Port [1815–1860]. New York: Charles Scribner's sons, 1939.
Albion, Robert Greenhalgh and Jennie Barnes Pope, *Sea Lanes in Wartime.* New York: W. W. Norton and Company, 1942.
Anderson, Benjamin M. *Economics and the Public Welfare.* New York: D. Van Nostrand Company, 1949.
Andrew, A. Piatt, "The Treasury and the Banks under Secretary Shaw." *Quarterly Journal of Economics* 21 (August 1907), pp. 519–68.
  "Hoarding in the Panic of 1907." *Quarterly Journal of Economics* 22 (February 1908), pp. 290–9.
  "Statistics for the United States, 1867–1909." Senate Doc. No. 570, 61st Cong., 2nd session. Washington, DC: Government Printing Office, 1910.
Ashton, Thomas S. *An Economic History of England: The 18th Century.* London: Methuen & Co., 1955.
Atkin, John. "Official Regulation of British Overseas Investment, 1914–1931." *Economic History Review* 23, second series (August 1970), pp. 324–35.
Bank of England. "The Foreign Exchange Market in Great Britain." In Robert Z. Aliber, ed. *The International Market for Foreign Exchange.* New York: Frederick A. Praeger, 1969, pp. 86–91.
Bankers' Magazine 2 (March 1848); 1, new series (October 1851, February 1852); 60 (June 1900).
Bareau, Paul. "The London Gold and Silver Markets." In Thomas Balogh, ed. *Studies in Financial Organization.* Cambridge: Cambridge University Press, 1947, pp. 213–26.
Beckhart, Benjamin Haggott. *The Discount Policy of the Federal Reserve System.* New York: Henry Holt and Company, 1924.
  The New York Money Market. vol. III, *Uses of Funds.* New York: Columbia University Press, 1932.
Bigelow, Erastus B. *The Tariff Question.* Boston: Little, Brown, and Company, 1862.
Blakey, Roy G. and Gladys C. Blakey. *The Federal Income Tax.* London: Longmans, Green and Co., 1940.

314

Bloomfield, Arthur I. *Capital Imports and the American Balance of Payments, 1934–39.* Chicago: University of Chicago Press, 1950.

   Monetary Policy under the International Gold Standard: 1880–1914. New York: Federal Reserve Bank of New York, 1959.

Board of Governors of the Federal Reserve System. *Banking and Monetary Statistics, 1914–1941.* Washington, DC, 1943.

   Banking and Monetary Statistics, 1941–1970. Washington, DC, 1976.

Bolles, Albert S. *The Financial History of the United States.* vol. II, *From 1789 to 1860,* 4th edn; vol. III, *From 1861 to 1885,* 2nd edn. New York: D. Appleton & Company, 1894.

Borts, George H. "Review of *International Financial Transactions and Business Cycles,* by Oskar Morgenstern." *Journal of the American Statistical Association* 55 (March 1960), pp. 223–8.

Bowen, Frank. C. *A Century of Atlantic Travel.* Boston: Little, Brown, and Company, 1930.

Brigham, Clarence S., ed. *British Royal Proclamations Relating to America, 1603–1783.* Worcester, MA: American Antiquarian Society, 1911.

Brown, Harry Gunnison. *International Trade and Exchange.* New York, The Macmillan Company, 1914.

Brown, William Adams, Jr. *England and the New Gold Standard 1919–1926.* London: P. S. King & Son, 1929.

   "The Government and the Money Market." In Benjamin Haggott Beckhart, James G. Smith, and William Adams Brown, Jr. *The New York Money Market.* vol. IV, *External and Internal Relations,* part 2. New York: Columbia University Press, 1932.

   The International Gold Standard Reinterpreted, 2 vols. New York: National Bureau of Economic Research, 1940.

Brock, Leslie V. *The Currency of the American Colonies, 1700–1764.* New York: Arno Press, 1975.

Bullock, Charles J., John H. Williams, and Rufus S. Tucker, "The Balance of Trade of the United States." *Review of Economic Statistics* 1 (July 1919), pp. 215–66.

Bureau of the Census. *Historical Statistics of the United States: Colonial Times to 1970.* Washington, DC: US Government Printing Office, 1975.

Cairncross, Alec and Barry Eichengreen. *Sterling in Decline.* Oxford: Basil Blackwell, 1983.

Calmoris, Charles W. and Larry Schweikart. "The Panic of 1857: Origins, Transmission, and Containment." *Journal of Economic History* 51 (December 1991), pp. 807–34.

Cameron, Rondo. *Banking in the Early Stages of Industrialization.* New York: Oxford University Press, 1967.

Cannan, Edwin. *The Paper Pound of 1797–1821.* London: P. S. King & Son, 1925.

Carothers, Neil. *Fractional Money.* New York: John Wiley & Sons, 1930.

Catterall, Ralph C. H. *The Second Bank of the United States.* Chicago: University of Chicago Press, 1902.

Chandler, Lester V. *Benjamin Strong, Central Banker.* Washington, DC: The Brookings Institution, 1958.

Clapham, Sir John. *The Bank of England*, 2 vols. Cambridge: Cambridge University Press, 1945.

Clare, George. *A Money-Market Primer*, 2nd edn. London: Effingham Wilson, 1906.

Clark, Arthur H. *The Clipper Ship Era*. New York: G. P. Putnam's Sons, 1920.

Clark, Truman A. "Violations of the Gold Points, 1890–1908." *Journal of Political Economy* 92 (October 1984), pp. 791–823.

Clarke, Stephen V. O. *Central Bank Cooperation 1924–31*. New York: Federal Reserve Bank of New York, 1967.

Clay, Sir Henry. *Lord Norman*. London: Macmillan, 1957.

Cole, Arthur H. "Evolution of the Foreign-Exchange Market of the United States." *Journal of Economic and Business History* 1 (May 1929a), pp. 384–421.

　　"Seasonal Variation in Sterling Exchange." *Journal of Economic and Business History* 2 (November 1929b), pp. 203–18.

Commercial and Financial Chronicle. Various issues.

Committee on Commerce. "Branch Mint, New York [Phoenix Report]". House Report No. 490, 31st Cong., 1st session, September 14, 1850.

Congress of the United States. *Annals*, 5th Cong. Washington, DC: Gales and Seaton, 1851.

Cornwallis, Kinahan. *The Gold Room*. New York: A. S. Barnes & Co., 1879.

Craig, Sir John. *The Mint: A History of the London Mint from A.D. 287 to 1948*. Cambridge: Cambridge University Press, 1953.

Cross, Ira B. *Domestic and Foreign Exchange*. New York: The Macmillan Company, 1923.

Cumby, Robert E. "Is it Risk? Explaining Deviations from Uncovered Interest Parity." *Journal of Monetary Economics* 22 (September 1988), pp. 279–99.

Cutler, Carl C. *Queens of the Western Ocean*. Annapolis, MD: United States Naval Institute, 1961.

Davis, Lance E. and Jonathan R. T. Hughes. "A Dollar–Sterling Exchange, 1803–1895." *Economic History Review* 13 (August 1960), pp. 52–78.

Del Mar, Alexander. *The History of Money in America from the Earliest Times to the Establishment of the Constitution*. New York: The Cambridge Encyclopedia Company, 1899.

Deutsch, Henry. *Arbitrage*. London: Effingham Wilson, 1910.

　　Transactions in Foreign Exchanges. London: The Financial Handbooks Publishing Company, 1914.

de Vries, Margaret Garritsen. *The International Monetary Fund 1972–1978*. vol. I, *Narrative and Analysis*. Washington, DC: International Monetary Fund, 1985.

Dewey, Davis Rich. *Financial History of the United States*, 12th edn. New York: Longmans, Green and Co., 1934.

Director of the Mint. "Letter . . . to Hon. A. A. Sargent in Relation to the Proposed Repeal of the Gold Coinage Charge." Senate Miscellaneous Document No. 109, 43rd Cong., 1st session May 18, 1874.

　　Annual Report. Washington, DC: Government Printing Office, 1895, 1942.

Dunbar, Charles Franklin. *Economic Essays*. New York: The Macmillan Company, 1904.

(revised by Oliver M. W. Sprague). *The Theory and History of Banking*, 5th edn. New York: G. P. Putnam's Sons, 1929.

Dutton, John. "The Bank of England and the Rules of the Game under the International Gold Standard: New Evidence." In Michael D. Bordo and Anna J. Schwartz, eds. *A Retrospective on the Classical Gold Standard, 1821–1931*. Chicago: University of Chicago Press, 1984, pp. 173–195.

The Economist. Various issues.

Eichengreen, Barry. "Central Bank Cooperation under the Interwar Gold Standard." *Explorations in Economic History* 21 (January 1984), pp. 64–87.

Golden Fetters. New York: Oxford University Press, 1992.

Eichengreen, Barry, Mark W. Watson, and Richard S. Grossman. "Bank Rate Policy under the Interwar Gold Standard: A Dynamic Probit Analysis." *Economic Journal* 95 (September 1985), pp. 725–45.

Einzig, Paul. "The Gold Points of the Exchanges Today." *Economic Journal* 37, (March 1927a), pp. 133–9.

"Present and Future Gold Export Points." *Economic Journal* 37 (September 1927b), pp. 480–3.

"International Gold Movements." *Economic Journal* 38 (December 1928), pp. 662–5.

"Gold Points and Central Banks." *Economic Journal* 39 (September 1929a), pp. 379–87.

International Gold Movements. London: Macmillan and Co., 1929b.

International Gold Movements, 2nd edn. London: Macmillan and Co., 1931.

The Theory of Forward Exchange. London: Macmillan and Co., 1937.

A Dynamic Theory of Forward Exchange. London: Macmillan and Co., 1962.

The History of Foreign Exchange, 2nd edn. London: Macmillan and Co., 1970.

Elliot, Jonathan. "The Funding System of the United States and of Great Britain." House of Representatives Executive Document No. 15, 28th Cong., 1st session. Washington, DC: Blair and Rives, 1845.

Entz, John F. *Exchange and Cotton Trade between England and the United States*. New York: E. B. Clayton, 1840.

Evitt, Herbert E. *A Manual of Foreign Exchange*. London: Sir Isaac Pitman & Sons, 1936.

Escher, Franklin. *Elements of Foreign Exchange*. New York: The Bankers Publishing Company, 1910.

Foreign Exchange Explained. New York: The Macmillan Company, 1918.

Modern Foreign Exchange. New York: The Macmillan Company, 1933.

Fama, Eugene F. "Efficient Capital Markets: A Review of Theory and Empirical Work." *Journal of Finance* 25 (May 1970), pp. 383–417.

Feavearyear, Sir Albert. *The Pound Sterling*, 2nd edn. Oxford: Clarendon Press, 1963.

Federal Reserve Bank of New York. "The Foreign Exchange Market in the United States." In Robert Z. Aliber, ed. *The International Market for Foreign Exchange*. New York: Frederick A. Praeger, 1969, pp. 98–107.

Federal Reserve Board, *Annual Report, 1925–31*. Washington, DC: Government Printing Office, 1926–32.

Federal Reserve Bulletin 14 (May 1928), 15 (September 1929).

Fels, Rendigs. *American Business Cycles, 1865–1897.* Chapel Hill: University of North Carolina Press, 1959.

Financial Register of the United States. 1838.

Financial Review. Various issues.

Fraser, Herbert F. *Great Britain and the Gold Standard.* London: Macmillan and Co., 1933.

Friedman, Milton. "Bimetallism Revisited." *Journal of Economic Perspectives* 4 (Fall 1990a), pp. 85–104.

"The Crime of 1873." *Journal of Political Economy* 98 (December 1990b), pp. 1159–94.

Friedman, Milton and Anna Jacobson Schwartz. *A Monetary History of the United States 1867–1960.* Princeton, NJ: National Bureau of Economic Research, Princeton University Press, 1963.

Garber, Peter M. and Vittorio U. Grilli. "The Belmont–Morgan Syndicate as an Optimal Investment Banking Contract." *European Economic Review* 30 (June 1986), pp. 649–77.

Giovannini, Alberto. "Bretton Woods and Its Precursors: Rules versus Discretion in the History of International Monetary Regimes." In Michael D. Bordo and Barry Eichengreen, eds. *A Retrospective on the Bretton Woods System: Lessons for International Monetary Reform.* Chicago: National Bureau of Economic Research, University of Chicago Press, 1993, pp. 109–47.

Goodhart, Charles A. E. *The New York Money Market and the Finance of Trade, 1900–1913.* Cambridge, MA: Harvard University Press, 1969.

Hallwood, C. Paul, Ronald MacDonald, and Ian W. Marsh. "Credibility and Fundamentals: Was the Gold Standard a Well-Behaved Target Zone?" In Tamim Bayoumi, Barry Eichengreen, and Mark P. Taylor, eds. *Modern Perspectives on the Gold Standard.* Cambridge: Cambridge University Press, 1995.

Hammond, Bray. *Banks and Politics in America.* Princeton, NJ: Princeton University Press, 1957.

Haupt, Ottomar. *Arbitrages et Parités*, 8th edn. Paris: Librairie Truchy, 1894.

Hardy, Charles O. *Credit Policies of the Federal Reserve System.* Washington, DC: The Brookings Institution, 1932.

Hawtrey, Ralph G. *Currency and Credit*, 4th edn. London: Longmans, Green and Co., 1950.

Hepburn, A. Barton. *A History of Currency in the United States.* New York: The Macmillan Company, 1924.

Herndon, John Goodwin, Jr. "The Development of International Reciprocity for the Prevention of Double Income Taxation." Ph.D. dissertation. Philadelphia: University of Pennsylvania, 1932.

Hidy, Ralph W. "The House of Baring and the Second Bank of the United States, 1826–1836." *Pennsylvania Magazine of History and Biography* 68 (July 1944), pp. 269–85.

Hodrick, Robert J. *The Empirical Evidence on the Efficiency of Forward and Futures Foreign Exchange Markets.* Chur, Switzerland: Harwood Academic Publishers, 1987.

Holmes, Alan R. and Francis H. Schott. *The New York Foreign Exchange Market.* New York: Federal Reserve Bank of New York, 1965.

Horton, S. Dana. *The Silver Pound.* London: Macmillan and Co., 1887.

Horsefield, J. Keith. *British Monetary Experiments, 1650–1710.* Cambridge, MA: Harvard University Press, 1960.

House of Commons. "Minutes of Evidence taken before the Committee on the High Price of Gold Bullion." British Parliamentary Papers, vol. 3, 1810.

"Reports from Committees: The Bank of England Resumption of Cash Payments." Session 21 January–13 July 1819. vol. 3, Appendix C.1., 12th May 1819.

"Report from the Committee of Secrecy of the Bank of England Charter." Session 6 December 1831–16 August 1832. Reports from Committees, vol. 6, Appendix No. 96, 11 August 1832.

"Minutes of Evidence taken before Select (Secret) Committee on Commercial Distress." British Parliamentary Papers, vol. 8, parts 1 and 3, 1847–8.

"Evidence taken before the Select Committee on the Bank Acts." Reports from Committees, vol. 10, part I, session 2, 1857.

Huntington, Andrew T. and Mawhinney, Robert J., eds. "Laws of the United States Concerning Money, Banking, and Loans, 1778–1909." Senate Document No. 580, 61st Cong., 2nd session. Washington, DC: Government Printing Office, 1910.

"International Monetary Conference." Senate Executive Document No. 58, 45th Cong. 3rd session. Washington, DC: Government Printing Office, 1879.

Jaeger, Ruth M. "Stabilization of the Foreign Exchanges." Ph.D. dissertation. New York: Columbia University, 1922.

Johnson, Joseph French. *Money and Currency,* rev. edn. Boston: Ginn and Company, 1905.

"Banking Principles." In Joseph French Johnson, Howard McNayr Jefferson, and Franklin Escher. *Banking*, part 1. New York: Alexander Hamilton Institute, 1911.

Kaminsky, Graciela and Peruga, Rodrigo. "Can a Time-Varying Risk Premium Explain Excess Returns in the Forward Market for Foreign Exchange?" *Journal of International Economics* 28 (February 1990), pp. 47–70.

Kemmerer, Edwin Walter. *Gold and the Gold Standard.* New York: McGraw–Hill Book Company, 1944.

Keynes, John Maynard. *A Treatise on Money*, 2 vols. London: Macmillan and Co., 1930.

Kindleberger, Charles P. *A Financial History of Western Europe,* 2nd edn. New York: Oxford University Press, 1993.

King, Wilfred T. C. *History of the London Discount Market.* London: George Routledge & Sons, 1936.

Kirdaldy, Adam W. *British Finance During and After the War, 1914–21.* London: Sir Isaac Pitman & Sons, 1921.

Knox, John Jay. *A History of Banking in the United States.* New York: Bradford Rhodes, 1900.

Krooss, Herman E., ed. *Documentary History of Banking and Currency in the United States*, 4 vols. New York: Chelsea House, 1969.

Krugman, Paul. "Target Zones and Exchange Rate Dynamics." *Quarterly Journal of Economics* 106 (August 1991), pp. 669-82.

Kupferman, Martin and Maurice D. Levi. "Taxation and the International Money Market Investment Decision." *Financial Analysts Journal* 34 (July–August 1978), pp. 61–4.

Laughlin, J. Laurence. *The History of Bimetallism in the United States*, 4th edn. New York: D. Appleton and Company, 1900.

Levi, Maurice D. "Taxation and 'Abnormal' International Capital Flows." *Journal of Political Economy* 85 (June 1977), pp. 635–46.

Levich, Richard M. "Empirical Studies of Exchange Rates: Price Behavior, Rate Determination and Market Efficiency." In Ronald W. Jones and Peter B. Kenen, eds. *Handbook of International Economics*, vol. II. Amsterdam: North-Holland, 1985, pp. 979–1040.

Li, Ming-Hsun. *The Great Recoinage of 1696 to 1699.* London: Weidenfeld and Nicolson, 1963.

Lindsay, William Schaw. *History of Merchant Shipping and Ancient Commerce*, vol IV. London: S. Low, Marston, Low, and Searle, 1874.

Lowrie, Walter and Matthew St. Clair Clarke. *American State Papers*, vol. V. Washington: Gales and Seaton, 1832.

Macaulay, Frederick R. *The Movements of Interest Rates, Bond Yields and Stock Prices in the United States since 1856.* New York: National Bureau of Economic Research, 1938.

Macesich, George. "Sources of Monetary Disturbances in the United States, 1834–1845." *Journal of Economic History* 20 (September 1960), pp. 407–34.

Maginnis, Arthur F. *The Atlantic Ferry.* London: Whittaker and Co., 1892.

Margraff, Anthony W. *International Exchange.* Chicago: Geo. E. Marshall & Co., 1904.

Martin, David A. "1853: The End of Bimetallism in the United States." *Journal of Economic History* 33 (December 1973), pp. 825–44.

Martin, Joseph G. *A Century of Finance. Martin's History of the Boston Stock and Money Markets, One Hundred Years.* Boston: privately printed, 1898.

McCormick, Frank. "Covered Interest Arbitrage: Unexploited Profits?" *Journal of Political Economy* 87 (April 1979), pp. 411–17.

McGrane, Reginald Charles. *The Panic of 1837.* New York: Russel & Russel, 1965.

Merchants' Magazine 1 (July 1839), 19 (September 1848).

Miller, Hugh F. R. *The Foreign Exchange Market.* London: Edward Arnold & Co., 1925.

Mitchell, Brian R. *British Historical Statistics.* Cambridge: Cambridge University Press, 1988.

Mitchell, Wesley Clair. *A History of the Greenbacks.* Chicago: University of Chicago Press, 1903.

   Gold, Prices & Wages under the Greenback Standard. Berkeley: University of California Press, 1908.

Moggridge, Donald E. *British Monetary Policy 1924–1931: The Norman Conquest of $4.86.* Cambridge: Cambridge University Press, 1972.

Morgan, E. Victor. *Studies in British Financial Policy, 1914–25.* London: Macmillan & Co., 1952.

Morgenstern, Oskar. "The Validity of International Gold Movement Statistics." Special Papers in International Economics No. 2. Princeton, NJ: Princeton University, International Finance Section, 1955.

International Financial Transactions and Business Cycles. Princeton: National Bureau of Economic Research, Princeton University Press, 1959.

Myers, Margaret G. *The New York Money Market.* vol. I, *Origins and Development.* New York: Columbia University Press, 1931.

A Financial History of the United States. New York: Columbia University Press, 1970.

Nettles, Curtis Putnam. *The Money Supply of the American Colonies Before 1720.* Studies in the Social Sciences and History No. 20. Madison: University of Wisconsin, 1934.

The Emergence of a National Economy. New York: Holt, Rinehart and Winston, 1962.

New York Times. Various issues.

Newcomb, Simon. *Principles of Political Economy.* New York: Harper & Brothers, 1886.

North, Douglass C. "The United States Balance of Payments, 1790–1860." In *Trends in the American Economy in the Nineteenth Century.* Princeton, NJ: National Bureau of Economic Research, Princeton University Press, 1960, pp. 573–627.

"Sources of Productivity Change in Ocean Shipping, 1660–1850." *Journal of Political Economy* 76 (September–October 1968), pp. 953–70.

Noyes, Alexander D. "The Treasury Reserve and the Bond Syndicate." *Political Science Quarterly* 10 (December 1895), pp. 573–602.

Forty Years of American Finance, 2nd edn. New York: G. P. Putnam's Sons, 1909.

Nussbaum, Arthur. *Money in the Law: National and International.* Brooklyn, NY: The Foundation Press, 1950.

A History of the Dollar. New York: Columbia University Press, 1957.

Officer, Lawrence H. "The Floating Dollar in the Greenback Period: A Test of Theories of Exchange-Rate Determination." *Journal of Economic History* 41 (September 1981), pp. 629–50.

"Dollar–Sterling Mint Parity and Exchange Rates, 1791–1834." *Journal of Economic History* 43 (September 1983), pp. 579–616.

"Integration in the American Foreign-Exchange Market, 1791–1900." *Journal of Economic History* 45 (September 1985), pp. 557–85.

"The Efficiency of the Dollar–Sterling Gold Standard, 1890–1908." *Journal of Political Economy* 94 (October 1986), pp. 1038–73.

"The Remarkable Efficiency of the Dollar–Sterling Gold Standard, 1890–1906." *Journal of Economic History* 49 (March 1989), pp. 1–41.

"Gold-Point Arbitrage and Uncovered Interest Arbitrage under the 1925–1931 Dollar–Sterling Gold Standard." *Explorations in Economic History* 30 (January 1993), pp. 98–127.

"Market Efficiency and Regime Efficiency under the 1925–1931 Dollar–Sterling

Gold Standard." In Tamim Bayoumi, Barry Eichengreen and Mark P. Taylor, eds. *Modern Perspectives on the Gold Standard.* Cambridge: Cambridge University Press, 1995.

Officer, Lawrence H. and Thomas D. Willett. "The Covered-Arbitrage Schedule: A Critical Survey of Recent Developments." *Journal of Money, Credit and Banking* 2 (May 1970), pp. 247–57.

Patterson, E. L. Stewart. *Domestic and Foreign Exchange.* New York: Alexander Hamilton Institute, 1917.

Perkins, Edwin J. *Financing Anglo-American Trade.* Cambridge, MA: Harvard University Press, 1975.

"Foreign Interest Rates in American Financial Markets: A Revised Series of Dollar–Sterling Exchange Rates, 1835–1900." *Journal of Economic History* 38 (June 1978), pp. 392–417.

The Economy of Colonial America. New York: Columbia University Press, 1980.

Persons, Warren M., Pierson M. Tuttle, and Edwin Frickey. "Business and Financial Conditions Following the Civil War in the United States." *Review of Economic Statistics* 2 (supplement, July 1920), pp. 5–55.

Peters, Richard, ed. *Public Statutes at Large of the United States of America.* Boston: Charles C. Little and James Brown, vols. 1–2, 1848; vols. 3–4, 1846; Little, Brown and Company, vols. 4–5, 1860.

Pierson, Nikolaas G. *Principles of Economics*, 2 vols. London: The Macmillan Company, 1913.

Poole, William. "Speculative Prices as Random Walks: An Analysis of Ten Time Series of Flexible Exchange Rates." *Southern Economic Journal* 33 (April 1967), pp. 468–78.

Public General Statutes, 1870, vol. V. London: Queen's Printers, 1870.

Public General Acts, 1938–39, vol. I. London: King's Printer, 1940.

Redish, Angela. "The Evolution of the Gold Standard in England." *Journal of Economic History* 50 (December 1990), pp. 789–805.

Redlich, Fritz. *The Molding of American Banking: Men and Ideas.* New York: Hafner Publishing Company, 1951.

Reuss, W. F. *Calculations and Statements Relative to the Trade Between Great Britain and the United States of America.* London: Effingham Wilson, 1833.

Richman, Peggy Brewer. *Taxation of Foreign Investment Income: An Economic Analysis.* Baltimore: Johns Hopkins Press, 1963.

Sanger, George P., ed. *Public Laws of the United States of America*, 1862–3, 1863–4, 1864–5, 1869–70. Boston: Little, Brown and Company, 1863, 1864, 1865, 1870.

Sayers, Richard S. *Bank of England Operations, 1890–1914.* London: P. S. King & Son, 1936.

The Bank of England 1891–1914. Appendixes. Cambridge: Cambridge University Press, 1976.

The Bank of England 1891–1914. Cambridge: Cambridge University Press, 1986.

Secretary of the Treasury. "Report Respecting the Relative Value of Gold and Silver, &c." House Document No. 117, 21st Cong., 1st session, May 29, 1830.

"Report . . . in Compliance with a Resolution of the Senate Relative to the Means of Supplying the Mint with Bullion and Foreign Coins for Coinage." Senate Document No. 162, 24th Cong., 1st session, February 15, 1836.

"Report . . . Transmitting Statements of the Rates of Exchange and Prices of Bank Notes at Different Periods." Senate Document No. 457, 25th Cong., 2nd session, May 28, 1838.

"Report Showing . . . the Rates of Foreign and Domestic Exchange, and the Prices of Bank-Notes and Specie, at New York and Philadelphia, During the Years 1838, 1839, and 1840." Senate Document No. 69, 26th Cong., 2nd session, January 13, 1841.

Annual Report, 1900, 1920, 1922, 1926. Washington, DC: Government Printing Office, 1901, 1921, 1923, 1927.

Seidman, Jacob S. *Seidman's Legislative History of Federal Income Tax Laws, 1938–1861.* New York: Prentice-Hall, 1938.

Select Committee on Coins. "Gold and Silver Coins." House of Representatives, Report No. 496, 22nd Cong., 1st session. In *Reports of Committees of the House of Representatives*, vol. V. Washington, DC: Duff Green, 1832.

Seyd, Ernest. *Bullion and Foreign Exchanges.* London: Effingham Wilson, 1868.

Shaw, William A. *The History of Currency 1252 to 1894*, 2nd edn. New York: G. P. Putnam's Sons, 1896a.

Select Tracts and Documents Illustrative of English Monetary History, 1626–1730. London: Wilsons & Milne, 1896b.

Shepherd, James F. and Gary M. Walton. *Shipping, Maritime Trade, and the Economic Development of Colonial North America.* Cambridge: Cambridge University Press, 1972.

Shrigley, Irene. *The Price of Gold.* London: P. S. King & Son, 1935.

Silberling, Norman J. "British Prices and Business Cycles, 1779–1850." *Review of Economic Statistics* 5 (October 1923), pp. 223–61.

Simon, Matthew. "The Hot Money Movement and the Private Exchange Pool Proposal of 1896." *Journal of Economic History* 20 (March 1960), pp. 31–50.

"The Morgan–Belmont Syndicate of 1895 and Intervention in the Foreign-Exchange Market." *Business History Review* 42 (Winter 1968), pp. 385–417.

Smith, Walter Buckingham. *Economic Aspects of the Second Bank of the United States.* Cambridge, MA: Harvard University Press, 1953.

Smith, Walter Buckingham and Arthur Harrison Cole. *Fluctuations in American Business, 1790–1860.* Cambridge, MA: Harvard University Press, 1935.

Soetbeer, Adolf. *Edelmetall-Produktion.* Gotha: Justus Perthes, 1879.

Southard, Frank A. *Foreign Exchange Practice and Policy.* New York: McGraw-Hill Book Company, 1940.

Spalding, William F. *Foreign Exchange and Foreign Bills.* London: Sir Isaac Pitman & Sons, 1915.

The London Money Market, 2nd edn. London: Sir Isaac Pitman & Sons, 1922.

A Primer of Foreign Exchange. London: Sir Isaac Pitman & Sons, 1925.

Dictionary of the World's Currencies and Foreign Exchanges. London: Sir Isaac Pitman & Sons, 1928a.

Foreign Exchange and Foreign Bills, 7th edn. London: Sir Isaac Pitman & Sons, 1928b.

Tate's Modern Cambist, 28th edn. London: Effingham Wilson, 1929.

Spaulding, Harrison B. *The Income Tax in Great Britain and the United States.* London: P. S. King & Son, 1927.

Spiller, Pablo T. and Robert O. Wood. "Arbitrage during the Dollar–Sterling Gold Standard, 1899–1908: An Econometric Approach." *Journal of Political Economy* 96 (August 1988), pp. 882–92.

Sprague, Oliver M. W. "History of Crises under the National Banking System." Senate Document No. 538, 61st Cong., 2nd session, Washington, DC: Government Printing Office, 1910.

"The Crisis of 1914 in the United States." *American Economic Review* 5 (September 1915), pp. 499–533.

Spraos, John. "The Theory of Forward Exchange and Recent Practice." *Manchester School of Economic and Social Studies* 21 (May 1953), pp. 87–117.

Stanley, Robert. *Dimensions of Law in the Service of Order: Origins of the Federal Income Tax, 1861–1913.* New York: Oxford University Press, 1993.

Statutes at Large of the United States of America. August 1893 to March 1895, vol. 28; March 1909 to March 1911, vol. 36, part 1; May 1919 to March 1921, vol. 41, part 1; April 1921 to March 1923, vol. 42, part 1. Washington, DC: Government Printing Office, 1895, 1911, 1921, 1923.

Stewart, Frank H. *History of the First United States Mint.* Camden, NJ: privately printed, 1924.

Strauss, Albert. "Gold Movements and the Foreign Exchanges." In *The Currency Problem and the Present Financial Situation.* New York: Columbia University Press, 1908, pp. 63–87.

Studenski, Paul and Herman E. Krooss. *Financial History of the United States*, 2nd edn. New York: McGraw-Hill Book Company, 1963.

Sumner, William Graham. *A History of American Currency.* New York: Henry Holt and Company, 1874.

Svensson, Lars E. O. "The Simplest Test of Target Zone Credibility." International Monetary Fund *Staff Papers* 38 (September 1991), pp. 655–65.

Swoboda, Otto. *Die Arbitrage.* Berlin: Haude & Spenersche, 1928.

Sylla, Richard. "The United States 1863–1913." In Rondo Cameron, ed. *Banking and Economic Development.* New York: Oxford University Press, 1972, pp. 232–62.

"Monetary Innovation in America." *Journal of Economic History* 42 (March 1982), pp. 21–30.

Taus, Esther Rogoff. *Central Banking Functions of the United States Treasury, 1789–1941.* New York: Columbia University Press, 1943.

Taxay, Don. *The US Mint and Coinage.* New York: Arco Publishing Company, 1966.

Taylor, George Rogers. *The Transportation Revolution, 1815–1860.* New York: Holt, Rinehart and Winston, 1951.

Taylor, Mark P. "Risk Premia and Foreign Exchange: A Multiple Time Series Approach to Testing Uncovered Interest-Rate Parity." *Weltwirtschaftliches Archiv* 123 (1987), pp. 579–91.

Temin, Peter. *The Jacksonian Economy.* New York: W. W. Norton & Company, 1969.

Lessons from the Great Depression. Cambridge, MA: The MIT Press, 1989.

Timberlake, Richard H. *Monetary Policy in the United States.* Chicago: University of Chicago Press, 1993.

Tooker, Elva. *Nathan Trotter, Philadelphia Merchant, 1787–1853.* Cambridge, MA: Harvard University Press, 1955.

Triffin, Robert. *Gold and the Dollar Crisis.* New Haven: Yale University Press, 1960.

Tucker, George. *The Theory of Money & Banks Investigated.* New York: Sentry Press, 1839.

Tyler, David Budlong. *Steam Conquers the Atlantic.* New York: D. Appleton-Century Company, 1939.

Warren, George F. and Frank A. Pearson. *Wholesale Prices for 213 Years, 1720 to 1932.* Ithaca, NY: Cornell University Agricultural Experiment Station, 1932.

Gold and Prices. New York: John Wiley & Sons, 1935.

Watson, David K. *History of American Coinage.* New York: G. P. Putnam's sons, 1899.

Watson, Jesse P. *The Bureau of the Mint.* Baltimore: The Johns Hopkins Press, 1926.

Weinstein, Allen. "Was There a 'Crime of 1873'?: The Case of the Demonetized Dollar." *Journal of American History* 54 (September 1967), pp. 307–26.

Whitaker, Albert C. *Foreign Exchange.* New York: D. Appleton and Company, 1919.

Foreign Exchange, 2nd edn. New York: D. Appleton-Century Company, 1933.

White, William H. "Interest Rate Differences, Forward Exchange Mechanism, and Scope for Short-Term Capital Movements." International Monetary Fund *Staff Papers* 10 (November 1963), pp. 485–501.

Willem, John M., Jr. *The United States Trade Dollar.* New York: privately printed, 1959.

Williams, David. "London and the 1931 Financial Crisis." *Economic History Review* 15 (April 1963), pp. 513–28.

Williams, T. Taliesin. "The Rate of Discount and the Price of Consols." *Journal of the Royal Statistical Society* 75 (March 1912), pp. 380–400.

Wright, Chester Whitney. *Economic History of the United States.* New York: McGraw-Hill Book Company, 1949.

Yeager, Leland B. *International Monetary Relations: Theory, History, and Policy.* New York: Harper & Row, 1976.

York, Thomas. *International Exchange.* New York: The Ronald Press Company, 1923.

Index

abrasion, 134, 138
  See also gold points; gold-point estimates
acceptance
  bankers', 62
  derived from time bill of exchange, 61
  no market in New York, 63
Adams, John (President), 20
Adams, John Quincy (Secretary of State
    and President), 50–1, 52–3
    (table), 293
adjustable-peg system. *See* gold-exchange
    standard
Albion, Robert Greenhalgh, 123, 125, 126,
    127, 135, 157, 166, 167, 168,
    185, 295, 301, 303
alloying. *See* mint procedures
Anderson, Benjamin M., 302
Andrew, A. Piatt, 100, 159, 291, 304
  exchange-rate series, 65, 68, 74, 80, 89–90
    (table), 97–8 (tables)
angel. *See* Mint, British
Anglo-French War (1790s)
  effect on international integration, 200
  war-determined normal profit plus risk
    premium, 185
  war-risk insurance premium, 185
Anne (Queen), 50
arbitrageurs
  gold-point, dominant, 108–9, 195, 222
  interest, dominant, 223, 242
  See also covered interest arbitrage; gold-
    point arbitrage; uncovered
    interest arbitrage
Ashton, Thomas S., 292
Assay bars. *See* bars; Federal Reserve Bank
    of New York; New York Assay
    Office
Assay Office of New York. *See* New York
    Assay Office

assaying. *See* mint procedures
Atkin, John, 32

Baltimore
  dominant foreign-exchange market, 60,
    91
  exchange-rate series, 66–8, 81–7
    (including tables), 91, 96–100
    (including tables)
  location of House of Brown, 202
  premium of specie over currency, 78
    (table)
Bank of England
  coinage of bullion at Mint, 292 (note
    19)
  early history, 40
  exchange-market intervention, 63, 176,
    264–6 (including table), 276
  interest-free advances, 170–1 (including
    table) issuer of banknotes, 37
  manipulation of gold points, 237–40
  moral suasion, 45
  notes, 37–8, 40, 42
  purchase of gold, 39–40, 43, 140–5
    (including tables)
  right to transact in bullion, 39
  sale of gold, 39–40, 43, 45, 147, 149–52
    (including tables), 154–5
    (including table)
  transactor in gold, versus market, 141,
    142, 149, 152, 154
  See also Bank Rate; monetary policy
Bank of the United States. *See* Second
    Bank of the United States
Bank Rate
  data, 163, 263
  use in converting time to demand bill, 69,
    71–2
Bank Restriction Period. *See* paper

326